TRANSLOCAL LIVES AND RELIGION

The Study of Religion in a Global Context

SERIES EDITORS

Satoko Fujiwara
EXECUTIVE EDITOR
UNIVERSITY OF TOKYO

Katja Triplett
SERIES EDITOR
LEIPZIG UNIVERSITY

Alexandra Grieser
MANAGING EDITOR
TRINITY COLLEGE DUBLIN

The series, published in association with the International Association for the History of Religions, encourages work that is innovative in the study of religions, whether of an empirical, theoretical or methodological nature. This includes multi- or inter-disciplinary studies involving anthropology, philosophy, psychology, sociology and political studies. Volumes will examine the continuing influence of postcolonial, decolonial and intercultural dynamics, as well as contemporary responses from intersectional studies. They will also address the relevance and application of more recent approaches such as cognitivist, as well as ones concerned with aesthetic culture—art, architecture, media, performance and sound.

PUBLISHED

Philosophy and the End of Sacrifice:
Disengaging Ritual in Ancient India, Greece and Beyond
Edited by Peter Jackson and Anna-Pya Sjödin

The Relational Dynamics of Enchantment and Sacralization:
Changing the Terms of the Religion Versus Secularity Debate
Edited by Peik Ingman, Terhi Utriainen, Tuija Hovi and Måns Broo

Translocal Lives and Religion:
Connections between Asia and Europe in the Late Modern World

Edited by
Philippe Bornet

Published by Equinox Publishing Ltd.

UK: Office 415, The Workstation,
     15 Paternoster Row, Sheffield,
     South Yorkshire S1 2BX
USA: ISD, 70 Enterprise Drive, Bristol, CT 06010

www.equinoxpub.com

First published 2021

© Philippe Bornet

All rights reserved. No part of this publication may be reproduced or transmitted in any form or by any means, electronic or mechanical, including photocopying, recording or any information storage or retrieval system, without prior permission in writing from the publishers.

Published with the support of the Centre interdisciplinaire en histoire et sciences des religions, University of Lausanne.

British Library Cataloguing-in-Publication Data

A catalogue record for this book is available from the British Library.

ISBN-13: 9781781795828 (hardback)
ISBN-13: 9781781795835 (paperback)
ISBN-13: 9781781795842 (e-PDF)

Library of Congress Cataloging-in-Publication Data

Names: Bornet, Philippe (Historian of religions), editor.
Title: Translocal lives and religion : connections between Asia and Europe in the late modern world / edited by Philippe Bornet..
Description: Bristol, CT : Equinox Publishing Ltd, 2021. | Series: The study of religion in a global context | Includes bibliographical references and index.
Identifiers: LCCN 2019021251 (print) | LCCN 2019981193 (ebook) | ISBN 9781781795828 (hardback) | ISBN 9781781795835 (paperback) | ISBN 9781781795842 (pdf)
Subjects: LCSH: Asia—Religion. | Europe—Religion. | East and West.
Classification: LCC BL1033.T73 2020 (print) | LCC BL1033 (ebook) | DDC 200.9—dc23
LC record available at https://lccn.loc.gov/2019021251
LC ebook record available at https://lccn.loc.gov/2019981193

Contents

PRELIMINARIES

    List of Figures   vii

    Foreword   ix
    SUJIT SIVASUNDARAM

    Editor's Preface   xi
    PHILLIPE BORNET

PART I: INTRODUCTION

1. From Comparative to Connected Religion: Translocal Aspects of Orientalism and the Study of Religion   3
   PHILLIPE BORNET

PART II: TRANSNATIONAL TRAJECTORIES AND INDIVIDUAL APPROPRIATIONS OF RELIGION

2. "In-Between" Religiosity: European *Kālī-bhakti* in Early Colonial Calcutta   35
   GAUTAM CHAKRABARTI

3. The Making of the Ideal Transnational Disciple: Unravelling Biographies of Margaret Noble/Sister Nivedita   57
   GWILYM BECKERLEGGE

4. The Curious Case of the Drs. d'Abreu: Catholicism, Migration and a Kanara Catholic Family in the Heart of the Empire, 1890–1950   89
   DWAYNE RYAN MENEZES

5. Religion and the "Simple Life": Dugald Semple and Translocal "Life Reform" Networks   123
   STEVEN SUTCLIFFE

6. Re-discovering Buddha's Land: The Transnational Formative Years of China's Indology — 149
   MINYU ZHANG

PART III: RELIGIONS ON THE MOVE

7. Charles Pfoundes and the First Buddhist Mission to the West, 1889–1892: Some Research Questions — 171
   BRIAN BOCKING

8. Travelling through Interstitial Spaces: The Radical Spiritual Journeys of Pandita Mary Ramabai Saraswathi — 193
   PARINITHA SHETTY

9. A "Christian Hindu Apostle"? The Multiple Lives of Sadhu Sundar Singh (1889–1929?) — 219
   PHILIPPE BORNET

10. The Chen Jianmin (1906–1987) Legacy: An "Always on the Move" Buddhist Practice — 253
    FABIENNE JAGOU

PART IV: IN SUMMARY

11. Afterword — 275
    MAYA BURGER

    Index — 291

List of Figures

Figure 2.1	Antony Firingee, dir. S. Banerjee, India, 1967.	41
Figure 3.1	Sister Nivedita's statue installed in the city of Salem, Tamil Nadu, India, to mark the 150th anniversary of her birth.	58
Figure 4.1	Dr. John Francis d'Abreu.	94
Figure 4.2	Dr. J.F. d'Abreu, with his wife Teresa and three daughters (c. 1900).	95
Figure 4.3	Pon and Elizabeth, with two daughters, c. 1945.	97
Figure 4.4	Frank and Ann at their wedding, 2 June 1945.	98
Figure 4.5	Angelo Saldanha (aka E.C. Francis) in Western Australia.	114
Figure 4.6	Angelo Saldanha, Daily News [Perth], 11 April 1929.	115
Figure 5.1	Dugald Semple's "Wheelhouse" colony, Beith, c. 1930.	125
Figure 5.2	Dugald Semple preaching the "Simple Life" c. 1940.	129
Figure 5.3	Semple's photograph of Gandhi at lunch, London 1931.	130
Figure 5.4	Madeleine Slade (Mirabehn) visiting Semple at "Wheelhouse," Beith, North Ayrshire, 1931.	131
Figure 8.1	Anant Shastri with his family.	196
Figure 8.2	Photograph of an inmate of Mukti Sadan "before and after" her arrival.	202
Figure 8.3	Ramabai at work on her translation of the Bible into popular Marathi.	214
Figure 9.1	"I was thirsty and you gave me to drink" in *Mitteilungen der Schweizerischen Hilfskomitees für die Mission in Indien*.	221
Figure 9.2	Eugène Burnand (1850–1921), "Go forth into all the world and preach the gospel to all creatures" 1915.	231
Figure 9.3	Sundar Singh in Lausanne 1922.	232
Figure 9.4	Sadhu Sundar Singh in Saanen, March 1922.	235
Figure 9.5	"As you look for me wholeheartedly, I will let myself be found by you [Jeremiah 29: 13]," *Mitteilungen der Kanaresischen Mission* 4.4, July 1922.	236
Figure 10.1	Chen Jianmin.	263
Figure 10.2	Chien Jianmin's *Five Elements Stūpa*, Taipei.	266

Foreword

Sujit Sivasundaram

The search for authenticity and purity has often necessitated a sojourn to somewhere far away while setting aside the known. Yet if archaic forms of pilgrimage, ascetic wandering and evangelism were already characterized in this way, such longings were accelerated by the late modern period as this volume makes clear in great detail. On the one hand the acceleration of a search for authenticity and purity in far away places came to be because of the possibilities provided by new technologies. On the other hand, it was also connected with a period of intensified territorial imperialism radiating outwards from Europe and an intensified stage of capitalism. Yet if these are infrastructural, political and financial changes, the volume before us pays less attention to these themes and focuses instead on the individual in the midst of this period of profound change. A recurrent idea is that this individual life is "interstitial," "in-between" and "hybrid." It is not fully formed and its twisting paths denote a characteristic feature of religious practice of this age.

There are different ways of explaining this interstitiality. One might point to the reconsideration of what religion is, and the redefinition of specific religions, or even "world religion," in the light of new knowledge and ethical commitments as well as secularism and the demarcation of the non-religious. But the life in transit in this set of decades also comes to be because of new modes of association and institutionalisation, about which this volume provides plenty of evidence. Circulating lives were also generated partly from late-modern political expression and fraternity which had dizzying axes of coordination as the authors of this volume demonstrate. Additionally, the vast migrations of this era were bringing people into contact, while making it possible for people to "pass" between identities. At the heart of this passing and mutation of significations were religious beliefs and the solidarities that they provided across other identities. Together with these individuals on the move, there also travelled vast numbers of texts and chronicles of various kinds, for this was an intense period of translation, printing and comparative studies and religious texts were at the heart of this programme and scholarly networks. The "global" could also come to characterise the imagination of religions in this period as they were cartographically imagined and statistically computed.

Yet in the midst of all of these potentialities which were new and which pertained to the definition of religion as well as its texts, institutions and membership; and the ideological context and globality of religiosity; there was much failure. The dreams of global conversation were unmet. The interstitial often did not move into one or other form or character, falling back into exceptionality rather than wide representative width. In this sense the stories told here were often subaltern or marginal ones, even though it is important to be clear that many of the actors here are elites of some kind or the other. For religiosity and class-status or social aspiration often went together in this period. Given recent critiques of connected histories, it is pleasing to see attention to the limits of connection in this volume as well as connectivity's underside in capitalism, commerce and privileged modes of access to incessant travel.

In reading this volume, one wonders then how it opens a vista back again on disconnected histories of religion; or for instance a religious practice which is articulated as determinedly local. For if this period was one of religious nomadism, it is certainly the case that less universalist and less absorptive ages of religiosity soon followed in the later twentieth century. At the same time another mode of subalterneity involved religious and millenarian revolt of various kinds. Rather than romanticising this age of the high modern, might it then be said that the two phases of connection as well as disconnection, or for that matter what might in turn be described first as localism and second as repeated mobility, are inherently related? In the modern, does one set the context for the other?

For opening up such a rich vista of histories of experience while foregrounding religion, which surely is a key theme in late modern history, while placing these at the heart of connected approaches, the authors of this volume deserve congratulations. This is a volume that is worthy of wide reading by Asianists, global historians and scholars of religious studies and should be read from start to finish; the intertwining of cases generates an assembly which is telling for this age. This assembly gets to the contortions of this period with subtlety and nuance.

About the author

Sujit Sivasundaram is Professor of World History and Fellow, Gonville and Caius College, Cambridge University. His most recent book is *Waves Across the South: A New History of Revolution and Empire* (University of Chicago Press, 2020).

Editor's Preface

PHILIPPE BORNET

The project

This book gathers contributions originally presented at a double panel entitled "Transnational Encounters and Religion: Following the threads of connected histories (nineteenth-twentieth centuries)" of the International Association for the History of Religions Congress in Erfurt, July 2015. All contributions have been reworked to integrate results of the rich exchanges that took place at this occasion. A few authors joined the project after the initial panel: Gwilym Beckerlegge, Gautam Chakrabarty, Parinitha Shetty, Steven Sutcliffe and Minyu Zhang. The international profile of the contributors mirrors an important aspect of the methodological project proposed in the book: to bring into relation records spread in different locations and telling different aspects of a same story. This logically implies to seek the expertise of people who happen to be proficient with one or the other set of documents, in one or the other language, in a collaborative fashion.

About the book

The first part, "Transnational Trajectories and Individual Appropriations of Religion" focuses on various actors who interacted with religious frameworks, appropriated them for different idiosyncratic purposes and ended up creating original combinations in the fringes of religious institutions. In his chapter, "'In-Between' Religiosity," Gautam Chakrabarti, deals with the figure of Anthony Firingee (?–1836) and his religious activities in colonial Calcutta. Himself of Portuguese origin, and a product of colonial translocal networks, Firingee appropriated the vocabulary of local rituals addressed to Kālī and Durgā before passing it to a broader audience. Focusing on the notion of hybridity, this is a case, not so much of "religion on the move" (since the religious practice remains in Bengal and retains its Bengali provinciality), but of how an imperial context such as colonial Bengal could work as a space of hybridization, inflecting a tradition in new directions.

In the contribution of Gwilym Beckerlegge, "The Making of the Ideal Transnational Disciple," we are invited to revisit the translocal biography of one of Vivekananda's disciples. Deviating from standard narratives emphasizing the fulfilment of Margaret Noble's spiritual quest by her guru and her Irish origins that would explain her involvement with the Indian struggle for Independence, Beckerlegge focuses on her formative years in London. Through various encounters with prominent figures active in education, religion and politics, she developed an interest for educational policies, social activism, and alternative forms of religion that would then develop during her stay in India. Her life itself can be considered as a translocal space, aggregating and rearranging ideas and practices borrowed from various contexts.

The chapter of Dwayne Ryan Menezes, "The Curious Case of the Drs. D'Abreu," explores the opportunities offered to local individuals by religious transnational networks. It is argued that Catholicism provided both geographical mobility and a respectable identity to Indian migrants settling in Great Britain towards the beginning of the twentieth century. It helps to reflect on the role of global religious networks such as Catholicism (and more specifically, Jesuits) in the strategic (re-)negotiation of social roles shaped in a colonial context. Methodologically, Menezes' contribution is a perfect example of a work that brings together documents spread in distant archives, from India to Great Britain, Australia and the USA, so as to reconstitute the puzzle of transnational biographical itineraries.

In his contribution, "Religion and the 'Simple Life'," Steven Sutcliffe deals with a Scottish exponent of the "simple life" within early twentieth-century networks of life reform or *Lebensreform*. Analysing Semple's highly idiosyncratic synthesis, opposed to any form of institutionalized religion and including elements borrowed to popular conceptions of Tolstoy and Gandhi, Sutcliffe argues that such a combination was made possible by a series of translocal exchanges. It focuses on different forms of transnational communication, such as travels along the network of an institution, interpersonal contacts and publications. This chapter shows eloquently how intellectual interactions, not systematically mediated through religious institutions, can produce religious reconfiguration and change.

In the last chapter of this part, "Re-discovering Buddha's Land," Minyu Zhang explores how translocal networks linking Germany, India and China contributed to the formation of Indian studies in China. The author demonstrates the impact of three interrelated networks in this history: that of the revived and mythologized Buddhist China-India connection, that of the scholarly network around Western, particularly German orientalists—with the example of Ji Xianlin, (1911-2009) bringing back German textual criticism to China—and a political "Asiatist" network interested in socialist and anti-imperialist ideology. Exploring the interface between the academic study of "subject matters" and the ways these studies have been put to practical use, the chapter makes it clear that social sciences about India and Indian religions in China have been mirroring major social and political concerns.

The second part of the book, "Religions on the Move," is interested in figures of individuals who acted as "religious entrepreneurs" (a terminology used in Nile Green's work, Green 2015) by actively promoting a set of concepts and practices related to "religion" and attempting to build a community of followers around it. In his chapter, "Charles Pfoundes and the Forgotten First Buddhist Mission to the West," Brian Bocking revives the memory of the first (1889) Japanese Buddhist Mission to the West. Building on results of a thorough empirical investigation, he brings to light different general questions that are helpful for dealing with cases of "transnational religious interactions": for example, the issue of declared vs. actual results of the religious activity, with a particular attention to the creative results coming out of "failed" projects; the role of travel infrastructure (roads, rail) and the question to whom it was accessible as favourable factors—or on the contrary, as negative constraints—for the pursuit of transnational religious projects; the idiosyncratic conception of religion (or "Buddhism," or "Christianity" etc.) of "religious entrepreneurs," and the necessity to question those encompassing labels, or the role of the telegraph as a "Victorian internet," enabling the promoters of religious projects to communicate almost immediately with partners, since at least the end of the nineteenth century. All these questions provide a welcome conceptual framework that helps to delineate the specificities of the late nineteenth and early twentieth century for the circulation of religious practices on a global scale, beyond religious affiliations.

In the next chapter, "Travelling through Interstitial Spaces," Parinitha Shetty explores the tumultuous life of Pandita Ramabai. Having encountered multiple socio-religious frameworks (her birth into the Citpāvan Brahmin caste, her exposure to the Prārthanā Samāj and Brahmo Samāj, her encounter with Protestant Christianity), she strove to find opportunities to build for herself a "liminal location." Neither here nor there, her original trajectory witnesses both the opportunities offered by the interaction with institutional forms of religion and the difficulties to get a message through while inhabiting a liminal space. The case also offers insights into the gendered aspects of "religious translocality": Pandita Ramabai not only travelled through heavily gendered networks but also addressed the issue of gender in front of her various, international audiences.

In his chapter, "A 'Christian Hindu Apostle'?," Philippe Bornet focuses on Sadhu Sundar Singh (1889-1929?) and on the way he crossed various borders:

religious, political, social, geographical. Recontextualizing first Sundar Singh in his local context, it is argued that the concept of *sādhu* functioned as a key to unlock an "interstitial space" not controlled by external forms of authority and filled with elements borrowed from different sources. Focusing then on his tour in Switzerland, 1922—a tour out of which came an impressive number of publications that would have a lasting effect—it appears that the tour produced creative encounters with members of different movements in the margins of "institutional religions." Overwhelming the intentions of the tour's organizers, Sundar Singh's performances led in part to creative reconfigurations (e.g. with the Swedenborgian Church) and in part to open conflict (e.g. with Protestant liberal circles, as represented by the pastor O. Pfister).

In the last chapter of this part, "The Chen Jianmin Legacy," Fabienne Jagou follows the complex biographical itinerary of a Buddhist master, Chen Jianmin, focusing on his original synthesis of Chinese, Indian and Tibetan traditions. She then analyses the construction of Chen Jianmin's successful legacy through disciples spread in various locations who more often than not, did not know each other and would not agree with each other. This is a great case to analyse the translocal consequences of the encounter of a traditional scheme to perpetuate a legacy with modern communication techniques, with consequences felt up to the contemporary West.

The afterword by Maya Burger, originally provided as a response to the panel and thoroughly reformulated, pushes the discussion further and gives an important summary of issues that emerge from the diversity of the cases. It is both a fitting concluding chapter and an invitation for additional research in the same general direction.

A few questions

In his *Birth of the Modern World*, and surveying the period from 1780 to 1914, Christopher Bayly noted that the three domains of "religious travel," print and "religious buildings" underwent radical changes in the nineteenth century on a worldwide level, transcending boundaries between religions and contributing to the building of what he calls "global 'empires of religion'" (Bayly 2004, 351). While this general claim certainly calls for empirical studies on specific cases, it appeared that beyond the diversity of geographical, cultural and religious contexts explored in each contribution, one can discern similar patterns about the circulation of ideas and practices related to religion. Inspired by B. Bocking's contribution in the present volume, the following questions appeared as *leitmotivs* that connect most of the cases explored here.

1. How did the developments in media and transports of the beginning of the twentieth century (postal mail, telegraph, train, the opening of the Suez Canal) affect the transmission of "religious" ideas and practices?

2. How did the actual location (regions, cities, or smaller spatial entities) of contacts contribute to the global circulation of discourses and practices about "religion"? In what way did specific locations such as London, Calcutta or Kalimpong make interactions (and which) possible and specific?
3. How were conceptions or practices about "religion" endowed with new meanings, instrumentalized or rejected in the different contexts they crossed? Is there any regularity in the way these processes happened?
4. Did translocal relations involving religious aspects provide opportunities to fight against specific power structures, in particular in the colonial context of the early twentieth century?
5. Are "religious exchanges" patterned by gender in a way that is specific to the period? Are female voices easier to hear then rather than earlier? If so, how and with what effects on the available documentation?
6. Considering the development of scholarly studies about religion in the beginning of the twentieth century, did such encounters contribute to building stereotyped conceptions of "religion" or did they, on the contrary, extend the range of possible ideas on "religion"?
7. Finally, what are the consequences of these micro-stories of religious exchanges for the history of the study of religion and for theorizing in the field? Is it possible to "generalize" about religion from the different cases in any way, or are we stuck with a juxtaposition of particular stories with similar patterns? What models of comparison, networks or translation could possibly be helpful?

Reference

Bayly, Christopher A. 2004. *The Birth of the Modern World: 1780-1914: Global Connections and Comparisons*. Malden: Blackwell.

Green, Nile. 2015. *Terrains of Exchange: Religious Economies of Global Islam*. Oxford: Oxford University Press.

About the author

Philippe Bornet is Senior lecturer in South Asian studies at the Department of South Asian Languages and Civilizations, University of Lausanne, Switzerland. After stays in Tübingen and at the University of Chicago, he completed a PhD in the comparative history of religions on rituals of hospitality in Jewish and Indian texts. His current research deals with interactions between India and Europe and more specifically, Swiss missionaries in South India in the beginning of the twentieth century. Recent publications include *Rites et pratiques de l'hospitalité*, 2010, *Religions in Play*, 2012 (ed. with M. Burger) and *L'orientalisme des marges* (ed. with S. Gorshenina), 2014.

PART I

Introduction

— 1 —

From Comparative to Connected Religion: Translocal Aspects of Orientalism and the Study of Religion

Philippe Bornet

Introducing the notion of "connected history" and situating it among other related approaches ("global history," "comparative history," "entangled history," "cultural transfers," etc.), the chapter examines the potentialities as well as the challenges it presents for the comparative study of religions. Building on recent considerations about a critical "comparative religion," it is argued that a "connected religion" approach has the potential to both criticize classical taxonomies and construct alternative ways to think about concepts and practices about religion. In order to assess the approach, two examples are introduced and contrasted: Looking at F.M. Müller's involvement with Bengali (Dwarkanath Tagore, Debendranath Tagore, Keshub Chandra Sen), Marathi (Behramji Malabari) and Japanese scholars (Nanjo Bunyu and Kenjiu Kasawara), it is argued that the orientalist project is not only better understood when re-contextualized in this global context, but that it also had consequences beyond the scholarly world, offering opportunities to all involved actors. The second example explores the encounter of a Swiss missionary, Jakob Urner, with specialists of the Vīraśaiva literatures such as Channappa Uttangi. In so doing, attention is paid to the often discordant and oppositional dynamics constitutive of political and religious processes, to the development of scholarly representations (mainstream or marginal), and to their impact on the study of religions as an academic discipline. It is also suggested that such an approach is better carried out in a collaborative framework, since it generally involves dealing with sources that stem from various cultural, institutional or linguistic backgrounds.

Translocal, transnational, entangled, crossed, connected, and other kinds of histories

In recent years, much attention has been devoted to issues related to the study of "transnational" or "translocal" topics in history, with a particular interest for flows of people, objects, ideas or practices across geographical and political boundaries.[1] This renewed interest is evident in the apparition of a flurry of labels such as "transnational history," "entangled history" (Mintz 1985), "cultural transfers" (Espagne 1999), "crossed history" ("histoire croisée," Werner and Zimmermann 2006), "symmetric history" ("histoire à parts égales," Bertrand 2011), along with "guide books" and their "companions" (Iriye and Saunier 2009). Even if this is nothing entirely new, considering early attempts at weaving historical narratives over vast spatial areas such as early histories of the so-called silk-roads (Herrmann 1910) or Fernand Braudel's classical study of the Mediterranean (Braudel 1949), these different approaches result from historiographical debates of the late twentieth century that can be considered as a "transnational turn." They perceive themselves as various, though not always clearly distinguished from each other, antidotes to the epistemological implications of territories being divided along borders that reflect the modern formation of nation-states.[2] Despite typical objects of the study of religions being often "translocal" or "transnational"—whether pilgrims, books or relics—the significance of this turn for theorizing about religion might not have been fully acknowledged yet. In this introduction, I would like to explore a few implications of recent reflections about "entangled" or "connected" histories for the study of religion before assessing the program it invites us to through two examples.

From comparative history to connected histories

In his essay on comparative history published in 1928 (Bloch 1928), the French historian of the Annales school, Marc Bloch (1886–1944), distinguished a type of comparison that works on distinct societies in time and space from another type that presupposes mutual relations between neighbouring societies—a kind of comparison that is actually not "really" comparison, since in the end, the compared elements are shown to belong to a single historical process (Bloch 1928, 17–19). Mentioning J.G. Frazer's *Golden Bough* as an instance of the first type, Bloch prefers the precision of the second. He goes on with a comparative study of the "individualization" of agrarian exploitations in early modern England and France, and shows the benefits of the comparative method for both discovering documents on a local scale and for

---

1. "Translocal" has been preferred for the volume's title, because it does not necessarily imply contacts across national borders and suggests interactions across other types of borders (language, race, socio-economical class, religion) within a given political or spatial entity.
2. As Bayly *et al.* (2006, 1441–1442) observed, the shared purpose of these different types of history is to "break out of the nation-state or singular nation-state as the category of analysis, and especially to eschew the ethnocentrism that once characterized the writing of history in the West." Bayly's (2004) own attempt at writing a revised "global history" of the modern world is a good illustration.

their interpretation. He concludes that historians should expand the spatial area of their interests and move further away from national frames.³

This conception of comparative history—itself followed by an impressive number of case studies—has come under criticism in the last two decades, especially among historians specializing in the one or the other style of "transnational history." For example, Michel Espagne noted that in many comparative studies, there is a tendency to discard the diachronic dimension to the profit of an imagined synchrony of the compared constellations. He added that the comparative process almost inevitably freezes the poles of the comparison and reifies the very political or social entities it is supposed to deconstruct (Espagne 1994, 112–115). In the end however, Espagne does not substantially diverge from Bloch: he insists on the one hand on the necessity to break away from the national framework, emphasizing that "only a focus on the genealogical mechanisms that led to the reification of oppositions can define a supra-national historiographical space" (Espagne 1994, 119). On the other hand, he recommends an approach reminiscent of Bloch's work on societies that have been in contact. Espagne's own contribution to the debate is his theorization (with M. Werner) of "cultural transfers," a concept which invites historians to "privilege phenomena of re-appropriation and re-semantization of an imported cultural good, considering what this process reveals about the context of importation and paying a particular attention of the socio-cultural background of mediators" (Espagne 2005).

Equally critical of both national and comparative history, Serge Gruzinski writes that

> Comparative history appeared for a long time as a workable solution and it was at the origins of fruitful exchanges. The perspectives it brings to light, however, are sometimes only illusions: the choice of objects to compare, the selected frames, criteria and determinisms ..., the interpretative frameworks of underlying problems ... still rely on philosophies or theories of history that already provide the answers to the raised questions. In the worst case, comparative history is only an insidious resurgence of Euro-centrism. (Gruzinski 2001, 86)

As a way out of the issues of comparative history, Gruzinski and Sanjay Subrahmanyam introduce a notion of "connected histories" which consists in "reconnecting" records that have been artificially separated by historiographical (often nationalist) preferences. Focusing on events occurring in distant geographical spaces or between historical records of a same event kept in

---

3. "Therefore, the most evident, and perhaps, necessary teaching of comparative history is that it might be time to think about breaking the outdated topographic compartments in which we pretend to encase social realities." (Bloch 1928, 44, my translation).

distant archival spaces, the program is not entirely at odds with that of "cultural transfers."[4] It however comes with a few specificities of its own. The most important is (1) a focus on *micro-histories* that are re-contextualized into a larger, global framework: this contrasts with "world history" or "global history" in the sense that it does not attempt to write single events into a general (and often diffusionist) narrative. It also contrasts with "purely" local histories, since they are shown to be an aspect of wider processes.[5] A second specificity (2) is an attention to change as observed in various *situations of interaction*: often working at a biographical level, connected histories entail not only the study of networks centred on specific actors, practices, ideas, but also a study of how these practices and ideas are modified, re-semanticized in the various contexts they travel to or in.[6] Thirdly (3), the approach generally requires a *multiple contextualization* to shed light on the divergent local or regional dimensions of an object (or a person) in movement.[7] Since archives have often been constituted in specific political or religious configurations, they implicitly tend to mirror and reinforce the institution they represent. As Deacon *et al.* (2010, 3) noted, in order to retrieve the "messiness" of specific trajectories, one needs to work "in the interstices of the archive." From an historiographical point of view, this is all the truer when dealing with connections between distant areas whose records were kept by distinct historiographical regimes. The challenge is then to work across different archives, places, documents, languages, to bring them together into a single scholarly output, much in the sense of Romain Bertrand's "symmetric history" (Bertrand 2011) or Sujit Sivasundaram's "cross-contextualization" (Sivasundaram 2010).

---

4. To my knowledge, the first use of the expression "connected history" goes back to Strayer's collective work (Strayer 1989). Methodological implications are set forth in the works of S. Subrahmanyam (1997) and S. Gruzinski (2001).

5. Potter and Saha (2015)'s plea for "connected histories of empire" goes in the same direction. The authors stress that "Connected histories of empire grounded in specific places and concerned with particular individuals might help us avoid the simplifications encouraged by the planetary scale of analysis that absorbs many Global historians." Examples of historical narratives focusing on individual trajectories inscribed in larger settings include works of historians of the *microstoria* school, such as C. Ginzburg's *The Cheese and the Worms* (Ginzburg 1980) or E. Grendi's studies about the city of Genoa.

6. This is different from the study of the circulation of commodities, which constitutes the main topic of S. Mintz's "entangled history" of sugar (Mintz 1985).

7. This is akin to Sivasundaram's notion of "cross-contextualization" (Sivasundaram 2010, 154, in particular: "[F]or a more globally representative history of science to emerge, it is necessary to experiment with divorcing sources from their usual sites of contextualization so as to take them to quite different contexts, at a distance from their obvious authors and readers.")

This is of course not an attempt at producing a "neutral narrative" or at constructing an Archimedean point of objectivity, but rather an effort at multiplying perspectives and reconstructing the different, often diverging, sides of a single event or biographical trajectory. Since the selection of relevant documents is entirely left to the scholar, the corpus will necessarily reflect his or her position and invites to reflexive comments and revision. A typical example of connected history is Subrahmanyam's study of Vasco da Gama (Subrahmanyam 1998) in which the standard, nationalist, narrative of the Portuguese explorer is re-evaluated in the light of a wide array of sources. Re-contextualizing the expedition into the larger setting of Indian Ocean and South Indian history, Subrahmanyam's study provides a welcome correction to nationalist retellings of the same. The approach also encourages the integration of scholars who happen to be more familiar with some corpuses or with some languages rather than with others on a collaborative mode: this is then an invitation to internationalize an academic discipline such as history or the study of religions.

From early to late modernity

If the notion of "connected history" has been originally developed in the framework of the "early modern period," it can be extended well beyond the eigthteenth century. As Subrahmanyam puts it:

> It is true that this approach is essentially confined to works dealing with the period from the sixteenth to the eigthteenth century. It did not have much effect yet on the nineteenth and twentieth centuries, especially because of the control exerted by national history, much stronger for this period. ... If done for the nineteenth and twentieth centuries, I imagine that this would be called "transnational history" or something similar.0 I do not care: the way one calls it does not matter; the approach does.
> (Subrahmanyam 2012, n.p.)

A major difference between the early modern and the late modern period, however, is that in the latter case (and with the possible exception of studies working on the relations between two or more European regions in contact, such as Espagne 1999), the approach will almost inevitably encounter debates marked by postcolonial studies. In the wake of Edward Said's seminal book *Orientalism* (1978), two different sets of attitudes emerged: on the one hand, studies have analysed different contexts in which Western representations have maintained and reinforced structures of power, through various mechanisms and in various registers, from architecture, law, medicine to political institutions and religion (for example Inden 1992, Cohn 1996 or Dirks 2001). On the other hand, out of critical observations formulated shortly after the publication of Said's essay, studies outlined processes of interaction

(Kopf 1980), exploring the "dialogical" construction of historical situations (Irschick 1994), the contribution of non-European history to the construction of European modernity (Bayly 2004) or the different modes of the circulation of knowledge (Raj 2007).

Each array of studies comes with its specific risks: in putting an emphasis on the power imbalances between the "West and the Rest" (S. Hall), analyses are exposed to a certain one-sidedness, focusing the attention on the agency of Western actors with the unintended effects of silencing their local interlocutors and reifying the poles of the interaction, such as Europe—Asia/Africa, colonizers—colonized etc. (Stoler and Cooper 1997, 9). The second set of approaches has been criticized for not giving sufficient consideration to the asymmetries of power and presenting as a "dialogue" what should rather be described as a monologue forced upon dominated groups (Dirks 2001, 303–315).[8]

Connected histories are of course closer to the second set of approaches, but do need to take seriously the concern of irenicism and the fact that in forced encounters, not all possible actions are available to all agents (Asad 1993, 15–16). There is certainly a possible middle way between the quasi deterministic character of Foucault's "discourse" (which leaves little space to individual agency or movements of resistance) and a view that would optimistically emphasize the agency of individual actors, ignoring all of the external socio-political factors affecting (but not determining) their actions.[9]

Connected histories of "religion" and religion

Conceptual boundaries in the study of religion

What can we learn from this for the study of religion specifically? How does this relate with current conversations about theory in the discipline? Like history has its evils, so does the study of religion, in at least two related domains. There is first a tension that is consubstantial to the project of a non-religious history of religion. As Bruce Lincoln observed (Lincoln 1996, 225), religious traditions tend to present themselves in transcendent and unchanging terms and have generally a teleological conception of their own history—in a way similar to nationalist narratives, except, arguably, for the added reference to a transcendent authority. Conversely, history as a discipline insists on disruptions, changes, processes of borrowing, thus running almost inevitably

---

8. These risks are evident in Subrahmanyam's analysis (2007, 43–44) of the opposed readings of B. Cohn and W. Pinch about the encounter of the British ambassador Thomas Roe (1581–1644) with the Mughal emperor Jahangir.

9. This "middle path" seems to be the perspective taken in recent studies, for example in Peabody's study of the Rajasthani kingdom of Kota (2003), in the work of Dodson (2007a) on the "double practices" of Hindu Sanskrit scholars to the service of the East India Company, or in that of Manjapra (2014) on the cultural relations between Indians and Germans, and their position towards the British.

against a "religious" point of view. For the study of religion, there is then a basic need to question the conceptual boundaries erected by the traditions themselves—particularly so because many of them have efficiently organized their own archives and constructed narratives about their past, be it in the form of Sri Lankan Buddhist chronicles (on which see Bornet 2019) or Christian ecclesiastical history.

The second tension can be felt in the academic study of religions itself, with tendencies to compartmentalize or isolate the objects along boundaries such as institutions (Christianity, Islam, etc.), regions, languages or ethnic groups. It can be the result of a scholarly appropriation of religious, "emic" discourses, as in the case of "world religions" with their implied exclusivity and homogeneity, resulting in grouping together material meant to belong to a specific tradition while excluding what is thought to belong to others (Masuzawa 2005 and Fitzgerald 2000). A similar process is at work in "orientalist" works that tend to reify and categorize Asian traditions, often creating artificial oppositions and boundaries (King 2006 and Bornet 2014b).[10] More pragmatically, it can also be an effect of the organization of departments (with chairs either specialized in areas or in "religions"), it can be related to linguistic difficulties (sticking to the language one is familiar with and not looking beyond) or to epistemological preferences, such as C. Geertz's notion of "religion as a system of symbols" which paves the way for an apprehension of religions as discrete and stable institutions, encouraging scholars to look for causes and consequences of religion within the same system (and not, for example, in political or social realms).[11]

Comparative and connected religion

Against such biases, comparison certainly offers potential ways out, provided it is done with a minimum of carefulness (Freiberger 2019). In one of several essays on the topic and echoing Bloch's distinction, J. Z. Smith differentiated between "analogical" and "genealogical" modes of comparisons (Smith 1990, 47). He warned against the risks entailed by genealogical projects that compare two historically related objects: while in principle workable and usefully undermining claims about the "purity" of a given tradition, a genealogical approach might conceal the scholar's own "interests and activities" and reconstruct teleological pedigrees.[12] For Smith, the analogical project,

---

10. For example, Smith (1995) and Prothero (2010) defend opposite views but share a same conceptual framework made of reified, and thus "disconnected" religious traditions.
11. Asad (1983) severely criticized Geertz's notion of religion as a "system of symbols." More recently, Bornet (2016a) proposed a critical assessment of a model of religion based on C. Geertz in the light of Ram Mohan Roy's views about religion.
12. Smith (1990, 51) observed that "'genealogy' disguises and obscures the scholar's interests and activities allowing the illusion of passive observation." In an afterword

consisting in comparing two unrelated sets of data, remains the best way to critically contribute to the discipline. Giving up entirely the search for similarities to be explained by a common origin, and interested in both similarities and differences, analogical comparison can lead to critical contributions on the conceptual and theoretical level, and works as an antidote against ethno-, Euro-, Christian-, and other centrisms.[13] The main difficulty lies in the need to master not only the languages relevant to each context, but also two unrelated socio-historical frameworks, so as to avoid the "freezing" and de-historicizing effect pointed out by Espagne. It implies to work inductively from sources that are precisely contextualized, so that the comparative project becomes a comparative study of two sets of documents.[14]

Without contesting the virtues of the analogical approach, that there is a possibility for a viable instantiation of a genealogical project.[15] Analysing the various inputs that constitute a specific situation on a "genealogical mode," an approach of "connected religion"—as one might call it—challenges the claims of actors about the purity or unchanging nature of their tradition. Looking at processes that construct a tradition from different angles and involving a multiple contextualization (as does the framework of "cultural transfers"), it addresses the concern about de-historicizing the data. Moreover, the single operation to bring together documents that were not meant to be read in the light of each other plays a role similar to the intent behind Smith's analogical comparison[16]: it disturbs the stability of each document taken separately and draws the attention on the scholar's own intellectual

---

to a book on comparison in the study of religion, Smith noted that preconditions for a sound "genealogical comparison" are "not fulfilled in the usual comparison of religious phenomena, but [added that] there is nothing, in principle, to prevent [a] successful deployment." (Smith 2000, 238)

13. With a similar idea, Lincoln (1989, 172) observes: "[T]he only alternative to comparison is one brand of parochialism or another: That is, the stance of those who privilege the data with which they happen to be familiar while ignoring, and thus remaining ignorant of, the rest. Among the most prevalent brands are ethnocentrism, androcentrism, Eurocentrism, and the other centrisms as yet unnamed (e.g., those of class, temporality, and genre), all of which yield generalizations of a highly prejudicial nature—and not accidentally so."

14. On this "weaker" type of comparison as a tool to "de-provincialize" the study of religion, see Freiberger 2009, Holdrege 2010, Bornet 2010, Lincoln 2012 and Bornet 2016b.

15. This conception of "genealogy" is close to Bergunder's "genealogische Praxis" (Bergunder 2011, 46 and 54).

16. Smith 2014, 180: "[I]f I am right, what we do with comparison is to take something out of its place, something else out of its place, and put them in a place that is in our head. ... Our way to doing it is by putting them by neighbours that they never intended to have and to see what happens."

operations. By rewiring separate historiographical traditions, a "connected religion" framework acts as a powerful antidote against the reproduction of narratives that sedimented along the lines of the archives they are part of. In this sense, working at the level of sources, this particular type of genealogical work is precisely able to counter teleological tendencies and not to reinforce them. Its difficulties are similar to the ones noted above about the analogical perspective (mastering languages, socio-historical contexts etc.), making it equally well suited for collaborative work.

Given this, there are at least two levels of analysis where a "connected religion" approach can be particularly relevant. First, one can follow the journeys of categories, classifications, practices, theories formulated by actors with a notion of "religion" (or "sacred," "mysticism," "ritual" etc.), paying a special attention to processes of appropriation, re-semantization, hybridization etc. It is then possible to re-evaluate the narrative of categories manufactured in metropolitan centres before globally spreading—more often than not, along the lines of colonialism and Christian missions—under a more dynamic light: not only the history of uniquely Western categories being consistently (mis)applied to non-Western contexts, but also (or, rather) a complex history of appropriations, rejections, and subversions on a global scale, in processes that could be described as dialogical (Irschick 1994) rather than unilateral. This could be called "connected 'religion'," with quotation marks around "religion," indicating that the conceptualization of data as "religious" is the work of the actors under study ("religion" as an emic category) and not that of the scholar.

Second, and removing the quotation marks, one can follow the circulation of religious currents, worldviews, practices on a global scale, across traditional labels, committing to one or the other working definition of "religion."[17] There is certainly no need to limit oneself to ideas and practices labelled as "religious" by their actors. On the contrary, studying religious discourses, ideas and practices expressed by various terms in different vernacular languages (and their transformations when moving across cultures, languages and political formations) is, as Michael Pye noted, crucial for fighting Eurocentric tendencies in the field (Pye 2003).[18]

---

17. One will naturally be careful as to how the concept is formulated. The important point is that, as a heuristic device, it is not bound to be designed after a specifically Christian or European model. This position has been convincingly argued by Sweetman (2003).

18. In this perspective, Pye (1994), 122 analyzed the use of the Japanese term *shūkyō* as an equivalent of "religion" in Tominaga Nakamoto's work (eighteenth century). The discussion about extra-European concepts functionally and semantically similar to that of "religion" has been clearly framed by Kollmar-Paulenz (2012 and 2013) and is further elaborated in the research group "Multiple Secularities—Beyond the West,

Here, one can begin by observing that religious communities are among the oldest "translocal communities" and that processes of globalization are by no way specifically modern but were largely anticipated by religious actors: Buddhist, Christian, Jaina or Manichean monks, Christian or Muslim pilgrims, Buddhist and Christian missionaries represent excellent examples of actors whose activity went across geographical and political boundaries since the beginnings of their respective institutions. Examples of "connected religion" in this perspective include Wilhelm Halbfass's masterly work on the relations between India and Europe (Halbfass 1981), Silk Road studies dealing with the various changes religious ideas and practices underwent while moving spatially (Klimkeit 1998 and Foltz 1999), the study of works conceptualizing religious diversity in the context of their redaction, such as the seventeenth century *Dabistān-i-Maẕāhib* of Mubad Shah (Behl 2010), Subrahmanyam's study of millenarist currents in Eurasia around 1500 across linguistic, political and religious affiliations (Subrahmanyam 1997), examinations of the early encounters between Portuguese administrators and Buddhists in colonial Sri Lanka (Berkwitz 2013), or micro-studies about ancient or early modern contacts in the Indian Ocean (Singh and Dhar 2014).

The neat theoretical distinction between religion with and without quotation marks, however, is not entirely unproblematic, especially considering the fact that categories and discourses easily move from one level (i.e. scholarly) to another (i.e. practical), so that "religion" becomes religion and conversely, for example when groups redefine themselves and their practices with reference to "scholarly terms" or when scholars are influenced by elite religious practitioners. At least from the nineteenth century on, it is not possible to strictly distinguish between the two perspectives, since scholarly categories and discussions about religion travelled widely along with practices and doctrines. This "fluidity" is particularly evident in re-evaluations of the role of missionaries as mediators of scientific conceptions in the Pacific Ocean (Sivasundaram 2005), in interactions between British (Evangelical) orientalists and Muslim scholars in colonial contexts (Green 2015), or in the history of religiously (and politically) engaged transnational and scholarly movements such as Theosophy (Burger 2014 and Yoshinaga 2009).

For both levels of analysis, the most interesting actors are different mediators who regularly crossed borders, such as missionaries, members of diaspora communities, monks, pilgrims, scholars, tourists, translators, or travelling revolutionaries, who all played key roles in disseminating and reconfiguring notions and practices about religion. Looking at various appropriations at an individual level, the approach pays a particular attention to

---

Beyond Modernities" (http://www.multiple-secularities.de).

creative reinventions, change and discontinuity.[19] As explored in the present book, the lives of individuals can represent valid entry points into processes that connect local and global dimensions, provided one does not lean into the linearity and teleological tendency of autobiographies, but rather emphasize discontinuity, change and strategies that construct identities through a multiple contextualization (Bourdieu 1986).[20]

If the focus is on "primary actors," it should not obliterate the role of "secondary" players in the encounters: interpreters, language teachers, local informants, or diggers working on the behalf of Western archaeologists, whose agency has often been downplayed because they are largely absent or marginal in the records—a phenomenon that Tavakoli-Targhi aptly termed "orientalism's genesis amnesia," calling for studies that examine actors from "peripheral zones" or subaltern actors (Tavakoli-Targhi 1996).[21] By multiplying historiographical perspectives on a given topic and retrieving archival documents that have been left unexplored, a "connected religion" framework increases the chance that such figures re-emerge.[22]

Two connected histories of religion

I would like now to exemplify the approach through two actual examples: the case of a rather sedentary scholar, Friedrich Max Müller (1823–1900), and that of a Swiss missionary to India, Jakob Urner (1887–1965).[23]

A non-travelling literatus: Max Müller (1823–1900)

In her biographical study of Friedrich Max Müller, Tomoko Masuzawa observed that "Müller never left the great libraries of Europe to experience in his own person 'the real India'" concluding that in this "somber nave of his biblioworkshop ... he continued to contemplate the possibility of pure, lit-

---

19. The focus on the aspect of individual appropriations echoes recent analyses about "lived religion" (McGuire 2008 and Rüpke 2016).
20. The cases explored by Bocking and Menezes in the present volume emphasize the fluidity of identities, perceptible in the way individuals chose pseudonyms for themselves so as to gain consideration among certain circles.
21. With a similar idea, Bornet and Gorshenina (2014a) encourage to look at what they call an "orientalism from the margins" and Green (2015, 103–138) sheds light on the crucial role played by a number of lesser-known "co-operators" of Western scholars.
22. For example, Subrahmanyam's study of Vasco da Gama pays a particular attention to the crucial roles played by Gama's Gujarati (?) pilot embarked in Malindi or by the convert Gaspar da Gama (Subrahmanyam 1998, 123–128 and 147–154)—figures largely ignored in nationalist retellings of the expedition.
23. The second case has been studied in the framework of a project on the relations between India and Switzerland in the twentieth century, directed by Prof. M. Burger (Lausanne) and Prof. A. Malinar (Zurich) and funded by the Swiss National Fund (SNF 147342).

eral signification, free of figures, beyond all names" (Masuzawa 1993, 59; 75). It is absolutely correct, of course, that Müller never travelled to India and it could seem at first that he is the worst possible example for an experiment in "connected religion." However, even if Müller indeed accomplished most of his career in European libraries, studying a textualized India and calling the Veda "his friend" (Müller 1899a, xii), there are signs suggesting that his contacts—certainly not with any "real India"—but with a few Indian scholars from select elitist circles, exerted at least some influence on his own views. In addition, his works were widely translated and moved along the transnational networks of major British publishers, deploying effects well beyond European and American academic circles. The ivory tower might be more porous than what has sometimes been asserted.

In an autobiographical volume, *Auld Lang Syne: My Indian Friends* (1899), Müller writes that when in Paris, in 1844, as he was working with Eugène Burnouf (1801–1852), he met an important member of the Brahmo Samāj, Dwarkanath Tagore (1794–1846), grandfather of the better-known Rabindranath Tagore (1861–1941). With him, Müller no doubt discussed Brahmo Samāj views about religion and differences between Indian and Western cultures. We know at least about one particular encounter, staging Müller playing the pianoforte and accompanying Tagore who was singing French or Italian classical songs. Upon Müller's repeated requests, Tagore played "real Indian music," provoking the perplexity of the German orientalist. Seeing his reaction, Müller tells us, Tagore expressed the following thoughts:

> You [Europeans] say our religion is no religion, our poetry no poetry, our philosophy no philosophy. We try to understand and appreciate whatever Europe has produced, but do not imagine that therefore we despise what India has produced. ... And if you would study our poetry, our religion, and our philosophy, you would find that we are not what you call heathens or miscreants, but know as much of the Unknowable as you do, and have seen perhaps even deeper into it than you have!"
>
> (Müller 1899a, 7–8)

Müller added: "He was not far wrong," implying that for him, any abstract definition of "religion," "poetry" or "philosophy" should be sufficiently ductile to account for Indian instantiations of the category. In his later work, Müller took the Indian material as a source of inspiration for his own theorizing, as he clearly states in his *Lectures on the Origin and Growth of Religion* (1878):

> I do not think therefore that I am exaggerating when I say that the sacred books of India offer for a study of religion in general, and particularly for the study of the origin and growth of religion, the same peculiar and unexpected advantages which the language of India, Sanskrit, has offered for the study of the origin and growth of human speech. It is for

that reason that I have selected the ancient religion of India to supply the historical illustrations of my own theory of the origin and growth of religion. That theory was suggested to me during a lifelong study of the sacred books of India; it rests therefore on facts, though
I am responsible for their interpretation. (Müller 1878, 135-136)

Even if based on a comparison between linguistics and religion that would be problematic by today's standards, Müller's theorization about religion is described as inductively rooted in the study of "the ancient religion of India." Of course, Müller tends to represent himself as having reached his conclusions independently, through his own philological work. By taking a closer look, however, it appears that Müller's views about religion were very similar to those circulating among Brahmo Samāj circles, such as the priority given to personal intuition in experiencing religion or the theistic postulate of a higher power, perceptible in all religions, and particularly so in ancient Indian traditions.[24]

The vehicles for the circulation of such ideas would not be hard to identify. After the early encounter with Dwarkanath Tagore, Müller remained in epistolary contact with leaders of the Brahmo Samāj (and its various offshoots), such as Debendranath Tagore (1817-1905), Protap Chandra Majumdar (1840-1905) and particularly Keshub Chandra Sen (1838-1884) from their encounter in London in 1870 until his death in 1884.[25] In the address he gave in 1883 for the 50th death anniversary of the Brahmo Samāj founder, Ram Mohan Roy (1772-1833) in the Bristol museum, Müller calls himself Roy's "sincere fol-

---

24. See Müller (1879, xxxvii-xxxviii): "Our powers of perceiving, of reasoning, and of believing may be more highly developed, but we cannot claim the possession of any verifying power or of any power of belief which they did not possess as well. ... The question is, whether there is or whether there is not, hidden in every one of the sacred books, something that could lift up the human heart from this earth to a higher world, something that could make man feel the omnipresence of a higher Power, something that could make him shrink from evil and incline to good, something to sustain him in the short journey through life." Compare with Sen (1876, 4 and 10): "If you search the ancient scriptures of the Hindus, you will find there the most sublime and beautiful conceptions of the Great Spirit will meet with sparkling texts pointing to Him Unseen. ... The Infinite Father above and the eternal home before, meet in one focus in the eye of faith, and may be said to be apprehended together in the intuitive consciousness."

25. On Sen's controversial figure, Kopf (1988, 107-108) observed: "Keshub, Rammohun Roy, Rabindranath Tagore, to name but three of the intellectual giants who emerged out of the so-called Bengal renaissance, underwent extreme changes of identity because they were neither simplistic Westernizers nor rabid nativists, but were highly-sophisticated cosmopolites with subtle, eclectic or synthetical intellects. ... In my judgment, only when we view Keshub as an interpreter of East-West encounter—and a very sensitive one at that—can we begin to appreciate his apparent aberrations and contradictions in their larger significance."

lower" (Müller 1884, 23).²⁶ Rhetorical effect of the declaration aside, he shows a real admiration for the "originator of the Indian Reformation," noting in particular his rejection of "idolatry" and his interest for the Veda, largely concordant with his own (Müller 1884, 30–31). Throughout the address, Müller displays a profound knowledge of Roy's life and work. Several notes indicate that he was in personal contact with Sophia Collet, a "real follower" of Roy in Great Britain who was then collecting material on him and subsequently published a biography (Collet 1914 [1900]) that became standard (Müller 1884, 14, 15 and 24).

In his later days, Müller developed a strong interest for Ramakrishna (1836–1886) and demonstrably became one of the earliest figures accountable for the spread of ideas about the Ramakrishna movement among Western audiences (Müller 1896, 1899b). Not expressing any criticism at this stage and operating a careful selection in Ramakrishna's works, Müller presented him as "an authentic expression of the sublimest form of India's heritage—Vedanta." This was a bidirectional relation since, as Beckerlegge noted, "Müller's interest was seen by members of the Ramakrishna movement as a significant indication of the recognition now being given to their master, and, of course Müller's standing as a scholar assured an attentive reception for his researches among academics" (Beckerlegge 2000, 8–9 and 15).²⁷

Judging in which measure Roy's, Sen's, Majumdar's or Ramakrishna's views percolated in Müller's conceptualization of religion is a tricky task, since these views are themselves already a blend of European Enlightenment ideas about religion (independently shared by Müller), reinterpretations of Upanishadic notions, as well as of early nineteenth-century Christian, Muslim, or even Parsi conceptions about religion (Halbfass 1981, 200–216 and 223–227, Mitter 1987, 189–196), to the point that the threads of influence might be impossible to disentangle. It is however clear that this context played at least some role and that traditional intellectual biographies of Müller might be in need of some revision.²⁸

---

26. In a letter sent to B. Malabari in March 1879, Müller writes: "I should like to write a life of Rammohun Roy. I have many materials for it, but I want more. He was a really great man, much greater than the world imagines, and we here in Europe have to learn from him quite as much as you in India" (in Müller 1902, 62). Even if Müller did not produce a book-length life of Rammohun Roy, he wrote a biographical essay in 1883 (Müller 1884, 1–46).

27. As a sign of the rapid spread of the ideas published in Müller's book on Ramakrishna (Müller 1899b), see Sylvain Lévi's review the same year (Lévi 1899) and the influence of Müller's exposition of Ramakrishna on Romain Rolland (Bridet 2014, 226).

28. For example, Kippenberg's otherwise very well-informed handbook does not make any mention of the contacts Müller had with Indian intellectuals altogether (Kippenberg 1997, 60–79).

In the opposite direction, Müller's works found an important echo in India.[29] In particular, three works need to be mentioned in that context: (1) the critical edition of the Ṛg Veda, (2) philosophical works on religion such as the above-mentioned *Lectures on the Origin and Growth of Religion*, and (3) his essay designed as a compulsory reading for civil servants about to serve in India, *India, What Can It Teach Us?* (1883). Müller's edition of the Ṛg Veda (first edition in 1849-1875) brought many reactions: after the publication of the first volume (1849), Müller received a letter from a Bengali scholar—another non-traveling scholar—Radhakanta Deb (1784-1867), who had published the famous Sanskrit lexicon, *Śabdakalpadrumaḥ* (1821) and was head of a conservative Bengali party, the Dharma Sabhā.[30] He wrote that even if himself and Vaidika Pandits found it curious that a *mleccha* from Great Britain released an edition of the Ṛg Veda on the banks of the Thames rather than those of Ganges (what he took as an evident sign of the Kālīyuga),[31] he was glad that such a text was now available to the pandits (letters of 1851 and 1855).[32] Incidentally, the second edition of Müller's Ṛg Veda edition could be published thanks to the patronage of the Maharaja of the Princely State of Mysore, Chamarajendra Wadiyar X (1863-1894) who also sponsored Vivekananda's travel to Chicago in 1893

---

29. On the reception of German orientalist scholarship in India, see Van der Veer (2001, 116-122).

30. On this episode, Müller (1899a, 27) writes: "Among the first to recognize my edition of the Rig-Veda was the Râjah Râdhâkânta Deva, and his recognition was all the more important to me as he stood at the head of the strictly orthodox and conservative party in Bengal." Halbfass (1981, 343) gives a good overview of the *Dharma Sabhā* and similar parties in early nineteenth-century Bengal.

31. As Radhakanta Deb wrote in a letter of November 1851: "It is surely, a very curious reflection on the vicissitudes of human affairs that the descendants of the divine Rishis (prophets) should be studying on the banks of the Bhagirathi (Ganges), the Yamuni (Jumna), and the Sindhu their Holy Scriptures as published on the banks of the Thames by one whom they regard as a distant Mlechchha, and this Mlechchha, the descendant of the degraded Kshattriyas (noblemen), according to our Shastras, and claiming a cognate origin with the Hindus, according to the investigations of the modern philologists, who will ere long rise to the rank of a Veda-Vyâsa (arranger and revealer of the Veda) of the Kaliyuga. ... As Yavanacharya (a Greek teacher) gave to the Hindus his system of astronomy many centuries ago, so the German Bhatta (Doctor) is now giving them his edition of the Rig-Veda, and will, as he promises, furnish them with his commentaries upon them." (in Müller 1899a, 32-33)

32. Dodson (2007b, 52-53) mentions several critical responses such as Pramadadasa Mittra (active around 1860-1880) and Siva Prasad. Among the major critics were of course Dayananda Saraswati and prominent members of the Ārya Samāj, about which Dodson (2007b, 56) writes: "But the most ardent critic of European interpretations of the Vedas in the late nineteenth century was Guru Datta Vidyarthi (1864-90), leader of the 'Gurukul' wing of the Hindu reformist organization, the Ārya Samāj. Dayananda Sarasvati accused Max Müller of being largely ignorant of Vedic Sanskrit."

(Müller 1899a, 158–159).³³ Müller's work thus enjoyed a certain popularity in contemporary Indian elitist circles, providing them with a version of the Ṛg Veda that was printed and endowed with the prestige of Western science.³⁴ At the same time, Müller perceived himself as a kind of reformer, opening up to the multitude a tradition that had been so far restricted to the few:

> For years, for centuries, nay for thousands of years, this Veda on which their whole religion was founded had been to them a kind of invisible power, much as the Bible was in the early centuries of the Papacy, when the privileged only were supposed to know it and were allowed to interpret it. In discussions between Brahmans and Christian missionaries, this Veda had always been the last stronghold to the Brahmans. ... And now the book was there, handled by everybody, and set out more or less successfully by anybody acquainted with Sanskrit. (Müller 1899a, 44–45)

Comparing his own work on the Veda to Luther's translation of the Bible, Müller considered that he was contributing, in a more or less direct way, to the development of a movement of reform in India. Adding actual evidence to this, Müller mentioned Brahmins from Pune who "called an assembly in which a man, not a Brâhman, read out my edition, and all the Brâhmans corrected whatever MSS. they possessed, according to the text as settled in the distant University of Oxford" (Müller 1899a, 25). One could of course question whether this anecdote can really be taken as illustrative of the publication's broader effect in India—in its double dimension of altering textual practices and upturning hierarchies. Given the persistence of traditional Vedic schools with a teaching strictly based on the oral tradition, this is rather unlikely. It is however clear that the edition was received in India and that it contributed to open up the text to people external to the traditional circles of its transmission, such as women and lower castes.

Other works such as the *Lectures on the Origin and Growth of Religion* found a wide audience in India, with more direct effects. The text exposes the notion of religion as a "sense of the infinite," frontally opposing the Hume-De Brosses line of argument on the polytheist or fetishist origins of religion.³⁵

---

33. In the preface of the Ṛg Veda edition, Müller writes that the work is not meant for the "general scholar, but only for those who make Sanskrit their special study, and for those among the natives of India who are still able to read their own Sacred Books in the language of the original" (Müller 1890, viii, my translation).

34. Van der Veer (2001, 107) noted the same, emphasizing the use of philology in India as "an authoritative science for the transformation of Hindu traditions."

35. Müller (1901 [1878], 186) acknowledges clearly the role of the Indian case for his theorizing about religion: "I have selected the ancient religion of India to supply the historical illustrations of my own theory of the origin and growth of religion. That theory was suggested to me during a lifelong study of the sacred books of India; it rests therefore on facts, though I am responsible for their interpretation."

On the one hand, it is deploying a "proto-phenomenological" program that can be read as heretic (or very liberal) Christian theology. On the other hand, the text could be employed not only as a pamphlet against evangelical mischaracterizations of "Hindu traditions" as more or less elaborate forms of savagery, but also as a way to confirm the core doctrine of several movements of reform, such as, precisely, the Brahmo Samāj.[36] A figure who engaged himself in different social struggles and published a number of articles to this end in several Indian periodicals, the Parsi Behramji Malabari (1853-1912), contributed to spread this text widely in India: he translated it in Gujarati (Müller 1881) and organized its translation in yet other languages, Bengali, Hindi, Tamil and even Sanskrit.[37] Müller himself was sympathetic to these efforts and wrote the following to Malabari:

> I am deeply interested in the effect which my Hibbert Lectures will produce in India. When writing them I was often thinking of my friends in your country more than of my audience at Westminster.

And in a letter of February 1882:

> I wanted to tell those few at least whom I might hope to reach in English, what the true historical value of their ancient religion is, as looked upon, not from exclusively European or Christian, but from a historical point of view. I wished to warn against two dangers: that of undervaluing or despising the ancient national religion, as is done too often by your half-Europeanized youths; and that of overvaluing it, and interpreting it as it was never meant to be interpreted, of which you may see a painful instance in Dayananda Sarasvati's labors on the Veda.

Finally, other figures active in the national freedom struggle made a strategic use of Müller's views about India, especially those that could be construed as speaking of a consubstantial relation between colonizers and colonized. In this context, the essay *India, What Can It Teach Us?* (1883) received a great deal of attention. Müller wrote for example that

> If I were asked under what sky the human mind has most fully developed some of its choicest gifts, has most deeply pondered on the greatest problems of life, and has found solutions of some of them which well deserve the attention even of those who have studied Plato and Kant, I should point to India. (Müller 1883, 24)

---

36. Gidumal is the author of a biography of Malabari (1892) with selected added texts from him. Even if this is arguably difficult to check, both Malabari (1903) and Menant (1907) emphasize the influence of Müller's Hibbert lectures in India.

37. Müller sent Malabari a copy of his essay (Müller 1902, 61-62) and was then informed about the initiative (1902, 126-127). Of the mentioned languages, only the Gujarati (Müller 1881) and the Hindi versions were ever completed.

The phrase caught the attention of M. K. Gandhi, who used it as an argument in legal procedures against the colonial government, for example when underwriting petitions to extend Indian interests. In his writings about religion, Gandhi equally re-used Müller's views on "Aryanism," emphasizing the racial and spiritual proximity between Indian and British peoples (Chidester 2014, 49–50).

While these cases only relate to India, Müller's auto-biographical writings also signal privileged contacts with other regions and actors, such as the Japanese Buddhist monks Nanjo Bunyu (1849–1927) and Kenjiu Kasawara (1851–1883) who stayed in Oxford and worked with Müller (Müller 1884, 178–219). In particular, Nanjo Bunyu had an extremely influential and prolific activity after his return to Japan in 1884, using the skills learned in England to edit and print an important number of Chinese and Sanskrit Buddhist texts. There would be ample material for further research as it is clear that the collaboration had long lasting consequences and that Japanese scholars were an important part of Müller's wide and eclectic epistolary network.[38]

As Rabault-Feuerhahn well demonstrated (Rabault-Feuerhahn 2008), oriental studies in the nineteenth century were largely organized as transnational networks, and India as well as China were definitely part of this network, next to France, Germany and Great Britain. It is not unreasonable to assume that the same "orientalist networks" channelled conceptions about religion traveling, as the scholars, in both directions. In this framework, and in spite of the fact that he did not travel himself beyond Europe, Müller appears as an important node in the connected history of religion(s) between Asia and Europe. Of course, the relationship is fraught with asymmetry in the sense that he was in a more powerful position to impose his views than his interlocutors—notably through privileged relations to prestigious editors with a wide, though certainly not global, diffusion, and through personal relations with high rank British officials. As already mentioned, a "connected religion" approach does not obliterate power dynamics in any way. It encourages on the contrary a close analysis that looks at situational constellations of power and knowledge moving across boundaries with actors and books.[39]

---

38. Cf. the contributions of M. Zhang (this volume, p. 152) for further elements on Nanjo Bunyu in the context of a connected history of Chinese Indological studies, and of B. Bocking (also this volume, p. 186) on Takakusu Junjiro's stay by Max Müller in Oxford.

39. Chidester (2014, 51) expresses a similar view: "Gandhi's use of imperial theory was situational, deploying Max Müller's research on religion within local and colonial struggles over Indian citizenship and trading rights in South Africa. Imperial theory, therefore, was not always controlled by the metropolitan center."

A travelling literatus: Jakob Urner (1883-1961)

Jumping now to the 1920s, let us focus on the region around Dharwad, Karnataka for a case that is strikingly symmetrical to Müller's. In this post-war period, German missionaries of the Basel mission had been forced to leave the territory and their Swiss colleagues remained alone on the field, giving an increasingly large share of their responsibilities to Christian Indians. Among these Swiss missionaries, one figure—Jakob Urner (1883-1961)—stands out, because he developed a strong interest for the Vīraśaiva tradition and its texts, along with the necessary linguistic skills. His time in India coincides with a period of deep changes on the local level, with the deliquescence of the mission as a white European institution and the emergence of nationalist and regionalist movements (and notably, in that region, the revival of the Vīraśaiva tradition)—illustrating the process of groups that redefine themselves according to borrowed terms that are soon not felt borrowed anymore.

Whereas one would typically imagine that, as a missionary, Urner relentlessly tried to press his views on his interlocutors, a closer examination shows that even if there was indeed such an intention, practical circumstances made the whole enterprise much more precarious and ambiguous. The "failure" of the evangelical prospects had however creative effects that are seen for example in the figure of the missionary's language teacher (*munshi*), Channappa Uttangi (1881-1962), from whom Urner learned the Kannada language.[40]

This encounter had at least two important lasting consequences: (1) Working on Kannada reading exercises, Urner became particularly interested in the so-called *vacana* literature of the Vīraśaivas, finding what he perceived as astonishing similarities between these texts and his own theological views. These texts—which since then became crucial in the identity construction of modern Karnataka—seemed to support an egalitarian, anti-caste ideology, as well as a religious practice centred on the individual devotion to a single divinity. A full collection had been published in 1923, edited by one important actor of the local revivalist movement, Phakirappa Gurubasappa Halkatti (1880-1964) (Halkatti 1923).[41] Supposed to date back to the twelfth century, the corpus was actually a collection of texts belonging to different places and times, selected for their progressive ideology and fitting to the beginning of the twentieth century.[42] First imagining a Christian influence, Urner pro-

---

40. For further elements reconsidering the positive effects of "failed projects," see Bocking's contribution, *infra*, p. 161.
41. A few of Basava's *vacanas* were published in the *Indian Antiquary*, edited and translated by Halkatti and another Christian missionary, John Nicol Farquehar (Halkatti 1922).
42. Boratti (2010) gives a good description of the constitution of this corpus and of the

gressively developed a genuine interest for these texts and as soon as 1923, translated a series of them in English and German, probably helped by his language teacher.[43] In the end, he came to see in them a roadmap for social progress for Karnataka and possibly for India as a whole, a roadmap that was particular since it was not only not Christian, but also largely deviated from the standard Vedāntic conception of Indian religions that was then gaining a prominent status. In this sense, Urner largely echoed the views of his language teacher. (2) A second effect was that the *munshi* learned from Urner how to apply a philological approach to the texts, and discovered through him the work of an important *vacanakāra* named Sarvajña. Uttangi embarked on a major work of manuscript collection and edition, and became a recognized reference in the domain. Later, he developed a syncretic theology, conciliating his Christian identity with regionalist and nationalist views, partly using to this end works in comparative religion that had been sent to him by Urner such as William James's *Varieties of Religious Experience* (1901–1902).[44]

In conclusion

By contrast to Müller, Urner was in contact not so much with a Westernized, Indian elite, but with non-elite groups fighting for recognition in the political and religious arenas of both the region and the nation. The situation in their respective contexts of activity mirrors this difference. Whereas Müller was in a dominant position, Urner was clearly marginalized: in his "home country," he was in the margins of academic Indian studies; in India, he was never part of the local political dynamics that composed the context of his work, and he was not particularly successful in accomplishing evangelical goals either. Another difference is in the relation to the language: Urner learned Kannada "on the field," with a local scholar, whereas Müller learned his Sanskrit with European scholars and in European libraries.

Nevertheless, Müller and Urner both acted within specific transnational institutions (academia for Müller, Christian mission for Urner) that were dealing with issues of religion. Both also produced important effects on the local context, calling for a multipolar contextualization of their work, ideally pursued in different languages (English, German, Bengali, Gujarati, Kannada, Sanskrit etc.). In quite unexpected ways, they both mirror, in their respective works, powerful local political and religious dynamics (Brahmo Samāj / Vīraśaiva revivalism) of which they somehow became spokespersons, almost on a ventriloquist mode, while of course not giving up entirely a norma-

---

underlying interests that framed it.
43. The texts are kept in the archives of the Basel Mission, BMA C-10.89.
44. Sebastian (2005/6) provides a useful analysis of Uttangi's intellectual and political profile.

tive standpoint (confidence in the superiority of science for Müller, desire to propagate Christianity for Urner). Both cases also show well how easily scholarly discourses about religion can move across different epistemic levels or genres, from "religion" to religion and the way back.[45] Finally, it is noteworthy that the "actual travel" of actors is not a necessary prerequisite for a "connected history," considering other kinds of structuring networks, such as that of the circulation of books, letters or students. In sum, the "connected religion" approach helps to see Müller not as a recluse in his library, but as an important node in a transnational network which channelled conceptions of religion. Similarly, Urner appears not only as a missionary imparting and preaching a religious doctrine on future converts, but also as an actor whose views were themselves altered by the situation of contact.

To conclude, the proposed framework opens new ways into the historiography of the study of religions, to be reconsidered under the lens of interactions with different circles of religious (and non-Christian) actors, texts or practices on a global scale. The approach is able (1) to develop alternative perspectives on topics that have already been studied by bringing together separate historiographical traditions; (2) to criticize a "world religions" model and stereotyped conceptions about "oriental religions" by focusing on processes of changes and individual appropriations; (3) to bring nuance to historical accounts of the study of religion and to intellectual genealogies which often remain exclusively confined to Europe. Müller's case shows —I contend—that intellectual genealogies focusing on a specifically European tradition in the study of religion (Gladigow 1995) might greatly benefit by widening their scope outside of Europe. It becomes then possible to go beyond a mere criticism of the "orientalism" that has characterized much of the early production in the comparative study of religions and towards a less Eurocentric conception of the discipline's own genealogy—and, one hopes, of its future.

Acknowledgements

I thank Professors M. Burger, P. Schreiner and all participants to the panel "Transnational encounters and religion: Following the threads of connected histories (nineteenth–twentieth centuries)" at the IAHR Erfurt congress for insightful comments on previous versions of this text.

---

45. In that sense, the traditional narrative of the history of the study of religion is in need of some revision, to frame it in a more global context than usually acknowledged and to take into account the contribution of actors involved in religious agendas (see Habermas 2010, for an argument about the contribution of missionaries to the construction of a secular "science of religion").

References

Asad, Talal. 1983. "Anthropological Conceptions of Religion: Reflections on Geertz." *Man,* New Series 18(2): 237–259. https://doi.org/10.2307/2801433

———. 1993. *Genealogies of Religion: Discipline and Reasons of Power in Christianity and Islam.* Baltimore, MD: The Johns Hopkins University Press.

Barrett, Tim H. 2016 "Michael Pye, Translating Drunk—and Stark Naked: Problems in Presenting Eighteenth Century Japanese Thought." *Journal of the Irish Society for the Academic Study of Religions* 3: 236–249. https://jkapalo.files.wordpress.com/2016/06/michael-pye-translating-drunk-e28093-and-stark-naked-problems-in-presenting-eighteenth-century-japanese-thought-pdf.pdf

Bayly, Christopher A. 2004. *The Birth of the Modern World: 1780–1914: Global Connections and Comparisons.* Malden, MA: Blackwell.

———. et al. 2006. "AHR Conversation: On Transnational History. Transnational History: A Review of Past and Present Scholarship." *The American Historical Review* 111(5): 1441–1464. https://doi.org/10.1086/ahr.111.5.1441

Beckerlegge, Gwilym. 2000. *The Ramakrishna Mission: The Making of a Modern Hindu Movement.* Delhi/Oxford: Oxford University Press.

Behl, Aditya. 2010. "Pages from the Book of Religions." In *Notes from a Maṇḍala*, edited by L. Patton and D. Haberman, 113–149. Newark, NJ: University of Delaware Press.

Bergunder, Michael. 2011. "Was ist Religion? Kulturwissenschaftliche Überlegungen zum Gegenstand der Religionswissenschaft." *Zeitschrift für Religionswissenschaft* 19(1/2): 3–55. https://doi.org/10.1515/zfr-2011-0001

Berkwitz, Stephen C. 2013. *Buddhist Poetry and Colonialism: Alagiyavanna and the Portuguese in Sri Lanka.* Oxford: Oxford University Press. https://doi.org/10.1093/acprof:oso/9780199935765.001.0001

Bertrand, Romain. 2011. *L'histoire à parts égales.* Paris: Seuil. https://doi.org/10.14375/NP.9782021050172

Bloch, Marc. 1928. "Pour une histoire comparée des sociétés européennes." *Revue de synthèse historique* 46: 15–50.

Boratti, Vijay. 2010. "The 'Discovery' of Vachanas: Notes on Fakirappa Gurubasappa Halakatti's Secular Interpretation of the Texts and the Lingayath Community in Colonial Karnataka." *South Asia: Journal of South Asian Studies* 33(2): 177–209. https://doi.org/10.1080/00856401.2010.493279

Bornet, Philippe. 2010. *Rites et pratiques de l'hospitalité.* Stuttgart: Steiner.

———. 2014b. "Review of Guides to South Asian Religions." *Asiatische Studien* 68(3): 849–854. https://doi.org/10.1515/asia-2014-0059

———. 2016a. "Die mehrfachen Ebenen der Religion Rammohan Roys (1772–1833)." In *Einheit und Differenz in der Religionswissenschaft: Standortbestimmungen mit Hilfe eines Mehr-Ebenen-Modells von Religion*, edited by K. Lehmann and A. Jödicke, 119–131. Würzburg: Ergon-Verlag.

———. 2016b. "Comparison as a Necessary Evil: Examples from Indian and Jewish Worlds." In *Interreligious Comparisons in Religious Studies and Theology. Comparison Revisited*, edited by A. Nehring and P. Leukel-Schmidt, 72–92. London: Bloomsbury.

———. 2019. "From the Emic to the Etic and Back Again: Archaeology, Orientalism, and Religion from Colonial Sri Lanka to Switzerland." In *"Masters" and "Natives": Digging the Others' Past*, edited by S. Gorshenina, P. Bornet, C. Rapin et M. Fuchs. Berlin/Boston: De Gruyter. https://doi.org/10.1515/9783110599466-009

Bornet, Philippe and Svetlana Gorshenina, eds. 2014a. *L'orientalisme des marges: perspectives de l'Inde et de la Russie*. Lausanne: Etudes de lettres.

Bourdieu, Pierre. 1986. "L'illusion biographique." *Actes de la recherche en sciences sociales* 62(1): 69–72. https://doi.org/10.3406/arss.1986.2317

Braudel, Fernand. 1949. *La Méditerranée et le monde méditerranéen à l'époque de Philippe II*. Paris: Armand Colin.

Bridet, Guillaume. 2014. *L'événement indien de la littérature française*. Grenoble: Presses Universitaires de Grenoble. https://doi.org/10.4000/books.ugaeditions.506

Burger, Maya. 2010. "Encountering Translation: Translational Historiography in the Connected History of India and Europe." In *India in Translation through Hindi Literature: A Plurality of Voices*, edited by M. Burger and N. Pozza, 25–45. Bern: Peter Lang.

———. 2014. "Marge ou centre? Où chercher la vérité? L'orientalisme d'une Russe en Inde: Helena Petrovna Blavatsky." In *L'orientalisme des marges*, edited by P. Bornet and S. Gorshenina, 297–321. Lausanne: Etudes de lettres. https://doi.org/10.4000/edl.761

Chidester, David. 2014. *Empire of Religion: Imperialism and Comparative Religion*, Chicago, IL: University of Chicago Press. https://doi.org/10.7208/chicago/9780226117577.001.0001

Cohn, Bernard. 1996. *Colonialism and its Forms of Knowledge: The British in India*, Princeton, NJ: Princeton University Press.

Collet, Sophia D. 1914 [1900]. *The Life and Letters of Raja Rammohun Roy*. Calcutta: Loan Stack.

Cooper, Frederick, Stoler, Ann Laura. 1997. *Tensions of Empire: Colonial Cultures in a Bourgeois World*. Berkeley: University of California Press. https://doi.org/10.1525/9780520918085

Deacon, D., P. Russell and A. Woollacott, eds. 2010. *Transnational Lives: Biographies of Global Modernity, 1700–present*. New York: Palgrave McMillan. https://doi.org/10.1057/9780230277472

Dirks, Nicholas. 2001. *Castes of Mind: Colonialism and the Making of Modern India*. Princeton, NJ: Princeton University Press. https://doi.org/10.1515/9781400840946

Dodson, Michael S. 2007a. *Orientalism, Empire and National Culture: India 1770–1880*. New York: Palgrave Macmillan. https://doi.org/10.1057/9780230288706

———. 2007b. "Contesting Translations: Orientalism and the Interpretation of the Vedas." *Modern Intellectual History* 4: 43–59. https://doi.org/10.1017/S147924430600103X

Espagne, Michel. 1994. "Sur les limites du comparatisme en histoire culturelle." *Genèses* 17: 112–121. https://doi.org/10.3406/genes.1994.1266

———. 1999. *Les transferts culturels franco-allemands*. Paris: Presses universitaires de France. https://doi.org/10.3917/puf.espag.1999.01

———. 2005. "Les transferts culturels." In *Connections* 19.01.2005. Available online: www.connections.clio-online.net/debate/id/diskussionen-576

Fitzgerald, Timothy. 2000. *The Ideology of Religious Studies*. Oxford: Oxford University Press.

Foltz, Richard. 1999. *Religions of the Silk Road: Overland trade and cultural exchange from Antiquity to the fifteenth century*. New York: St. Martin's Griffin.

Freiberger, Oliver. 2009. *Der Askesediskurs in der Religionsgeschichte: Eine vergleichende Untersuchung brahmanischer und fruhchristlicher Texte*. Wiesbaden: Harrassowitz.

Freiberger, Oliver. 2019. *Considering Comparison: A Method for Religious Studies*. Oxford: Oxford University Press. https://doi.org/10.1093/oso/9780199965007.001.0001

Gidumal, Dayaram. 1892. *Behramji Malabari, a Biographical Sketch*. London: T.F. Unwin.

Ginzburg, Carlo. 1980. *The Cheese and the Worms: The Cosmos of a Sixteenth-Century Miller*. Baltimore, MD: The Johns Hopkins University Press.

Gladigow, Burkhard. 1995. "Europäische Religionsgeschichte." In *Lokale Religionsgeschichte*, edited by H.G. Kippenberg, 21–42. Marburg: Diagonal Verlag.

———. 1997. "Vergleich und Interesse." In *Vergleichen und Verstehen in der Religionswissenschaft*, edited by H.-J. Klimkeit, 113–130. Wiesbaden: Otto Harrassowitz.

Green, Nile. 2015. *Terrains of Exchange: Religious Economies of Global Islam*. Oxford: Oxford University Press. https://doi.org/10.1093/acprof:oso/9780190222536.001.0001

Gruzinski, Serge. 2001. "Les mondes mêlés de la Monarchie catholique et autres 'connected histories'." *Annales HSS* 56(1): 85–117. https://doi.org/10.1017/S039526490000007X

Habermas, Rebekka. 2010. "Wissenstransfer und Mission: Sklavenhändler, Missionare und Religionswissenschaftler." *Geschichte und Gesellschaft* 36(2): 257–284. https://doi.org/10.13109/gege.2010.36.2.257

Halbfass, Wilhelm. 1981. *Indien und Europa: Perspektiven ihrer geistigen Begegnung.* Basel: Schwabe.

Halkatti, Phakirappa Gurubasappa. 1923–1951. *Vachana Śāstra Sāra*, 3 vol.

Halkatti, P. G. 1922. "Vachanas Attributed to Basava." *Indian Antiquary* 51: 7–12; 36–40, 54–57.

Herrmann, Albert. 1910. *Die alten Seidenstrassen zwischen China und Syrien.* Berlin: Weidmann.

Holdrege, Barbara. 2000. "What's Beyond the Post? Comparative Analysis as Critical Method." In: *A Magic Still Dwells: Comparative Religion in the Postmodern Age*, edited by K. C. Patton and B.C. Ray, 77–91. Berkeley: University of California Press. https://doi.org/10.2307/j.ctv11hpsn2.10

———. 2010. "The Politics of Comparison: Connecting Cultures Outside of and in Spite of the West." *International Journal of Hindu Studies* 14(2–3): 147–175. https://doi.org/10.1007/s11407-011-9090-y

Inden, Ronald. 1992. *Imagining India.* Oxford: Blackwell.

Iriye, Akira. 1965. *After Imperialism: The Search for a New Order in the Far East, 1921-1931.* Cambridge, MA: Harvard University Press.

———. with Saunier, Patrick, ed. 2009. *The Palgrave Dictionary of Transnational History: From the Mid-nineteenth Century to the Present Day.* London: Palgrave. https://doi.org/10.1007/978-1-349-74030-7

Irschick, Eugene. 1994. *Dialogue and History: Constructing South India, 1795-1895.* Berkeley: University of California Press.

King, Richard. 2006. *Orientalism and Religion: Postcolonial Theory, India and "the Mystic East."* London: Routledge.

Kippenberg, Hans G. 1997. *Die Entdeckung der Religionsgeschichte: Religionswissenschaft und Moderne.* Munich: C.H. Beck.

Klimkeit, Hans-Joachim. 1988. *Die Seidenstraße: Kulturbrücke zwischen Morgen- und Abendland.* Cologne: DuMont.

Kollmar-Paulenz, Karénina. 2012. "Aussereuropäische Religionsbegriffe." In *Religionswissenschaft*, edited by M. Stausberg, 81–94. Berlin: De Gruyter.

———. 2013. "Lamas und Schamanen: Mongolische Wissensordnungen vom frühen 17. bis zum 21. Jahrhundert. Ein Beitrag zur Debatte um aussereuropäische Religionsbegriffe." In *Religion in Asien? Studien zur Anwendbarkeit des Religionsbegriffs*, edited by P. Schalk, M. Deeg, O. Freiberger, C. Kleine, and A. van Nahl, 151–200. Uppsala: Uppsala Universitet.

Kopf, David. 1979. *The Brahmo Samaj and the Shaping of the Modern Indian Mind*. Princeton, NJ: Princeton University Press.https://doi.org/10.1515/9781400869893

———. 1980. "Hermeneutics Versus History." *The Journal of Asian Studies* 39(3): 495–506. https://doi.org/10.2307/2054677

———. 1988. "Neo-Hindu views of Unitarian and Trinitarian Christianity in Nineteenth Century Bengal: The Case of Keshub Chandra Sen." In *Neo-Hindu Views of Christianity*, edited by A. Sharma, 106–119. Leiden: Brill.

Krech, Volkhard and Steinicke, Marion, eds. 2012. *Dynamics in the History of Religions between Asia and Europe in Past and Present Times: Encounters, Notions and Comparative Perspectives*. Leiden: Brill. https://doi.org/10.1163/9789004225350

Lévy, Sylvain. 1899. "Book Review: Râmakrishna. His Life and Sayings." *Revue de l'histoire des religions* 40: 287–288.

Lincoln, Bruce. 1989. "Unconcluding Postscripts." In *Discourse and the Construction of Society: Comparative Studies of Myth, Ritual, and Classification*, 171–174. Oxford: Oxford University Press.

———. 1996. "Theses on Method." *Method and Theory in the Study of Religion* 8(3): 225–227. https://doi.org/10.1163/157006896X00323

———. 2012. "Theses on Comparison." In *Gods and Demons, Priests and Scholars*. Chicago, IL: University of Chicago Press, 121–130. https://doi.org/10.7208/chicago/9780226035161.001.0001

Malabari, Behramji. 1903. "Recollections of Max Muller and His Hibbert Lectures." *East and West*: 327–338, 475–482.

Manjapra, Kris. 2014. *Age of Entanglement: German and Indian Intellectuals across Empire*. Cambridge, MA: Harvard University Press. https://doi.org/10.4159/harvard.9780674726314

Masuzawa, Tomoko. 1993. *In Search of Dreamtime: The Quest for the Origin of Religion*. Chicago, IL: University of Chicago Press.

———. 2005. *The Invention of World Religions, or, How European Universalism Was Preserved in the Language of Pluralism*. Chicago, IL: The University of Chicago Press. https://doi.org/10.7208/chicago/9780226922621.001.0001

McGuire, Meredith. 2008. *Lived Religion: Faith and Practice in Everyday Life*. Oxford: Oxford University Press.

Menant, D. 1907. "Influence of Max Müller's Hibbert Lectures in India." *The American Journal of Theology* 11(2): 293–307. https://doi.org/10.1086/478685

Mintz, Sidney W. 1985. *Sweetness and Power: The Place of Sugar in Modern History*. New York: Penguin Books.

Mitter, Partha. 1987. "Rammohun Roy and the New Language of Monotheism." *History and Theory* 3: 177–208. https://doi.org/10.1080/02757206.1987.9960784

Müller, Friedrich Max. 1901 [1878]. *Lectures on the Origin and Growth of Religion as Illustrated by the Religions of India*. London/Bombay: Longmans, Green and.

———. 1881. *Dharmanī utpatti tathā vṛddhiviṣenāṃ bhāṣaṇa*. Korṭa Priṇṭiṅga Presa [in Gujarati].

———. 1883. *India: What Can It Teach Us?* London/Bombay: Longmans and Green.

———. 1884. *Biographical Essays*. New York: Charles Scribner's Sons.

———, ed. 1890. *Rig-Veda Samhitâ: The Sacred Hymns of the Brâhmans Together with the Commentary of Sâyanâkârya*. Second Edition. London: Henry Prowde.

———. 1896. "A Real Mahatman." *Nineteenth Century* 40: 306–319.

———. 1899a. *Auld Lang Syne: My Indian Friends*. New York: Charles Scribner's Sons.

———. 1899b. *Râmakṛiṣhṇa: His Life and Sayings*. New York: Charles Scribner's Sons.

Müller, Georgina, ed. 1902. *The Life and Letters of the Right Honourable Friedrich Max Müller*. London: Longmans, 2 vol.

Peabody, Norbert. 2003. *Hindu Kingship and Polity in Precolonial India*. Cambridge: University of Cambridge.

Pollock, Sheldon. 2010. "Comparison Without Hegemony." In *The Benefit of Broad Horizons: Intellectual and Institutional Preconditions for a Global Social Science*, edited by H. Joas and B. Klein, 185–204. Leiden: Brill. https://doi.org/10.1163/9789004192874_012

Potter, Stephen J. and Saha, Jonathan. 2015. "Global History, Imperial History, and Connected Histories of Empire." *Journal of Colonialism and Colonial History* 16(1). https://doi.org/10.1353/cch.2015.0009

Prothero, Stephen. 2010. *God Is Not One: The Eight Rival Religions that Run the World—and Why their Differences Matter*. San Francisco, CA: Harper.

Pye, Michael. 1994. "What is 'Religion' in East Asia." In *The Notion of "Religion" in Comparative Research: Selected Proceedings of the XVI IAHR Congress*, edited by U. Bianchi, 115–122. Rome: "L'Erma" di Bretschneider. https://doi.org/10.1057/9780230379411_8

———. 2003. "Overcoming Westernism: The End of Orientalism and Occidentalism." In *Religion im Spiegelkabinett. Asiatische Religionsgeschichte im Spannungsfeld zwischen Orientalismus und Okzidentalismus*, edited by P. Schalk, 91–114. Uppsala: Uppsala University.

Rabault-Feuerhahn, Pascale. 2008. "Voyages d'études et migrations savantes. Paris, lieu fondateur et provisoire de l'indianisme allemand." *Revue germanique internationale* 7: 2–15. https://doi.org/10.4000/rgi.405

Raj, Kapil. 2007. *Relocating Modern Science: Circulation and the Construction of Knowledge in South Asia and Europe, 1650-1900*. New York: Palgrave Macmillan. https://doi.org/10.1057/9780230625310

Roy, Ram Mohan. 1818. *Translation of an Abridgement of the Vedant, or Resolution of All the Veds the Most Celebrated and Revered Work of Brahminical Theology; Establishing the Unity of the Supreme Being, and That He Alone is the Object of Propitiation and Worship*. Calcutta.

Rüpke, Jörg. 2016. *On Roman Religion: Lived Religion and the Individual in Ancient Rome*. Ithaca, NY: Cornell University Press. https://doi.org/10.7591/9781501706264

Said, Edward. 1978. *Orientalism: Western Conceptions of the East*. New York: Pantheon.

Sebastian, Mrinalini. 2005/2006. "Chennappa Uttangi: A *Drishtanta* for the Resolution of Conflicting National, Regional and Communal Identities." *Journal of Karnataka Studies* 2.2/3.1.

Sen, Keshub Chandra. 1877. *Our Faith and Our Experiences. A Lecture Delivered on the Occasion of the Forty-Sixth Anniversary of the Brahmo Samaj at the Townhall, Calcutta*. Calcutta: Indian Mirror Press.

Sengupta, Syamalendu. 1990. *A Conservative Hindu of Colonial India: Raja Radhakant Deb and His Milieu (1784-1867)*. New Delhi: Navrang.

Singh, Upinder and Dhar, Parul Pandya. 2014. *Asian Encounters: Exploring Connected Histories*. Oxford: Oxford University Press.

Sivasundaram, Sujit. 2005. *Nature and the Godly Empire: Science and Evangelical Mission in the Pacific, 1795-1850*. Cambridge: Cambridge University Press.

———. 2010. "Sciences and the Global: On Methods, Questions and Theory." *Isis* 101: 146–158. https://doi.org/10.1086/652694

Smith, Huston. 1995. *The Illustrated World's Religions: A Guide to Our Wisdom Traditions*. San Francisco, CA: Harper.

Smith, Jonathan Z. 1990. *Drudgery Divine: on the Comparison of Early Christianities and the Religions of Late Antiquity*. London: SOAS.

———. 2000. "The 'End' of Comparison: Redescription and Rectification." In *In Comparison a Magic Dwells: Comparative Religion in the Postmodern Age*, edited by K. Patton and B. Ray, 237–241, Berkeley: University of California Press. https://doi.org/10.2307/j.ctv11hpsn2.20

———. 2014. "Interview with J. Z. Smith." In *Magie de la comparaison*, edited by D. Barbu and N. Meylan, 175–195. Geneva: Labor et Fides.

Stoler, Ann Laura and Cooper, Frederick. 1997. "Between Metropole and Colony: Rethinking a Research Agenda." In *Tensions of Empire: Colonial Cultures in a Bourgeois World*, 1–56. Berkeley: University of California Press. https://doi.org/10.1525/california/9780520205406.003.0001

Strayer, Robert W., ed. 1989. *The Making of the Modern World: Connected Histories, Divergent Paths. (1500 to the Present)*. New York: St. Martins Press.

Subrahmanyam, Sanjay. 1997. "Connected Histories: Notes towards a Reconfiguration of Early Modern Eurasia." *Modern Asian Studies* 31(3): 735–762. https://doi.org/10.1017/S0026749X00017133

———. 1998. *The Career and Legend of Vasco da Gama*. Cambridge: Cambridge University Press.

———. 2007. "Par delà l'incommensurabilité: pour une histoire connectée des empires au temps modernes." *Revue d'Histoire Moderne et Contemporaine* 54–55 (5): 34–53. https://doi.org/10.3917/rhmc.545.0034

———. 2012. "Le goût de l'archive est polyglotte: interview with Anne-Julie Etter and Thomas Grillot." Available online: http://www.laviedesidees.fr/Le-gout-de-l-archive-est.html

Sweetman, Will. 2003. "'Hinduism' and the History of 'Religion': Protestant Presuppositions in the Critique of the Concept of Hinduism." *Method and Theory in the Study of Religion* 15: 329–353. https://doi.org/10.1163/157006803322697407

Tavakoli-Targhi, Mohamad. 1996. "Orientalism's Genesis Amnesia." *Comparative Studies of South Asia, Africa and the Middle East* 16(1): 1–14. https://doi.org/10.1215/1089201X-16-1-1

Van der Veer, Peter. 2001. *Imperial Encounters: Religion and Modernity in India and Britain*. Princeton, NJ: Princeton University Press. https://doi.org/10.1515/9781400831081

Werner, Michael and Zimmermann, Bénédicte. 2006. "Beyond Comparison: Histoire Croisée and the Challenge of Reflexivity." *History and Theory* 45: 30–50. https://doi.org/10.1111/j.1468-2303.2006.00347.x

Yoshinaga, Shin'ichi. 2009. "Theosophy and Buddhist Reformers in the Middle of the Meiji Period: An Introduction." *Japanese Religions* 34(2): 119–131.

About the author

Philippe Bornet is Senior lecturer in South Asian studies at the Department of South Asian Languages and Civilizations, University of Lausanne, Switzerland. After stays in Tübingen and at the University of Chicago, he completed a PhD in the comparative history of religions on rituals of hospitality in Jewish and Indian texts. His current research deals with interactions between India and Europe and more specifically, Swiss missionaries in South India in the beginning of the twentieth century. Recent publications include *Rites et pratiques de l'hospitalité*, 2010, *Religions in Play*, 2012 (ed. with M. Burger) and *L'orientalisme des marges* (ed. with S. Gorshenina), 2014.

PART II

Transnational Trajectories and Individual Appropriations of Religion

— 2 —

"In-Between" Religiosity:
European *Kālī-bhakti* in Early-Colonial Calcutta

GAUTAM CHAKRABARTI

"You'll find Mother in any house.
Do I dare say it in public?"
(Nathan and Seely 1982, 60)

One of the most engaging socio-cultural traits in late eigthteenth- and early nineteenth-century India was the disarmingly engaged and comparativist manner in which European travellers responded to the multi-layered and deeply syncretic field of devotional spirituality in eastern India. The predominantly-*śākta* orientation of early modern Bengali configurations of religious devotion led, especially in the vicinity of the rather-heterodox city of Calcutta, to the familiarization of European migrants to the Goddess Kālī, Herself representing a certain subaltern, *tāntrika* aspect of Hindu devotional practices. Antony Firingi, (Æntōnī Phiringī) originally Hensman Anthony (?–1836), was a folk-poet/bard, who, despite being of Portuguese origin, was married to a Hindu Brahmin widow and well-known throughout Bengal for his celebrated Bengali devotional songs addressed to the Goddesses Kālī and Durgā, towards the beginning of the nineteenth century. He was also celebrated for his performance in literary contests known as *kabigān* (bardic duels) with the then elite of Bengali composers. His *āgamani* songs, celebrating the return of Goddess Durgā to her parental home are immensely-popular till today and he was associated with a temple to Goddess Kālī in the Bowbazar-area of North Calcutta that is nowadays famous as the *Phiringī Kālibāri* (foreigner's Kālī temple). In this essay, the literary-cultural construction of a religious hybridity, operating between and cross-fertilizing Indo-European cultural conjunctions, is examined through the study of individual, "in-between" religious agency, in this case of Hensman Anthony, who comes across as a figure representing the condition of the transcultural subaltern.

One of the most interesting and characteristic socio-cultural traits in late eigthteenth- and early nineteenth-century India was the engagingly-involved and comparativist, some would even venture to say ethnographical, manner in which European travellers responded to the multi-layered and richly-syncretized field of devotional spirituality in eastern India. The predominantly (though, by no means, exclusively) *śākta* orientation of early modern Bengali configurations of religious devotion led, especially in the vicinity of the rather-heterodox city of Calcutta, to the familiarization of European migrants to the Goddess Kālī, Herself[1] representing a certain subaltern, tāntrika configuration of Hindu devotional rituals and practices. Antony Firingi,[2] (Æntōnī Phiringī) originally Hensman Anthony (?–1836), was a folk-poet/bard, who, despite being of Luso-Indian origin, was married to a Hindu Brahmin widow and achieved considerable fame for his much-feted devotional songs, addressed to the Goddesses Kālī and Durgā, in Bengali towards the beginning of the nineteenth century. He was also celebrated for his redoubtable performance in literary face-offs, more often than not of a competitively-scurrilous nature, known as *kabigān* (bardic duels) with the then crème de la crème of Bengali composers (Kuśa 2000, 87). His *āgamani* songs, celebrating the return of Goddess Durgā to her parental home—a process that is ritually central to the Bengali autumn-festival of Durgā Pūjā—are immensely-popular till today and he was instrumental in the construction and engaged in the maintenance of a temple to Goddess Kālī in the Bowbazar-area of North Calcutta that became and remains, till date, famous as the *Phiringī Kālibāri* (foreigner's Kālī temple). In the present essay, this literary-cultural construction of a religious hybridity, operating between and cross-fertilizing Indo-European cultural conjunctions, will be examined through the study of individual, "in-between" religious agency, in this case of Antony, who does come across as a transcultural subaltern, if one may so frame it. The attempt, thus, is to take a closer look at an "in-between," intensely-intercultural figure, who is intangible both to contemporary scholars of early-colonial India—not least due to the paucity of relevant biographical and archival material—and to the increasingly shrill rhetoric of the self-(re-)definition of inter-religious relations across the globe.

It is, therefore, especially interesting to attempt a conceptualization of notional expressions of interiorized and externalized minorityhood through a text-oriented literary-cultural prism, as is necessary to reconstruct the life

---

1. I consciously use the initial capital letter while referring to the Goddess and other divine entities, for instance, G-d/God/Goddess/Deity/Divinity, among others. The orthographic distinction between 'God' and the 'gods' is, in my opinion, one that confirms and seeks to perpetuate—unwittingly or otherwise—epistemological, noetic, theological and spiritual hierarchies and distinctions between the so-called poly- and monotheistic faiths and belief-systems.

2. The word *firingi* is said to be derived from the Persian *frangui*, for the "Franks," which was a generic name for European-origin people. As Rosinka Chaudhuri notes, in an end-note to her essay, "[t]he appellation 'Firingi' denoted a foreigner, usually of Portuguese origin, in Bengal. ... Further, the name is spelt, when written in English, as Antony rather than Anthony in all the standard histories." (Chaudhuri 2013, 207)

and works of Antony. It may, in fact, be salient to this discussion to consider ideas of Eurasian literary and cultural syncretism, if not in terms of a "new or third race," at least in those of a European and Russian[3] engagement with Indian spiritual and philosophical phenomena and concepts, especially with the noetic template of *bhakti*.[4] Since some scholars have sought to explain it away as merely a reflection of the European/Christian "need" to articulate a doctrinally- and conceptually-sound response to the possibly-bewildering smorgasbord of Indic Goddesses, Gods, ideals and sects through devotional spirituality, the meta-syncretic[5] co-constitution of liminal, "in-between" and "third space" (Bhabha 2004) religious experiences and their literary-cultural expressions has been explored much less. The attempt here, however, is not to look at the possible motivations and drives behind this phenomenon but to acknowledge, in the figure of Antony, an individual example of what Stephen Greenblatt *et al.* (2010) call "cultural mobility" and Hubert Seiwert views as "human creativity that broadened the realm of possibilities." (Seiwert 2017, 15) Thus, the role of religion, especially as perceived from the analytical prism of its functional relationship with human (re-)productions of culturally-constituted frameworks of sociality, lends itself to semantic interpretation at a microcosmic level, that of a border-crossing individual's experience of both ritual and literary and/or musical expressions of devotional spirituality.

Given this, it may be worth considering the life of Antony, as a non-Anglophone European practitioner and creator in a Bengali Hindu folk-idiom, in his peripheral subject-position as a transcultural participant in the social expression of religious feeling in early-colonial Bengal. That his transcending and, to some extent, transgressive creativity had, at least initially, taken place in a tumultuous urban setting that encouraged and, perhaps even celebrated heterodox cosmopolitanism in cultural taste and socio-religious practice, highlights the enmeshed idiosyncratic response of a border-crossing individual to Indic socio-religious practices. Antony's initial tenuous leverage with both the Anglophone masters of Calcutta and his later patrons amongst the landed mercantile gentry of the Bengali nouveaux riches lends credence to the idea

---

3. Here, the examples of Gerasim Lebedev's (1749–1817) "intercultural enthusiasms" (Chakrabarti 2015) and, much earlier, the almost-picaresque commercial travels of Afanasius Nikitin (?–1472) come to one's mind.

4. *Bhakti* ("devotion, adherence" in Sanskrit and many Indian languages) is one of the forms of yogic and other religio-spiritual practice, where the individual soul seeks liberation and succour through an intense and often expressive devotion to a Divine or semi-divine figure or personage, as may be represented by a specific icon or idol or a typical set of ritual practices.

5. The term "meta-syncretic" is used here in the sense of going beyond the ritual and conceptual mélange of theological syncretism in actual practice.

that his existence may be characterized by a certain transcultural subalternity that transcends both race and class. One may, from this perspective, arrive at a more nuanced and variegated view of the development of devotional spirituality in early/mid-colonial Bengal, with the active and passive participation of multiple foreign actors, who may have had different levels of access to and understanding of the basic conceptual and practitional parameters of Indic spiritualities. That, however, is beyond the scope of this essay, which seeks to analyse the interplay of transcultural enthusiasms and cosmopolitan transgressions as a hybrid pathway of socio-religious expression.

Antony, seen thus, stands out as a rather idiosyncratic, perhaps even exceptional interlocutor between the so-called binaries of "East" and "West," without, given his exact historical situation, having to struggle against "the fixity and fetishism of identities within the calcification of colonial cultures [, which might] recommend that 'roots' be struck in the celebratory romance of the past or by homogenizing the history of the present" (Bhabha 2004, 13). His life and work in Calcutta could serve as an illuminating, if occasionally contrapuntal, sidelight to the socio- and cultural-historical footprint of the "rooted cosmopolitans" (Appiah 1997, 618) of the so-called Bengal Renaissance,[6] like Michael Madhusudan Datta (1824–1873), who were seeking to combine the classical Sanskritic cognitive and cultural heritage with the brave new world of exciting transcultural possibilities and intercultural enthusiasms. If, as Stuart Blackburn and Vasudha Dalmia say, "[e]ver since Clifford Geertz transformed the drama of Balinese cock-fighting into a text, and new historicism made the complementary gesture of returning culture to the centre of literary studies" (Blackburn and Dalmia 2004, 1), there has, indeed, been a conceptual, methodological and referential convergence between literary and cultural historiography, one area in which this development should be of significant help is that of researching Antony's contribution to the transcultural mélange of early-colonial Calcutta.

As may be concluded from the little verifiable information—mainly descended through oral history and anecdotes—that exists on his life, Antony's personal and creative biographies often coalesce into a composite narrative, which is not bereft of its bipolar surprises. This maverick Luso-Indian singer-composer is said to have been born in a salt merchant's family

---

6. The term "Bengal Renaissance" has had a contested reception over the last two centuries, with Indian and foreign scholars debating its provenance. According to David Kopf, the comparison to the Italian Renaissance was first made by Raja Ram Mohan Roy, the eminent social and religious reformer: "Though it is by no means certain when the term renaissance was first used in nineteenth-century Calcutta, Rammohun Roy ... allegedly told Alexander Duff, the missionary, that 'I began to think that something similar to the European renaissance might have taken place here in India'" (Kopf 1979, 3).

in Sutanuti, one of the three originary constituent villages of Calcutta, to a Bengali mother; his grandmother is also supposed to have been Bengali. It is unclear, from the historiographical record or, rather, the sketchiness of it, as to why he chose to become a performer; it seems, however, that his ethnic and religious background was no hindrance to his choice. When one seeks to understand Calcutta's "urban folklore," especially in the domain of "*kabig[ā]n*, the poetical contests, and its sub forms like *kheur* [that] flourished in Calcutta in the nineteenth century," (Sen 2010, 59) through the prism of its heterodox early-colonial caste- and professional interactions, one sees a consistent pattern of consolidation amongst "professional group[s] of performers coming from different caste[-] and religious groups. While Bhabani Bene was from the lower caste of spice dealers, Bhola Moira belonged to the sweetmeat maker caste, Horu Thakur was a brahman, Ram Basu, a *kāyastha* and Antony Firingi, a Portuguese Christian." (Sen 2010, 59) While this phenomenon is, indeed, a trope of professional and performative group-formation in a milieu that challenged traditional caste-hierarchies, one should not overlook the subversive and transgressive role played by individual talent, which could and did transcend traditional norms, and its creative expression. Often the latter was seen as a function of the depth of the artist's personal commitment.

While it could be suggested that such cultural border-crossing is more characteristic of the hybridizing forces unleashed by colonization, one should not be oblivious to the potential implicit in pre-colonial literary-cultural forms and tropes to trigger and leverage dynamic and nuanced articulations of protean normativities in narratives of identity-formation in the early-colonial period. One cannot deny, to paraphrase Indira Viswanathan Peterson, "[t]he ability of traditional scholars to transform literary genres in response to new patrons and worldviews." (Blackburn and Dalmia 2004, 9) In an essay on a nineteenth-century Tamil Christian poet and playwright, Vedanayaka Sastri, Peterson demonstrates how transitional and interstitial literary personalities can adapt "prevailing poetic and performance conventions for new ritual and devotional roles." (Blackburn and Dalmia 2004, 10) This is echoed in Rosinka Chaudhuri's description of Antony's songs as being "devotional lyrics with a secular message, capturing the humanist-universal-folk of the Bengali syncretistic tradition in lines that were uncannily reminiscent of the songs of Bauls such as Lalan Fakir or of the aphorisms of Ramkrishna" (Chaudhuri 2013, 198). Thus, cultural products of India's "colonial modernity" appear to be framed by what Chaudhuri calls "the confluence of Western and Indian modes," (Chaudhuri 2013, 198) which demonstrate no marked deference to the restrictive and hierarchizing internal dynamics of colonial power-relations and, thereby, problematize—as in Antony's case—all easy theorizations of the nature of colonial modernity in early nineteenth-century India. His life and work open up, for scholars today, spaces that were not seen either to exist or be valuable to the creation of spatio-temporal frameworks for the critique of older dogmas, both social and religious, for sweeping away the old order and for creating new templates of religio-cultural sociality. One may also attempt, through a historico-cultural exploration of Antony's life and work, a theorization of the transcultural and border-crossing circulation of Indic religio-cultural texts and tropes that had been facilitated by economic and technological revolutions,[7] which, in turn, had enabled what Pascale Casanova calls "the bourse of literary values" and Paul Valéry categorizes as "the spiritual economy" (Casanova 2004, 12). This would facilitate a nuanced intellectual framing of the historiography of what was a period of multivalent religio-cultural possibilities through what can be called the perspective of transcultural subalternity, as residing in the experiences, observations, lifestyles, life events, and creative agencies of individuals caught between two or more worlds, inhabiting the liminal and often-precarious interstices of globalizing spaces and moments, as in early-colonial Calcutta.

In order to understand the interstitial and somewhat unique position of Antony in the popular *imaginaire* of Bengali culture, it is crucial to delink the historical figure from that of the romantic icon fictionalized in *Antony Firingee* (1967), a commercially-successful Bengali film, which had an all-star cast, including the legendary Uttam Kumar, Bengali cinema's first and, arguably, only real mega-star, and Tanuja. This film, especially through its many songs that had been composed by the historical Antony and were sung by renowned playback-singers like Manna Dey, seems to have crystallized a rather charismatic and epoch-making image of the Luso-Indian bard in the popular imagination (Figure 2.1).

The film ascribes to Antony the role of a person who, through what has been described as "devotional songs to '*ma Kali*' or Durga in secular performative spaces," (Chaudhuri 2013, 199) bridges the "old" world of vernacular religio-cultural performativity, within the public domain, and that of the "new" one that was seen to be defined by colonial modernity, notwithstanding the conceptual problems of the term, and the Anglo-European civility it claimed to introduce to Bengal. As Chaudhuri writes,

> In the case of Antony, we have almost an inverse career path, featuring movement away from bourgeois Western respectability –wonderfully captured in the film by Antony's cravat and tight trousers, carriage and furniture, language and mercantile activity—toward an increasingly "indigenous" or Indian identity, revealed by his gradual abandonment of the accoutrements of Western life for the village, the *dhoti-kurta*, the

---

7. These enabling paradigm shifts, which played a significant role in the global circulation of religious ideas and practices as discursive vehicles in the nineteenth century (Bayly 2004), could have provided the backdrop for Antony's cross-cultural engagement with Indic religious praxis.

"In-Between" Religiosity

worship of the mother-goddess Durga and absorption in Sanskrit hymns and the Bengali *kabi* tradition. (Chaudhuri 2013, 199)

While it is difficult, given the paucity of archival and biographical evidence, to ascertain the truth-claim of this image of a "return" to the vernacular roots of religio-spiritual belief and expression, it may be argued that Antony's *oeuvre* did constitute a shift that was rather uncharacteristic of the *Zeitgeist*, which had a quite clear developing prejudice against the traditional world of folk-religion and popular and public performance of religious devotion. Thus, the *Weltanschauung* of the English-educated Brahmo scholar-

Figure 2.1 Stills from Bannerjee, *Antony Firingee* (5:25; 2:21:20), dir. S. Bannerjee, 1967.

mercantile agent/newspaper-editor/lawyer/other professional, who—when not completely denying any positive value to the folk- and popular idioms of religious expression—was wont to view the Indic "old" and the European "modern" as necessarily opposed to each other and also to privilege the latter over the former. As Rosinka Chaudhuri further observes,

> Rajnarain Basu's *Se Kal Ar E Kal* ("Then and Now," 1874) contains exactly such a demarcation, with a section on Antony ... as belonging to the past and Derozio[8] as representative of the future ... [however], that binary is one that does not retain its validity in the face of the complex shape of the modern as it was coming into being at this time.
>
> (Chaudhuri 2013, 199)

This discursive opposition would play a significant role in the self-characterization of the Bengal Renaissance and the anti-colonial movement, with its insistence on a secular faith-neutrality that was continually self-performative, which was to emerge out of it and provide a discursive template for (post-)colonial Indian modernity. Thus, formulations of anti-colonial solidarity and post-colonial societal, cultural, ideological and political discourses were, quite often, significantly influenced by this early-colonial conceptualization of modernity as being difficult to reconcile with traditional forms of religious and spiritual expression. The latter, despite being tolerated, cultivated, encouraged and even promoted—whatever be the motives for it—by the postcolonial state and civil society, remained contrapuntal to the truth-claims of Indian modernity.

One is, thus, inclined to opine that this oppositional framing of the space between the "old" and the "new," the "traditional" and the "modern" is somewhat misleading in the quest for a holistic understanding of the frenetic cross-cultural and border-crossing enthusiasms of early-colonial Bengal. The dogmatic religio-ideological imperatives that were so characteristic of what Joachim Küpper calls "the conditioned effacement of concrete materiality" (Küpper 2003, 365–366), with regard to the Spanish conquest of New World, seem to have been much less dichotomous in the early-colonial Indian context. The much-discussed and -debated mercantile orientation of Europe's expansion into the newly-discovered spaces of the post-*Descobrimento* world was especially and specifically true for the British entrée into the geopolitical equations of the Indian subcontinent. From early on, the English East India

---

8. Henry Louis Vivian Derozio (1809–1831), "whose mother was English and grandfather was variously described as 'Native Protestant' and 'Portuguese Merchant,'" (Chaudhuri 2013, 195) was a charismatic Luso-Indian poet and educator, having taught at the Hindu College, Calcutta, where a group of his devoted and intelligent students formed themselves into a radical societal-cultural reform movement called "Young Bengal." His famous poem "To India—My Native Land" (1828) is arguably the first modern Anglophone poetic articulation of anti-colonial Indian nationalism.

Company had subdued its evangelical sympathies to the profit-imperative and acknowledged the practical hurdles involved in proselytizing a subcontinent as rich and diverse in millennial religio-cultural traditions as India. Thus, Anglo-Indian colonial modernity, howsoever multivalent and/or polemical that term may be, was necessarily grounded in a negotiatory "in-between" space "in which several times compete[d] and coexist[ed]." (Chaudhuri 2013, 199) The apparent seamlessness with which societally-constituted cultural choices and predilections did overlap with each other in what Chaudhuri calls "an ambiguous space containing both the traditional and what we might call the new urban folk" (Chaudhuri 2013, 199) highlights the need to unpack the conceptual framing of colonial modernity as having occurred "in multiple ways within specific local contexts." (Dodson and Hatcher 2013, 4) The currency of alternative conceptualizations of colonial modernity through, among others, the theoretical prism of "multiple modernities," (Eisenstadt 2000) should convince us of the pressing need to attempt a reconfiguration of the cultural history of early-colonial India from the perspective of transcultural individual agency, as seen in the case of Antony, that had a parallel and complementary and/or contingent role *vis-à-vis* British colonialism. The resultant enmeshed hybridity operated both as a locus of the interplay of two contrasting but parallel responses to the societal, cultural, ethical and religious challenges of colonialism and as the primary platform for "the complex inauguration of the Indian modern." (Chaudhuri 2013, 199) Hence, it might just make more historiographical sense to look at the phenomenon that is referred to as colonial modernity as a synthesized, even synthetic concept that bridges the gap between the demands of an ideologically-configured future that sought to break with, to a certain extent, a constructed past and the irredentist pull of this meta-territorial history.

Such a polyvalent understanding of the notional currency of colonial modernity would do well to engage with Partha Chatterjee's description of the time of Antony and Derozio as "the age of transition" (Chaudhuri 2013, 199), an age that is "not teleologically predetermined by the ascendance of the colonial modern." (Aquil and Chatterjee 2008, 5) It would, thus, stand to reason that one needs to theorize the conceptual emergence and geopolitical expansion of colonial modernity as not being necessarily linked to the interstitial societal-cultural overlaps and syncretic encounters that were central to lives like that of Antony. More often than not, such lives do seem to defy neat ideological allocation to one or the other discursive trajectories that instrumentalize figures, movements, events and contingencies in keeping with one or the other teleological imperative, whether or not the latter is implicitly or explicitly articulated. As Chaudhuri observes, "Antony participated in a new, vulgarized vernacular public culture that would later be frowned upon by the students of Derozio" (Chaudhuri 2013, 199), who, under the influence of colonial interrogations of what was beginning to be disenfranchised as the vernacular, could be seen as having attempted "to distinguish a high culture from the 'low' indigenous traditions—an attempt that was bound, inevitably, for failure" (Chaudhuri 2013, 199). In fact, within at least the Anglicized intellectual elites of early-colonial Calcutta, so powerful and dominant was this need to construct a prescriptive hierarchy of literary-cultural taste and acceptability that it would take almost a century and a half for literary-cultural historians to attempt critical analyses of this noetic infrastructure. A Luso-Indian born-again worshipper of Goddess Kālī was, hence, doubly compromised for the early-colonial Anglicized intellectual; he was an embarrassing and, hence, forgettable reminder of the vigorous intensity of certain aspects of their spiritual-intellectual legacy. Antony was not only singing paeans to a Goddess seen, by the Reverend Alexander Duff, a Scotsman who was one of the most charitable and influential European missionaries in India, as, "[o]f all the Hindu divinities, ... the most cruel and revengeful" (Duff 1839, 241) and "[t]he Patroness of thieves and murderers" (Duff 1839, 195). He was also composing his works in poetic idioms that had double uses: they could be deployed as vehicles of both spiritual and erotic expression, and were seen, by these intellectuals, as having had a corrosive influence on public morals and not deemed fit for either religious explorations or literary-cultural creativity.

Thus, it appears that Antony's self-linking to a subaltern precolonial discourse of the "folk"[9] idiom of devotional spirituality, which was looked upon with considerable disfavour by the emerging early-colonial Bengali intellectual (semi-)consensus, put him in an intermediary position of negotiated self-positioning between quite disparate worlds. What is even more interesting about his life and work is that he seems to redefine, in terms of societal-cultural transactionality, the contiguous but rather dissonant spaces straddled by him. While he comes with the baggage of an as yet nascent racialization of colonial sociality, with the emerging hegemonies, power-relations, hierarchies and normativities being European and Europhone in nature, he appears to be uninterested in the Pauline art of preaching to the Heathen, as practised by the missionaries, and "go native" in dress, food-habits, cultural choices and marital decisions. Moreover, he seems to seek to interpret the spatial presence of the Goddess Kālī in what is, as argued by some local historians, a city named after Her[10] as a trope of the psycho-emotional framing of fields

---

9. Not, of course, to be read in conjunction with the German *völkisch*, with its ideational and ideological charges.
10. Calcutta<Kolikātā<Kālighāt<Kālikṣetra, the last-two toponyms meaning river-bank-steps or area of the Goddess Kālī. This etymology of the city's name, one of the three main theories in circulation, is mentioned in the "Kolkata"-entry of the *Encyclopaedia Britannica* (https://www.britannica.com/place/Kolkata).

of belonging. What Margrit Pernau identifies as "the contested character of emotions linked to specific spaces ... [and] the role of power in resolving these contestations" (Pernau 2014, 545), is as true of early-colonial Calcutta as of pre- and post-1857 Delhi, which is what she is writing about. In the case of the former, figures like Antony proceed from a position of implicit and assumed hegemonic cultural sway to that of enthusiastic self-acculturation and active participation in the religious and cultural lives of their adoptive homes. While moving from an urban Europhone to a rural *zamindāri*[11]-milieu (and in between them), performing his poetic compositions in the sacral and secular courtyards and inner spaces of Bengali landholding households seems to become, for Antony, a self-fashioning exercise characterized by expressive literary-cultural shape-shifting.

"Hindoo" Stuart: A British Antony Firingi?

This intriguing—especially so to the denizens of societal-cultural reform in early- and mid-colonial Bengal—example of "going native" was not just a case of a European migrant's (for colonist is certainly not how Antony saw himself) self-identification with Bengal's syncretic and, more often than not, heterodox devotional culture, and is certainly not to be analysed on the same lines as the so-called "white Mughals" (Dalrymple 2002) of Delhi and Hyderabad, *viz.* Sir David Ochterlony, James Achilles Kirkpatrick *et al.* Though one may compare his life and work and, certainly, the way he was perceived by his average European fellow-Calcuttans, with Major-General Charles "Hindoo" Stuart (c. 1758–1828), there are certain reasons to see Antony's engagement with Bengali Hindu culture as being somewhat more nuanced and lyrical—at least, in terms of his engagement—than Stuart's. Stuart became (in)famous due to his efforts to make the British and other European women in Calcutta adopt the sari as their main article of dress, citing health-, beauty- and other reasons for this suggested sartorial shift. He was also known to take a daily morning-bath in the Ganga, have acquired a range of Hindu idols with which he was buried, according to his wishes, at the Park Street Cemetery in Calcutta, and be favourably disposed to those of his soldiers who wore full-blown Rajput moustaches and sported caste-marks on their foreheads. (Dalrymple 2002, 42–44, 496) Stuart was also consistently and openly critical of missionary efforts at evangelizing Hindus within British India, pre-eminently in his *Vindication of the Hindoos* (1808), in which he wrote: "the Hindoo system ... little needs the meliorating hand of Christian dispensations,

---

11. The *zamindār* ("landholder" in Persian) was the principal tax-collecting and/or revenue-farming authority in rural North India throughout the periods of Mughal and British ascendancy; absentee landlords, based in Calcutta and its environs, are widely acknowledged to be the prime movers of early- and mid-colonial societal and religious reform.

to render its votaries, a sufficiently correct and moral people." (Stuart 1808, 9) He also furnishes evidence from scriptural and other textual sources of Hinduism in support of his argument "that, if the Hindoos are not already blessed with the virtues of Morality, it can in no wise be attributed to the want of an ample system of Moral Ordinances, for the regulation of their conduct in society." (Stuart 1808, 2) Thus, "Hindoo" Stuart's engagement with his adoptive spirituality and cultural enthusiasms was not just skin-deep and cosmetic, anchored in conceptualizations and appropriations of the exotic and the alien(ating). Not unlike Antony, he seems to have been swayed by what he saw, "in the vast region of Hindoo Mythology, [as] Piety in the garb of Allegory: and ... Morality, at every turn, blended with every tale"; (Stuart 1808, 97) Stuart goes on to make the categorical assertion that Hinduism "appears to be the most complete and ample system of Moral Allegory, that the world has ever produced." (Stuart 1808, 97)

What, however, appears to distinguish Antony's approach from Stuart's is the fact of the former's interest in Hinduism being more artistically nuanced, through his focus on musical and literary creativity, than the latter, who seems to have been more engaged with the quest for a fair and just British socio-political engagement with the faith-systems of the majority of their Indian subjects. Stuart's Hinduphilia was that of an admirer, an enthusiast, a fellow-traveller, actually a sort of collector of Hindu worlds, whereas Antony's was a less *ex cathedra* and more enmeshed approach to what must have been, for both of them, a somewhat bewildering, if richly variegated and exquisitely layered plethora of Divinities, Deities, rituals and concepts. In his *Vindication*, Stuart returns repeatedly to the theme of the inherent moral qualities of the average Hindu and seeks to counter missionary calls for the state-supported (if not -sponsored) evangelization of the Hindu subjects of the East India Company. In fact, his stand definitely had political overtones, as shown by the presence, in his pamphlet, of a section on the strategic mistake and "danger of attempting to convert the natives of India." (Stuart 1808, 153) He goes on, further, to write that he has "no hesitation in declaring the dread moment to be arrived, when the absolute safety of the state requires that [the missionaries] should be for ever silenced." (Stuart 1808, 157) This focus on the security of British possessions and interests in India is what sets Stuart apart from Antony, with the latter having, as far as one may ascertain from his life and works, no interest in acknowledging the adversarial aspects of the Hindu-Christian encounter in Bengal. In one of his most well-known devotional duel-songs, made even more famous by the Bengali film discussed earlier, he writes: "There is no difference between Christ and Krishna / that men should follow only a name—I have never heard of such a thing / My *Khoda* is the same as the Hindu's *Hari* / Look there, see *Hari* is standing." The short song ends with an exhortation to Durgā: "Pity me mother, spare me a glance o mother Matangi[12] / I do not know how to worship you / by race I am a firingee" (Chaudhuri 2013, 198). Though this stylistic trajectory and devotional content cannot be said to be exceptional, especially since his Bengali has only minor idiosyncrasies, the lyrical content of his songs and his repeated self-referencing as "firingee" do make his compositions identifiable. (Paniker 1997) This is an attitude to the issue of Hindu-Christian dialogue and spiritual cohabitation that would, most certainly, baffle Stuart and irritate figures like Derozio, whose chosen lived reality was, unlike Antony's, that of the cosmopolitan hustle and bustle of metropolitan Calcutta, with its "commercial establishments, clubs, offices, periodicals, newspapers, theater-going and literary endeavor" (Chaudhuri 2013, 198).

In fact, it would be most instructive to pay attention to the multidimensional templates of urbanization—as a spatial discourse that has a transforming effect on religious practice and socio-cultural choices—in early-colonial Calcutta. One of the defining features of this process was the evolution of the folk-idiom, in its various generic manifestations, as a vehicle of societal and cultural expression for, primarily, the urban poor who were to find themselves increasingly distant, both spatially and ideationally, from the increasingly Anglophone and Anglophile upper classes, who would go on to constitute the famed *bhadralok*.[13] As some scholars of Bengali folk-culture have argued, the widening and deepening of the religio-cultural gap between different socio-economic classes, especially between the metropolitan socio-cultural elites and the emerging urban poor, was often the result of re-constituted caste- and class-hierarchies stemming from rural Bengal and re-framed within the dynamics of proto-industrial urbanization (Banerjee 1989). These new urban subaltern formations, drawing from their past rural (mostly as artisans and craftspeople) cultural milieus and inheritances, would—increasingly in the period under consideration—find themselves to be unaccounted for in the *bhadralok* conceptualization of the new moral order. This would push them in the direction of catering to their own psycho-emotional needs by taking recourse to recycling and recalibrating their rural belief-systems that were quite foreign to the Europhile (re-)configuration of religiosity as carried out by the Hindu social reformers of the early-colonial period, pre-eminently

---

12. The Goddess *Mātaṅgī*, who has been seen as the *Tāntrika Sarasvatī* and, hence, a facilitator of the spoken and sung word, is one of the *Daśamahāvidyās* (Ten Forms into which the Mother Goddess replicates Herself). According to one iconographic representation, she "is black. Her eyes roll in intoxication, and she reels about like an impassioned elephant." (Kinsley 1988, 163)

13. "A term (literally, 'civilised people') used, till quite recently, to denote the Bengali middle classes, which cultivated a specific aura of eclectic cultural and intellectual tastes, despite their social conservatism; often, this leisured urbane sophistication was bought by economic pelf." (Chakrabarti 2012, 256)

those belonging to the Brahmo Samāj. In a paradoxical development that defines the Bengali, if not the entire Indian, upper- and middle-class attitude to religion and religiosity in the early days of British ascendancy in the subcontinent, the need to respond to the demands of colonial modernity was addressed by a rather schematic and selective reading of "ancient" texts that were supposed to be definitive in terms of intellectual provenance and philosophical rigour. It was an attempt at creating a certain template of, primarily, a Hindu way of life that would be presentable to a "western" audience. Of course, this need not mean that the reformers' agenda was necessarily straitjacketed into revisionist and reductionist paradigms.

Often, reform movements like the Brahmo Samāj would actually (re-)deploy various poetic and musical tropes and other literary-cultural signifiers from earlier devotional configurations. To give just one prominent example, the Brahmo-saṅgīt that formed the base of the Samaj's services and went on—through the poetry and musical compositions of Rabindranath Tagore—to define the norm of what constitutes musical refinement in Bengal had, as its core, a pre-Brahmo Vaiṣṇava *kīrtan*[14] tradition. As David Kopf observes:

> Rabindranath Tagore, also a Brahmo, later brought this musical art to its perfection, and through him and his songs, middle-class Bengali Hindu society accepted it as their own—though by dropping off Brahmo and calling these songs Rabindra sangit. Their importance ... was that they conveyed the ideology of Brahmoism directly and simply through the ears of people accustomed to the Vaishnava kirtan. (Kopf 1979, 238–239)

This was, then, the trajectory followed by the reformers in their musical expression of reformist spiritual positions, as nuanced by their intellectual processing of both the challenges and the opportunities of colonial modernity, as manifested in the frenetic urban churning of early-colonial Calcutta. It could be interesting to compare Antony's poetical and musical compositions with the poetic *oeuvre* of the afore-mentioned Derozio, who was almost deified by his students and other followers, and is widely credited with having influenced and formed the minds of a number of the leading lights of the Brahmo and more radical social reformers. Derozio's poetry, which had a strain of ardent patriotism that was very Anglophone in tone—with more

---

14. The word *kīrtan(a)* ("narrating, declaiming, describing, elocution") connotes a musical and/or recitative genre of encomium, usually directed—with devotional fervour, as in the Vaiṣṇava case—towards a Divinity but also, through parody and inversion, towards despised individuals, objects, practices. It is said to be derived from the Vedic practice of *anukīrtana* (renarration), which "captures the essential meaning of the original more powerfully than imitation." (Lal 2009, 423) In Vaiṣṇava devotional practice, this mode of musical retelling often acquires mystical fervour, through an intensely performative recitative exploration of the notable attributes of the Divinity concerned.

than a hint of Sir Walter Scott's rousing fervour—was directed towards a Bengal, even India, considered by Derozio as having somehow lapsed from her past glory. As is evident from what he writes in his most famous poem "To India—My Native Land" (1828), this young Luso-Indian poet-cum-educator appears to have identified a mission for himself, prefiguring the reformist movement that was to evolve into the nationalist anti-colonial struggle later in the nineteenth century:

> Well—let me dive into the depths of time,
> And bring from out the ages that have rolled
> A few small fragments of those wrecks sublime,
> Which human eye may never more behold.
> (Mukhopadhyay *et al.* 2001, 99)

It was this mission, which sought to (re-)discover and glorify a personified idyll of the Motherland without acknowledging the religious subtexts—specifically contingent to the Indian situation—of that move, while critically evaluating and occasionally rejecting the manifestations of religio-cultural contemporaneity, that was largely adopted by the reformist and nationalist agendas in mid- and late-colonial India. A narrative like Antony's, doubly baffling and idiosyncratic in its rejection of the outward attributes of Europhone modernity and the post-Enlightenment rationalist discourse, and in its open and joyous acceptance and even championing of the literary-cultural idioms of an esoteric—to missionaries, repulsive—Indic devotional practice, was thus viewed as an exception to the norm.

Antony Firingi as a transcultural subaltern

It is in this context that it may be useful to look at Antony's life and work as an example of transcultural subalternity. This would be especially salient for his compositions in Bengali and his association with the Kālī Temple, in the Bowbazar neighbourhood of Calcutta. While this may involve extending the discursive domain of subalternity beyond the frameworks established by the Subaltern Studies Collective, especially as seen in the scholarship of Dipesh Chakrabarty (1992) and Gayatri Chakravorty Spivak (1988), one does not feel the required noetic leap to be too exaggerated. More often than not,

> [b]y assigning the agency in history to an elite that in its multiplicity could be clerics, secular intelligentsia, colonialist and social or political institutions, [historians] not only deny the agency of subaltern and its autonomous consciousness but also by adopting an essentialist approach they dehistoricize the process of social and cultural changes. ... Although the subaltern historians launched their project by criticizing the historiography of Indian nationalism, over the past twenty years it has evolved into a critique of historiography itself. (Atabaki 2003, 6)

Hence, it does seem that the possibility of expanding the concept of subalternity into the domain of transcultural liminality, thereby enabling the categorization of figures like Antony as subaltern, lies within the conceptual range of the framework of subaltern historiography. A similar and quite apposite example of this conceptual expansion would be Harald Fischer-Tiné's work on, among others, European courtesans and sex-workers in colonial India. It appears that the Anglo-European presence in India was characterized as much by internal class-hierarchies, with the so-called white subalterns—including the poor, vagabonds, criminals, prostitutes, soldier's widows, orphans and the insane—forming the baseline of a social pyramid (Fischer-Tiné 2009, 59), as it was by race-discourses. The transcultural nature of Antony's life and work, and the precarity of his interstitial existence between widely disparate socio-cultural and religious worlds in an in-between city that was, itself, the product of intercultural negotiation and compromise rendered—from the perspective of an individual's societal-cultural agency—his life and work as a European devotee of a Hindu Goddess quite vulnerable to the vagaries of both a bemused, at best, and suspicious, at worst, colonial administration and an initially incredulous indigenous clientèle. The latter, without much awareness of and sensitivity to the precariousness of Antony's European subjectivity—due, in large measure, to his being of Luso-Indian origin—might have seen in him another enthusiasm-filled and colourful *sāhib*[15] going native in pursuance of a passing fad. Though he was born into a wealthy Luso-Indian mercantile family and appears, initially, to have lived quite a luxurious life in the manner of the famous *nabobs*[16] of the English East India Company, his transformation into a Kālī-*bhakta* ("worshipper") and singer-composer, actually a travelling performance-artist taking part in intensely-fought bardic duels was as uncommon as it was impressive to the point of being incredible. Not only are his songs replete with *purāṇic* and *śāstric*[17] allusions that indicate

---

15. The Anglo-Indian word *sāhib* comes to English, Hindi, Bengali, Urdu, Marathi and other Indian languages, via Persian, from the Arabic *ṣāḥib* ("friend, lord"); it was used, during the colonial period, for European-origin people and for superiors in social and other hierarchies.

16. The Anglo-Indian word *nabob* comes from either the Bāṅglā *nabāb*, the Hindustani *navāb*, and/or the Portuguese *nababo*, all of which come, through Farsi, from the Arabic *nuwwāb*; the term was used extensively in Mughal and other pre-colonial Indian administrative contexts to denote a male provincial administrator. In the Anglo-Indian context, the *nabob* was "[a]n employee of the East India Company, [who] was perceived to have returned to Great Britain equipped with ill-gotten affluence, a ravenous appetite for extravagance, and aspirations to rise into elite spheres of power and influence." (Smylitopoulos 2012, 11)

17. The word *śāstra* ("academic treatise"), according to the Capeller's Sanskrit-English Dictionary, can mean "instruction, precept, rule, theory, a scientific or canonical work" (http://www.sanskrit-lexicon.uni-koeln.de/scans/CAEScan/2014/web/index.

an intuitive and substantial working knowledge of Hindu mythology and cosmogony, but he also displays a relish, not least in his style of bardic duelling, for idiomatic and self-ironic Bengali poetic composition. More often than not, in these duels between Antony and his Bengali competitors and fellow-poets, there were "personal vituperative comments to the enjoyment of the common listeners." (Paniker 1997, 843) As the following exchange between Anthony and Thakur[das] Singh[a], one of the most well-known and redoubtable practitioners of this genre in the early nineteenth century, should prove, the former could hold his own in poetic banter and verbal repartee, notwithstanding his "otherness."

Thakur Singh to Antony Firingi:

> One thing I want to know from you, Antony,
> Coming to this country, why have you not put on a *kurta* and a hat?

Antony Firingi to Thakur Singh:

> I am very glad to be in Bengali dress in Bengal,
> I have discarded *kurta*[18] and hat after being the son-in-law of Thakur Singh's father.

(Paniker 1997, 848)

Thus, it is perhaps not difficult to consider Antony as having succeeded in enmeshing himself vocationally and professionally—though it is difficult to view his initial participation in the poetic duels as a purely (if at all) professional act—in the indigenous religio-cultural milieux of early-colonial Calcutta. It is believed that his initial exposure to Hindu devotional practices was through his wife, whom he, according to one scholar, "saved from mounting the funeral pyre of her dead husband as Sati" (Sen 1962, 28) and who seems to have been a defining influence in his subsequent life as "almost a Hinduized Anglo-Indian in all tastes." (Sen 1962, 28) However, he soon acquires enough knowledge and awareness of Hindu beliefs and practices to not only sing paeans to the Mother Goddess but also, later on, compose songs on his own. As discussed earlier in this essay, Antony makes a reverse move, from the city—in his case, the French enclave of Chandernagore—to an adjacent

---

php, *s.v.*). The *Purāṇas* ("of ancient times") are ancient post-Vedic and early-medieval Sanskrit texts—with culturally-significant medieval translations into almost all the major vernacular languages of the subcontinent—dealing with the genealogies of the various Hindu Deities, semi-divine monarchs and heroic figures, along with their respective families and clans, sages and savants, for which they have been called "the true Bibles of Hinduism" (Klostermaier 2007, 15); they also serve as compendia that structure ancient and medieval knowledge of Hindu cosmogony, philosophy and sacred geography.

18. This was probably meant, as suggested by the context, as a "coat"—a synecdoche signifying European attire and, by extension, culture—rather than the *kurtā*, a collarless shirt-like North Indian and Bengali garment for the upper body.

village, Boruti. This is a marked and telling contrast to the steady Calcutta-bound migration, intellectual and cultural, professional and leisure-driven, from Bengal's villages and small and medium-sized towns that began in the early nineteenth century and continues till today. Though it does remain difficult to ascertain the degree to which he saw himself as a "Hinduized" subject of European origin, given the paucity of archival and other documentary material shedding light on the key events of his life, it is quite clear from the compositions with which he is associated that his life and work showed an undeniable pattern of attachment and devotion to the Goddess Kālī, as sacralized and worshipped in the Bengali Śākta-tradition. In one of his first compositions, sung during his duel with the renowned Bhola Maira, when both had received "an invitation from a millionaire at Chinsura on the occasion of Durga Puja" (Sen 1962, 28), Antony says: "*Bhajon pujon jāni ne Mā / Jātete Firingi / Jodi dayā kore kripā karo / He Śibā Mātongi*" ("I do not know, Mother, any sort of devotional and worship-rituals, being a foreigner; please have mercy and bestow your Grace on me, o Consort of Śiva, Mātangī"). It is interesting that he uses this particular name for the Mother Goddess—Mātangī is supposed to be the *tāntrika*-form of Sarasvatī, the Vedic Goddess of learning and the arts—and one may even take this as tentative evidence of Antony's knowledge of *tāntrika* mystical concepts and practices. On the other hand, it might also demonstrate the depth of his knowledge of Bengali literary-cultural sensibilities and expressive practices, a familiarity, in fact, even virtuosity that secures him a place in the annals of Bānglā literature and culture.

Be that as it may, one feels confident in looking at Antony's contribution to literary and musical practices of worshipping the Mother Goddess in Bengal as a statement of transcultural subalternity, which asserts its creative agency in a spatio-temporal locus of hybridity. This interstitial and even liminal voice seems to, occasionally paradoxically, transcend its double—religious and ethnic—distancing from the experiential realization sought by it through literary-cultural creativity. Antony Firingi, the maverick Luso-Indian poet-worshipper of the Divine Patroness of Calcutta, the awe-inspiring Goddess Kālī, has secured for himself a place in the religio-cultural pantheon of Bengal.

References

Appiah, Anthony Kwame. 1997. "Cosmopolitan Patriots." *Critical Enquiry* 23(3): 617–639. https://doi.org/10.1086/448846

Aquil, Raziuddin, and Partha Chatterjee, eds. 2008. *History in the Vernacular*. Ranikhet: Permanent Black.

Atabaki, Touraj. 2003. *Beyond Essentialism: Who Writes Whose Past in the Middle East and Central Asia?* Amsterdam: Aksant Academic Publishers.

Banerjee, Sumanta. 1989. *The Parlour and the Streets: Elite and Popular Culture in*

Nineteenth Century Calcutta. Calcutta: Seagull Books.

Bannerjee, Sunil, director. 1967. *Antony Firingee* [এন্টনী ফিরিঙ্গী]. National award winning movie, full HD. | *uttam kumar* | *tanuja*. https://www.youtube.com/watch?v=Lno9wIfouJE

Bayly, Christopher Alan. 2004. *The Birth of the Modern World, 1780-1914: Global Connections and Companions*. Oxford: Blackwell Publishing.

Bhabha, Homi K. 2004. *The Location of Culture*. Oxford: Routledge.

Blackburn, Stuart and Vasudha Dalmia, eds. 2004. *India's Literary History: Essays on the Nineteenth Century*. New Delhi: Permanent Black.

Casanova, Pascale. 2004. *The World Republic of Letters*, translated by M.B. DeBevoise. Cambridge, MA: Harvard University Press.

Chakrabarti, Gautam. 2012. "The *Bhadralok* as Truth-Seeker: Towards a Social History of the Bengali Detective." In *Cracow Indological Studies* XIV, edited by L. Sudyka, 255–268. Kraków: Księgarnia Akademicka. https://doi.org/10.12797/CIS.17.2015.17.06

———. 2015. "'Pure and Mixed' in East India: Gerasim Lebedev's Intercultural Enthusiasms." In *Cracow Indological Studies* XVII, edited by T. Dubyanskaya, 115–132. Kraków: Księgarnia Akademicka. https://doi.org/10.2307/2928652

Chakrabarty, Dipesh. 1992. "Postcoloniality and the Artifice of History: Who Speaks for 'Indian' Pasts?" *Representations* 37 (Winter): 1–26.

Chakravorty Spivak, Gayatri. 1988. "Can the Subaltern Speak?" In *Marxism and the Interpretation of Culture*, edited by C. Nelson and L. Grossberg, 271–313. Urbana: University of Illinois Press. https://doi.org/10.1007/978-1-349-19059-1_20

Chaudhuri, Rosinka. 2013. "Three Poets in Search of History: Calcutta, 1752–1859." In *Trans-Colonial Modernities in South Asia*, edited by M.S. Dodson and B.A. Hatcher, 189–209. Oxford: Routledge.

Dalrymple, William. 2002. *White Mughals: Love and Betrayal in Eighteenth-Century India*. New Delhi: Viking/Penguin Books India.

Dodson, Michael S. and Brian A. Hatcher, eds. 2013. *Trans-Colonial Modernities in South Asia*. Oxford: Routledge. https://doi.org/10.4324/9780203135396

Duff, D.D., Rev. Alexander. 1839 (2nd edition). *India and India Missions: Including Sketches of the Gigantic System of Hinduism, both in Theory and Practice; also Notices of Some of the Principal Agencies Employed in Conducting the Process of Indian Evangelization, andc. andc.* Edinburgh: John Johnstone.

Eisenstadt, Shmuel N. 2000. "Multiple Modernities." *Daedalus* 129(1): 1–29. https://doi.org/10.1177/03058298000290031201

Fischer-Tiné, Harald. 2009. *Low and Licentious Europeans: Race, Class and White Sub-*

alternity in Colonial India. New Delhi: Orient BlackSwan.

Greenblatt, Stephen, Ines Županov, Reinhard Meyer-Kalkus, Heike Paul, Pál Nyíri and Friederike Pannewick. 2010. *Cultural Mobility: A Manifesto*. Cambridge: Cambridge University Press. https://doi.org/10.1017/CBO9780511804663

Kinsley, David. 1988. *Hindu Goddesses: Visions of the Divine Feminine in the Hindu Religious Tradition*. Berkeley: University of California Press. https://doi.org/10.1525/9780520908833

Klostermaier, Klaus K. 2007. *A Survey of Hinduism*. Albany: State University of New York Press.

Kopf, David. 1979. *The Brahmo Samaj and the Shaping of the Modern Indian Mind*. New Delhi: Archive Publishers. https://doi.org/10.1515/9781400869893

Küpper, Joachim. 2003. "The Traditional Cosmos and the New World." *MLN* 118(2): 363–392. Hispanic Issue. https://doi.org/10.1353/mln.2003.0045

Kuśa, Satyendra. 2000. *Dictionary of Hindu literature*. New Delhi: Sarup and Sons.

Lal, Ananda. 2009. *Theatres of India: A Concise Companion*. Oxford: Oxford University Press.

Mukhopadhyay, Abirlal, Amar Dutta, Adhir Kumar and Sakti Sadhan Mukhopadhyay, eds. 2001. *Song of the Stormy Petrel: Complete Works of Henry Louis Vivian Derozio*. Kolkata: Progressive Publishers.

Nathan, Leonard and Clinton B. Seely. 1982. *Grace and Mercy in her Wild Hair: Selected Poems to the Mother Goddess*. New York: Great Eastern.

Paniker, K. Ayyappa, ed. 1997. *Medieval Indian Literature: An Anthology. Vol. I: Surveys and Selections*. New Delhi: Sahiya Akademi.

Pernau, Margrit. 2014. "Space and Emotion: Building to Feel." *History Compass* 12(17): 541–549. https://doi.org/10.1111/hic3.12170

Seiwert, Hubert. 2017. "The Dynamics of Religion and Cultural Evolution: Worshipping Fuxi in Contemporary China." In *Dynamics of Religion: Past and Present*, edited by C. Bochinger and J. Rüpke, 9–29. Berlin: De Gruyter. https://doi.org/10.1515/9783110450934-002

Sen, Gopi Nath. 1962. "An English Kabiwala of Bengal." *Midwest Folklore* 12(1): 27–30.

Sen, Soumen. 2010. *Folklore, Tradition, Urbanity*. Kolkata: Anjali.

Smylitopoulos, Christina. 2012. "Portrait of a Nabob: Graphic Satire, Portraiture, and the Anglo-Indian in the Late Eighteenth-Century." *RACAR* 37(1): 10–25 (Montreal: Université du Québec à Montréal). https://doi.org/10.7202/1066730ar

Stuart, Charles ("A Bengal Officer"). 1808. *Vindication of the Hindoos*. London: R. and J. Rodwell.

About the author

Gautam Chakrabarti, PhD, is Postdoctoral Researcher and Lecturer at the Kulturwissenschaftliche Fakultät, Europa-Universität Viadrina, Frankfurt (Oder). He has previously worked for the ERC-Projekt "Developing Theater," Ludwig-Maximilians-Universität München. He has also taught Berlin- and German Studies, Comparative Literature, English and Anglophone Literature and Culture at the Freie Universität Berlin.

— 3 —

The Making of the Ideal Transnational Disciple: Unravelling Biographies of Margaret Noble/Sister Nivedita

Gwilym Beckerlegge

> This chapter departs from the representation of Margaret Noble/Sister Nivedita (1867–1911) popularized by emic biographies. These have tended to treat her eclectic spiritual life, with all its fluid complexity, as merely preparatory to her meeting Swami Vivekananda (1863–1902) in London, and to attribute the roots of her commitment to the cause of Indian nationalism, after her initiation as his disciple, to a deep-seated Irish nationalism inculcated by her family. Instead, by extending the concept of "translocalism," this chapter will explore Nivedita's life as a "translocal space." It will be suggested that the distinctive transnational course of Nivedita's life, between two seats of resistance to British colonial rule via the capital of the British Empire, gave rise to ambivalence and unresolved tensions that she exhibited in relation to her identity and the direction of her career.

Introduction

Margaret Noble's (1867–1911) life was dramatically transformed after encountering Swami Vivekananda (1863–1902) in London between 1895 and 1897. Although she had already established her own school, she followed Vivekananda, acknowledged as "one of the most important modern gurus" (Smith 2003, 173), after he returned to India in 1897. It was as Bhagini Nivedita, Sister Nivedita (the Dedicated), the name Vivekananda gave her when he initiated her as his disciple in 1898, that Margaret Noble came to be widely known and respected in India. This chapter will refer to Nivedita, rather than to Margaret Noble or Nivedita according to the phase of her life under discussion.[1]

Today, Nivedita's fame is largely confined to India and to those familiar with the Ramakrishna Math and Mission, the Hindu movement founded by

---

1. This chapter draws on Beckerlegge (unpublished) and Beckerlegge (2017), which was written for a non-specialist audience. See fn. 6 below.

Figure 3.1 Sister Nivedita's statue installed in 2017 at the Ramakrishna Ashram dispensary in the city of Salem, Tamil Nadu, India, to mark the 150th anniversary of her birth. Nivedita (1988, 368) referred to visiting the city of Salem in 1903.

Vivekananda, with which Nivedita was closely associated (but see Som 2017, ix). Yet, the breadth and impact of Nivedita's activities in India extended beyond her association with the Ramakrishna movement. In acknowledgment of this, the Government of India issued a postage stamp to mark the centenary of her birth. On the 150th anniversary of her birth in 2017, the state government of West Bengal, the home of the Ramakrishna Math and Mission, commemorated her life as did various Indian cultural associations, in addition to the Ramakrishna Math and Mission. There were public unveilings by state officials of statues in her honour in other parts of India. Nivedita's house in Kolkata has been restored and there are plans to open a research-centre in her name.

In the UK, English Heritage has marked Nivedita's house in Wimbledon with a "blue plaque," its recognition of the residences and workplaces of famous persons. Scholars of different disciplines and interests continue to examine the life of this remarkable individual and the influences held to be responsible for its course, as have her biographers.

Unravelling biographies of Nivedita

The most well-known, full-length biographies of Nivedita are Reymond (1953),[2] Pravrajika Atmaprana (1977 [1961]), and Foxe (1975). Lizelle Rey-

---

2. This was originally published in French as *Nivédita Fille de L'Inde* (Reymond 1945), and later serialized in Bengali in 1962.

mond had a long-standing interest in Indian spirituality and worked with the Ramakrishna Mission then involved in aiding refugees after Partition in 1947. Pravrajika Atmaprana wrote as a member of the Shri Sharada Math (the sister-organization of the Ramakrishna Math), and Barbara Foxe as a member of what was then the London Ramakrishna Vedanta Centre. These emic biographers enjoyed privileged access to members of Nivedita's family and other intimates, to other prominent devotees of Vivekananda, and to source materials, including Nivedita's diary (Foxe 175, 204), preserved by the Ramakrishna movement and its sympathisers. Consequently, these three biographies, published in English, have exercised a reverberating influence on emic and popular understandings of Nivedita's life, as well as on scholarly studies.[3]

Maina Singh (2006, 41) has aptly contrasted Atmaprana's "making of a saint" approach with Reymond stimulating the reader's curiosity about Nivedita's personal life. It is not clear what use the two later biographers made of Reymond's biography, which is the most detailed. Reymond's work appears in Atmaprana's bibliography, but Atmaprana (1977, vii) does not make explicit whether this was a study on which she relied or one she sought to correct. Foxe (1975) makes no reference to Reymond.

Of the three biographers, only Atmaprana has provided specific references as distinct from a general acknowledgment of sources and informants. The biographers completed their work, moreover, before a large part of Nivedita's correspondence had been brought together, a process initiated by Reymond and completed by Sankari Prasad Basu (1982). Without question an important source, much of Nivedita's correspondence comprises affectionate, sometimes chatty, newsletters to other intimates of Vivekananda, and exchanges with major Indian personalities of her day. The letters do not offer much detail about Nivedita's early life, formative influences, and family, or a systematic exposition of her ideas.

Charles Keyes (1982, 16) has observed that sacred biography generates a "model for emulation by others." The biographies of Nivedita are in tone and intent reverential and implicitly didactic, and favour commemoration/cele-

---

3. The publication of these three biographies in English has enhanced their accessibility in India. For this reason, I deal with Reymond's biography in this chapter in its English translation, rather than examining it in relation to its original publication in French and Reymond's other works on Hindu spirituality in French. Apart from some relatively minor variations in the details contained in these two versions, and some changes to breaks between chapters and chapter headings, the French and English versions of Reymond's biography of Nivedita are very similar. The French version of the biography offers no additional insights into that part of Nivedita's life on which this chapter will focus. I make limited reference in this chapter to studies heavily and uncritically dependent on the standard biographies because of these studies' uniform nature.

bration over critical description (see Hamilton 2007, particularly pp. 6–128).[4] What Nivedita's biographers celebrate is Nivedita as the ideal transnational disciple who stepped out of her old life as Margaret Noble to begin a new one as Nivedita under her guru in a new land, rather than Nivedita in terms of her own achievements as an educator and social and political activist. Even today, Nivedita is commonly cited within the Ramakrishna movement as a trustworthy source of information about Vivekananda, rather than as an authority in her own right.[5] Her biographers view her early life largely as preparation for her meeting with Vivekananda. Her eclectic spiritual life is presented as a sign of her, till then, fruitless quest for spiritual fulfilment, rather than in relation to the milieu in which she moved. The transformation of Margaret Noble, the London-based progressive educationalist, into Nivedita is explained primarily in terms of the charismatic nature of Vivekananda's presence and message.

Carl T. Jackson (1994, 170–173) has observed that even the more "meticulously researched" literature published by the Ramakrishna movement about its own history may appear "devoid of interpretation" through ignoring external factors and bypassing internal difficulties. These same characteristics are to be found in Nivedita's biographies, not least in their subservience to celebrating Vivekananda by celebrating his disciple. For example, Nivedita's life prior to meeting Vivekananda is covered relatively briefly by Reymond, and more briefly by Atmaprana and Foxe, possibly because regarded as of less significance or because of lack of information. The problem of available information, of course, diminished as Nivedita became more widely known in India and interacted with prominent personalities. Never holding official office, however, Nivedita was not an "elite" woman, and thus, like many women of that period, her life has not been captured in imperial and colonial archives (Ballantyne and Burton 2005, 4).

Any attempt to uncover Nivedita's life, therefore, inevitably leads to sources preserved within and published by the Ramakrishna movement. Vivekananda's (1989) *Collected Works* makes important references to Nivedita, as does the standard emic biography of Vivekananda (His Eastern and Western Disciples 1979), which was first published within a decade of Vivekananda's death, and the reports of Vivekananda in contemporary Indian newspapers compiled by Basu and Ghosh (1969). Later accounts produced within the Ramakrishna movement have largely echoed these sources, and

---

4. Reba Som's (2017, xxviii and 247) recent biography similarly sets out to celebrate Nivedita, here as *lokmātā* ("mother of the people")—the epithet conferred by Rabindranath Tagore—rather than to test claims made about her impact and reputation.

5. Volume 1 of *The Complete Works of Sister Nivedita*, published by the Ramakrishna movement begins with Nivedita's account of Vivekananda. Her writings prior to meeting Vivekananda do not appear until Volume 5.

the more systematic histories of Gambhirananda (1983) and Burke (1985 and subsequently). Burke drew on memoirs preserved within the movement and media reports, but essentially enriched rather than changed the direction of what had become a reverberating narrative. Turning to Nivedita's writings, as we have seen, it was her biographer, Reymond, who played a major part in gathering together Nivedita's correspondence (Basu 1982). Prior to the publication in 1967 of the *Complete Works of Sister Nivedita* to mark the centenary of her birth, those items of Nivedita's various writings, which had been previously published, had been published separately, some were out of print, and some items had never been published (Nivedita 1982a, xii). When it comes to that period of Nivedita's life before she found fame in India, it is even more difficult for the biographer to achieve an independent vantage point from which to test these sources and, equally important, to supplement the relatively limited information they contain.

Instead of offering another biographical overview of Nivedita's life in this chapter, I shall argue more specifically, that, to understand the making of Nivedita as Vivekananda's "ideal transnational disciple," it is important, in spite of the difficulties mentioned above, to consider the phase of her life in Britain, which has attracted less attention from her biographers and other scholars than her origins in Ireland and her later life in India. My starting point will be the way in which the British phase of Nivedita's life has been presented by her biographers, largely Reymond because her account is the most detailed.

Nivedita: The heroine of a "governess novel"?

Biographers regularly have recourse to imaginative evocation when re-creating the lives of their subjects, but are expected to base this on scrupulous attention to sources and context. Nivedita's biographers' lack of detail about her early life is compounded by, at times, shallow treatments of the settings in which she found herself, with some resulting inaccuracies, as in the account of her education. The three biographies state that Nivedita and her younger sister May attended Halifax College, possibly meaning simply a school in Halifax, Yorkshire, England, rather than a specific institution with this name. The sisters, in fact, were educated at Crossley Heath School in Halifax.[6]

---

6. Information about Margaret Noble's school-days was relatively recently made public by Crossley Heath School, Halifax, but then withdrawn from the school's website. The information included in this chapter was then available from http://www.crossleyheath.org.uk/school information/school-history/margaret-elizabeth-noble-sister-nivedita and "School History" http://www.crossleyheath.org.uk/school-information/school-history [accessed 04 November 2016]. The availability of this new information prompted O'Doherty (2017) and Beckerlegge (2017) independently to re-examine this phase of Nivedita's life in their respective contributions to the special issue of *Prabuddha Bharata* published to mark the 150th anniversary of Nivedita's birth

Comparing Reymond's account of Nivedita's schooldays with the information provided by Crossley Heath School, including the names of teachers mentioned (not always accurately) by Reymond, casts light on Reymond's approach.[7]

Reymond's account reads rather like a nineteenth century "governess novel's" re-creation of school-days in a Victorian charitable institution. This popular *genre*, of which Currer Bell's (Charlotte Brontë) *Jane Eyre* (first published in 1847) is the pre-eminent example, is said to have followed, although not exclusively, one of two basic patterns: the "romantic" (ending in marriage, often to the governess's employer) and "providential" (growing into a life of service in gratitude for God's providence) (Da Sousa Correa 2000, 99). This same pattern re-surfaces in Reymond's (1953, 15–19) account of the early life of Margaret Noble who, before she adopted a life of service as Nivedita, is said to have entertained hopes of marriage on more than one occasion prior to meeting Vivekananda.[8]

Familiar refrains in "governess novels" and Reymond's biography of Nivedita are explicable to an extent in terms of the common experiences of often vulnerable young women sent to charitable schools, and the conditions of the time. For example, like the fictional Jane Eyre, and many young women of Nivedita's generation, Nivedita experienced a disrupted family life, having lost a beloved parent at an early age, was sent away to a distant, charitable institution, and subsequently made her way in the world as a teacher. But, there are more specific parallels between these fictional and biographical "lives." Like one of Jane Eyre's fellow-pupils, the head-teacher is said to have cropped Nivedita's hair to combat perceived signs of pride. Like Jane Eyre, Nivedita was a serious and able student who became the protégé of a young, senior teacher, a Miss Angela Louisa Collins (later Headmistress of Crossley Heath School), who shaped her intellectually and spiritually, allowing her to express her "nascent mysticism" (Reymond 1953, 17–18).

When Reymond (1953, 15, 16) declared that a "stern" and "austere" life awaited them (the Noble sisters) at school in Halifax, perhaps she intended that those familiar with novels in the style of *Jane Eyre* should summon up their imagery of hardship and cruelty to appreciate what Nivedita is likely to have undergone while at school. Reymond's account, however, misrepresents this phase of Nivedita's life in certain crucial respects. Reymond does

---

("Sister Nivedita" 2017). They also question the emphasis placed on Nivedita's Irish roots in emic explanations of her commitment to the cause of Indian independence, which is discussed later in this chapter.

7. There are some inaccuracies in accounts of Nivedita's life, prior to her relocation to India, in other publications of the Ramakrishna movement, for example, the claim that she was educated in London (*Nivedita of India* 2002, 1).

8. On whether Nivedita had hopes of embarking on a romantic relationship with Vivekananda, see, for example, Sen (2016, 14–19), Sil (1997, 129–150), Som (2017, 23).

not make clear the significance of Nivedita having joined the school after the Education Act of 1870, which had a positive impact on the academic quality of girls' education by broadening the curriculum beyond preparation for domestic service. *Jane Eyre* was published nearly two decades before the 1870 Education Act. Crossley Heath School was not the horrific Lowood Institution conjured up by Charlotte Brontë, and nor was its head another Mr Brocklehurst, Lowood's sadistic benefactor and superintendent (O'Doherty 2017, 227). Nivedita, in fact, benefited from what was, by the standards of the day, a good education. This would enable her take up a career and so to gain financial independence and a measure of social standing. If Foxe's (1975, 16) reference to Nivedita's reaction against the "stifling idiocy of the formal Victorian education" is Foxe's own judgment, this too presents a de-contextualized view of educational opportunity of that period. Also, it does not square with the impression Foxe and other biographers give of Nivedita as a high-achieving, engaged student who we know, through the information made public by Crossley Heath School, to have been chair of the Students' Committee.

Our analysis of the popular biographical narrative of one chapter in Nivedita's early life suggests the need for caution when assessing the biographers' accounts of other aspects of her early life. This is an important consideration because, in addition to offering a questionable account of Nivedita's schooldays, which provided the mechanism that enhanced her social mobility, they present her Irish connection as a key factor in her preparation for encountering Vivekananda and her willingness to offer her life in service to India. Yet, this aspect of her life is one about which we know even less with any certainty than we do about her schooldays. Skating over the period of approximately seven years she spent in London, then the centre of the colonial power that held sway over both Ireland and India, moreover, diminishes the fluid and "translocal" nature of Nivedita's life.

Approaching Nivedita's life as a "translocal space"

Desley Deacon *et al.* (2010, 2) argue that biography has often been "pressed into the service of nation," which does less than justice to lives framed by "mobility, not nation," citing dictionaries of national biography as an example of this tendency. I hope to avoid this pitfall, having previously contributed the entry on Margaret Noble to the *Oxford Dictionary of National Biography* (Beckerlegge 2007)!

Drawing on the work of Tony Ballantyne and Antoinette M. Burton, Simon J. Potter and Jonathan Saha (2015) have argued that "whilst studying ... global interconnectedness we must also remain attentive to the related production of 'translocal' spaces." They encourage the re-conceptualization of local places as "translocal" spaces: "specific arenas of interaction reproduced across the world through the establishment, maintenance and contestation of empires."

Such an approach, according to Potter and Saha, counteracts the tendency in connected history to focus on imperial networks, making "local" places appear static, spaces merely to be crossed. Attention is drawn instead to the way in which the "production of global spaces of connection, by implication, involves the production of fraught local spaces of interaction."

Vivekananda, was prescient in his recognition of the impact of what we would now commonly refer to as globalizing forces, and highly adept in using the transport and communication systems of his day (see Beckerlegge 2004). The course of Nivedita's life and mission was no less dependent on imperial networks of transport and communication. Hers was a body "in motion," "in subjection," "in struggle," and "in action" (Ballantyne and Burton 2005, 8). Her life itself could be described metaphorically as a "translocal space," and, as we shall see, a no less fraught personal space of interaction, in this instance, of ideas and personal aspirations.

Even before Nivedita moved to London in 1890, her mobile lifestyle after she completed her education in Halifax had taken her from the north of England, to North Wales, and briefly to the Midlands of England. These regions widened her horizons, prompting her early writings, including an article on the living conditions of workers and their families in Wrexham in which, before she met the reality in Calcutta, she spoke about the threat of disease and the risk to public health (Nivedita 1975, 5, 420–424). The emerging campaigning tone in her articles on women's rights (Nivedita 1975, 5, 379–411) perhaps anticipated what she would later refer to in 1902(?) as "woman-making," suitably adapting Vivekananda's slogan of "man-making education" (Basu 1982, 1, 482). This was the entry-point into her social activism, which became more pronounced in London and the hall-mark of her life in India. Similarly, and perhaps surprisingly at that time, it was her experience in North Wales and provincial England, before she moved to the capital, that began to deepen her exposure to ideas with distant origins. These currents of thought were far from provincial and were indicative of the slowly but surely accelerating globalization of ideas.

Nivedita's "extraordinary, fluid, disruptive and yet ordinary" life

The adjectives "extraordinary, fluid, disruptive and yet ordinary," which Deacon *et al.* (2010, 1) use to describe "transnational lives" that refuse to be confined by gender-based or national boundaries, could all be applied to Nivedita's life. Indeed, she was perceived by some of her contemporaries as transgressive in the way in which she crossed social and moral boundaries. Foxe (1975, 16) has traced this tendency, which sometimes resulted in censure, to Nivedita's early experience, following the death of her father (see for example *More Letters of Sister Nivedita* 2016, 31). Foxe suggests that this led Nivedita to exhibit a degree of independence, both intellectually and of necessity in her personal life through her enforced travelling between Ireland and England, which would have been unusual in a young woman of that time. Nivedita's report of her initial dealings with Vivekananda and his assessment of her suggest that, in her late twenties, she had matured into an assertive and strong-minded individual. These were characteristics of an independence, which Nivedita was later to discover, society in general did not value in women and thus did not encourage, according to Foxe (1975, 14).

By the time she left school, although supportive as a child of the pastoral work of her father, Nivedita had begun to react against the dogmatic Christianity of her mother, and possibly against the austere Bible-based, non-conformist Christianity of her first head-teacher at Crossley Heath School (Nivedita 1975, 2, 460; cf. Reymond 1953, 16–18). Singh (2006, 47) states that Nivedita "…inherited from her family both religious fervour and a zeal to fight for the cause of political freedom" (a judgment attributed elsewhere to Nivedita's brother, Richmond Noble: see Mukherjee 1997, 1). I would suggest that Nivedita's spirituality was shaped far more by her encounters en route from Dugannon to, eventually, Calcutta, and that its development was perhaps initially fostered by Miss Collins, her teacher at Crossley Heath School. During her teens and while in her first teaching post at Keswick, Nivedita was drawn to High Anglicanism and contemplated conversion to Roman Catholicism, which would have been quite a leap from her Irish family's non-conformism. Through the circles in which she moved during her time at Wrexham in North Wales, she was introduced to New England Transcendentalism. It was quite possible that this would have provided her first introduction to Hindu thought. At much the same time, she began to study Buddhist teaching. Foxe (1975, 16) sees this as signalling her movement away from Christian belief.[9] At the very least, this pattern suggests that, by the time Nivedita arrived in London, where she allied herself to the Broad Church wing of the Anglican Church, she was, in her own words, "not very orthodox," in fact, like others there who were drawn to Vivekananda.

The Broad Church comprised members of the nineteenth-century Anglican Church who were committed to a liberal and thus "broader" understanding of the Church's doctrines and creeds. Christians of this conviction sought to reach an accommodation with critical studies of the Bible and contemporary scientific discoveries, not least the impact of Darwinism on the understanding of creation and human nature. Some were also inclined to display more sympathy towards other religions. Thus, when Nivedita (1975, 331) stated in an interview reported in 1902 that "I was then a member of the Church of England, and held 'Broad' views," she knowingly identified herself with a

---

9. It is evident that Nivedita's acquaintance with Hindu texts soon widened through her interaction with other supporters of Vivekananda, in addition to the teaching she received directly from Vivekananda (Reymond 1953, 41).

theological position that would have been recognizable to Anglicans of her day. This identification, moreover, overlapped with that of others in the circle of admirers Vivekananda first attracted in London and in which Nivedita increasingly moved in an orbit around Vivekananda. Speaking of that time, Vivekananda (1989, 5, 221) claimed to have found that "... about thirty English Church clergymen agree entirely with me on all points of religious discussion." We know the name of one senior clergyman associated with the Broad Church, Hugh Haweis, the Canon of St James, Marylebone, London, who, like Vivekananda, had attended the World's Parliament of Religions, and who referred to Vivekananda in his sermons and invited Vivekananda to speak to a gathering at his home (Basu and Ghosh 1969, 495).

Another woman in the circle who met Vivekananda in 1895, together with Nivedita, is described by Nivedita as "perhaps the least unconventional of the group in matters of belief," and as a friend and disciple of the Anglican theologian F. D. Maurice, also a leading figure in the Broad Church. According to Eric Sharpe (1975, 146–147), Maurice exhibited in his writings a degree of interest in, and sympathy for, different religions that was "unusual at that time." Nivedita (1982, 20) referred only to this woman as having an "historic name" and did not identify her explicitly. Marie Louise Burke (1985, 281–285) later argued that this person was probably Lady Ripon, wife of Lord George Ripon, former Secretary of State for India and former Viceroy of India.

It was to such an audience that Vivekananda (1989, 2, 329–235) offered a message that he presented as being "broad" (in the sense of being able to accommodate different kinds of minds), following reason, and providing the basis for a universal religion. It was one that appeared to respond to the religious concerns of his hearers in London. Some of the dilemmas they faced were, in fact, common to those among them who retained their Christian convictions through their alignment with the liberal positions of the Broad Church, and to those who, to use Nivedita's words, were "not very orthodox" to the point of being increasingly sceptical about religious claims.

Understanding Nivedita's description of her brand of Christian belief as "Broad," therefore, sheds further light on what her experience in London is likely to have added to her earlier, growing revolt against the conservative Christianity of her mother and some of her teachers. It is suggestive of the milieu in which she moved and the circles in which she would have expected to find like-minded and sympathetic individuals. Nivedita's willingness to assess the level of "orthodoxy" of those drawn to Vivekananda, including her own, is as revealing as her confession of the attraction she felt for the "Church of Rome," striking in an Irish-born Protestant and one who placed herself within the Broad Church, and the speed with which she recognized Vivekananda as her guru.

Nivedita (1972, 1, 22) spoke of the relative rapidity of her decision to address

Vivekananda as "Master" against the backcloth of her declared religious scepticism in relation to the teaching of the Christian churches (Nivedita 1982a, 20; Nivedita 1988, 389). She also acknowledged how little she knew of Vivekananda at that time (Nivedita 1982a, 17). Nivedita's adoption of the title "Master," referred to as a "new functionary in western religion" by Steven Sutcliffe (2013, 431) in his study of the Rosicrucians some two decades later, reflects more than just her increasing proximity to a Hindu guru and gradually to Hindu custom. It speaks of a spiritual life that, well before meeting Vivekananda led her to India, had become increasingly complex and hybrid, thus defying rigid categorization.

Atmaprana (1977, 6) has described Nivedita as spiritually unsatisfied when she arrived in London, having long been a "seeker after truth" (1977, 6–9; 1995, 123). In this respect, Nivedita had much in common with others attracted to Vivekananda in both London and the United States. But, for many their seeking, often not limited to traditions familiar in Europe, was not solely symptomatic of a deep-rooted spiritual dissatisfaction. They placed a positive value on seeking as part of their ongoing spiritual quest. They were "serial" or "multiple" seekers, as characterized by Sutcliffe (1998), who were prepared to take eclectically, rather than exclusively, from different teachings and teachers. Nivedita (1975, 2, 460–461) spoke of her unhappiness following her doubts about Christianity, but, like other seekers she placed value on the process of her quest, which had a cumulative quality even before she met Vivekananda.

The process of seeking helps to explain how pre-existing religious convictions and allegiances to social causes could dictate how individual sympathisers, not least Nivedita, received Vivekananda's message and what they took from it. Their journeys to Vivekananda and his interpretation of the Hindu philosophy of Vedānta (often referred to as Neo-Vedānta), which for some would not be their final destination, often followed similar paths, typically via New England Transcendentalism, New Thought, Christian Science, and Theosophy (see Beckerlegge 2004).[10] Recognizing different patterns of seeking helps to explain why Vivekananda's early admirers in London and the United States were drawn to different aspects of his message, and, arguably, the degree of fluidity and consequent instability in the groups that formed around Vivekananda in New York and London (see Beckerlegge 2000, Chapters 7 and 8).

Nivedita's willingness to take the step of accepting a Hindu guru as her spiritual guide and to re-make her life in India as his initiated disciple was

---

10. Malachi O'Doherty (2017, 229) calls for more research into the influence of Christian Science on Nivedita. His abbreviated quotation (Basu 1982:1, 13), omitting "... in Mrs Jonson's hands ...," however, makes Nivedita's observation appear more general than she might have intended. On Mrs Jonson (Johnson), see Beckerlegge (2000, 145–179) and later in this chapter.

hardly what was expected of a white, Christian-educated woman of that period. As I have emphasized elsewhere (Beckerlegge 2004), contrary to the popular image of Vivekananda's early followers in London and the United States looking to the "East," only a minority of these engaged deeply with the Indian dimension of his mission. Only a few of these formally accepted Vivekananda as a guru through initiation. What drew the majority to him, and some only transiently, was his brand of universalism. For several, this chimed with their own ongoing quests for a more generous form of Christianity beyond that offered by the historic institutionalized churches.

Nivedita (1982a, 21) captured the different degrees of commitment among Vivekananda's sympathisers when she reflected on their first meeting with Vivekananda in 1895. She noted "The doctrine that while no one religion was true in the way commonly claimed, yet all were equally true in a very real way, was one that commanded the immediate assent of *some* of us" [emphasis added], implying that not all were as open as she was to Vivekananda's style of religious universalism. This would also seem to imply that Vivekananda's teaching added a structure and name to an aspiration, a position, that Nivedita already held, having arrived at it independently as a "serial seeker."[11] In this same spirit, Nivedita would later urge others to find their own "'Master'—your own *Ishta* as I would rather say" (Basu 1982, 2, 688). It is clear from the above that such a view, which Nivedita later chose to express in Hindu terms, would have been consistent with her outlook in 1895 when she first encountered Vivekananda. Nivedita presumably took the term "*ishta*" from *iṣṭa devatā*, "chosen deity," which refers to the practice followed by some Hindus of adopting a particular deity for worship and devotion but without implying any rejection of other deities. On such a basis, Nivedita was able to accommodate "Vedāntins" who retained existing commitments, for example, to Christianity, and who felt unable to accept Vivekananda as their "Master," their "*ishta*," as wholeheartedly as she had.

Nivedita stood out in the extent to which she was complicit in Vivekananda's efforts at "Hinduizing" or "Indianizing" her outlook (His Eastern and Western Disciples 1979, 337). But it is important to appreciate that what drew Nivedita to act on Vivekananda's message in the first instance, although she would later imbibe more of his Neo-Vedāntin teaching, was her desire to serve women through the field of education. This, and more generally being active in the world for the welfare of others, was what Vivekananda intended for her (Vivekananda 1989, 7, 501, 510–513). He also valued her skill as a speaker and writer, which he hoped to put to the service of the Ramakrishna movement (Vivekananda 1989, 8, 447).

---

11. See, for example, Nivedita's article "The Christ Child" and its reflection on the "common soul of human genius," which was written before she met Vivekananda (Nivedita 1975, 372–373).

The Making of the Ideal Transnational Disciple

Nivedita was not unusual, given her circumstances at that time, in making a career as a teacher. Her involvement as a child in her father's pastoral work and her later move into progressive education could well have inclined her towards a path of social activism. Nevertheless, although life in the British Empire at that time offered some women opportunities they would not have had in Britain, the route Nivedita took into a life of service dedicated to India could hardly have been anticipated from the course of her life to that point. It distinguishes her from other British women activists in India who were drawn to India because of concern about the condition of Indian women but, in common with Nivedita, were "outside the formal establishment" (Ramusack 1990, 119).

Like the other women activists in Barbara Ramusack's study of the period 1865–1945, Nivedita had received an above-average education for a woman of that time. She was, however, from a less financially secure and socially privileged background, and thus to a greater degree had to make her own way in the world. Her relationship to a Hindu guru, who had opened her eyes to the educational needs of Hindu women, set her apart from the other women activists considered by Ramusack, some of whom came from political families. Also, although Nivedita dedicated herself to serving the people of India, this was not the result of contact with a leader or an organization with a general reformist agenda for India, whether Christian, as in the case of the Unitarians, or Hindu, as in the case of the Brahmo Samāj. Unlike other British women activists of her day, Nivedita offered her service by allowing herself to become "Hinduized" or "Indianized" under the influence of her guru, rather than seeking to improve the lives of Indian women by advancing a reformist agenda for India and, more particularly, Hindu practice and belief.

Nivedita is generally acknowledged both in emic sources and by external commentators, including Indian newspapers of the time, as a major personality in the nascent Ramakrishna movement, not least because of her standing as Vivekananda's disciple and her increasing visibility in India. Her participation, as a white woman, in efforts to improve public sanitation following an outbreak of plague in Calcutta brought more attention to the Ramakrishna movement's early forays into public acts of service (*sevā*) (Gambhirananda 1983, 105; Basu 2007, 2, 762, 805–806; Beckerlegge 2006, 30). Her prominence, however, should not be allowed to overshadow the fact that she could be a highly divisive figure.

Nivedita's public defence in Calcutta of the worship of the goddess Kālī, a popular practice criticized by Hindu reformers, prompted strong reactions among Vivekananda's remaining followers in London. Henrietta Müller had been one of those responsible for inviting Vivekananda to visit London and for funding his visit from the United States where he had attended the World's Parliament of Religions in 1893. In a letter of September 1899, she reproached Nivedita's "shameful public defence" of "idolatry" (Burke 1987a, 101). Mrs Ethel Ashton Johnson (sometimes given as Jonson), another leading light in the London-based circle of Vivekananda's admirers and one-time chair of its meetings, was no less critical of Nivedita's "worship at Swami's feet," which she found "... so deplorable as to be quite unspeakable from an English woman's point of view" (Burke 1987a, 105, cf. 106).[12]

Speaking of Nivedita after her death, Aurobindo Ghose (1872–1950), the Hindu philosopher and former activist in the nationalist cause, referred to her as "practically an Indian in belief, culture, and aspirations" (quoted in Boehmer 2002, 41). Yet, in 1900 Nivedita stated that "It is wholly a mistake to suppose that I have renounced either my nationality or my religion in becoming a sister of the order [Ramakrishna movement]. Christianity is the nursery in which my spiritual thought was trained" (Burke 1987b, 289). Again, in 1902 Nivedita reasserted in *The Bengalee* that "I have never broken with my position as a member of the Church of England nor is there any reason why I should do so" (Basu and Ghosh 1969, 283). Thus, when introducing Nivedita in her study of British women activists in India, Ramusack (1990, 313) characterized her as one of "two extraordinary Irish Protestant social and political activists," rather than as a Neo-Vedāntin. It is possible, of course, that Nivedita implicitly relied on the concept of *iṣṭa* (see above) as a device to rationalize her repeated declarations of her own continuing adherence to the Anglican Church.

Another striking feature of the fluid course of Nivedita's life, and arguably indicative of a degree of tension at its heart, was her decision on the death of Vivekananda in 1902 to sever her formal links with the Ramakrishna Math and Mission. Committed to the revival of India and an acknowledged inspiration for many involved in the struggle for Indian independence, Vivekananda nevertheless ruled that he and his followers should abstain from direct political activity. The Ramakrishna Math and Mission has remained publicly committed throughout its history to this policy of non-intervention in politics.[13] Nivedita's public, formal act of disassociation enabled her to devote herself to the Indian independence movement without implicating the Ramakrishna movement or being subject to its direction or censure. It did not imply any rift for she remained on close and warm terms with it and its adherents. Held to be one of Vivekananda's most ardent disciples, Nivedita's decision might suggest that, because of her loyalty and obedience to him, her own understanding of what service to India might and should entail at that time only

---

12. See also Basu (1982, 1, 296), which refers to conflict with Mary Hale, an American devotee, over Nivedita's way of working.

13. See, for example, Vivekananda (1989, 5, 46, 218; 6: 406). The movement's standard, emic history states that Vivekananda directed the movement to "steer clear of politics and violent social reform" (Gambhirananda 1983, 162).

found full expression after Vivekananda's death.[14] Her life subsequently took another direction subject to the priorities of her political activism.

As with her public identification with Hindu belief and practice, controversy has surrounded the question of the nature and extent of Nivedita's involvement with the violent wing of the Indian independence movement. The popular image of Nivedita as an "Irish nationalist" because of her origins, and her acceptance of the theories of the anarchist Peter Kropotkin and her interest in the Pan-Asianism of Kakuzo Okakura, however, have arguably inflated claims made about her involvement in, and influence on, revolutionary politics in Bengal. Of the three biographers, Reymond has provided the most sensationalistic account of Nivedita's political activity, which in turn has influenced other authors, and Atmaprana has sought, rather implausibly, to distance Nivedita from such activity. It is beyond doubt that Nivedita worked closely with militant nationalists, as is evident from her close relationship with Aurobindo. She was subject to surveillance, and her return to Britain in 1907 might have been the result of fear of arrest, as might the concealed nature of her return in 1908 (see *More Letters of Sister Nivedita* 2016, 71–73, 79). On the other hand, her health had started to deteriorate in the period before she left India, and, despite her high profile, she was not arrested. As Elleke Boehmer (2002, 44) puts it, although Nivedita might well have moved in circles that planted bombs, there is no evidence to suggest that she did or incited others to do so. Peter Heehs (1998, 74) has noted that the view of her being actively involved in such politics, and the violence some groups adopted, has been rejected by all professional historians who have considered it.

After her death, elements in Nivedita's controversial essay *Aggressive Hinduism* have been taken up by supporters sympathetic to the cause of Hindu nationalism (*Hindutva*), which has been criticized for stoking communalism in post-Independence India.[15] In this essay she declared "our work is not now to protect ourselves but to convert others. Point by point, we are determined not merely to keep what we had but to win what we never had before" (Nivedita 1990, 495). By the last decade of the twentieth century, Nivedita had been installed in the Mother's Shrine of the Bhārat Mātā Temple at Hardwar. The worship of Bhārat Mātā (Mother India) has been largely propagated in recent years by Hindu nationalists (McKean 1996, 147).[16]

---

14. After Vivekananda's death, Nivedita was spoken of by some as his successor as the leader of the Ramakrishna movement (Basu 2007, 2, 815).

15. Madhav Sadashiv Golwalkar (1906–1973), the second leader of the Rashtriya Svayamsevak Sangh or RSS (the National Volunteer Association), has acknowledged this essay's influence within the RSS, the popular flag-bearer of the Hindu nationalist cause (Golwalkar 1966, 368).

16. Vivekananda's contribution to Hindu nationalism has been re-evaluated as part of the greater scholarly interest prompted by this ideology's increasing popular appeal,

Yet, just as in her role of Vivekananda's disciple Nivedita continued to profess her identity as a member of the Church of England, so too, although born in Ireland, she always spoke of herself as an Englishwoman (Foxe 1975, 12). Similarly, although she came to be increasingly involved in the struggle for Indian independence, she nevertheless, even after her arrival in India, continued to identify herself not simply as English but with England (cf. *More Letters of Sister Nivedita* 2016, 11–12). Nivedita (1982a, 287) recalled that she "startled" Vivekananda in 1898 by her passionate declaration of attachment to the "English flag" (cf. Nivedita's letter of 1898 in which she referred to herself as having been "the most loyal Englishwoman that ever breathed in this country [India]," Basu 1982, 1:11). Several weeks after this incident he told her "Really, patriotism like yours is a sin!" (Nivedita 1982a, 287). Her repeated affirmation of her English identity stands in contrast to the position of Annie Besant, her contemporary who, although born in London, shared Nivedita's Irish roots and was also active in, among other things, the causes of Irish and Indian independence. The limited and tenuous evidence of Nivedita's active involvement in the struggle for justice and freedom in Ireland stands in contrast, for example, to Besant's published opposition to the Coercion Acts (to contain and suppress resistance) and the eviction of tenants. Besant declared "Three quarters of my blood and all my heart was Irish" (quoted in Taylor 1992, 1).[17]

The ways in which Nivedita chose to articulate her national and religious identity, and her position in relation to Britain's imperial role reflect a life lived in passage between Ireland, England, and India. It also, I would argue, illustrates what I meant when I referred earlier to her life as itself a "translocal space," a fraught personal space of interaction of not altogether consistent ideas and personal aspirations, both religious and political, shaped through her experience of "the establishment, maintenance and contestation of empires" (Potter and Saha 2015).

For the emic biographers we have considered, the major factor extraneous to the transformative impact of Nivedita's meeting with her future guru and her acceptance of him in this role is her birth and family history in Ireland (for example, Reymond 1953, 9; Atmaprana 1977, 2; Foxe 1975, 12–13). This family history is similarly regarded by other emic studies as crucially formative in Nivedita's acceptance of Vivekananda and adoption of a life of service to India. According to Foxe, who acknowledged that Nivedita identified herself as English, Nivedita inherited from her family her "fiery Irish nature" and her "Irish fighting spirit," which were fed by her family's stories of the "heroism of Irish patriots fighting for Home Rule" (1975, 14). Nivedita's "Celtic blood"

---

and its influence on contemporary Indian politics. See, for example, Sharma (2013).

17. Nor was Nivedita engaged while in London in the range of social and feminist causes as was Henrietta Müller (referred to above in this chapter), who later disassociated herself from Vivekananda. See Beckerlegge (2000, 180–201).

also recommended her to Vivekananda (1989, 7, 511). Significantly, from an emic perspective, this account does not diminish the impact that Vivekananda had upon her. It does explain why this late nineteenth-century, London-based teacher was able to identify so immediately and effectively with a Hindu guru's message and his vision for India. According to this view, Nivedita was, in effect, already a fully-formed nationalist, shaped by Ireland's anticolonial struggle, who was thus able to identify strongly with India's growing resistance to British rule. The powerful, quasi-explanatory image of Nivedita's "Irishness," has been pervasive in popular literature about her life.

There are several problems with her biographers' transposition to India of Nivedita as a fully-formed, "fiery," Irish nationalist, where she transplanted and acted on these convictions under Vivekananda's spell (cf. Boehmer 2006, 64). The first, as noted earlier in this chapter, relates to the nature of the sources on whom her biographers were able to draw as a basis for their representation of the formative influence of her Irish ancestry on her life.

Nivedita was born in Dungannon, Co. Tyrone, Ireland. The timing of the arrival of her paternal family in Ireland several generations earlier, and possibly their reported antipathy to Roman Catholics, suggests that they could have been part of the Plantation, the strategic settlement from the sixteenth century, of Protestants from England and Scotland, particularly in the North of Ireland. The consequences of this process, in effect, the colonization of Ireland by the English crown, included the creation of a Protestant Anglo-Irish ruling elite (known as the Protestant Ascendancy), and the undermining of the Irish language and Irish culture.

Not yet one year of age, Nivedita was left in Ireland with her maternal grandmother while her father, Samuel Noble, completed his training in England to join the Wesleyan ministry. She re-joined her family in England at the age of four, after her father had been given a church in Oldham, Lancashire. There she met her three-year-old, younger sister, May, for the first time. Their younger brother, Richmond was considerably, approximately 10 years, younger than Nivedita, and was born in Devon after the family had made a further move to a kinder climate prompted by Samuel Noble's declining health. After their father's death, Nivedita's sister May accompanied her to Crossley Heath School, and May, therefore, would have been well-placed to have been a source of information about that phase of her sister's life. According to May's grandson, however, she "promised Sister N [Nivedita] never to reveal anything of their time at that school" (Sarkar 2017a, 684). The ages and experiences of Nivedita's younger siblings, neither of whom were born in Ireland, inevitably have a bearing on what independence and reliability they could have brought to any account they gave of her early life, particularly in relation to their family's experience in Ireland (see Foxe's (1975, 230) acknowledgment). A flavour of Richmond's recollections is given in Burke (1985, 309–312).

The second problem relates to the fact that, in addition to leaving Ireland when she was four, apart from school holidays, England was Nivedita's home until she left for India in 1898. Her entire, immediate family, moreover, had moved to England by the late eighteen-eighties. In some ways even more telling, given that Nivedita was by then a fully independent adult, is the limited nature of her contact with Ireland on the occasions when she left India for Britain or the United States (see for example *More Letters of Sister Nivedita* 2016, 41–43), a factor that her brother is said to have regarded as indicative of her diminishing interest in the Irish cause (for example, Foxe, 1975, 202). Nivedita made relatively few references to Ireland in her writings, mostly to different landscapes.

The third problem relates to the claimed active involvement of both Nivedita's grandfathers in the struggle for Irish Home Rule. In Reymond's (1953, 9–10) account, Nivedita's paternal grandfather John Noble, a Wesleyan minister like her father, is presented as being of national standing, "fighting" relentlessly in common cause with Catholics against the pro-English Church of Ireland. The choice of the term "fighting" could have been intended to imply non-violent political action. Set in a paragraph where mention is made of bombs being thrown, patriots' meeting being broken up, and patriots being hanged, it rather suggests his involvement in a militant armed struggle. Nivedita's father and maternal grandfather (referred to simply as Hamilton) are similarly said to have been active in the cause. The latter "fought" for Home Rule, being the "undisputed head of the Young Ireland movement," which, unlike the Loyal National Repeal Association led by Daniel O'Connell, did not renounce force in pursuit of its objectives. Thus, linked to the more militant Young Ireland movement, Hamilton is said to have risked death and imprisonment "ten times over" in the cause of land-reform, and as a reader and distributor of the Young Ireland movement's clandestine newspaper *The Nation* (Reymond 1953, 18–19). These members of Nivedita's family, however, do not feature in accounts produced independently of the Ramakrishna movement of prominent leaders of the Young Ireland, land-reform, and Home Rule movements. Interestingly, the Eire Vedanta Society (Eire Vedanta Society 2011) makes relatively little of Nivedita's Irish origins in its account of her life. The claims made about the political activism of Samuel Noble, Nivedita's father, moreover, are difficult to square with his decision to leave Ireland to take up theological training for the ministry in England.

Recently published correspondence between members of Nivedita's family considerably diminishes the aura of authority lent to the depictions of Nivedita by Reymond and Foxe, until then bolstered by the authors' acknowledgements of privileged access to recollections by Nivedita's relatives, and items such as Nivedita's diary. The correspondence that bears directly on this chapter's concerns is that between Ruth Olave Wilson (known as Grancy), the daughter of May (Nivedita's sister), and Isabel Noble, the daughter of Richmond Noble (Nivedita's brother), and that between Grancy and William Noble, the son of Richmond Noble. This correspondence dates from the 1970s, by which time Isabel and William were in their sixties and Grancy, the daughter of Richmond's elder sister, presumably would have been older. This correspondence, which was made available by the grandson of Nivedita's sister (see Sarkar 2017a, 683–685), was published while this chapter was being prepared (see also *More Letters of Sister Nivedita* 2016).

From the correspondents' more general discussion of their family, we learn about Richmond's wounds incurred during the First World War and his dislike of the Church, William's own wartime experience, and tensions between different wings of a family much larger and far more widely-spread than is apparent from Nivedita's biographies. The correspondents returned regularly to the subject of their famous aunt, Sister Nivedita. What appears to have provoked this discussion was the publication and dissemination of the most popular biographies of Nivedita, Reymond's in English in 1953 and Foxe's in 1975, which Grancy and her cousins were evidently keen to read critically. It is possible that this conversation was triggered by Grancy's letter of 5 May 1977 to her cousins in which she declared "I have been more than disturbed by the letters [not explained by the writer] and also in the beginnings of the two books—the Lizelle Reymond and the Barbara Foxe" (Sarkar 2017a, 685). Grancy suggests that Foxe might have attempted to conform Nivedita too closely to her own "devotion for the Yoga and modern devotions and the desire for meditations," failing to understand as a result the nature of Nivedita's acceptance of Hinduism and Vivekananda (Sarkar 2017a, 685–686). As we shall see, Isabel was familiar with Reymond's *The Dedicated*, and William asked Grancy in 1977 to send him a copy of the earlier French version of Reymond's biography, *La Fille d'Inde* (Sarkar 2018, 303–304). It is not possible to say from the exchange whether William was unfamiliar with Reymond's account at this point, which seems unlikely given his sister's knowledge of it, or whether this is evidence of his desire to compare it with the later, English version. There is no explicit mention of Atmaprana's (1977) biography, possibly because its publication in India made it less accessible. Isabel, however, referred to a "short life put out by the Sister Nivedita School in Calcutta," which would not be an accurate description of Atmaprana's biography (Sarkar 2018, 308). The antecedent to Atmaprana's biography was published in 1959 but only in Bengali. Barbara Foxe's account attracts the most comment, again possibly because it would have been the easiest to access because of its provenance but more likely because of Foxe's contact with the family. It was not only how Nivedita had been represented by her biographers that drew the correspondents' attention but also the difficulties in gathering detailed and reliable accounts of their family history and Nivedita's place in it.

In a letter of May 1978, Grancy recalled that her mother (Nivedita's sister, May) "... *denied* a good deal of her childhood ..." and that consequently Grancy knew little about certain aspects of her mother's early life. As if by way of explanation, Grancy added that "Mother—when I asked questions—always said that Aunt Margaret [Nivedita] begged that no publicity should be given about their childhood" (Sarkar 2017b, 781; cf. Sarkar 2017a, 684). This raises the question of what family members of Nivedita's generation would have been prepared to reveal about her youth, although May appears to have been willing to share some of her and Nivedita's past with her grandson (Sarkar 2017a, 683–684). Grancy also recalled that Nivedita was "never *really* one of us—it was as if she was on a higher plane of evolution," but she acknowledged that Nivedita had absorbed more from having lived "for some time" with her family in Ireland than even they had realised (Sarkar 2017b, 781). Grancy mentioned in passing Barbara Foxe as somebody who might be interested in her private letters (Sarkar 2017b, 782).

In her response to her cousin's letter (not dated but offering Christmas greetings), Isabel also touched on their aunt, as well as discussing the family more generally. She urged Grancy to make the effort to write, perhaps implying that Grancy was not in good health, because "You are the only link to correct some of the inaccuracies that have cropped up in the accounts of our grandparents' lives!" (Sarkar 2017b, 786). William also thanked Grancy for responding to his requests for more information about the family's history, but made clear that he regarded his sister, Isabel, as more knowledgeable than he was about their family's history (Sarkar 2018, 299, 303). It is evident that all three had devoted considerable efforts to gathering information from older members of their family but not always successfully (see, for example, Sarkar 2018, 308).

Isabel referred in her letters to Grancy to finding mistakes "in every biography of aunt Margot" (Sarkar 2017b, 786), and to her annoyance at finding inaccuracies in the accounts of her aunt's early life, adding "... and I wish I had some basic dates to put it right at least in my copy..." (Sarkar 2018, 308). It is not clear from the context whether Isabel's latter comment also referred to biographies of her aunt in general or one in particular. Mentioning specifically Reymond's *The Dedicated*, Isabel stated that "great grandfather Rev John Noble" (Nivedita's paternal grandfather) was born in 1798, according to her father, Richmond Noble, and not 1825 as given in *The Dedicated*. She continued:

> The most idiotic account of ... Richard Hamilton [Nivedita's maternal grandfather] working all his life for the "Irish cause"; Margot going on rounds with him peddling a clandestine paper inciting rebellion.
> This I find impossible to swallow. (Sarkar 2017b, 786).

The Making of the Ideal Transnational Disciple

The family discussion of Nivedita's biographers' representations of her Irish nationalism continued in exchanges between Grancy and her cousin, William, the son of Nivedita's brother. William referred in a letter of 28 March 1977 to having just received a book on "Aunt Margot," which he intended to send to Grancy. The date of the letter and the fact that both Grancy and William referred to Barbara Foxe suggest that book was probably Foxe's biography, published in 1975. In a subsequent letter dated 2 May but not completed and posted until after 8 May, William expressed pleasure on hearing in a letter from Grancy of 2 May (not published) that the book had arrived. Presumably responding to an observation made by Grancy (possibly in her letter of 2 May or even her letter of 8 May cited above—depending on when William and Grancy posted their letters), he wrote "I had the same feeling about Aunt Margot's background—no life and pathetically little of it. So regrettably, there was obviously no material to work upon" (Sarkar 2018, 303). One is left wondering what the biographers had in the way of reliable source material.

In a more general discussion of the family's history, William observed that his father, Richmond "... having been born so long after Aunt Margot and your Mother (Aunt May), and also not having known his father or his paternal grandparents means there is quite a blank as far as information is concerned" (Sarkar 2018, 299).

William then noted that his father had spent more time with the Hamiltons about whom William consequently knew much more. Foxe's (1975, 230) reliance on William Noble and his daughter, Mrs. R Whitney, and Richmond Noble's recollections as sources now has to be viewed in the light of William's observations about the extent of his own and his father's knowledge. The same holds true of Reymond's (1953, vi-vii) reference to the "Rich contributions to this vast store of material...made with alacrity by Nivedita's brother and sister...." The difficulty created by these biographers' way of acknowledging their sources is that the reader is left unsure as to the extent to which this "vast store of material" covered all the distinct and varied phases of Nivedita's life and more particularly, for our purposes, her early life in Ireland and the north of England.

William then turned to Barbara Foxe's biography, musing "I wonder if Barbara Foxe is right in saying in her book that Aunt Margot's "grandparents were enthusiastic supporters of the agitation for Home Rule..." (Sarkar 2018, 300). He then gave an extended but abridged quotation from Foxe (1975, 12-13), which is the core of her portrayal of a family committed to the cause of Irish Home Rule. He continued:

> I am quite certain that some of the above is wrong, and I am doubtful about the rest. It is not clear from the book which grandparents are referred to, the Nobles or the Hamiltons. I should not have thought, although cannot be certain, that the Noble grandparents were keen on

the fight for Home Rule, but I am quite certain that Grandmother (Mary Hamilton)...was not "reared on Home Rule"—all the Hamilton background was the very reverse of all this. (Sarkar 2018, 301)

Foxe's account can no longer be taken at face value, in the light of the documented reservations about its accuracy expressed on separate occasions by William Noble, one of Foxe's acknowledged sources, and his sister, Isabel.

All three correspondents acknowledged limits to their knowledge of their famous aunt's life while in Ireland, and, indeed, to their knowledge of the lives of their immediate family. No less significantly, they also recognised the limits of their parents as sources of information about Nivedita's early life in Ireland, despite being her siblings. Yet, there are grounds for accepting the exchanges between these younger members of Nivedita's family as a corrective to the accounts provided by Reymond and Foxe. The three correspondents may lay some claim to a degree of authority in these matters because of their place in Nivedita's family, and their access to whatever recollections their parents, Nivedita's siblings, chose or were able to share. Also, the provenance of this correspondence is known, unlike the specific sources of information used by Reymond and Foxe in their accounts of Nivedita's early days. I have not referred to Atmaprana here because she says little about Nivedita's life prior to her meeting Vivekananda.

William Noble spoke of his inherited knowledge from his father of the Hamilton side of the family, and all three correspondents had tried to gather information about their family's history, if only on occasion from each other. The period when these letters were written, and the ages of the correspondents are, on balance, likely to have encouraged a disinterested curiosity about lives and events of over half a century earlier. Their approach is largely measured with close reference to the biographies they had read, and the judgements they shared appear to have been arrived at independently. They referred respectfully to Vivekananda but their tone was more that of family members curious about a famous relative than of devotees. William Noble, in fact, confirmed in a letter of May 1977 to Grancy that she was right in her assumption that "I am not so interested in Swamiji himself—I am only interested in the Hindu religion in so far as Aunt Margot was concerned, but I am extremely interested in all that she did" (Sarkar 2018, 303). Finally, in relation to the sensitivities of the Irish political context, at the time when they exchanged letters, none of the correspondents were in Ireland, being in South Africa (Grancy), the United States (Isabel), and England (William). Also, as it appears that Nivedita's biographers have both greatly inflated her family's involvement in the campaign for Irish Home Rule and painted her own politics in a more extreme light than the available evidence suggests was the case, there would have been no reason for the cousins to have written defensively about either Nivedita or their family as a whole.

The Making of the Ideal Transnational Disciple

I noted earlier in this chapter that Nivedita's biographers' accounts of her early years, including her education in England, are marked by shallow treatments of the settings in which Nivedita found herself, with resulting inaccuracies. I suggested that, possibly in the absence of sufficient, accurate, and detailed information, Reymond developed a narrative informed in part by popular images of the plight of vulnerable young women sent away to distant, charitable schools, which featured in nineteenth-century literature. In seeking to explain her eventual commitment to the cause of Indian independence, Nivedita's biographers invoked a romanticised image of her "fiery" patriotism as the product of a Celtic and Irish ancestry (see, for example, Foxe 1975, 14), possibly influenced in this by Vivekananda's own attribution of qualities he admired in Nivedita to her "Celtic blood." Consequently, their exploration of Nivedita's political position in relation to the Irish campaign for greater political autonomy, like their treatment of her education, suffers from inadequate contextualisation. Her biographers fail to make clear, for example, the distinctive concerns of the Home Rule and the nationalist, separatist movements.

Nivedita's Ireland was not the Ireland of immediately before and after the Easter Uprising of 1916—she died in 1911. It was Ireland after the Potato Famine and the ensuing further loss of population through emigration. Reymond (1953, 9) refers baldly to conflicts between Roman Catholics and Protestants in early nineteenth-century Ireland, as if these were rooted in doctrinal differences, rather than to the abusive exercise of power by Protestant landlords over powerless, largely Roman Catholic tenants, which did provoke outbreaks of violent resistance. The growing sense of injustice and inequality in late nineteenth-century Ireland would fuel the campaign for Irish independence.

It was the cause of Irish Home Rule, we are told, that was actively supported by Nivedita's family. At that time, the goal of the Home Rule movement, devolution of powers to a legislative assembly in Ireland, was distinct from that of the separatist, nationalist movement for complete independence from Britain. In the latter decades of the nineteenth century, the campaign for Home Rule had become a party-political matter under leaders such as Charles Parnell and John Redmond. Nivedita's political position in relation to Ireland at that time was, thus, closer to the moderate mainstream than to what was then the more radical nationalist, separatist cause. Although it is reported that Nivedita spoke in favour of the Irish Home Rule Bill in London, this is not in itself indicative of a radical political position at a time when the principle of Irish Home Rule had been accepted by the Liberals under William Gladstone. This situation changed when the Home Rule Bill was voted down in the House of Lords in 1893 and the Liberals lost power in 1895. Home Rule, however, remained a popular cause in Ireland until the second decade of the twentieth century, the closing years of Nivedita's life, when Protestant opposition to Home Rule intensified as did nationalist agitation for independence.

Nivedita's experience in London, almost a quarter of her lifetime prior to her departure for India, had a significant impact on shaping her style of social and political activism, even though she had yet to become an "Indian nationalist." It was only once in India, when she had reports of Vivekananda being monitored by the police and directly witnessed racist behaviour (Basu 1982, 1, 11), and particularly from 1899 when she began to react increasingly vehemently against the policies of Lord Curzon, then the Viceroy of India, that she grew progressively more disillusioned with British rule in India. In committing herself to its overthrow (for example, Basu 1982: 1, 126, 435–438 and Basu 1982, 2, 540, 647, 721), she turned her back on the gradualist political agenda of Home Rule, with which she had become familiar in relation to the Irish cause from her days in London. Yet, in 1900 during a period in London, in an address to the Sesame Club she referred to speaking "in the interests of England and as an English woman" (Nivedita 1988, 441). In this same address, she was still prepared to explore the "building up of the British Empire by sure ways," here by going with love to India (Nivedita 1988, 441). She declared (p. 442) "The words 'British Empire' mean neither more nor less than the British opportunity to choose the noblest part ever played in the drama of the world..."

In many respects, Nivedita's ambivalent mixture of acceptance, at times even admiration, and resistance in response to Britain's rule of India could be said to have parallels with the attitudes of those Indians who once favoured a gradualist route to greater political autonomy. Looking as much to idealism and individual transformation as to structural change, she followed in the footsteps of her Master, Vivekananda (see, for example, Beckerlegge 2000, 46–48). In espousing the cause of Indian nationalism by choosing the path of political action, however, this close and most trusted of Vivekananda's disciples went her own way, whether prompted by her diagnosis of India's changed needs or her previous experience as an activist, rather than following the path marked out by Vivekananda for his followers.

Working towards a new understanding of "Indian nationality"

By the time Nivedita moved to London, she was, as we have seen, liberal in her religious opinions as she continued her "seeking." She was progressive to an extent in her social attitudes. This is evident from her early published interventions on behalf of the poor and the rights of women, and her adoption of the educational theories of Pestalozzi and Froebel led to the invitation to help establish a progressive school in London.[18] The name of her own school,

---

18. See Nivedita's commendation of the kindergarten system for development in India (Basu 1982, 2, 574–580), and her writings on education more generally (for example, Nivedita 1975, 1–75). She recognized that she would have to tailor her educational philosophy to the needs of young Hindu women at the girls' school she opened in Calcutta in 1898 (see, for example, Burke 1987b, 290).

the Ruskin School, reflected her acquaintance with John Ruskin's ideas from her time at Wrexham and was indicative of her broad familiarity with the Arts and Crafts Movement shaped by, among others, William Morris and Ruskin. This movement's appreciation of traditional crafts and forms of artistic production would prepare the ground for Nivedita's later thinking not just about art but also about co-operation, mutual aid, economics, and education (under the influence of Peter Kropotkin, which increased over the following decade).[19] These were values that would be central to the phase of the *swadeshi* movement triggered by the Partition of Bengal in 1905. Kumari Jayawardena (1995, 193) has noted that "Nivedita's vitality was to inspire many others—Indian politicians, artists, poets, scientists," reflecting the breadth of Nivedita's interests, her networking abilities, and thus the extent of her both direct and indirect influence in Bengal in the first decade of the twentieth century. This pattern of activity is consistent with her brother's testimony that, wherever Nivedita went, a "literary club was sure to spring up" (quoted in Reymond 1953, 28). If not the founder of groups during her years in England, Nivedita was assiduous in joining societies in London and enjoyed an extensive network of contacts, which were habits she maintained in Calcutta. At the Sesame Club in London, founded in 1895 and aimed particularly at professional women, Nivedita heard Vivekananda lecture and, as we have seen, contributed to its programme of talks and discussions. There she also met, among other prominent people with links to Ireland, William Butler Yeats who, although raised as a member of the Protestant Ascendancy (see above), was an Irish nationalist and a member of the Irish Republican Brotherhood, and George Bernard Shaw who, in contrast, was a supporter of Irish Home Rule and thus of remaining within the British Empire.

Once in India, it is evident that Nivedita put the creative arts in the service of the campaign for Indian freedom in a manner reminiscent of the Irish Literary Revival. This important feeder into the Irish nationalist movement aimed at countering the undermining of the Irish language and Irish culture under British rule. The Revival had been gathering momentum since the middle of the nineteenth century, and, through the efforts of Yeats, had also been promoted in London since the early 1890s. Nivedita's familiarity with the rippling effects of the Irish Literary Revival would have preceded her acquaintance with the fruits of the Bengal Renaissance under Vivekananda's tutelage.

---

19. Nivedita's letters in the early 1900s indicate her increasing exposure to the influence of Peter Kropotkin and Guiseppe Mazzini (for example, Basu 1982:1, 3, 381; Basu 1982, 2, 539, 560, 566). Her most specific references were to Kropotkin, despite his rationalist expectation that religion would die out. Nivedita returned to Kropotkin's emphasis on self-sufficiency and his theory of "mutual aid" on several occasions in her writings.

Nivedita encountered the Irish Literary Revival in London, not Ireland, through her contacts in the Sesame Club, her participation in groups like the Free Ireland group she joined, according to the emic biographical narrative, on moving to London, and her friendship with Octavius Beatty, the editor of the *Wimbledon News*, a mouthpiece of Irish organizations to which, along with other publications, she is said to have contributed pro-Boer articles.[20] Public debate about the Boer War might well have been an important factor in developing Nivedita's growing sense of unease about British colonialism, and one that provided an important bridge between her sympathy for the Irish Home rule movement and her active support for the cause of Indian independence.

By the time of the Second Boer War (1899–1901), Nivedita had already established herself in India. Although supported by the British Establishment and the British public in general, the Second Boer War generated considerable criticism of Britain's actions by other nations and gave rise to a vociferous anti-war movement. Vivekananda himself (1989, 6, 422) commented implicitly on the Boer War. Writing to Nivedita in December 1899, he spoke of looking to a time when the "blood-letting," Britain's conduct of the Boer War, would be over and people would return to thinking about "better" and "higher" things. He also expressed the hope that Britain would lose the Cape Colony so that Britain could "concentrate her energy on India."

The risk of creating "another Ireland" through the occupation and colonial rule of South Africa, with its minorities, was one of the arguments deployed by those in Britain opposed to the Boer War. Given her background, Nivedita might be expected to have been sensitive to such a parallel, but, when she referred to the Boer War (an "individual and general degradation" driven by British greed) in a letter of July 1901 (Basu 1982, 1, 434), Nivedita addressed this solely in relation to the governance of India. It is evident from her scathing criticism of colonial officials and reference to this "awful doing of my nation to you [India]," that by this point Nivedita had come to hold British colonial rule responsible for India's condition (Basu 1982, 1, 435). She eagerly anticipated the replacement of colonial rule by an Indian government, no matter what its faults, and implied that this could be through violence and that she would have a role in this (for example, Basu 1982, 1, 11, 436).

What appear to be parallels in the strategies adopted respectively by the supporters of the Irish and the Indian struggles for independence illustrate the recognition in different colonial settings of the crucial linkage between the undermining of traditional culture by the colonial power, the need to revive language and the arts, the need for an appropriate style of education

---

20. Octavius Beatty is yet another name that seems to have been kept alive through its recycling in the Ramakrishna movement's literature and other works dependent on it (cf. Basu 1982: 1, 35, 36). Som (2017, 5) notes that Nivedita also published in the pacifist-inclined, pro-Boer *Daily News* and *Review of Reviews*.

to facilitate this revival, and the need to regain political independence to ensure these things happened.

Nivedita looked particularly, but not exclusively, to the role of national and civic art in contributing to the development of a new understanding of "Indian nationality" in which "Hindu and Mohammedan must become one" (for example, Nivedita 1982b, 205-206; 1975, 147-153; Basu 1982, 2, 553). Collaborating closely with E. B. Havell, Superintendent of the Government School of Art in Calcutta, and Ananda Coomaraswamy, she sought to defend Indian art. Fiercely critical of the European style of art popularized in India by the eminent painter and print-maker, Raja Ravi Varma, she strove to promote the growth of the "national" art movement in Bengal, known as the New Calcutta School or the Neo-Bengal School, centred on the work of Abanindranath Tagore, among others.

In *Aggressive Hinduism*, frequently cited as evidence of her commitment to a form of Hindu supremacy, Nivedita (1990, 503-504) declared in 1905:

> But far more, on behalf of India herself, do we need artists ... who can wake in us the great new senses. We want men of the Indian blood who can portray for us the men of old, — Bhishma and Yudhisthira, Akbar and Sher Shah, Pratap Singh and Chand Bibi, — in such a fashion as to stir the blood. We want through these to feel out, as a people, towards the new duties of the time to be.[21]

Conclusion

In exploring Nivedita's life as a "translocal space," a fraught personal "space" of interaction of ideas and personal aspirations, we have traced a life that moved, via an extended period in the capital of the British Empire, between two countries under British rule, both of which had embarked on campaigns to regain, if not independence, then at the least far greater autonomy. Hers was a life shaped by personal adversity, transnational opportunities, and colonial struggles.

The complexity of Nivedita's life was reflected, as we have seen, in the way in which it was punctuated by several striking changes of course, in the ways in which she chose to identify herself, and in her ambivalent attitude to the British Empire. The reality of her life was certainly more complex than the popular image of her as a "fiery" Irish nationalist transplanted to India, which is why I have argued in this chapter that it is necessary to give more weight to the considerable period of her life spent in Britain, and particularly London. It was here that she was first exposed to Indian thought, before she met Vivekananda, and where her social activism first found expression.

---

21. On Indian art in the service of Hindu apologetics shaped by Vivekananda and Nivedita, see Beckerlegge (2008).

It was where British national pre-occupations with Ireland, the Boer War, and India began to foster what would become increasing, although not entirely consistently voiced, misgivings about British colonialism.

Margaret Noble's encounter with Vivekananda was undeniably at the heart of her transformation into Nivedita. The "making" of Nivedita as Vivekananda's ideal, transnational disciple, however, had its roots in the very social activism, which developed around her role as an educator in Britain. Vivekananda recognized the potential of Nivedita's sense of vocation and what she could contribute as a worker in India, and it was his vision of how to transform Indian society that initially drew her most powerfully to his message and thus to become his disciple.

It is the mark of her life, perhaps even an irony at its heart, that it was only through her participation in literary circles in London that the Irish-born Nivedita appears to have engaged more closely with the cause of Irish freedom. Yet, although undoubtedly sympathetic to the Irish Home Rule movement, she did not make this, or the cause of Irish independence, the focus of her social and political activism. There is no evidence of a level of engagement with the cause of Irish freedom, whether through Home Rule or independence, comparable to her activism in support of the cause of Indian independence, including her constant commentary on conditions in India in her writings and letters.

It was the cause of social uplift in India and subsequently India's independence to which Nivedita committed the greater part of her considerable energy for the remainder of her life, and where she truly became an activist rather than remaining a progressive, social commentator.

References

Atmaprana (Pravrajika). 1977. *Sister Nivedita*. Calcutta: Sister Nivedita's Girls' School.

Ballantyne, Tony and Antoinette M. Burton. 2005. "Introduction: Bodies, Empires, and World Histories." In *Bodies in Contact: Rethinking Colonial Encounters in World History*, edited by T. Ballantyne and A M. Burton, 1–15. Durham, NC: Duke University Press. https://doi.org/10.1215/9780822386452-001

Basu, Sankari Prasad and Sunil Behari Ghosh, eds. 1969. *Vivekananda in Indian Newspapers 1893-1902*. Calcutta: Basu, Bhattacharya and Co.

Basu, Sankari Prasad. 1982. *Letters of Sister Nivedita*, 2 vols. Calcutta: Nababharata Publishers.

Basu, Sankari Prasad, ed. 2007. *Swami Vivekananda in Contemporary Indian News (1893-1902) with Sri Ramakrishna and the Mission*, vol. 2. Kolkata: Ramakrishna Mission Institute of Culture.

Beckerlegge, Gwilym. 2000. *The Ramakrishna Mission: The Making of a Modern Hindu Movement.* Oxford: Oxford University Press.

———. 2004. "The Early Spread of Vedanta Societies: An Example of 'Imported Localism'." *Numen* 51(3): 296-320. https://doi.org/10.1163/1568527041945526

———. 2007. "Noble, Margaret Elizabeth [Sister Nivedita] (1867–1911)." In *Oxford Dictionary of National Biography*, Oxford University Press. http://www.oxforddnb.com/view/article/95037

———. 2008. "The Swami and the Artist: The Use of Indian Art in Swami Vivekananda's Apologetics." In *Colonialism, Modernity and Religious Identities*, edited by G. Beckerlegge, 213-238. Oxford: Oxford University Press.

———. 2017. "The 'Irishness' of Sister Nivedita." *Prabuddha Bharata* 122(1): 118-136.

———. Unpublished. "Unravelling Biographies of Margaret Noble/Sister Nivedita," paper presented at the annual conference of the British Association for the Study of Religions in September 2017.

Bell, Currer (Charlotte Brontë). 1847. *Jane Eyre: An Autobiography.* London: Smith, Elder & Co.

Boehmer, Elleke. 2002. *Empire, the National, and the Postcolonial 1890-1920: Resistance in Interaction.* Oxford: Oxford University Press.

———. 2006. "Friable Transnationalism: The Question of the South African Gandhi and the Irish Nivedita." In *Ireland and India: Colonies, Culture and Empire*, edited by T. Foley and M. O'Connor, 58-67. Dublin: Irish Academic Press.

Burke, Marie Louise. 1985. *Swami Vivekananda in the West New Discoveries: The World Teacher* Part One. Calcutta: Advaita Ashrama.

———. 1987a. *Swami Vivekananda in the West New Discoveries: A New Gospel.* Part One, (3rd edition). Calcutta: Advaita Ashrama.

———. 1987b. *Swami Vivekananda in the West New Discoveries: A New Gospel* Part Two, (3rd edition). Calcutta: Advaita Ashrama.

Da Sousa Correa, Delia. 2000. "*Jane Eyre* and Genre." In *The Nineteenth-Century Novel: Realisms*, edited by D. Da Sousa Correa, 87-116. London: Routledge.

Deacon, Desley, Penny Russell and Angela Woollacott. 2010. "Introduction." In *Transnational Lives: Biographies of Global Modernity, 1700-Present*, edited by D. Deacon, P. Russell and A. Woollacott, 1-11. Basingstoke: Palgrave Macmillan. https://doi.org/10.1057/9780230277472_1

Eire Vedanta Society. 2011. "Sister Nivedita." https://rkmireland.org/about-us/sister-nivedita

Foxe, Barbara. 1975. *Long Journey Home: A Biography of Margaret Noble (Nivedita).* London: Rider.

Gambhirananda (Swami). 1983. *History of the Ramakrishna Math and Ramakrishna Mission*. 3rd revised edition. Calcutta: Advaita Ashrama.

Golwalkar, Madhav Sadashiv. 1966. *Bunch of Thoughts*. 2nd impression. Bangalore: Vikrama Prakashan.

Hamilton, Nigel. 2007. *Biography: A Brief History*. Cambridge, MA: Harvard University Press. https://doi.org/10.4159/9780674038226

Heehs, Peter. 1998. *Nationalism, Terrorism, Communalism: Essays in Modern Indian History*. Oxford: Oxford University Press.

His Eastern and Western Disciples. 1979. *The Life of Swami Vivekananda by His Eastern and Western Disciples*, vol. 2. 6th edition. Calcutta: Advaita Ashrama.

Jackson, Carl T. 1994. *Vedanta for the West: The Ramakrishna Movement in the United States*. Bloomington: Indiana University Press.

Jayawardena, Kumari. 1995. *The White Woman's Other Burden*. New York: Routledge.

Keyes, Charles F. 1982. "Introduction: Charisma and Sacred Biography." In *Charisma and Sacred Biography*, edited by M.A. Williams, 1-22. Journal of the American Academy of Religion Thematic Studies 48(3–4). Chambersburg, PA: American Academy of Religion.

McKean, Lise. 1996. *Divine Enterprises: Gurus and the Hindu Nationalist Movement*. Chicago, IL: University of Chicago Press.

More Letters of Sister Nivedita. 2016. Kolkata: Sri Sarada Math.

Mukherjee, Santana. 1997. *Sister Nivedita in Search of Humanity*. Calcutta: Minerva.

Nivedita (Sister). 1975. *Complete Works of Sister Nivedita*, vol. 5. Calcutta: Sister Nivedita's Girls' School.

———. 1982a. *Complete Works of Sister Nivedita*, vol. 1. 3rd impression. Calcutta: Sister Nivedita's Girls' School.

———. 1982b. *Complete Works of Sister Nivedita*, vol. 4. 2nd edition. Calcutta: Sister Nivedita's Girls' School.

———. 1988. *Complete Works of Sister Nivedita*, vol. 2. 3rd edition. Calcutta: Sister Nivedita's Girls' School.

———. 1990. *Complete Works of Sister Nivedita*, vol. 3. 3rd impression. Calcutta: Sister Nivedita's Girls' School.

Nivedita of India. 2002. Kolkata: The Ramakrishna Mission Institute of Culture.

O'Doherty, Malachi. 2017. "Nivedita." *Prabuddha Bharata* 122(1): 224-234.

Potter, Simon J. and Jonathan Saha. 2015. "Global History, Imperial History, and Connected Histories of Empire." *Journal of Colonialism and Colonial History* 16(1). https://doi.org/10.1353/cch.2015.0009

Ramusack, Barbara N. 1990. "Cultural Missionaries, Maternal Imperialists, Feminist Allies: British Women Activists in India, 1865-1945." In *Western Women and Imperialism—A special issue of Women's Studies International Forum*, edited by N. Chaudhuri and M. Strobel, 13 (4): 309-321. https://doi.org/10.1016/0277-5395(90)90028-V

Reymond, Lizelle. 1945. *Nivédita Fille de L'Inde*. Paris / Neuchâtel: V. Attinger.

———. 1953. *The Dedicated—A Biography of Nivedita*. New York: John Day.

Sarkar, Sarada. 2017a. "Sister Nivedita's Unpublished Letter and Family Papers." *Prabuddha Bharata* 122(10): 683–705.

———. 2017b. "About Sister Nivedita by Her Niece and Three Unpublished Letters of Sister Nivedita." *Prabuddha Bharata* 122(12): 779–787.

———. 2018. "Her Family Remembers Sister Nivedita and Some Other Papers." *Prabuddha Bharata* 123(2): 299–315.

Sen, Amiya P. 2016. *An Idealist in India: Selected Writings and Speeches of Sister Nivedita*. Primus Books: Delhi.

Sharma, Jyotirmaya. 2013. *A Restatement of Religion: Swami Vivekananda and the Making of Hindu Nationalism*. New Haven, CT: Yale University Press.

Sharpe, Eric. 1975. *Comparative Religion: A History*. London: Duckworth.

Sil, Narasingha P. 1997. *Swami Vivekananda—A Reassessment*. Selinsgrove: Susequehanna University Press/Associated University Presses.

Singh, Maina. 2006. "Political Activism and the Politics of Spirituality: The Layered Identities of Sister Nivedita/Margaret Noble (1867-1911)." In *Ireland and India: Colonies, Culture and Empire*, edited by T. Foley and M. O'Connor, 39-57. Dublin: Irish Academic Press.

"Sister Nivedita: Offered to India." 2017. *Prabuddha Bharata* 122(1).

Som, Reba. 2017. *Margot: Sister Nivedita of Vivekananda*. Gurgaon: Penguin Random House India.

Sutcliffe, Steven. 1998. "Seekers, Networks and 'New Age'." *Scottish Journal of Religious Studies* 18(2): 97-114.

———. 2013. "'Rosicrucians at Large': Radical Versus Qualified Invention in the Cultic Milieu." *Culture and Religion* 14(4): 424-444. https://doi.org/10.1080/14755610.2013.838801

Taylor, Anne. 1992. *Annie Besant: A Biography*. Oxford: Oxford University Press.

Vivekananda (Swami). 1989. *The Complete Works of Swami Vivekananda*, 8 vols. Calcutta: Advaita Ashrama

About the author

Gwilym Beckerlegge is Professor Emeritus of Modern Religions in the Discipline of Religious Studies at the Open University, UK. He has published extensively on Swami Vivekananda's legacy, particularly Vivekananda's promotion of *sevā* (service to humanity), with reference to the Ramakrishna Math and Mission and the Vivekananda Kendra. For details of selected publications, see Gwilym Beckerlegge's web page http://www.open.ac.uk/Arts/religious-studies/beckerlegge.shtml and entry under Open Research Online http://oro.open.ac.uk/view/person/gtb2.html.

— 4 —

The Curious Case of the Drs. d'Abreu: Catholicism, Migration and a Kanara Catholic Family in the Heart of the Empire, 1890–1950

Dwayne Ryan Menezes

> In the late nineteenth and early twentieth centuries, several Catholics from South Kanara in British India, whether as British subjects or Indo-Portuguese Catholics, journeyed across the wider British, Portuguese and Catholic worlds. Wherever they travelled or settled, they often strategically deployed their Catholicism (more precisely, Roman Catholicism), distinctive Anglo-Luso-Brahmin culture and ambiguities about their racial heritage to overcome structural barriers to the mobility and assimilation of South Asians. Catholicism, with its numerous institutions, lay and clerical transnational networks, and doctrinal emphasis on universalism emerged as a particularly valuable tool that some could deploy for the purpose of assimilation. Catholicism would not only facilitate intermarriages with Catholics of other ethnicities, but also enable racial "passing" and other forms of strategic ethnic reidentification. By focusing on the d'Abreu family from Mangalore, members of which journeyed to the British Isles since 1890, this study shall uncover the forgotten history of an Indo-Portuguese Catholic family that embedded itself within the heart of British society. It shall explore how, by strategically emphasizing the Catholic and Portuguese markers of their multifaceted identities and connecting to Catholic institutions and networks, the pioneering d'Abreu immigrant could embed himself within local Catholic society in Birmingham as a successful, presumably Portuguese, medical doctor, while his sons could acquire an education at Stonyhurst, become prominent surgeons, and marry into the British gentry and aristocracy. It shall explore both the transnational practices and networks of Catholicism and investigate the extent to which Catholicism could facilitate migration and aid assimilation.

This chapter invites its readers to journey back in time to visit two immigrant families that lived in the English Midlands in the 1890s. The first is the Edalji family in Shropshire, whose much-discussed story may already be familiar to the reader. The second is the d'Abreu family of Handsworth, whose story is just as important but that—for reasons this chapter shall outline—has escaped the attention of both the communities of scholars and the wider public. While this chapter recounts the history of the Edaljis in Britain rather briefly, it primarily seeks to recover and present in much greater depth the little-known history of the d'Abreu family. In the light of the d'Abreu history, the chapter shall explore the role that Catholicism, as well as the instrumentalist deployment of Catholic identity and racial ambiguity, could play in facilitating migration and aiding assimilation. It should be clarified at the offset that the terms "Catholicism" and "Catholic," used throughout the chapter, refer specifically to Roman Catholicism and Roman Catholic.

The history of the Edaljis in England began when Shapurji Edalji (c.1842–1918), a Parsi man born in Bombay around 1842, converted to Christianity under the influence of a Free Kirk missionary in 1856 and journeyed to St. Augustine's College, Canterbury, in 1866 to train as a missionary (Barnes 2005; Oldfield 2010; Weaver, 2006). He remained in England after his training and accepted temporary posts at the parishes of Burford, Oxford, Farnworth, Liverpool, St Levan and Bromley St Leonard, before being appointed vicar of St Mark's Church, Great Wyrley (Weaver 2006, 22). It was while acting as curate for the Reverend G. A. Sandberg, the vicar of St Clement's in Toxteth, Liverpool, that he grew acquainted with the vicar's friend, the Reverend Thompson Stoneham, himself the vicar of the parish of Ketley in Shropshire, and his daughter, Charlotte Stoneham. In 1874, Shapurji and Charlotte would marry at a ceremony led by the bride's uncle, the vicar of Hillesley, while another uncle, the vicar of St Mark's in Great Wyrley, arranged for his ministry to pass eventually to Shapurji as a wedding gift (Weaver 2006, 22). In December 1875, the Edaljis arrived in Great Wyrley to assume the ministry, with Shapurji consequently becoming the first South Asian known to have served as vicar of an English parish. This, however, did not sit well with the local population.

In January 1876, as Shapurji Edalji settled into his new role, Charlotte gave birth to their first son, George (1876–1953). Alongside the matters concerning his growing family and his demanding ministry to which he had to attend, the Reverend also found himself having to wrestle with the enemies he had cultivated among some influential parishioners with vested interests who did not find the new vicar as acquiescent as his predecessor (Weaver 2006, 24–29). In 1888–1889, the Edaljis received anonymous letters that featured threats to smash the windows of the vicarage and later even shoot Shapurji if he did not comply with their demand to order a particular newspaper. When Shapurji did not give in to the threats, there were windows broken, graffiti slandering the Edaljis written on the walls of the vicarage, and threatening letters sent to their maidservant that made references to her "black master" and "black man" (Weaver 2006, 19–30). Between 1892 and 1895, the parish and the Edaljis in particular were once again the recipients of a wave of anonymous letters, some more obscene than others. The letters accused George Edalji, the son of the Reverend, and Fred Brookes, the son of a member of the Vestry Committee, of engaging in sexual relations with each other's sisters, despite George's sister Maud still being only 10 years of age at the time (Weaver 2006, 39–40). The Reverend himself received letters accusing him of criminal practices similar to those of Oscar Wilde—in other words, homosexual acts—and, at one time, even found the upper windows of his vicarage smeared with excrement (Weaver 2006, 37–72). The Chief Constable of Staffordshire, however, wrongly laid the blame both for the letters and for the vandalism on young George, despite the most sincere protestations by his parents that his involvement was not even plausible.

A little over 10 years later, in 1903, a number of horses, cows and sheep would be brutally slashed and mutilated in what would become infamous as the Great Wyrley Outrages. By this point, George Edalji had already studied the law and had established a law practice in Birmingham five years earlier. Nevertheless, as most of the gory incidents had occurred around the vicarage, George was once again brought up as the suspect and was arrested, found guilty, and sentenced to seven years in prison (Weaver 2006, 77–110). The accusations and charges against the Edaljis, as Weaver and others have demonstrated, may have been fuelled by grievances with the Reverend's style of administration and stance on various labour and educational issues, but they were rooted in racial bias and prejudice (Barnes, 2005; Oldfield 2010; Weaver 2006). After a protracted campaign which, at one point, even included a petition to the Home Office, with 10,000 signatures (including those of 1,000 solicitors), to support his innocence, the Home Office paroled George after three years, but did not grant him an official pardon (Weaver 2006, 180). It was only after Sir Arthur Conan Doyle, the celebrated author of the fictional detective series featuring Sherlock Holmes, would get involved and point out that, due to his near-sightedness, George could simply not have been guilty that it became apparent that the case was a farce.

George Edalji would be pardoned, but he would not receive compensation and would continue to be viewed with suspicion. With the long and recurring campaign of harassment, intimidation and misrepresentation against the Edaljis, and the frequent incrimination of George for crimes that he did not commit, their story is one that highlights the extent and the effects that racial prejudice and discrimination—both at the social and the institutional levels—could assume in the day. On more than one occasion, the Edaljis found themselves the victims of a grave travesty of justice, despite being a relatively well-established and certainly a well-educated family that shared, furthermore, the dominant religion of their locality to so visible a degree that the father in the family was also the vicar of the parish. While the clerical network to which Shapurji Edalji came to be connected through his ministry and his marriage facilitated his assimilation and even professional promotion within the clerical world to an extent, that embeddedness within the clerical world clearly did not translate as a warm and accepting embrace by the parishioners in Great Wyrley. Even one as sympathetic to the Edaljis as Sir Arthur Conan Doyle felt compelled to remark, "The experiment will not, I hope, be repeated, for though the vicar was an amiable and devoted man, the appearance of a coloured clergyman with a half-caste son in a rude, unrefined parish was bound to cause some regrettable situation" (Doyle 1924, 216).

Let us leave the Edaljis aside for the moment and consider the case of another migrant family that lived in the West Midlands in the same period. Dr. John Francis d'Abreu (1863–1911) was a "Portuguese" man who lived in the suburb of Handsworth in Birmingham. Following the great migrations from Ireland over the mid-nineteenth century, the industrial metropolis of Birmingham had become home to a considerable Irish immigrant population, many of whom were attracted to it by the employment opportunities it afforded, and it came to serve as the heart of the Catholic Midlands. Handsworth proved particularly popular with Irish immigrants and was catered to by the parish church St. Francis of Assisi (opened in 1894), which traced its origins to a convent St. Mary's Refuge that was founded in 1841 by the Irish Sisters of Mercy who were still active in the parish (Thomas n.d., 3 [Catholic Archdiocese of Birmingham Archives, St. Chad's Cathedral]). The local parish church was said to have catered to 3,500 Catholics by 1910, predominantly Irish, though also English, Iberian, Italian and French (Thomas n.d., 3 and 18). What evidence there is suggests that Dr. d'Abreu was well-integrated into the Catholic life of the suburb. In the Midlands, and in Birmingham in particular, there were Catholics to be found in every echelon, from streetsellers and miners to priests and doctors, as well as aristocratic landowners and wealthy manufacturers, making it possible for d'Abreu to establish himself locally in the familiar role of the "Portuguese" doctor. That d'Abreu would have been in regular contact with the Irish in Handsworth, and attached himself to their more established networks, can be gathered not just from his ties with the local church, but also his employment from 1898 as surgeon at the Hamstead Colliery & Co., where several of the miners were Irish.[1]

Furthermore, following a local church meeting, d'Abreu was introduced by the Rev. Lawrence Henry of St. Mary's Refuge to Teresa Noonan, an Irish Catholic, whom he would marry at the Church of Our Blessed Lady and St. Thomas of Canterbury in Dudley on 12 June 1895 (Church of Our Blessed Lady, entry

---

1. He was subsequently also a member of the British Medical Association, a Medical Referee of the Refuge and Pearl Assurance Companies, a Fellow of the Royal Institute of Public Health and later a Medical Officer of the Handsworth District West Bromwich Union. *Medical Registers and Directories*, from 1892 to 1911; *Kelly's Directory of Birmingham* 1899, 487 and 898.

The Curious Case of the Drs. d'Abreu

for 12 June 1895, and obituary of John Francis d'Abreu, *Mangalore*, 1911). The Noonans were an Irish Catholic family that had immigrated from Ireland in the mid-nineteenth century and that had since acquired some prosperity through a chain of drapery stores. They had established themselves as gentlemen's outfitters with shops in Dudley, Bilston, Kidderminster and Oldbury by the 1880s.[2] Both d'Abreu and Noonan were seen to be hailing from Catholic families in trade, medicine still considered as such. As the Noonans were based in Dudley, they would have been acquainted with the Rev. Lawrence Henry who had served at the local parish church there between 1892 and 1894, before transferring to Handsworth where d'Abreu lived (Whittington 1923, 152). In the case of both the Reverend Shapurji Edalji and Dr. John Francis d'Abreu, it is worth noting the role that Christian clergymen, whether Anglican or Roman Catholic, could play in facilitating introductions that led to marriages, especially when the immigrants concerned were Christian and connected to Christian institutions and networks in the local parish. It is also of interest to understand the extent to which intermarriage might have helped an immigrant assimilate in local society, especially in sections that shared one's religious and class background. While intermarriage had enabled Shapurji Edalji to embed himself within Anglican clerical networks, it had not proven to be a panacea that would save him from the many difficulties he would encounter later.

In what way would intermarriage influence the trajectory of Dr. John Francis d'Abreu as a Roman Catholic immigrant? The case of the d'Abreus suggests that, contrary to what one might imagine, assimilation in local Catholic society might have been advantageous in itself. As Catholics of other ethnic groups, including the more numerous Irish Catholics, were also seen to be outside the mainstreams of the predominantly-Protestant English or Scottish nations and were often the subject of anti-Catholic or anti-Irish prejudice themselves, assimilation into local Catholic society that continually brought together Catholics of different ethnicities—even if for no other reason than to find strength in numbers—may have proved slightly more feasible for a new and darker-skinned Catholic immigrant. Unlike Shapurji Edalji who was faced with the need to gain acceptance as an Anglican vicar of an English parish from ethnically English parishioners affiliated with the dominant religion of the land, John Francis d'Abreu sought to carve out a place for himself among his religious compatriots who were themselves negotiating their status in relation to the Protestant majority. The disadvantage, of course, was that while assimilation into local Catholic society may have translated as assimilation within British society as a whole through assimilation into one of its more accepted and welcoming—even if not equally privileged—components, it could serve to lock the new Catholic immigrant within the space that

---

2. Interview with and records of Jim Noonan in Birmingham, 15 October 2011.

Figure 4.1   Dr. John Francis d'Abreu.

had been traditionally carved out for Catholics. Nevertheless, as shall be seen in the case of the d'Abreus, the strength of Catholic networks, coupled with other factors such as education, occupation, racial background, and even agency with regards to self-identification and professional mobility, could enable Catholic immigrants to carve out careers for themselves that did not conform to the existing templates.

The Noonans were connected by marriage to well-established families such as the Plants, Hardmans and Hillmans that produced local mayors and were major Catholic donors. The d'Abreus had seven children—four girls and three boys—but as Dr. John Francis d'Abreu would die in 1911, while the youngest boys were both less than five, it fell on his wife Teresa d'Abreu (née Noonan) to look after the family. Owing to the strength of the family's local Catholic networks, the three sons of Dr. d'Abreu were sent to Stonyhurst College, a prestigious Catholic public school in Lancashire run by the Jesuits. Given the absence of adequate records, it is still not clear who precisely paid for their tuition and board, but what is known—at least from family accounts—is that a few of d'Abreu's friends and relations provided some assistance. While the eldest son was admitted to Stonyhurst prior to his father's early death in 1911, some of the d'Abreus's well-off Catholic connections, such as the Plants, Noonans and Hillmans, supposedly assisted Teresa in educating the two younger boys at Stonyhurst.[3] Following Stonyhurst, the two younger boys—Francis ("Frank") and Alphonsus ("Pon")—proceeded to Birmingham to study medicine, then joined the Royal Army Medical Corps (RAMC)—Supplementary Reserve of Officers and were called up at the outbreak of the Second World War, and eventually rose to be among Britain's

---

3. Interviews with grandchildren and relatives: with Veronica Barran in London on 9 September 2011 and 15 September 2011, and in Birmingham on 15 October 2011; with Francesca d'Abreu via email dated 12 August and 6 September 2011; with Jim Noonan and Mary Lander in Birmingham on 15 October 2011; with Cora Pollock in Loch Fyne, Scotland, on 20 September 2011; with Ouida Moliner in Loch Fyne, Scotland, on 20 September 2011 and in North Hatley, Canada, between 15 and 18 November 2011. Also, records of Stonyhurst College, Lancashire, and Catholic Archdiocese of Birmingham Archives.

The Curious Case of the Drs. d'Abreu

Figure 4.2   Dr. J.F. d'Abreu, with his wife Teresa and three daughters (c. 1900).

most prominent surgeons. The life trajectories of Lt. Col. Francis ("Frank") Arthur Philip d'Abreu KM ERD ChM FRCS (1904–1995) and Professor Alphonsus ("Pon") Ligouri d'Abreu CBE ChM FRCP FRCS (1906–1976) as the sons of a "Portuguese" immigrant are also of interest, just as the case of George Edalji was as crucial to the Edalji story as the experiences of Shapurji.

After graduating from the University of Birmingham in 1930 and holding resident and registrar appointments in the city, the youngest son Pon served in the Surgical Unit, Cardiff Royal Infirmary, University of Wales, as Junior Assistant from 1930 to 1933 and Assistant Director from 1933 to 1939.[4] During the Second World War, he served in the RAMC as a surgical specialist in general and thoracic surgery, earlier on with the First Army in North Africa and subsequently with the Eighth Army in Italy, eventually becoming Officer-in-Command of the Surgical Division of a British General Hospital with the Central Mediterranean Forces. He was promoted to the rank of Lieutenant-Colonel in 1942, awarded an OBE in 1944 and mentioned in the Dispatches. After the War, he returned to Cardiff where he served as Acting Professor of Surgery, 1945–1946, before moving back to Birmingham as Consultant Surgeon to the United Birmingham Hospitals. He served as Professor of Cardiothoracic Surgery at Birmingham from 1959 and also Dean, and later Chair, of the Faculty of Medicine. He was also a member of the Central Health Services Council, 1964–1971, and the Medical Sub-Committee of the University Grants Committee from 1964, President of the Section of Surgery at the Royal Society of Medicine in 1967, President of the Thoracic Society in 1968, and

---

4.   The principal source for this information is the biographical entry in Royal College of Surgeons of England 2014.

President of the Society of Thoracic and Cardiovascular Surgeons of Great Britain and Ireland in 1969–1970. He served on the Council of the Royal College of Surgeons for around two decades, including six years as a member of the Court of Examiners and two years as Vice-President, and was twice elected Hunterian Professor. He was also John Alexander Lecturer at University of Michigan in 1965, McLauchlin Galle Visiting Professor in Canada in 1966, Visiting Professor of Surgery at Harvard in 1967 and awarded a CBE in 1968. Additionally, he served as Honorary Colonel, RAMC (48th Division of the Territorial Army, West Midlands District), Deputy Lieutenant of Warwickshire and Vice-President of the Warwickshire County Cricket Club (The Royal College of Surgeons of England 2014). He was the author of the classic *A Practice of Thoracic Surgery*, first published in 1953, thereafter translated into many languages and renamed *d'Abreu's Practice of Cardiothoracic Surgery*, with a fourth edition published prior to his death.

While Pon took an active part in cricket and drama and acted with future Hollywood stars Laurence Olivier and Madeleine Carroll during his years in Birmingham, his elder brother, Frank, demonstrated a keen interest in sport. Apart from being Head of the Line (headboy) at Stonyhurst, he was captain of its rugby and cricket teams, and while at the medical school at the University of Birmingham, he won the intervarsity boxing championship at welterweight (The Royal College of Surgeons of England 2015). Upon graduating in 1929, he served as house surgeon and resident surgical officer at Birmingham General Hospital and then the Queen's Hospital. In 1932, he was elected to the Fellowship of the Royal College of Surgeons; and from 1934, he held the post of cancer registrar at St Bartholomew's Hospital in London, the first non-Bart's man to hold a junior surgical post there (Royal College of Surgeons of England 2015). Over the course of the Second World War, he served throughout and finished as Lieutenant-Colonel in the South-East Asia Command (King 1995). Following the Second World War, he was appointed Consultant General Surgeon to Westminster Hospital where he served until 1969. From 1950, he also served as Honorary Surgeon at the Hospital of St John and St Elizabeth in London, a charitable hospital affiliated with the Sovereign Military Order of Malta and managed by the Sisters of Mercy (Royal College of Surgeons of England 2015). He was an examiner at the Universities of Cambridge and London, and the Society of Apothecaries, as well as Chairman and member of the Court of Examiners at the Royal College of Surgeons. In addition, he served as Director of the Clerical and Medical Assurance Society and was a member of the Medical Appeals Tribunal. He retained his interest in sport, especially cricket, rugby and horse racing, and served as a member of the Board of Management of the Institute of Sports Medicine and medical adviser and examiner to the Jockey Club (King 1995). Like his brother, he remained a devout Catholic all his life; in recognition of his services to the Hospital of

St John and St Elizabeth, he was made a Knight of Malta in 1977.

In the early-1930s, the youngest son Pon was introduced by a mutual friend to Elizabeth Ursula Arienwen Throckmorton whom he would marry. The Throckmortons were one of England's oldest and most connected Catholic gentry families whose large estates in Warwickshire and Devon totalled well over 8000 acres, and whose family seat Coughton Court remains one of the most popular stately homes in the Midlands. Elizabeth's grandfather was the 10th Baronet (Throckmorton), and a nephew of Cardinal Acton as well as the historian Lord Acton. On her father's death, her uncle, who had married a daughter of the Duke of Rutland, inherited the title, but in the absence of an heir, Elizabeth emerged as the sole heiress to the estates. The marriage between Pon and Elizabeth was not without opposition, but the opposition had little to do with Pon being the son of a Portuguese man. Instead, Elizabeth's mother opposed the marriage on grounds that Pon had a trade, rather than gentry, background.[5] Nevertheless, Pon and Elizabeth had a happy marriage, worshipped for the most part at the Oratory of St. Philip Neri in Birmingham, and were prominent figures in Catholic society in the 1950s and 1960s. While Pon's swarthier skin did not go unnoticed and may have attracted the occasional comment, he would be remembered by former students and colleagues simply as a "Portuguese man" whose family moved "from Goa to Malta and then on to England" (Moody 2003, 18). Yet, this hardly seemed to matter, and despite also being the mixed-heritage son of a darker-skinned immigrant, Pon's experiences would prove remarkably different from that of George Edalji. Pon's eldest daughter, Clare, a British barrister and the current tenant of Coughton Court, married, first, Alan Tritton CBE, a Director of

Figure 4.3   Pon and Elizabeth, with two daughters, c. 1945.

---

5. Interviews with grandchildren and relatives: with Veronica Barran in London on 9 September 2011 and 15 September 2011, and in Birmingham on 15 October 2011; with Jim Noonan and Mary Lander in Birmingham on 15 October 2011.

Figure 4.4 Frank and Ann at their wedding, 2 June 1945.

Barclays Bank and High Sheriff of Essex, and, thereafter, John Andrew McLaren. His second daughter, Felicity, married the writer Roald Dahl in 1983 and has more recently served as the producer of the film adaptations of her late husband's works, *Matilda* and *Charlie and the Chocolate Factory*. In 1972, his third daughter, Veronica, a Deputy Regional Tribunal Judge, married the architect Marius Barran, whose father, Sir David Barran, was chairman of Shell.

A similar social trajectory would be reflected in the life of Pon's elder brother Frank d'Abreu (1904–1995). During the War, he came into contact with Margaret Ann Bowes-Lyon who served as an army nurse, and they would soon marry in 1945. Ann was the daughter of the British Wimbledon champion the Hon. Patrick Bowes-Lyon, son of the 13th Earl of Strathmore and Kinghorne, and her first cousin was Elizabeth Bowes-Lyon who married King George VI and who is remembered as Queen Elizabeth the Queen Mother. Like the Throckmortons, the Bowes-Lyons were a very well-connected family, with extensive estates that included Glamis Castle in Scotland; Streatlam Castle within County Durham; Gibside near Gateshead; and St Paul's Walden Bury. Through Ann's uncles, aunts and first cousins alone and their marriages, Frank and Ann found themselves connected to the royal family of Denmark, the Dukes of Hamilton and Leeds; the Earls of Crawford, Granville, Kinghorne and Strathmore, Portarlington, and Southesk; the Viscounts Anson and Astor; the Barons Clinton, de Longueuil and Elphinstone, to name only a few. Again, the d'Abreu-Bowes-Lyon marriage would not be without opposition, and this time, not simply because the prospective groom was in trade. Although Ann, against the wishes of her family, would convert to Catholicism prior to her marriage to Frank, Frank was nevertheless expected to present a genealogical chart to the Bowes-Lyons. However, this, their children point out, was not to ascertain whether or not he was of Portuguese patrilineal ancestry, but to ensure that he was not an illegitimate child given that his father would not be present at the wedding. Frank appears to have seized the opportunity, however, to establish once and for all that his patrilineal ancestry was Portuguese, a need he met by devising a fictive family tree.[6] Over the next decades, Frank and Margaret also grew prominent in London and Catholic society, with close relations maintained with the royal family.

Thus, we have two stories of migrant families in the Midlands, the Edaljis and the d'Abreus, unfolding simultaneously and yet in a significantly different fashion. Both families were Christian: the Edaljis, Anglican, and the D'Abreus, Catholic. Both Shapurji Edalji and John Francis d'Abreu, moreover, had married white European women from the British Isles—the first, English; the second, Irish. Perhaps surprisingly, hence, while the Anglican migrant—professedly Indian—and his mixed-race son suffered the most atrocious kinds of discrimination, the Catholic migrant—though not a shade lighter—and his mixed-race sons were able to deploy strategically their Southern European heritage and Catholic faith to place themselves successfully within wider conceptualizations of whiteness and assimilate much more easily into British society. What is so surprising about this conclusion, one might ask: the Portuguese, despite being swarthy, were Europeans, were regarded as white, had long lived in Britain, and had long married into British families, and one would be right, except that what has been presented so far—and what the d'Abreu brothers have bequeathed to us—is not the complete picture.

Let us return for a moment to the suburb of Handsworth and visit their father, Dr. John Francis d'Abreu, the original migrant. Prior to settling down in Handsworth, it appears that d'Abreu earned his qualifications in Edinburgh, Scotland, where he studied for the Conjoint Diploma of the Triple Qualification Scheme, which allowed candidates to qualify for Licentiates of the Royal College of Surgeons of Edinburgh, the Royal College of Physicians of Edinburgh and the Faculty of Physicians and Surgeons of Glasgow (Royal College of Surgeons of Edinburgh 1888-1897, 313 [entry for 27 October 1891]). While little is known about his experiences as a student, the network of people and institutions he appears to have been connected with provides some valuable insight into his early life in Britain. On the matriculation register, signed by hand in the summer of 1890, the oldest record of his life in Britain, his place of birth was presented not as Lisbon, Porto or any other place in Portugal, but as Mangalore, a town in the district of South Kanara on the southwest coast of India. Parish records in Mangalore reveal that a boy called John Francis Abreo, not d'Abreu, was indeed born around 1865 to a landed Catholic industrialist Anthony Abreo and his wife Mary Noronha. Likewise, academic records reveal that Abreo studied at the Jesuit St. Aloysius College in Mangalore and

---

6. Interviews with grandchildren and relatives: with Veronica Barran in London on 9 September 2011 and 15 September 2011, and in Birmingham on 15 October 2011; and with Francesca d'Abreu via email dated 12 August and 6 September 2011.

the Madras Medical College in Madras before setting out for Edinburgh (Royal College of Surgeons of Edinburgh, Schedule for Dr. John Francis d'Abreu). Dr. d'Abreu, it emerges, was not a Portuguese man as he or his sons claimed, but an Indo-Portuguese Catholic born, raised and educated in India, which, of course, offers a new perspective to the entire story.

While Abreo may have been the first Kanara Catholic student to settle permanently in Britain, the precise date of his entry is not known. There is also no mention of his name in the passenger lists of ships arriving in Britain between 1887 and 1893, which suggests that he might have journeyed to Abadan, Aden or the Suez by sea and then overland through Europe. What is certain is that his date of arrival was after mid-1889, which is when he completed his course of study and practice in Madras, and before 25 September 1890 when he registered at the Royal Colleges of Surgeons in Edinburgh (Royal College of Surgeons of Edinburgh, Schedule for Dr. John Francis d'Abreu). What complicates the matter further is that he presented his surname as d'Abreu on registration and later—most likely, by the time he moved to the Midlands around 1893—identified as "Portuguese." It is as d'Abreu, not Abreo, that he shall be addressed hereon.

Furthermore, the Conjoint Diploma of the Triple Qualification Scheme, for which d'Abreu sought to qualify in Scotland, had proven very popular with Indian students. Nevertheless, as both the Royal Colleges and the University of Edinburgh were generally non-residential at the time, students who did not live at home often lived with landladies who provided board and lodging (Anderson, Lynch and Phillipson 2003, 143–144). Marchmont, being an affluent neighbourhood of Edinburgh with large tenements well-suited to letting, grew particularly popular. It was in Marchmont that most Indian students in Edinburgh would reside, and yet it was not in Marchmont that d'Abreu would live earlier on. Instead, d'Abreu lived in the neighbourhood of Lauriston which was home to a large Irish immigrant population and which served as the heart of Catholic Edinburgh. In the "Schedule of the Course of Study" he had to fill out by hand in February 1891 prior to his appearance before the examiners in October that year, d'Abreu noted that he lived at 20 Lauriston Gardens, in the care of a certain "Johnstone" (Royal College of Surgeons of Edinburgh, Schedule for Dr. John Francis d'Abreu). The Scottish Census of 1891 reveals that this was an elderly Scottish widow, Esmee Johnston, who, along with her middle-aged spinster daughter, Georgina, hosted students in their flat as lodgers (Scotland, *1891 Scotland Census*, roll 352). Down the street, there stood a Catholic convent by the name of St. Catherine's that housed the Sisters of Mercy, and less than a five-minute walk away, on a parallel street, was the Catholic Church of the Sacred Heart. In the locality, there was also a Jesuit establishment which housed Jesuits serving in the parish. All of this reflects how the neighbourhood was home to several Catholic parishioners and opens up the possibility that d'Abreu, who hailed from the diocese of Mangalore that was under the Jesuits, may have deliberately chosen to live in the neighbourhood and attach himself to Catholic—particularly Jesuit—networks, though it must be said that the area was not unpopular with students. It also presents the possibility that d'Abreu may have been referred to the Johnstons by the religious or lay Catholics with whom he may have been in contact.

From the register of candidates who passed the examination of the Royal Colleges, one gathers that d'Abreu lived by 27 October 1891 at 25 Warrender Park Terrace in Marchmont, less than a ten-minute walk across The Meadows from his previous residence. The 1891-Census revealed that 25 Warrender Park Terrace constituted a block of 8 flats, half of which had lodgers. The flat into which d'Abreu moved had two rooms let out by Hugh Ritchie, a draper's clerk, who lived there with his wife Eliza, brother Robert, six daughters and one son. There were three Indian lodgers in the let rooms: Camille Saldanha, recorded as "living on own means," in one; and Joseph Michael Pereira and Pestanji Ukarji, medical students, in another. Of these, Saldanha and Pereira were Kanara Catholics and distant relations of d'Abreu; and Pereira had also been a contemporary of d'Abreu at Madras Medical College, graduating in the same year. While it is unclear whether d'Abreu already lived there (possibly sharing a room with Saldanha), but was away in April 1891 when the Census was taken, or moved in later, what is clear is that though he lived elsewhere at the start, he maintained contact with at least two other Kanara Catholics in Edinburgh and eventually moved in with them. Moreover, Pereira, in his correspondence with the Dean of Medicine at Edinburgh, specified that he left for Scotland in March 1890; and it is possible that d'Abreu and Saldanha journeyed with him (Pereira 1892).

While Pereira lived in Marchmont in April 1891, later records reveal that he lived by October 1893 at 108 Lauriston Place, less than a two-minute walk from the house in Lauriston in which d'Abreu first lived. Why Lauriston proved so pivotal to Kanara Catholic students is, of course, curious and can only be understood within the context of Edinburgh's Irish Catholic history. Although the Irish had been migrating to Scotland in significant numbers even in the early-nineteenth century, the exodus since the Great Famine of 1846–1847 witnessed the Irish-born population just in Edinburgh increase from 7,100 in 1841 to 12,514 in 1851 or from 5.3% to 6.5% of the total population (Aspinwall and McCaffrey 1985, 130–132). The high incidence of poverty in the Irish population compelled the Catholic bishops to recognize the necessity for a greater number of priests and nuns: accordingly, Bishop Gillis requested the English Provincial of the Society of Jesus in 1858 for Jesuit priests and brothers and the Sisters of Mercy (a Catholic order founded in Ireland) in 1860 for nuns to cater to the spiritual, social and educational needs of Edinburgh's Catholics. In 1859–1860, the incoming Jesuits established the Catholic Church in Lauriston Street, which, not only through masses, but also confraternities, sodalities and guilds, soon became the centre of Catholic life in the Scottish capital, while in 1861, the incoming Sisters established their presence in the Convent of St. Catherine of Siena on Lauriston Gardens.[7] The strength and number of Catholic institutions locally, along with the anti-Irish and anti-Catholic rhetoric that had grown increasingly commonplace in Scotland, fostered a strong sense of Catholic community among the Irish in the locality and provided a community to which Catholic immigrants of other ethnicities could also affix themselves.

Another question that looms over is the pecuniary status of Kanara Catholic students in Britain. Although Pereira had passed most of his examinations in Edinburgh by July 1892, he failed in Surgery, and though granted two further retakes, he failed on both occasions. In his plea for a special third sitting, he begged the Dean of Medicine to consider that "it [was] very difficult for Indians to get an unqualified assistancy in England" (Pereira 1893). "If I go back to India now without passing," he wrote in October 1893, "my life will be a ruined one. I would make not only myself but all relatives miserable by plunging them in debts" (Pereira 1893). His letter revealed that he had no sponsor save his brother, a priest in India, who did not have a salary but received a meagre sustenance fee of Rs.30 from his parishioners. "All the money to the amount of Rs.4000 which he sent me till last year was all borrowed from his friends through his priestly influence." He added that every time his brother was unable to send money, Rev. Whyte of the Catholic Church of the Sacred Heart took pity and assisted him. Nearly two weeks later, Rev. Whyte himself wrote to the Dean about how genuinely distressing Pereira's pecuniary circumstances were, and that if granted a special private examination, the Dean would be "[conferring] a very great boon on a poor, & I think, a deserving student" (Whyte 1893). While this illustrates the difficult circumstances in which several Indian students completed their education in Britain, it also provides insights into the role that personal links with Catholic institutions could play in providing Catholic students from India with at least an imagined, though often real, buffer against extreme hardships through greater social capital in home and host societies.

Rev. Whyte informed the Dean that Pereira's friends (most likely, d'Abreu and Saldanha, whose lives also centred around Lauriston) frequently wrote to him about Pereira's circumstances (Whyte 1893). D'Abreu and Saldanha, however, appear not to have relied on Catholic institutions for financial

---

7. Peter Anson (1970, 299) notes that the Jesuits were "given a missionary district comprising the south and west parts of the city of Edinburgh, extending into the country as far as the Pentland Hills, inclusive of the villages of Colinton, Juniper Green, Balerno and Ratho, in which Irish Catholic families had settled."

support, as Pereira did. D'Abreu's nephew, Abundius (also D'Abreu), who migrated to Ireland around 1918, wrote in his diaries that his uncle John Francis d'Abreu hailed from a relatively affluent landed family. His uncle's father and, thus, his own grandfather (Antony) was a "gentleman farmer" with substantial landholdings, and his uncle's mother and his own grandmother (Catherine) was the daughter and heiress of Christopher Lobo, the proprietor of a distillery that had a monopoly over the production and sales of liquor in South Kanara (Diaries of Dr. Abundius D'Abreu [hereafter, Diaries], entry for 8 August 1951). Following the early demise of his father, John Francis d'Abreu received a share of the estate which he sold to finance his passage to, and education in, Britain (Diaries, entry for 8 August 1951; also, 26 November 1960). This is not to suggest that John Francis did not have strong links to Catholic—particularly Jesuit—institutions himself, but simply that these links may not necessarily have been of a pecuniary nature. In fact, before proceeding to Madras, he had studied at the Jesuit St. Aloysius College (in Mangalore) of which his great-uncle, Lawrence Lobo Prabhu, had been principal benefactor. Saldanha, likewise, was a man of independent means, as the 1891-Scottish Census indicated. While Kanara Catholic students in Britain often hailed from relatively affluent families, that did not mean that their circumstances never changed once in Britain: of his maternal uncle Isidore Noronha who accompanied or immediately followed John Francis, Abundius wrote that "he died in Cheltenham in poor circumstances," largely because he did not qualify as a doctor and was "too fond of good-living, racing and jollification," spending "his share of the fortune" (Diaries, 8 August 1951).

Returning to the subject of d'Abreu's Catholic connections, it is evident that d'Abreu was familiar with the Jesuits who were responsible for the ecclesiastical jurisdiction of the diocese of Mangalore since the late-1870s, and it may have been his Jesuit contacts in India who introduced him to the Jesuits in Lauriston. It is also of interest that following his education in Edinburgh, Dr. John Francis d'Abreu moved to Handsworth, a suburb of Birmingham, which, as discussed earlier, had also seen an influx of Irish Catholics during the Famines. Given that d'Abreu had no relatives in Birmingham, that he should choose to head to Handsworth suggests that he may have been advised to do so by the Sisters of Mercy with whom he grew well-acquainted in Edinburgh and who were also active in Handsworth. D'Abreu may have known, or learnt from his Irish acquaintances in Edinburgh, of Birmingham's rising importance as a node within Irish Catholic networks in Britain and, hence, decided to carve out his career amidst a people whose social life and medical needs he had grown intimately familiar with in Lauriston. It is also noteworthy that it was the vicar of *St. Mary's Refuge*, Rev. Lawrence Henry, who introduced d'Abreu to Teresa Mary Noonan of Dudley, whom he would marry in 1895.

To put it more succinctly, records suggest that it was his Catholic upbringing and Jesuit education in Mangalore that enabled him to attach himself to Jesuit networks and the Sisters of Mercy in Lauriston. Likewise, it may have been his eventual integration within local Irish Catholic networks in Lauriston and his connectedness to the Sisters of Mercy there that prompted him, perhaps on being recommended, to relocate to Handsworth, where he would soon be in contact with the local Sisters of Mercy, be accepted into local Irish society and even take an Irish wife. Furthermore, Stonyhurst College, the Jesuit public school at which his sons were educated, also happened to be the institution where some of the Jesuit founders of St. Aloysius College in Mangalore were educated, St. Aloysius being where d'Abreu himself had studied. Following the Second World War, moreover, his son Frank—now Lieutenant-Colonel—was appointed consultant general surgeon to Westminster Hospital and, from 1950, also served as honorary surgeon to the hospital of St John and St Elizabeth in London, a charitable hospital run by the Sisters of Mercy in London and affiliated with the Sovereign Military Order of Malta (Royal College of Surgeons of England 2015).

Thus, Kanara Catholic students in Britain, while sharing some similarities with other Indian students, such as in their choice of subjects, often differed from them in various aspects, such as in their greater willingness to culturally identify with the West, stay on and even intermarry with Europeans, and their ability to affix themselves to local Catholic networks (Menezes, 2014). Particularly apparent in the case of Kanara Catholics such as the d'Abreus was the role that a Jesuit-influenced Catholicism, with its emphasis on universalism, the transnational organization of the Catholic Church and the transnational linkages between Catholic institutions, could play in facilitating the assimilation of Catholic immigrants from South Asia in Britain. Yet, while Kanara Catholic students shared religious and often cultural similarities with local (chiefly Irish, but also English and Scottish) Catholics, their swarthier skin tones and Portuguese surnames, while not necessarily restricting their assimilation into local Catholic society, prevented them from passing as "Irish," "English" or "Scottish," though they would not always identify as "Indian" either. For some, such as John Francis d'Abreu who stayed on in Britain following his medical education, "Portuguese" and even "Spanish" proved popular as self-identifications, more plausible in light of their history, names and appearance, and expedient in facilitating their absorption into the wider European fold. There had long been well-respected Portuguese doctors (often of Jewish origin), with surnames such as Gonsalves and Pereira, in cities like Birmingham and London, and Kanara Catholic doctors could take on the roles of the familiar Portuguese medical figures in local society. By around 1893, when d'Abreu moved to Handsworth, he would have been more intimately familiar with the racial hierarchies in Britain and the challenges they could have posed, and it is not too hard to surmise why he identified as Portuguese as he journeyed in pursuit of a new life. It is clear that d'Abreu settled rather comfortably among the Irish, stepping into the shoes of the familiar and long-accepted Portuguese medical figures. It is, thus, within a Catholic (particularly Irish and Portuguese), and not just Indian, migrant context that the experiences of Kanara Catholic migrants such as d'Abreu ought to be understood.

What also ought to be stressed is the consciousness evident among some Kanara Catholics about their subjective positioning in the racial hierarchies of their host societies and their ability to alter favourably their positioning by strategically embracing plausible alternative identities. In his diaries, Abundius D'Abreu noted: "Colour bar is a natural phenomenon. It operates mostly against the Negroes. The other colour brown is a shade of ranging degree [and] is not looked upon with aversion. As a matter of fact, it is appreciated as long as the features, the appearance are of the Aryan type." (Diaries, 7 April 1965) It was precisely a consciousness of the potentialities presented by their particular shades of brown that enabled John Francis d'Abreu to successfully pass as "Portuguese" and his sons to conceal even more resolutely their Indian racial heritage.[8] As seen, one son, Pon d'Abreu, would be remembered by former students and colleagues simply as a "Portuguese man" whose family moved "from Goa to Malta and then on to England" (Moody 2003, 18). There were times, however, when identifying as "Indian" was more expedient, such as Joseph Michael Pereira's request to the Dean for a special examination and a request put forward by a Camillo Norbert Saldanha to the Principal Secretary of State for Home Affairs for a grant or temporary employment on grounds of being in financial difficulties (Saldanha 1898). Several Kanara Catholics applying for scholarships would also have to stress their being Indian to qualify for scholarships reserved for Indians. The case of Francis Xavier D'Souza is particularly insightful in this regard, and it also showcases official attitudes to Kanara Catholics seen to be both "Brahmin" and "Catholic" (Menezes 2014).

Strangely, however, while the story of George Edalji is widely remembered, the visible minority man, the story of the d'Abreus is entirely forgotten, merged into the annals of white British history. While the d'Abreus were indeed quite exceptional in who they married, their case being one wherein Indian migrants effectively concealed their Indian origins so as to quickly and successfully assimilate within local European populations in their host societies and often not be seen or remembered as Indian migrants was hardly unique. Several Indian migrants would, likewise, by situationally over-emphasizing or understating different markers of their identity, whether race, religion, caste, class or gender, adopt embellished or wholly fictitious identities

---

8. Interviews with John Francis d'Abreu's grandchildren, Veronica Barran (London) and Mary Lander (Solihull), 15 October 2011.

and adjust favourably their subjective positioning along multiple intersecting axes of privilege and exclusion in India and their various destinations.

As noted, it was not just across, but also beyond, the British world that the Catholics of South Kanara travelled. Likewise, their routes and careers as migrants were shaped not solely by their legal-political status as British subjects, but also by their identities, affiliations and agendas as Catholics. The Roman Catholic Church was the archetype of a transnational religious organization connecting parishes in distant South Kanara with the Holy See and parishes the world over; and so were the Carmelite and Jesuit religious orders present in South Kanara, which linked local parishes with missionary-sending provinces in Europe and other missions-fields. In a recent study, Seema Alavi explored how "outlawed" Indian Muslim subjects from British India—by tapping into religious movements within Islam that long sought to unify the *umma* and utilising webs of connections deriving from older forms of Islamic connectivity (such as kinship ties, student contacts and religious commentaries)—could journey across, and locate themselves at the intersections between, the British, Ottoman, Dutch and Russian Empires (Alavi 2011). Similarly, Kanara Catholic British subjects, by leveraging notions of Catholic universalism and tapping into older forms of Catholic connectivity, could journey across the multiple empires of the day and locate themselves at the intersections between those empires and the Catholic world, grafting themselves on to imperial and religious networks, while carving out their own transnational networks. Such strategies were also common among Anglo-Indians and Indo-Portuguese Catholic migrants from Goa and South Kanara (Menezes 2014). In Bangalore, Bombay, Calcutta and Madras, but more so in the Anglophone West, it was not uncommon for Catholics from South Kanara with Portuguese surnames such as Farias and Noronha to identify as Portuguese or to anglicize their surnames to Ferris and Newnes and identify thereafter as English, Scottish, Irish or Welsh, albeit not always successfully.

In the case of the d'Abreus and other Kanara Catholics, their claim to be Portuguese was not entirely ungrounded, given the particular history of the Catholics in South Kanara and the perceived ambiguities concerning their racial heritage (Menezes 2014, 5–14). Nestled between Goa and Malabar along the southwest coast of British India, South Kanara had been the site of one of the earliest colonial encounters between Asia and Europe—more specifically, South Asia and Portugal. As early as 15 September 1498, the Portuguese explorer Vasco da Gama and his crew briefly stopped by some rocky islets just off the coast they referred to as Canara (or Kanara) and set up a *padrão* (commemorative stone pillar with a cross) there that they dedicated to *Santa Maria*.[9] While missionary activities ensued in the region from 1500, it was

---

9. This was the last of the three *padrões* they had been instructed by the King of Portugal to set up, the first two having been erected in Malindi and Calicut (Ravenstein 1898, 80).

once Portugal had acquired a stronghold over the local port-town of Mangalore that a regular Franciscan mission was established in Canara. Under the Portuguese Franciscans, churches were set up across Canara, which was placed under the ecclesiastical jurisdiction of Goa. After Goa fell to the Portuguese in 1510, the Portuguese governor Afonso de Albuquerue formally introduced the *politica dos casamentos* (marriage policy), which encouraged intermarriages between European settlers and indigenous women with the hope of securing the Portuguese presence. Likewise, as a result of the missionary endeavours of the Franciscans, Jesuits and Dominicans, as also Augustinians, Theatines and Carmelites, Christianity was soon firmly established in Goa, not simply among those of lower castes, but also their high-caste counterparts, such as the Brahmins and Kshatriyas who converted *en masse* in areas such as Divar and Carambolim (de Sousa 1710). Between the 1560s and 1760s, there were multiple waves of Catholic and Brahmin migration from Goa to Canara, where, despite there being a local Catholic presence already, those of Goan origin soon formed the majority.[10]

In the same period as Brahmins and Catholics had been emigrating from Goa, *nayaka*s and *poligar*s across the Malabar coast and Tamil country, as Susan Bayly noted, had been recruiting Brahmins and literate service people to settle in their expanding domains (Bayly 1989, 48, 57–58). In Canara, it were the *nayaka*s of Ikkeri (Keladi) and petty rajas who invited the Catholics and Brahmins leaving Goa, offering them lands for settlement and cultivation.[11] While such acts, as Bayly argued, were often strategic, enabling the ruler to enhance his prestige by "incorporating a new locus of power into his networks," it meant, nonetheless, that the Goan immigrants could integrate themselves within the shared social order in Canara under the patronage of its rulers (Bayly 1989, 397; Conlon 1977, 14–48). Moreover, Portugal, despite its general decline, remained a sufficiently important player in Canara to continue securing privileges for Catholics (who remained Portuguese subjects) in treaties with the *nayaka*s even as late as 1714.[12] Although deteriorat-

---

10. The reasons for emigrating from Goa were varied, but generally related to escaping famines, invasions by the Bijapur Adilshahis and Marathas, and the extension of the Portuguese Inquisition to Goa (1560) which targeted indigenous Catholics believed to have reverted to non-Christian customs in addition to *cristãos-novos* (Jewish and Muslim "converts"). Shastry 2000; Ames 2000; Farias 1999, 28–40. For more on Saraswat Brahmin migration to Canara, see Conlon 1977, 14–48;

11. For Frank Conlon, the Ikkeri *nayaka*s who were building their power on the remains of the Vijayanagara Empire may have also sought to recruit outsiders in revenue capacities to consolidate their control over and against local power structures (Conlon 1977, 32).

12. These privileges included protection of Catholics, their churches and missions. For Portugal, the Catholics now served as the means of perpetuating its own influence in Canara (Shastry 2000, 263).

ing Portuguese-*nayaka* relations left Catholics adversely affected on occasion, the treaties ensured that Catholic interests were largely secure. Thus, the Catholics could embed themselves within the indigenous social order, while remaining part of the wider Portuguese world. Even in the late nineteenth and early twentieth century, furthermore, their social organization reflected the persistence of caste identities among them, even if notions of ritual pollution had been abandoned.[13] As Rowena Robinson noted, the Christianity that entered the Konkan coast in the 16th century revealed a hierarchical vision of society (clergy, knights and labourers) prevalent in Catholic Europe that allowed Catholic beliefs and practices to accommodate what were regarded as local social hierarchies, even while officially proscribing indigenous religious rituals (Robinson 2003, 72). Hence, despite official strategies of cultural de-paganization and Lusitanization imposed *from above*, converts in Goa could "reconstruct their socio-cultural system" around churches and develop a whole hierarchical caste order *from below* that was tolerated by Portuguese missionaries even before Roberto de Nobili arrived in Madurai (Robinson 2003, 71–72). This Catholic caste system comprising of *Bamonn*s (Brahmins), *Chardo*s (*kṣatriyas-vaiśyas*) and *Sudir*s (*śūdras*), Robinson observed, was similar to, but separate from and not ideologically integrated with, the Hindu caste order (Robinson 2003, 71–72). When the Catholics of Goa migrated to Canara, their distinctive social organization was extended to a new, but similar, social landscape where it was incorporated into the region's shared social order.

By the late-nineteenth century, the Catholics in South Kanara comprised at least three loosely-defined groups formed along lines of language, caste and class. The first group comprised of Tulu- and Kannada-speaking local converts of the fishing and seafaring castes (generally known as *Gaudi*s), who, along with some *Sudir*s, also cultivated *Bamonn* lands. The second was much smaller and comprised of local converts (*Padval*s) supposedly of Jain origin. The third was the most numerous and culturally- and politically-dominant, comprising Konkani-speaking Catholics of Goan origin: mainly *Bamonn*s and *Charodi*s (*Chardo*s) who formed the landed, merchant and professional classes, and *Sudir*s (Shudras) who formed an artisan or service class.[14] It is mainly with the third group that this chapter is concerned.[15] Moreover, by the 1760s,

---

13. For further information on persistence of caste identities following conversion, see Fuller 1976; Mosse 1996; Oddie 2013, 6 and Powell 2013.
14. The *Bamonn*s, furthermore, were characterized by an internal hierarchical stratification, with *Sirudegar* as the highest subdivision, followed by *Aldhengar, Cutdnangar, Divodegar, Natnolegar, Sasragar, Puruvargar* and *Maidegar*. See Maffei 1883, 155.
15. Although notions of ritual purity and pollution no longer governed their social interaction, Catholics of different groups seldom intermarried, were concentrated in different areas, were often catered to by different parishes and, between 1850 and 1950, were increasingly drawn into a collaborative relationship.

both Portuguese power and *nayaka* rule had waned in Canara, which came under the Sultans of Mysore, whose authority was challenged over the next decades by the locally-ascendant British against whom Mysore waged four Anglo-Mysore Wars. Following the decisive defeat of Mysore in 1799, Canara ceded to the British East India Company and was incorporated as a district into the Madras Presidency of British India. In 1859-1860, it was bifurcated into North and South Kanara. Given the troubled relationship of the Catholics in Canara with Tipu Sultan of Mysore, Britain acquired in Canara a largely loyal Catholic population that had been under European and indigenous cultural influence for three centuries and could serve, as a Revenue Administrator noted, a "valuable connecting link" between Europeans and locals (Stokes 1885; Saldanha 1938, 80-81; Menezes 2014, 8). Likewise, the Catholics found in "neutral" Britain an accommodating partner and protector to replace a weakened Portugal still embroiled in bitter ecclesiastical rivalries with the Holy See, and to provide education, employment and trade opportunities across its vast empire. Although the nineteenth and early twentieth centuries witnessed the Catholics increasingly come under British cultural influence, assert their "Britishness" and identify as "loyalists," such alignment with Britain was often interest-driven. The Catholics were among the earliest beneficiaries of English education and government employment in the region, became key players in the imperial coffee and tile trade, and migrated across the wider British world often as imperial auxiliaries.

As the region had been under Portugal for nearly 300 years before ceding to Britain for nearly 150 years in 1799, the Catholics therein had developed a distinctively-hybrid culture that reflected varying degrees of Brahmanical, Portuguese and British influences. In Portuguese India, conversion to Catholicism and the adoption of Portuguese names and culture were often enough for Catholics to be seen as Portuguese, and when territories that were formerly Portuguese passed on to the British, it was not uncommon for Catholic families with a Portuguese religious, cultural and/or racial heritage therein to be identified simply as Portuguese. Nevertheless, as Catholic families in Kanara had stopped identifying as Portuguese by the 1830s, it was rather irregular and obviously strategic that Kanara Catholic families such as the d'Abreus would choose to identify as such as late as the early twentieth century when overseas. Likewise, as Kanara Catholics had been British subjects after 1799, their claims to have been British or Anglo-Indian were not entirely ungrounded. The 1911-census expanded the scope of the term "Anglo-Indian" to include Eurasians, while the Government of India Act (1935) reinforced this meaning through its definition of "Anglo-Indian" as "a person whose father or any of whose other male progenitors in the male line is or was of European descent but who is a native of India" (Gait 1913, 140; Government of India 1935, 216 and The People of India 1950, 162, Article

366/2). The new term, while ignoring persons with a European female progenitor, included in its scope patrilineally mixed-race descendants not just of the British, but also the Portuguese, Dutch and French. However, not just due to the privileging of English in the term, but also its former association with British persons residing in India (similar to Domiciled Europeans), most Kanara Catholics—like several Eurasians of non-English descent—perceived themselves excluded from its scope, identifying instead as "Indian Christian." Hence, such self-identifications as "British" or "Anglo-Indian" were also often strategically made to obscure one's Indian racial heritage and circumvent the structural barriers to geographic and professional mobility one might have faced as a result (Menezes 2014, 5–14).

While at first these cases might simply illustrate how identities in the colonial period may have been fluid, flexible and situational, and how the categories of colonizer and colonized as well were hardly fixed and exclusive, but permeable and negotiable, placing these cases within the historical context of Indian migration would offer different insights. In the late nineteenth and early twentieth centuries, India might have been regarded as Britain's most valuable possession, and Indians might have, in principle, enjoyed the legal-political status of British subjects. Yet, in practice, soon after they arrived on the shores of Britain, the White Dominions (Canada, South Africa, Australia and New Zealand) and the United States, most found themselves confronted with discriminatory immigration legislation and popular prejudices that illustrated the unevenness of a shared British subjecthood (Menezes 2014, 120–126; Banerjee 2010, 17). Much has been written about the discriminatory legislation against "Asiatic"/non-white immigration introduced in these destinations since the late-nineteenth century, particularly with respect to the Chinese, but also Indians albeit British subjects (De Lepervanche 1984; Baas 2010; Bald 2013). The Immigration Restriction Acts of New Zealand in 1899 and Australia in 1901, and the 1917-Immigration Act in the United States, for instance, classed British Indians as prohibited immigrants and almost entirely restricted their entry in the following period, though debates ensuing over implications of their status as British subjects compelled the eventual introduction of certain exceptions, such as exemptions from the infamous Dictation Tests and temporary admission to students, visitors and merchants (see Bilimoria and Ganguly-Scrase 1988, 7, 19 and actual cases in *Auckland Star*, 10 August 1912; Abercrombie 1919; Petition on behalf of Indians and Afghans 1903, 10–12). Nevertheless, the numbers of Indian immigrants steadily declined. In Australia, while the restrictive White Australia Policy was still in force, the number of India-born therein declined from 7000 in 1901 to 2900 in 1947; yet, there continued to be a small number of Indians who successfully immigrated, whether by taking advantage of loopholes in the law or even as seamen abandoning ships and soldiers deserting troops and often escaping surveillance thereafter (Blunt 2005, 139; McGillivray and Smith 1997, 31; De Lepervanche 1984).

Although Australia eventually made provisions for the entry of mixed-race Indians, the policies were just as restrictive. Even by June 1949, Anglo-Indians were required to be "predominantly European in race or descent," "predominantly European in appearance," and "European in outlook, accustomed to a European way of life and of a type who could be readily absorbed into an Australian community" just to be eligible for admission (Heyes 1949). While having predominantly European blood meant being over-50%-European by ancestry, which had to be established through documentary evidence, a surprisingly large number of applications still met this criterion. Hence, the rules were tightened even further, and by 1950, one had to be at least 75% European by ancestry even to be eligible (Blunt 2005, 44–45). Even before these changes, it was not unknown for those over-50%-European racially to be refused admission, if they were not sufficiently European by appearance; and the application form explicitly solicited information about the origins of parents and grandparents, the degree of Indian blood, and two photographs, often to ascertain European appearance. Nevertheless, more Anglo-Indians and even Indian Christians than official records suggest managed to circumvent the barriers, whether by assuming false names/identities, manipulating birth records, providing fictive genealogies, using light and cosmetics to alter their images and pass as European. This, however, makes it difficult to trace the Kanara Catholics who settled in Australia in this period, but as, so to speak, "invisible migrants."

Furthermore, as Indo-Portuguese Catholics, whether from Goa or South Kanara, journeyed to Australia as seamen long before and even after the introduction of the abovementioned legislation, it is difficult to identify who the first Kanara Catholic—outside the maritime professions—to visit Australia may have been. Family records in Mangalore suggest that a certain Peter Fernandes was the first to visit Australia in the period not as a seaman. While Australian newspaper records indicate that a Peter Fernandes did indeed journey to Australia in the 1930s, this Peter was supposed to have toured Australia and New Zealand in 1935 and 1938 as part of the All-India hockey team and the Prince of Manavadar's Indian hockey team respectively. These newspaper accounts noted that he lived in Sind, played hockey with the Bombay Customs Club and was a member of the Indian hockey team that won gold at the 1936 Berlin Olympics ("Hockey" 1938; "India v. Western Australia" 1938; "Indian Hockey Team" 1938; "Indian Hockey Team Will Play in Sydney" 1938; "Indians and N.S.W. XI" 1938; "Why Are Indians So Good" 1938; "Would Welcome Match Against Queensland" 1938). Further research into this Peter's background revealed that he was born on 15 September 1916 in Karachi; studied at St. Patrick's High School there, as did many Goan and Kanara Catholics in Pakistan; and also played for the Karachi Goan Association team. Consequently, the Karachi Goan Association, along with various Goan media outlets, has celebrated him since as the first Goan to represent India at the Olympics (Barretto 2000 and Rodriguez n.d.). However, whether Peter was really from the Goan Catholic community, or was just adopted as "Goan" by the Goan Catholics of Pakistan, or simply identified as "Goan" for the sake of convenience, as did many Kanara Catholics who lived in host regions with relatively tiny Indo-Portuguese Catholic communities, has yet to be verified.

What official records reveal is that, by 1931, a daughter of Dr. John Francis d'Abreu managed to enter Australia with her English husband and live in Melbourne without raising any suspicion about her origins (Commonwealth of Australia. State of Victoria 1931, 17). It was in 1930 that Kathleen d'Abreu (c. 1903–1990) married Eric Herman Booth, son of Norman Parr Booth and a graduate of the University of Melbourne, at the Oratory of St. Philip Neri in Birmingham ("Australians Abroad" 1930). It was incidentally at the Oratory that her brother Pon d'Abreu also worshipped while studying medicine at Birmingham University, prior to his graduation in 1930. The Booths were an English family that had settled in Australia in the mid-1920s and grown particularly prominent in the commercial and social life of Tasmania. Norman Booth, born in Yorkshire around 1879, had followed his father's footsteps to join Cadbury Brothers Limited at Bournville in Birmingham. In 1901, he joined the business as its first analytical chemist, and his research was central to the development of the company's now iconic Dairy Milk chocolate launched in 1905 and Bournville Cocoa launched in 1906 (Chapman 1979). By 1919, Cadbury had merged with its lead competitor J. S. Fry & Sons; and thereafter, it joined Pascall to establish its presence in Australia. By 1924, Norman moved with his family to Tasmania, where Cadbury's had opened its first overseas factory at Claremont in 1922, and took over as chairman and managing director of Cadbury-Fry-Pascall Ltd. Of Norman's two sons, the younger, Phillip, was a surgeon who was engaged at one point to Margaret O'Grady, daughter of Sir James O'Grady, the former Governor of Tasmania ("In the Social Realm" 1932 and "Miss Margaret O'Grady's Wedding" 1933). Phillip eventually married Winifred Daphne Booth (née Denny), daughter of Bernard Denny, a wealthy partner of the London Stock Exchange, and herself a philanthropist whose estate, through the W.D. Booth Trust, has provided nearly $6 million for charitable causes in Tasmania (Burgess 2017). Thus, though she had an Indian father, Kathleen, being British-born, light-skinned, married to an Englishman and known thence as Mrs. Kathleen Booth, a perfectly English name, managed both to migrate to Australia as an Englishwoman and assimilate within its highest echelons at a time when discriminatory legislation against "Asiatic" immigration was still rife.

To further illustrate how one could overcome structural barriers to their geographic or professional mobility through ethnic reidentification, a particularly curious case worth mentioning is that of a young Englishman by the name of E.C. Francis. In the Western Australian press, Francis was described as "a young graduate of Cambridge University" with "prospecting experience in the Northern Territory," who showed up in Perth one day in 1929 with fine stream tin specimens that he had supposedly obtained between Collier Bay and Camden Harbour in northwestern Australia. Soon, "several leading Perth businessmen" rushed to form a mining syndicate that at first they would call the Francis Syndicate, but later the Kimberley Exploitation Syndicate. The syndicate secured the first pick in the ensuing rush for mining concessions, obtaining 1.5 million acres between Harding River and York Sound that it then appointed Francis to prospect ("Tin in the North" 1929; "The North-West Big Mineral Concessions" 1929). His optimistic report supposedly sent the £1 shares soaring up to £30 in May 1929. On 18 January 1930, *The West Australian* reported that Francis, now described as "a permanent director of Kimberley Exploitations Limited":

> expressed optimism for Kimberley potentialities as a mining field. During the past nine years he has travelled over most of Australia, examining mineral deposits and exploring large tracts of country. In Western Australia he has visited all the existing gold sources, excepting the districts of Hall's Creek and Ravenswood. His work has taken him particularly into Northern Australia, and during the past five years he has spent much time in North-West Australia, Arnhem Land and the country surrounding the Gulf of Carpentaria.
>
> ("Kimberley Development" 1930)

In a statement issued the previous day, Francis reaffirmed his belief that "within the next decade the mineral value of North-West Kimberley will be demonstrated in a degree as yet unrealised," and clarified that "his immediate object is to examine more fully the certain discoveries of gold and tin on No. 1 Concession of his company" so he could report progress within that year to its shareholders. ("Kimberley Development" 1930)

Later that year, however, a mining engineer of another prospecting party questioned Francis's findings, declaring his optimism unjustified ("Mining" 1930; "In the Kimberley" 1930; "Kimberley Tin Fields" 1929; "Kimberley Exploration Syndicate" 1930). Rumours soon circulated that the man known as Edward Carey Francis may not have been who he claimed. *The Sunday Times* reported that not only did he bear a striking resemblance to a missing Angelo Francis J. Saldanha who worked in farms and orchards, but also he claimed to have been born in Kent (England) where Saldanha was also born. Moreover, Cambridge apparently did not issue the BSc degree that Saldanha claimed he had earned, and a letter from a genuine Edward Carey

Francis, a Cambridge-educated mathematician and CMS missionary in Kenya who was formerly Fellow and Lecturer at Peterhouse (Cambridge), established that there was no other person by that name in Cambridge following the War ("A Mystery of Names" 1930). On investigating the matter further, it becomes clear that a certain Angelo Saldanha did indeed journey to Fremantle in April 1922 as an assisted immigrant, whereafter he worked first for a farmer in Dudinin, then orchardists in York and Bridgetown, and then as a mining agent in Perth by 1925, before vanishing off the official record by the end of 1930 (Incoming passenger list to Fremantle on "Omar" 1922 and "Missing Friends" 1930). Further investigation revealed that this Saldanha was the British-born son of Martin Sebastian Saldanha, a Kanara Catholic barrister who had settled in England at the turn of the century and who had often identified as "Portuguese." Thus, being British-born, European in names and appearance, and obscuring one's Indian heritage (identifying one's Kanara Catholic parents as "British" or "Portuguese") opened up the possibility for the mixed-race children of Kanara Catholics (who may even have had 50% or more "Asiatic" blood) to pass as European and migrate to Australia. It is noteworthy, moreover, that Saldanha chose to adopt an English name soon after he left the hinterland for Perth, suggesting that while he did not see his Portuguese surname as a liability with respect to his entering Australia, he regarded having a British surname as more advantageous in terms of access to privilege and opportunity.

Figure 4.5 Angelo Saldanha (aka E.C. Francis) in Western Australia (Sunday Times [Perth], 26 May 1929, 7.

Interestingly, his British-born sister, Christina Saldanha, a teacher by profession, journeyed to New York in 1939, providing her nationality as "Portuguese," and remained in the United States thereafter (Passenger and Crew

Lists of Vessels 1897–1957, 1939, Serial T715, Roll 6420, Line 1, p. 94). Among the other Kanara Catholics that made their way to the United States since the late-1890s, one, Wilfred "Seuldane" (changed from Saldanha), a marine engineer, was provided as French by race and Indian by nationality during the first leg of his voyage in September 1906 from Karachi to Saigon, then just Indian by nationality on the second leg between Saigon and Moji (Japan), and finally, just English by nationality on the final leg between Moji and San Francisco, where he would work as a clerk before moving to Europe and eventually returning to India (Crew Lists of Vessels Arriving at San Francisco. 1905–1954, Serial M1416, Rolls 2, 4; *Crocker-Langley San Francisco Directory* 1909, 1423). Yet another, Ignatius Monteiro, who found employment on a ship sailing to the States and worked as a chef in New York later, had his race provided as "white" and birthplace "Portugal" in the 1940-US Census (U.S. Bureau of Census 1940, Place: New York, Roll: T627-2629, p. 2A).

What these cases demonstrate is that, throughout the colonial period, there were Indian immigrants who managed to circumvent the structural barriers they faced to their mobility and assimilation to access, and achieve their ends

Figure 4.6   Angelo Saldanha; Daily News [Perth], 11 April 1929, 1 [misspelled as D.C. Francis]).

within, regions otherwise restricted to Indians. While Kanara Catholics were not always successful at their attempts at "passing," they did not always take recourse to "passing" only to circumvent the structural barriers they faced either. At times, they appear to have so greatly appropriated notions of imperial citizenship that they also viewed the empire as an expanse for Kanara Catholic colonization under the British flag and asserted their equality in this respect with the English, Scottish, Welsh and Irish (Menezes 2014, 90–126). This was particularly evident across Central and Eastern Africa, Mesopotamia, Persia and the Persian Gulf, and Southeast Asia, which had a long history of Indian and particularly Goanese subimperialism. In these contexts, again, they identified as Portuguese or British mainly out of expedience, but not always to circumvent structural barriers.

At other times, Kanara Catholics were more subversive in their aims, such as in the case of Camille Saldanha who had accompanied John Francis d'Abreu to Edinburgh in the 1890s. The 1891-Census had listed him rather plainly as a gentleman living on independent means. While little was known of Saldanha's career, the author's research into the archives of the Dublin and London Metropolitan Police, as well as British and American intelligence records, revealed that though he came from a family celebrated in official circles in British India for their commitment to the imperial cause, he had become a registered overseas agent of the anti-British Swadeshi Party in India and shuttled between London, Dublin and New York in the early-1900s, serving as a secret undercover nexus between Irish, Irish American, Indian and Japanese anti-British revolutionaries. Later, it appears that he settled on the west coast of the United States, where the overseas South Asian revolutionary movement Ghadar was active, under a yet unidentified guise. Again, by situationally adopting various identities, "Indian," "Catholic," "British" and "Portuguese," Saldanha could access and embed himself simultaneously in several transnational imperial and anti-imperial networks, far beyond the pale of suspicion of British authorities and yet pursuing a most productive career towards Irish and Indian independence as a subversive revolutionary (Menezes 2014, 169–173).

To conclude, it ought to be clarified that while these cases were undoubtedly unique, they were not isolated and exceptional, and these microhistories are considered mainly to recreate the larger picture of the experiences of Kanara Catholic migrants, which these reflect. As members of both an empire and a church that spread across borders, Kanara Catholics were able to travel not simply as British subjects, but also as Catholics, and travel not just to Britain and the rest of the British Empire, but also to Rome and the rest of the Catholic world. Catholicism went beyond just facilitating migration to also aid assimilation. Wherever Kanara Catholics travelled or settled, they often found themselves able to access—and embed themselves within—stronger, wider or simply different Catholic networks through the strategic exercise of their Catholic identities and even by adopting alternative ethnic identities for which being Catholic was a necessary marker. They were able to join Catholic churches and associations, access Catholic facilities for healthcare and education, reside and practice in Catholic suburbs, and even intermarry Catholics of other ethnicities. That being said, not all Kanara Catholics sought to obscure their Indian heritage or were strategic in choosing their identifications, and certainly not all were successful in achieving their aims even if they did do so. It would also be incorrect to suggest that migrants always shifted proactively between their multiple orientations bearing potential advantages in mind, for such identity adjustment may have often proceeded as a reactionary strategy against structural barriers they faced, such as institutionalized discrimination and popular prejudices.

Even Catholicism, which emerged as their key resource for assimilation in several destinations, could also serve as a barrier to assimilation within the mainstreams of their respective societies, allowing some assimilation, but mainly within spaces reserved for Catholics. By highlighting the abovementioned cases, the intention is mainly to draw attention to how some—and more specifically, often elite—Kanara Catholic migrants could strategically deploy their legal-political status as British subjects, religious affiliation with the Catholic Church, familiarity with Catholic and British institutional and cultural resources, real or putative racial admixture as well as European names and culture, to access and attach themselves to more established local and Catholic European networks and render themselves invisible to the observer of South Asian migration. These cases demonstrate that the experiences of migrants were not entirely dependent on prevalent attitudes and policies in host societies and stress the need to consider migrant agency, an aspect strangely neglected in a voluminous literature that often appears preoccupied with the discriminatory mechanisms of border control. The neglect has also meant that the more complex task of tracking, enumerating and exploring the experiences of Indian migrants who may not have identified as Indian and may have assimilated into local populations also remains neglected, almost all research, hence, relating simply to visible Indian diasporas and not the substantial "invisible" migrant networks that developed alongside. Yet, without attending to the invisible migrants, this research makes clear, our understanding of South Asian migration can never be wholly accurate or complete.

Acknowledgments

This paper is based on research undertaken while the author was still a PhD candidate in the Faculty of History at the University of Cambridge. The paper was first presented at the Centre on Migration, Policy and Society (COMPAS) at the University of Oxford in 2014, while the author served as a Visiting Academic there. It was then presented at the XXI World Congress of the International Association for the History of Religions convened in Erfurt, Germany, in 2015, while the author served as Postdoctoral Research Fellow at Heythrop College, University of London. At the time of its publication, the author serves as Associate Fellow at the Institute of Commonwealth Studies, University of London, and Honorary Fellow at University College London. The author is grateful to all of the mentioned institutions and their staff. He is particularly indebted to Veronica Barran, the granddaughter of Dr. John Francis d'Abreu, for her generosity, support and cooperation while the research for this paper was still ongoing.

References

"A Mystery of Names: Echo of Kimberley Expedition." 1930. *Sunday Times*, 16 November 1930, 9.

Abercrombie, John W. 1919. Letter to Hon. H.G. Osborne, House of Representatives, Washington, DC, 18 January 1919, National Archives, Washington, DC, United States.

Alavi, Seema. 2011. "'Fugitive Mullahs and Outlawed Fanatics': Indian Muslims in Nineteenth Century Trans-Asiatic Imperial Rivalries." *Modern Asian Studies* 45(6): 1337–1382. https://doi.org/10.1017/S0026749X11000266

Ames, Glenn. 2000. *Renascent Empire? The House of Braganza and the Quest for Stability in Portuguese Monsoon Asia, c. 1640-1683*. Amsterdam: Amsterdam University Press. https://doi.org/10.5117/9789053563823

Anderson, Robert, Michael Lynch and Nicholas Phillipson. 2003. *The University of Edinburgh: An Illustrated History*. Edinburgh: Edinburgh University Press.

Anson, Peter. 1970. *Underground Catholicism in Scotland, 1622-1878*. Montrose: Standard Press.

Aspinwall, Bernard, John McCaffrey. 1985. "A Comparative View of the Irish in Edinburgh in the Nineteenth Century." In *The Irish in the Victorian City*, edited by R. Swift and S. Gilley, 130–157. London: Croom Helm.

"Australians Abroad." 1930. *The Australasian* (Melbourne, Victoria), 19 April 1930, 14.

Baas, Michiel. 2010. *Imagined Mobility: Migration and Transnationalism among Indian Students in Australia*. London: Anthem. https://doi.org/10.7135/UPO9781843313410

Bald, Vivek. 2013. *Bengali Harlem and the Lost Histories of South Asian America*. Cambridge, MA: Harvard University Press. https://doi.org/10.4159/harvard.9780674067578

Banerjee, Sukanya. 2010. *Becoming Imperial Citizens: Indians in the Late-Victorian Empire*. Durham, NC: Duke University Press. https://doi.org/10.1215/9780822391982

Barnes, Julian. 2005. *Arthur & George*. London: Jonathan Cape.

Barretto, Lenny. 2000. "Karachi Goans." Karachi Goan Association, 13 April 2000. https://karachigoans.com/sample-page

Bayly, Susan. 1989. *Saints, Goddesses and Kings*. Cambridge: Cambridge University Press. https://doi.org/10.1017/CBO9780511583513

Bilimoria, Purusottama and Ruchira Ganguly-Scrase. 1988. *Indians in Victoria, Australia: A Historical, Social and Demographic Profile of Indian Immigrants*. Geelong: Deakin University and the Victorian Ethnic Affairs Commission.

Blunt, Alison. 2005. *Domicile and Diaspora: Anglo-Indian Women and the Spatial Politics of Home*. Oxford: Blackwell.

Burgess, Julian. 2017. *A Woman of Charity—The Winifred Daphne Booth Story*, Launceston.

Chapman, Peter. 1979. "Booth, Norman Parr (1879–1950)." *Australian Dictionary of Biography*. Vol 7. Carlton South, Vic.: Melbourne University Press. http://adb.anu.edu.au/biography/booth-norman-parr-5292

Church of Our Blessed Lady & St Thomas of Canterbury. 1895. *Marriage register*. Dudley, Staffordshire. Catholic Archdiocese of Birmingham Archives, St. Chad's Cathedral.

Commonwealth of Australia. State of Victoria. 1931. *Commonwealth Division of Fawkner. State Assembly District of Prahran. Subdivison of South Yarra. Map of Subdivision and Roll of Electors*. Melbourne: H. J. Green. https://www.ancestry.com.au/interactive/1207/RDAUS1901_101260__0080-00269

Conlon, Frank. 1977. *A Caste in a Changing World*. Berkeley: University of California Press.

Crew Lists of Vessels Arriving at San Francisco. 1905–1954. *Records of the Immigration and Naturalization Service*, RG 85, National Archives, United States.

Crocker-Langley San Francisco Directory. 1909. San Francisco: Crocker.

De Lepervanche, Marie. 1984. *Indians in a White Australia*. Sydney: Allen, Unwin.

de Sousa, Francisco. 1710. *Oriente Conquistado a Jesu Christo*. Lisbon.

Doyle, Arthur Conan. 1924. *Memoirs and Adventures*. London: Hodder & Stoughton.

Farias, Kranti. 1999. *The Christian Impact in South Kanara*. Mumbai: CHAI.

Fuller, Christopher. 1976. *Nayars Today*. Cambridge: Cambridge University Press.

Gait, E. A. 1913. *Census of India, 1911*, vol. I, part I. Calcutta: Superintendent Government Printing. https://archive.org/details/censusofindiav1pt1indi

Government of India. 1935. "First Schedule." In *Government of India Act, 1935*, 210–231. http://www.legislation.gov.uk/ukpga/1935/2/pdfs/ukpga_19350002_en.pdf

Heyes. 1949. Letter to Lt. Col. N. W. W. Johnstone, Office of the High Commissioner in New Delhi, 9 June 1949. A 446/182, 1960/66167. National Archives of Australia.

"Hockey." 1938. *Cairns Post* (Cairns, QLD), 10 June 1938, 4.

"In the Kimberley." 1930. *Sunday Times*, 27 July 1930, 15.

"In the Social Realm." 1932. *Weekly Times* (Melbourne, Victoria), 2 January 1932, 14.

Incoming Passenger List to Fremantle on "Omar." 1922. K269, 2 APR 1922, OMAR, National Archives of Australia.

"India v. Western Australia." 1938. *The West Australian* (Perth, Western Australia), 24 May 1938, 13.

"Indian Hockey Team: Visit to Bathurst." 1938. *National Advocate* (Bathurst, NSW), 10 September 1938, 5.

"Indian Hockey Team Will Play in Syndney." 1938. *The Referee* (Sydney, New South Wales), 26 May 1938, 22.

"Indians and N.S.W. XI." 1938. *The Labor Daily* (Sydney, NSW), 4 June 1938, 14

Kelly's Directory of Birmingham and its Suburbs. 1899. London: Kelly & Co.

"Kimberley Exploration Syndicate." 1930. *Kalgoorlie Miner*, 1 August 1930, 4.

"Kimberley Tin Fields." 1929. *Western Argus* (Kalgoorlie, Western Australia), 18 June 1929, 5.

"Kimberley Development." 1930. *The West Australian* (Perth, Western Australia), 18 January 1930, 18.

King, Philip. 1995. "Obituary: Frank d'Abreu." *The Independent*, 2 December 1995. http://www.independent.co.uk/news/people/obituary-frank-dabreu-1523675.html

Maffei, Angelus. 1883. *An English-Konkani Dictionary: And A Konkani-English Dictionary*. Mangalore: Basel Mission.

McGillivray, Mark and Smith, Gary, eds. 1997. *Australia and Asia*. Oxford: Oxford University Press.

Menezes, Dwayne. 2014. "Identity, Agency and the Catholics of South Kanara, 1870–1950." Unpublished PhD thesis, University of Cambridge.

"Mining. Kimberley Exploitation." 1930. *Western Mail*, 7 August 1930, 33.

"Miss Margaret O'Grady's Wedding." 1933. *The Advocate* (Burnie, Tasmania), 25 September 1933, 2.

"Missing Friends." 1930. *Sunday Times* (Perth, Western Australia), 21 September 1930, 10.

Moody, William. 2003. "Professor Alphonsus (Pon) d'Abreu: The Unsung Hero of Cardio-Thoracic Surgery." Dissertation, University of Birmingham.

Mosse, David. 1996. "South Indian Christians, Purity/Impurity and the Caste System: Death Ritual in a Tamil Roman Catholic Community." *Journal of the Royal Anthropological Institute* 2(3): 461–483. https://doi.org/10.2307/3034898

Oddie, Geoffrey. 2013 [1997]. "Introduction." In *Religious Conversion Movements in South Asia*, edited by G. Oddie, 1–13. Oxford: Routledge. https://doi.org/10.4324/9781315026756

Oldfield, Roger. 2010. *Outrage: The Edalji Five and the Shadow of Sherlock Holmes*. Cambridge: Vanguard.

Passenger and Crew Lists of Vessels arriving at New York. 1897–1957. *Records of the Immigration and Naturalization Service*. National Archives, United States.

Pereira, J. M. 1892. Letter to J. R. Fraser, Dean of the Faculty of Medicine, University of Edinburgh, 12 April 1892. Edinburgh University Library, Scotland.

———. 1893. Letter to J.R. Fraser, Dean of the Faculty of Medicine, University of Edinburgh, 12 October 1893. Edinburgh University Library, Scotland.

Petition on Behalf of Indians and Afghans Resident in Western Australia to Viceroy of India. 19 January 1903. A1, 1903/5781. National Archives of Australia.

Powell, Avril. 2013. "Processes of Conversion to Christianity in Nineteenth Century North-Western India." In *Religious Conversion Movements in South Asia*, edited by G. Oddie, 15–56. Oxford: Routledge.

Ravenstein, Ernest George, ed., trans. 1898. *A Journal of the First Voyage of Vasco da Gama, 1497–1499*. London: Hakluyt Society.

Robinson, Rowena. 2003. *Christians of India*. New Delhi: Sage.

Rodrigues, Menin. n.d. "Goans of Pakistan: Hall of Fame" http://www.goansofpakistan.org/hof.htm

Royal College of Surgeons of Edinburgh. 1888–1897. *College Records, 15 December 1888 to 20 October 1897*. Royal College of Surgeons of Edinburgh Archives, Scotland.

Royal College of Surgeons of England. 2014. "d'Abreu, Alphonsus Liguori (1906–1976)." In *Plarr's Lives of the Fellows Online*. http://livesonline.rcseng.ac.uk/biogs/E006407b.htm

———. 2015. "d'Abreu, Francis Arthur (1904–1995)." In *Plarr's Lives of the Fellows Online*. http://livesonline.rcseng.ac.uk/biogs/E007884b.htm

Saldanha, C. N. 1898. Letter to Sir Matthew White Ridley Bart, 29 June 1898, India Office Records, British Library.

Saldanha, Jerome. 1938. *Origin and Growth of Konkani or Goan Communities and Language*. Bombay: Anglo-Lusitano Press.

Scotland. *1891 Scotland Census. Reels 1-409*. General Register Office for Scotland, Edinburgh, Scotland.

Shastry, B. S. 2000. *Goa-Kanara Portuguese Relations, 1498-1763*. New Delhi: Mittal.

Stokes, John. 1885. *Report on the Revision of Assessment, and on the Disturbances known as Koots in Kanara, 1830-1831*. Mangalore: Collectorate Press.

"The North-West Big Mineral Concessions." 1929. *Sunday Times*, 30 June 1929, 2.

The People of India. 1950. *The Constitution of India 1949*. https://www.wdl.org/en/item/2672

Thomas, Reginald. Undated. *The History of St. Francis Parish, Handsworth*. Catholic Archdiocese of Birmingham Archives, St. Chad's Cathedral.

"Tin in the North." 1929. *Western Mail* (Perth, Western Australia), 16 May 1929, 52.

U.S. Bureau of Census. 1940. *Census of the United States, 1940*, National Archives United States.

Weaver, Gordon. 2006. *Conan Doyle and the Parson's Son: The George Edalji Case*. Cambridge: Vanguard.

Whittington, A. E., ed. 1923. *The Official Catholic Directory of the Archdiocese of Birmingham 1923*. Birmingham: Burnes, Oates & Washbourne.

"Why Are Indians So Good." 1938. *The Labor Daily* (Sydney, NSW), 2 June 1938, 11.

Whyte, E.D.W. 1893. Letter to J. R. Fraser, 25 October 1893. Edinburgh University Library, Scotland.

"Would Welcome Match Against Queensland." 1938. *The Telegraph* (Brisbane, Queensland), 25 May 1938, 11.

About the author

Dr. Dwayne Ryan Menezes is an Associate Fellow at the Institute of Commonwealth Studies, University of London, and Honorary Fellow at University College London. He read Imperial and Ecclesiastical History at the LSE and the University of Cambridge, graduating from the latter with a PhD in History. He served as Researcher at the Centre of Governance and Human Rights (CGHR) at the University of Cambridge; Visiting Academic at the Centre on Migration, Policy and Society (COMPAS) at the University of Oxford; and as Postdoctoral Research Fellow at Heythrop College, University of London. Dr. Menezes also acted until recently as Consultant to the Secretary-General of the Commonwealth, Principal Consultant to the European Parliament Intergroup for Freedom of Religion or Belief and Coordinator of the All-Party Parliamentary Group for Yemen in the UK Parliament, and continues to serve as Founder and Director of Human Security Centre (HSC) and Polar Research and Policy Initiative (PRPI) and the Coordinator of the All-Party Parliamentary Group for Greenland in the UK Parliament.

— 5 —

Religion and the "Simple Life": Dugald Semple and Translocal "Life Reform" Networks

STEVEN SUTCLIFFE

This chapter presents a case study of a Scottish exponent of the "simple life," Dugald Semple (1884-1964), within early twentieth-century networks of life reform or Lebensreform. It argues that the underlying thread in Semple's "life reform" is a non-conformist, anti-clerical religious individualism which incorporated Transcendentalism into a broad Tolstoyan and Gandhian pacifism. A case study of Semple's career in dialogue with his European and South Asian interlocutors demonstrates the value of empirically based transnational enquiry at the level of individuals and networks for understanding the varied inflections of "life reform," particularly the religious roots of the phenomenon. It also contributes to the historiography of important currents in "alternative religion" which fed the post-world-war-two "new age," "eco" and commune movements.

Introduction

This chapter presents a case study of a Scottish exponent of the "Simple Life," Dugald Semple (1884-1964), whom I locate within translocal networks of *Lebensreform* or "life reform." Semple lived mostly in the rural hinterland of Glasgow, then the "second city" of the British Empire, although he also worked briefly in London and visited Norway, Switzerland and the US. Semple came from a large family. After leaving school he became exposed to progressive and radical political and cultural currents and, as a result, in 1907 he went "back to the land" (Marsh 1982) to live in a tent on the local heath. Semple began to fashion a career as an authority on the "Simple Life," practising pacifism, vegetarianism and nature study influenced by Tolstoy, Thoreau and later Gandhi. I argue that the underlying thread in Semple's biography is a form of non-conformist, anti-clerical piety which shows affinities with the *Lebensreform* movement of the early twentieth century. His case study shows the value of understanding biography within wider translocal networks. Thus I agree with Deacon *et al.* (2010, 5, 3) when they argue that "the focus on an individual life ... shows clearly that it is impossible to segregate the public from the intimate, the economic from the cultural or the political from the personal," yielding an approach which "emphasizes connections" and "attends to regional as well as global scales."

I begin with a discussion of problems in researching the life of a practitioner like Semple where primary sources are obscure and scattered, including an account of my own chance rediscovery of his work, followed by a discussion of how best to reconstruct his biography. Attention to Semple's career shows the methodological value of a finely grained study of local religious nonconformities in the context of European, Nordic and South Asian connectivities. I argue that Semple's apparently idiosyncratic "Simple Life," largely forgotten by local audiences and neglected by historiographical authorities, represents a Scottish variation on a wider cluster of themes which in turn anticipate the organic, ecological and commune cultures of the later twentieth century.

Rediscovering Semple: Source problems

Despite his relative obscurity at the time of writing,[1] Dugald Semple was well known in his lifetime as a vegetarian, conscientious objector and naturalist, certainly in Scotland and the UK, and further afield within food reform networks. From c. 1907 until c. 1962 he worked as a journalist, photographer and public speaker, publishing around twenty books and pamphlets, often reusing material from his newspaper columns. He served briefly as secretary for the London Vegetarian Society and subsequently as an honorary office holder for the Scottish Vegetarian Society and the International Vegetarian Union. On his death in 1964 Semple left a substantial bequest for local senior citizens and a "Semple Centre," acquired for this purpose, continues to function as a community centre in the village of Fairlie on the Clyde coast where he spent his final years (Newton 2014).

Around 2000 I chanced upon a copy of *A Free Man's Philosophy* (Semple 1933) in a second-hand bookshop. The spine on the shelf caught my eye because the publisher was C.W. Daniel whose list in the first half of the twentieth century forms an important record of nonconformist politics and religion

---

1. Semple's books are out of print but UK copyright libraries in Edinburgh (National Library of Scotland) and London (British Library) hold a representative selection. There are scattered references to Semple in the historiography on vegetarianism and veganism (for example Twigg 1981, Leneman 1999, 223) but the main extant published sources are Moore (2014) and Sutcliffe (2018). The library of the Vegetarian Society in Altrincham, England, contains books by Semple; the website of the International Vegetarian Union carries archival material on Semple at http://www.ivu.org/history/societies/scottish.html and elsewhere; there is also a Wikipedia entry at https://en.wikipedia.org/wiki/Dugald_Semple.

Religion and the "Simple Life"

Figure 5.1 Dugald Semple's "Wheelhouse" colony, Beith, c. 1930 (Semple archive).

(Gassert 2000, Walter 2011). I was struck by the personal and affective tone of the foreword: "My earnest desire has been to write not only about what I know, but about what I feel about life, believing that wisdom is more of the heart than of the head"; accordingly, the book is presented as a record of "the actual doings of my experiment in living" (Semple 1933, n.p.). The chapter titles continue in the same uncomplicated language: "In Search of Truth," "Looking for Land," "The Health Garden," "Our Kinship with Animals," "Some Social Remedies" and "A Better Way to Live." The book includes a photographic plate of Semple's small-holding in the 1930s, complete with visiting tents and campers, which is subtitled "the open air life" (see Figure 5.1), and a photograph of M. K. Gandhi in London in 1931 (Figure 5.3, which I discuss below).

This book by a self-described "free man" confirmed my interest in the interwar period as a significant yet understudied matrix of alternative religious culture (Sutcliffe 2007). Yet I could find little hard information about Semple. I searched for his small holding in the North Ayrshire countryside unsuccessfully using his photographs and a contemporary map: as I later discovered, the land was later acquired by a quarry and his cottage, now ruined, is only approachable by foot across fields. Circumstances were conspiring against easy recovery. I published a short account of his career as part of an argument on the complexity of "post-Presbyterian" self-identity (Sutcliffe 2010). In 2011 I discovered a Wikipedia site created by Roger Griffith who had independently stumbled upon Semple.[2] He took me to the site in February 2012 for a field visit with local historian Donald Reid. Mr. Griffith was subsequently contacted by Mazda Munn, an artist living on the Isle of Cumbrae off the Clyde coast, who had found the Wikipedia site. In 1983 Ms. Munn had befriended Jessica Shepard (1905-?) who worked as Semple's secretary from the early 1950s until his death in 1964. Around 1995 Ms. Shepard gave Ms. Munn the remains of Semple's personal archive, consisting in three scrapbooks of newspaper cuttings, assorted postcards and books by Semple, a handful of publications by other authors from his personal library, and around 200 glass plate images, mostly of his own photographs, used for "magic lantern" projection to illustrate his talks (Munn 2015).

I narrate this series of coincidences because it formed a crucial part of my reconstruction of a life that "escape[s] the national biographer's net" because (as will become clear) it "drew emotional energy, ideological conviction [and] practical understanding from eclectic, transnational experience" and as such can only be found "in the interstices of the archive" (Deacon et al. 2010, 2, 3). A rough method for exploring these "interstices" is described by Matless (1998, 7) in his cultural geography of landscape when he explains that "second-hand bookshops ... offered space for exploration" and "general wanderings by car, bike or foot ... prompted things." The Wikipedia site and Semple's personal archive, independently presented by third parties, confirmed my hunch that Semple was an interesting figure who had fallen into the interstices.

Following these modest breakthroughs, Moore (2014) published an important article on Semple as a nature journalist based on the archive. I also located new sources. First, I discovered Semple's correspondence with Roland Muirhead (1868-1964), a Renfrewshire businessman and politician who organized his family's tannery according to the progressive working practices of the Welsh social reformer, Robert Owen (1771-1858), following Muirhead's sojourn as a young man in an Owenite colony in Washington state (Finlay 2004). Muirhead was a politically left-wing pacifist who moved in radical Liberal circles before co-founding the National Party of Scotland in 1928 which in 1934 merged with the Scottish Party to form the Scottish National Party; in 1950 he set up the Scottish National Congress as a pressure group for Scottish self-government. Muirhead acted as witness for Semple at the Paisley military tribunal which heard Semple's appeal against conscription

---

2. Griffith's interest in Semple "came from a habit of taking an interest in the 'overlooked'" (E-mail message to author, 23 December 2016). While researching the flax industry in North Ayrshire he saw a photograph of Semple's small holding reproduced in a local history publication (Reid 2000); "the sheer eccentricity of the man also added to the interest and the fact that a memory of him lingered locally" (E-mail message to author, 23 December 2016). Griffith created the Wikipedia site on 19 September 2011.

in March 1916. Muirhead was also involved with Semple in the "No Stipend" campaign in the 1930s against continuing privileges of land tax enjoyed by the Church of Scotland, and Semple and Muirhead remained in peripatetic communication (for example, Semple 1951).

Second, Semple's later books, including *Be Your Own Doctor: Natural Cures for Common Ailments* (c. 1945), *Looking at Nature* (1946) and his memoir *Joy in Living: An Autobiography* (1957)—significantly issued "with no rights reserved"— were published in Glasgow by William MacLellan (1915-1996). MacLellan, a conscientious objector in the 1939–45 war and a supporter of the Scottish National Party, published radical Scottish writers in Glasgow from around 1940 into the 1980s.[3]

Third, Semple was befriended in the 1950s by the Glasgow-born poet and essayist Kenneth White (b. 1936) who was evacuated from Glasgow to the coastal village of Fairlie during the 1939-1945 war. White's account illustrates Semple's exposure to information on South Asia and also the significance of contemporary print media in which "life reform" information circulated. As a young man White met Semple when updating the local register of voters:

> When I knocked at the door of a certain cottage ... this old longwhite-haired fellow appeared on the threshold, and on learning what my business was, told me point blank he wasn't going to sign. ... Over a cup of dandelion tea and an oatcake, we talked about the theory of anarchism [and] about Whitman and Thoreau [and] his relationship to Gandhi.
> (White, pers. comm. 18 June 2014)

White recalls the importance of books to Semple's project:

> That very first day, Dugald showed me his library, full of books such as Ralph Waldo Trine's *In Tune with the Infinite*, which I borrowed and read. Even at that time, this kind of literature seemed to me all too vapourish. But there were references in it here and there to original texts: sutras and upanishads. Thereafter, with the little pocket money I had, I began ordering books direct from a bookshop in New Delhi ... Later ... I translated German pamphlets on nature therapy for him.
> (White, pers. comm. 18 June 2014)

One pamphlet translated by White is by Walter Fliess (1857-?), a naturopath working in Hamburg, called "Why Medicines Fail!"[4] Fliess writes that "there is no doubt that Nature's remedies are best" since "Nature gives us herbs, water, air, light and animal magnetism, and it is the duty of every nature

---

3. On MacLellan as a publisher, see Third Eye Centre 1987 and "Bill MacLellan" 1996.
4. No date is given for the German source (presumably also a pamphlet), but a subtitle is given as "Extracts from 'Disorders of the Stomach and of the Bowels and the Natural Treatment of Same'" which appears to be a translation of Fliess 1897. Thanks to Bernadett Bigalke for information on Fliess.

healer to utilize these natural healing powers." After quoting various negative testimonies on scientific medicine, Fliess urges his reader to become aware of the "simple laws of health" and to follow "hygienic and natural remedies." As we will see, Fliess's pamphlet includes key themes in the *Lebensreform* movement.

In addition to borrowing *In Tune with the Infinite* (1897) by the American "New Thought" writer, Ralph Waldo Trine (1866-1958), White also borrowed Gilbert White's *The Natural History of Selborne* (1789) and Edward Carpenter's *From Adam's Peak to Elephanta: sketches in Ceylon and India* (1892). Selborne is a rural parish in Hampshire, England, and Gilbert White's contemporary account of its natural history is considered a pioneering publication which may also have influenced Semple's nature journalism. Edward Carpenter (1844-1929) was an English exponent of the "simple life" (Rowbotham 2008) who wrote many books and essays including *Civilization: its Cause and Cure* (1889) and *The Simplification of Life* (1905). Semple probably knew these and other titles since he met Carpenter twice in the early 1900s, in Glasgow and in London (Semple 1933, 16), a period when Carpenter had become "well known without ever being quite mainstream" (Rowbotham 2008, 335). Carpenter incorporated South Asian motifs into his own project for the "simplification of life" through his friendship with the Sinhalese Tamil reformer, Ponnambalam Arunachalam (1853-1924), whom he met at Cambridge university and who sent him a copy of the *Bhagavad Gītā* in the early 1880s (Rowbotham 2008, 42, 63-64, 70). In October 1890 Carpenter sailed to Colombo to visit Arunachalam and in January 1891 crossed to India. *From Adam's Peak to Elephanta*, the book which White borrowed from Semple in the mid-1950s, was a record of Carpenter's travels which included meetings with Arunachalam's guru Ramaswamy and a visit to the Elephanta caves off Bombay dedicated to Siva (Rowbotham 2008, 151-160). A material emblem of Carpenter's Indian sympathies was the Kashmiri sandals sent by his friend Harold Cox in 1885, which Carpenter used as inspiration to make his own sandals, thereby "creating a prototype" for later bohemian footwear (Rowbotham 2008, 99). A famous photograph of Carpenter in 1905 shows him proudly displaying his sandals (Rowbotham 2008, 272) and it is instructive to compare Semple's preferred footwear (just visible in Figure 5.2).

Although (with one exception) India does not appear as a major source of inspiration for Semple, he makes approving references. These are couched in "orientalist" terms, such as when he cites the Sanskrit "Salutation to the Dawn" to model the right way to start the day, or more generally commends the "reverence for sentient life which is held by Eastern nations" (Semple 1957, 37). He often quotes epigrams by "Buddha"; thus an advertisement in his late pamphlet *The Simple Teaching of Jesus* lists a forthcoming publication by him entitled "Buddha, the Compassionate One" (Semple c. 1952, endpaper;

no evidence of publication). In his early career Semple talked regularly on "Buddhism": for example, to the Theosophical Society in Glasgow (Semple 1957, 92) and to the Bridge of Weir literary society, on 7 March 1911 (Bridge of Weir Literary Society 1910). As a generalist who lectured on a variety of "life reform" topics, Semple probably had broad knowledge of the "religions of the world" from contemporary popular publications and talks. For example, he recalls attending talks on "The Soul of India" and "Indian Drama and Epic Poetry" by Edmund Russell, whom he describes as "a close friend of Sir Edwin Arnold" (Semple 1957, 51); Arnold was the author of "The Light of Asia," a popular narrative poem about the life of the Buddha published in 1879. Semple's approving but condescending tone transposes into comment on "indigenous" cultures: for example, his reference to being "well informed about the Red Indians," and his homiletic aside about "the African" who complains to his "Massa" [i.e. "Master"] that "all our troubles began when we put on clothes" (Semple 1957, 146, 118).

Figure 5.2 Dugald Semple preaching the "Simple Life" c. 1940 (Semple archive).

The exception is Mohandas Gandhi (1869-1948), mentioned by Kenneth White as the subject of his very first conversation with Semple, who planned to include Gandhi in his "Little Wisdom" pamphlet series (alongside Jesus and the Buddha) under the title "Gandhi, the Great Soul." Semple's contact with Gandhi was both personal and textual and through it he developed his most sustained commentary on Indian affairs. Semple's interest had been triggered by Gandhi's position on the board of the London Vegetarian Society for which Semple worked as secretary in 1916-17. Semple later refers to correspondence with Gandhi in which he learned of Gandhi's admiration for Tolstoy; thereafter Semple "watched Gandhi's progress with great interest" including reading Gandhi's journal *Young India*, published between 1919 and 1931, which he describes as "always a great inspiration" (Semple 1933, 120).

Figure 5.3 Semple's photograph of Gandhi at lunch, London 1931 (Semple archive).

During Gandhi's visit to London in 1931 to attend a roundtable conference on constitutional reform in India, Semple met him "on several occasions [when] I had the pleasure of discussing ... various topics" (Semple 1933, 120) including dietary reform, such as whether it was legitimate for vegetarians to use milk from goats or cows (Semple 1933, 68). Semple refers to Gandhi as "my friend" (Semple 1933, 68) and reproduces his informal photograph of Gandhi eating lunch in *A Free Man's Philosophy* (1933) and in *Joy in Living* (1957) (Figure 5.3). During his 1931 visit to the UK, Gandhi's acolyte, Madeleine Slade (1892-1982), known as "Mirabehn" on joining Gandhi's ashram in 1925, visited Semple at his colony in North Ayrshire (Semple 1957, 81-82) and the Semple archive includes a photograph of her with Semple taken during that visit (Figure 5.4).

Semple's interest continued after Gandhi's assassination in 1948, as glimpsed in correspondence with Roland Muirhead in 1951. Muirhead had set up the Scottish National Congress in Glasgow in 1950 to explore non-parliamentary approaches to Scottish independence. After reading about this new body, Semple wrote to Muirhead on 3 February 1951: "I am so glad to see that you favour non-violent methods ... I still get Gandhi's paper 'Harizan' [sic], and feel his victory was a real example to the world that good can overcome evil." Muirhead replied to Semple on 7 February 1951, writing that, in respect of the goal of Scottish self-determination, "our best hope is to use methods employed by the Indian National Congress." Muirhead fleshed this out on 24 February 1951: "the Congress idea is now to use methods adopted by Gandhi so far as they are suitable for Scotland ... keeping in view the need to use civil disobedience as a means to make things very troublesome for the [British] Government." On 28 February 1951 Semple applied to join the Scottish Congress and looked forward to attending its upcoming conference in Glasgow on 17 March, at which he also hoped "to speak a little if possible," on the grounds that "I knew Gandhi as you know, and discussed Scottish affairs with him" (Semple 1951).

When these scattered biographical sources are combined, a composite picture emerges of Semple as a freethinker who challenged established authorities, practised conscientious objection to military service and other state intrusions upon the individual, emphasized the reform of everyday life practices such as diet and exercise, took inspiration from charismatic nonconformists like Tolstoy and Gandhi, and looked to the natural world for transcendental meaning.

Four main disciplinary approaches to Semple are possible to contextualize this portrayal. The first is through the history of vegetarianism. Many themes in the historiography of Victorian vegetarianism are recognizable in his biography, including the twin modernist concepts of reform and consumption which themselves only became possible once "stable and secure food supplies" had become established (Gregory 2007, 190). Julia Twigg's "The Vegetarian Movement in England 1847-1981" (Twigg 1981) emphasizes the structural interdependence of vegetarianism with other reform movements, and this is confirmed by Semple's longstanding involvement in vegetarian societies which was also a significant mechanism in his transnational connectivity as I argue below.

A second approach to Semple is via the history of conscientious objection to military service. Although there is a large literature there is no mention of Semple in the study of the UK military tribunal system which examined conscientious objectors between 1916-1919 by Rae (1970), nor in Scottish studies of war resistance by Kenefick (2007) or by Duncan (2015). A major obstacle is the systematic destruction of tribunal records after the 1914-1918 war, with only one complete archive surviving in Scotland (covering the Lothian and Peebles area around Edinburgh). Until recently the sole extant material on

Figure 5.4   Madeleine Slade (Mirabehn) visiting Semple at "Wheelhouse," Beith, North Ayrshire, 1931 (Semple archive).

Semple was a short, hostile account by Reid (2016, 181-187) in a local history of military mobilization in the village of Bridge of Weir, where Muirhead's tannery was located and where Semple camped for several years, in which Muirhead is caricatured as an "odd-ball" and Semple is dismissed as "an old rogue" Reid (2016, 182, 187). A wider lens is provided by Alston's (2014) history of the Tolstoyan movement which informed many objections to military conscription, including Semple's as we shall see, and she footnotes Semple's introduction to a 1939 utopian novel by the Tolstoyan writer, Arthur St. John, whom Semple met in London (Alston 2014, 252).

A third approach is via the history of natural history. Moore (2014) provides a thorough analysis of Semple's nature journalism and photography, focusing on his role first as a popularizer of natural history and second as contributor to an established newspaper genre (Moore 2014, 209; see also Allen 1978). Moore identifies Semple's main contribution as the "Nature note," a short column traditionally contributed to local and national newspapers by "amateur enthusiasts" (Moore 2014, 210). Moore commends Semple's photography and describes his journalism as written "straightforwardly" and to practical effect (Moore 2014, 218).

The fourth approach, which I take here, is interdisciplinary and treats the preceding historiographies as ingredients for a synthetic study of Semple as a practitioner of *Lebensreform* or "life reform" in which Semple's passionate quarrel with Presbyterian tradition—"the religion of my fathers" (Sutcliffe 2010) –is a decisive factor. Until recently this historiography has been dominated by a question arising from the particularities of the German experience on whether *Lebensreform* was inherently anti-modern or even reactionary. For example, Thoms (2010, 152-157) discusses the ambiguities of vegetarian practice under the Third Reich, while Stone (2004, 185) writes in the UK of a form of "organo-fascism" arising from the confluence of "back to the land" ruralism with ultra-conservative politics. In contrast, Rohkrämer argues that *Lebensreform* was capable of expressing an "alternative modernity" ("eine andere Moderne"). This approach, which I broadly follow, represents *Lebensreform* as a nuanced and differentiated phenomenon occurring across the political spectrum, including anarchist and socialist expressions, rather than only conservative or reactionary values.[5]

We are now ready to appreciate a more finely-grained biography of Semple which will demonstrate his candidacy for inclusion within translocal Lebensreform networks.

---

5. *Lebensreform* as a form of "alternative modernity" in Germany is further explored in Anglophone sources by Jefferies (2003), Treitel (2004, 2017), Williams (2007) and Sharma (2012).

Dugald Semple 1884-1964: How to live the "Simple Life"

According to his own account in *A Free Man's Philosophy* (Semple 1933) and *Joy in Living* (Semple 1957), Semple was born in 1884 to a large family belonging to the rising bourgeoisie in the small town of Johnstone, Renfrewshire, close to the industrial centres of Paisley and Glasgow. His mother came from a farming family and his father, Robert Semple, was a tailor and also a Church of Scotland Elder and Sunday School superintendent. Semple served his apprenticeship as an engineering draughtsman during which time he came into contact with progressive politics and non-religious philosophies in an area known for its grassroots radicalism (Leonard 1990). Following a camping holiday which "quite enthralled me with the life of the open air" and in a spirit of transcendentalism influenced by Thoreau (Semple 1957, 15), he began to live in a tent, and later in an abandoned omnibus, on Linwood Moss outside Paisley. Shortly thereafter he was offered a site in Bridge of Weir by the Muirhead family who ran the local tannery. In 1910 he became a fulltime public speaker and journalist, writing for local newspapers such as *The Paisley and Renfrewshire Gazette* and the *Glasgow Herald* and for niche publications such as *The Vegetarian Messenger and Health Review* and *The Christian Commonwealth*, a "religious paper with a very broad and progressive outlook" (Semple 1933, 19). He gave talks to small societies ranging from his local literary association (on Buddhism, Tolstoy and Swedenborg) to natural history societies (for example, in Paisley) and on dietary issues to meetings of the Patriotic Food League, established in 1915.[6] Semple enjoyed lecturing: in an echo of his Presbyterian upbringing he writes "I much prefer the spoken word even to the art of writing" (Semple 1957, 92). An early leaflet advertises his availability to speak on a wide range of "reform" topics with titles like "The Simple Life," "The Simple Teaching of Jesus," "The Return to Nature," "Diet and the Simple Life," "The Vaccination Delusion," "Forward to the Land," "A Simple Religion," "How to be Healthy," "Fruitarianism," "Camping," "Anarchist Communism," and "Buddhism" (Semple c. 1912). As he remarks drily: "Were I to state the subjects that I have lectured upon, probably you would think I have been travelling for a new kind of encyclopaedia" (Semple 1957, 92).

In February 1916 Semple moved to London to take up a post as Secretary to the London Vegetarian Society (Semple 1933, 10) whose membership included

---

6. For the topics of Semple's lectures to the Bridge of Weir Literary Association between 1911 and 1915, see the syllabi in the membership cards held in the Roland Muirhead archive in the National Library of Scotland (Acc. 3721 Box 153 / 2). By his own account, Semple started the association and served as its secretary until moving to London in 1916 (Semple 1957, 31-32). For Semple's contributions to Paisley Naturalists' Society between 1925 and 1932, see Moore (2014, 216); on his lectures for the Patriotic Food League in Johnstone, Barrhead, Glasgow, Greenock and Paisley—which he writes were "well reported in the Press"—see Semple (1957, 48-49).

George Bernard Shaw, Ernest Bell and Valentine Knaggs amongst others, with Gandhi on its board. When universal military conscription was introduced in March 1916 Semple applied for exemption on grounds of conscience. His case was heard at a military service tribunal in Paisley where Roland Muirhead acted as his representative. Muirhead replied to the tribunal's question "Does he belong to any sect?" by saying "I think he is a Tolstoyan." Muirhead reported Semple's position to be "that war was inconsistent with Christian teaching [and] that war was contrary to loving one's enemies … [I]n his writing and lectures he [Semple] had shown that he was always opposed to war." Muirhead added: "He is a vegetarian. He carries his principles, and in his diet does not even take butter, cheese or milk. He maintained people could not get these things without killing something."[7] The tribunal was not convinced and allocated Semple non-combatant service. But Semple appealed against this ruling on May 15 and was granted "conditional exemption … as long as [he] continued to convert the people to eat less during the war" in accordance with his talks for the Patriotic Food League.[8]

In *A Free Man's Philosophy* Semple expresses mixed feelings about London: "my experiences in the great metropolis were invaluable in many ways, although I must confess that they were not always too pleasant' (Semple 1933, 10-11). On the one hand, he enjoyed attending lectures on "subjects of a progressive nature," naming speakers such as Walter Walsh of the Free Religious Movement, Bertrand Russell, and gatherings at "the Ethical Society, the Theosophical Society, and a strange group called the Sufi Society"[9]; he also met Edward Carpenter, as noted, and gave an address to mark the centenary of Thoreau's birth in July 1917 (Semple 1933, 14, 16; Willis 1999, 47-48, 52-53). He met the publisher C.W. Daniel whom he describes as "a man worth knowing, especially for his courage in publishing pacifist literature"; became aware of Gandhi through the London Vegetarian Society board; and met prominent Tolstoyans such as Arthur St. John and Aylmer Maude (Semple 1957, 53-55). On the other hand, he found the metropolis overbearing: "those miles and miles of streets were most monotonous, with people rush-

---

7. As reported in "Simple Lifer's Appeal Refused" Paisley and Renfrewshire Gazette, April 1, 1916. Muirhead is not named but correspondence in the Muirhead archive confirms his presence on behalf of Semple who did not attend, citing work commitments in London. Due to the systematic destruction of tribunal records after the war, local newspaper reports are often the sole means of reconstructing proceedings. For a detailed account of Semple's application and appeal, based on newspaper reports and correspondence in the Muirhead archive, see Sutcliffe 2018.
8. "Dugald Semple Not For the Army: 'Simple Lifer' Impresses Appeal Court," Paisley and Renfrewshire Gazette May 20, 1916.
9. Probably the Sufi Order in the West, founded in London by Inayat Khan (1882-1927) through publication in 1914 of *Sufi Message of Spiritual Liberty* (Sedgwick 2016, 163).

ing here and rushing there, and yet rushing nowhere in particular" and he concluded that London is "far too removed from Nature" (Semple 1933, 12, 18). Semple says he spent two years in London (Semple 1933, 18) but it seems more likely that it was eighteen months, from February 1916 to September 1917 when he resigned from his position as Secretary (Semple 1933, 19, 20). He returned to Scotland with his new wife, Cathie Tuckwell, a widower, via a "cross-country journey" (Semple 1933, 21) which included visits to various English and Welsh "simple life" colonies, most notably Whiteway, the Tolstoyan colony in Gloucestershire whose founders in 1898 burned their title deeds (Semple 1957, 57-58; Shaw 1935; Green 2000, 55-58; Taylor 2016).

Back in his natal environment, and evidently stimulated by these visits, Semple decided to "try some kind of social experiment" (Semple 1933, 24). Around early 1918 he "called together a little public meeting of friends in Glasgow" to discuss the possibility of establishing "no less than a Simple Life Colony" (Semple 1933, 24). Around thirty people attended, presided over by John M. Biggar (1874-1943), a Co-Operative Party candidate for Paisley in the 1918 general election and later a Lord Provost of Glasgow (Semple 1959, 58). They agreed a plan "to purchase a piece of land, and that each member should rent his portion from the parent society" (Semple 1933, 25). A "Simple Life Fellowship" was formed, membership of which "increased to over a hundred ... mostly drawn from city folks with no experience of country life" (Semple 1957, 59). The Fellowship drew up "a syllabus of lectures" and organized "summer rambles and outings to see suitable land sites" (Semple 1957, 59). However, it was not successful in securing a plot, partly due to slow progress in land reform after the war despite renewed appetite for access (as shown by the Land Settlement (Scotland) Act of 1919: Leneman 1989, 20-37) and partly because landowners "thought we were just a lot of theoretical cranks" (Semple 1957, 59).

Semple himself became "disappointed at our slow progress, especially after spending so much time visiting places ... and acting as a kind of labour exchange to proposed colonists" (Semple 1933, 26). The Fellowship had been offered a ten-acre small holding near Beith but turned it down for being too small. In 1920 Semple and his wife Cathie acquired it themselves, reasoning that it "would be invaluable for any future group action, and meanwhile might act as a centre for campers and lovers of the open air," although he acknowledges that this was the "final blow" to the larger colony sought by the Fellowship (Semple 1933, 27). The Semples farmed this small holding as a couple for the next two decades, first as an arable plot and later as a fruit farm, gradually incorporating visitors, helpers and sub-tenants into a loose co-operative. Cathie died in 1941 but Semple continued to live on the small holding until 1945 when he moved to Fairlie. Additionally, in 1937 he had a wooden hut named "Sunrise" built for summer sojourns on the Kintyre coast where "I study nature, take photographs, and enjoy the quiet life of the open air" (Semple 1957, 141). This followed in a tradition of rural "hutting" which developed in the west of Scotland after the 1914-1918 war as another aspect of new land use.[10]

Semple continued writing and lecturing from his "Wheelhouse" colony and from his "Sunrise" hut. In 1933 he added *A Free Man's Philosophy* to a list of publications which included *Simple Life Visitors* (1909), *Living in Liberty* (1911), *Joys of the Simple Life* (1915) and *Life in the Open* (1919). *Diet and Good Health* (1925) anticipated the bias in later publications towards practical dietary and nature cure advice, such as *Be Your Own Doctor* (1945?), *The Sunfood Way to Health* (1956), and his wife Cathie's *Wheelhouse Good Health Recipes* (1938). Semple's final book was the memoir *Joy in Living* (1957), issued with "no rights reserved," echoing in print media the rejection of title deeds at the Whiteway colony.

Joy in Living gives an insight into Semple's lifelong argument with his native Presbyterian culture. As a young man he describes himself as an "ardent socialist" and a "keen vegetarian." The "question of religion" preoccupied him from an early age, precipitating "long arguments ... after family worship on Sabbath evenings." His father threatened to burn his books "dealing with Tolstoy, Plato, Descartes, and ... Rationalist Press literature" and local ministers "tried to corner me with their quotations from the Scriptures." As a result, "I came to look on Sunday as a day of horror" (Semple 1957, 13-14). This growing antipathy is bolstered by anticlerical comments such as "whenever a man buttons his collar behind instead of in front [i.e. wears a clerical collar], he is usually going that way himself" (Semple 1957, 121). As early as 1911, in a chapter called "A Simple Religion" in *Living in Liberty*, Semple decried "Bible fetishism" and rejected the "God of Calvin" whom he described as "a God of anger who elects His children to everlasting punishment" (Semple 1911, 125, 128).

Semple's quarrel resurfaced in 1935 when, together with his mentor Roland Muirhead, he organized a grandly-titled "Scottish No-Stipend League" against the Church of Scotland's continuing practice of levying a tithe on landowners. This practice offended Semple's voluntarism by appearing to confirm the politically established nature of the Presbyterian church. In his pamphlet *Scottish No-Stipend League: an appeal for freedom*, Semple writes:

> Reader, do you not think with me ... that this stipend business is a disgrace to the name of religion? Think on how our covenanting forefathers suffered for the principles of religious tolerance ... To compel a Jew, Catholic or Agnostic to support one particular faith because he happens to be a landowner is not religion but intolerance of the worst kind.
>
> (Semple 1935, n.p.)

---

10. For example, the colony at Carbeth to the north of Glasgow, founded 1920, which survives today: see <http://www.carbethhutters.co.uk>

Ironically, by invoking the dissenting tradition of "our covenanting forefathers," known for defending the fledgling institutions of Presbyterianism against Episcopacy in the seventeenth century, Semple appeals to the authority of Scottish nonconformism. As I have argued elsewhere, this underscores the culturally Presbyterian flavor of his reform even as it travels in a "post-presbyterian" direction (Sutcliffe 2010).

Semple's ambiguous relationship with his Presbyterian formation is tempered by curiosity towards more "exotic" religion. He admires Quakers for "their simple sincere faith," Swedenborgians for their "New Church principles," and his father-in-law, a liberal Church of Scotland member with Unitarian leanings, for "his broad outlook" (Semple 1957, 14-15). During his life Semple met or corresponded with many alternative religionists, including Tolstoyans, Theosophists, Buddhists and Sufis; nature cure practitioners, vegetarians and fruitarians; and, as we have seen, charismatic reformers like Edward Carpenter and Mohandas Gandhi (Semple 1915, 23, 61, 75-76, 85; Semple 1933, 120-125; Semple 1957, 52).

Alongside this curiosity in "the other," facilitated through personal contact and consumption of print media, he emphasizes virtues of conscience, sobriety, frugality and self-reliance which have been widely attributed to "reformed" Christian traditions. The balance of the relationship between self and other remained fluid for Semple throughout his life. Although in *A Free Man's Philosophy* he stresses his early solidarity with co-operative socialism, Tolstoyan personal piety became increasingly formative: "the more I read [Tolstoy] ... the more I felt it was true that all true reform began with the individual, and that the kingdom of heaven must be realised within first," and this was to be realised through "the voice of conscience speaking within the sanctuary of the human soul" (Semple 1933, 105). In this vein he reflects in *Joys of the Simple Life* that "the real problem is mostly with ourselves" and that we must "get right within first" (Semple 1915, 12, 26). It follows that the "healthy religious person" should express "a code of his own making" in contrast to those who remain "priest-ridden" (Semple 1915, 79).

Hence while sympathetic to the idea of anarchist and socialist utopias, Semple's idea of "reform" is increasingly constituted as an ecology of upright moral relationships between individual persons. He anticipates this individualist bent as early as 1911 in *Living in Liberty*, when he writes that, although he is a "convinced Socialist" in legislative matters, in social matters "we are as much the slaves of our own bidding as to that of any taskmaster" and therefore "to know reform you must live reform" (Semple 1911, 151-152). This appeal to conscience informed Semple's objection to war service, and it also resolved the problem of authority presented to him by the religious pluralism which he encountered as he set out "in search of truth" (Semple 1933, 9), in that it identified the reform of the individual as *fons et origo* of real change.

As he put it in his final publication: "it is not another Messiah that is needed but more obedience to the living voice within" (Semple 1957, 142-143).

The "Simple Life" as an expression of *Lebensreform*

Semple provides a rich case study of a Scottish "simple life" project which in isolation may appear idiosyncratic. Yet almost all his ideas and interests can be documented amongst *Lebensreform* practitioners in continental Europe.[11] This is not an obvious connection to make for several reasons: the literature on *Lebensreformbewegung* makes little if any reference to the UK; discussions of UK phenomena which might qualify as "life reform" go under a local name such as "simple life" or "back to the land" (MacCarthy 1981; Marsh 1982, Gould 1988) and are confined to English examples. Peeters (2011, 22) mentions "Britain" alongside Germany, France and Belgium as a key *Lebensreform* site, but actually gives no examples. Rohkrämer (2013) interestingly interprets John Ruskin, Edward Carpenter and William Morris as proponents of *Lebensreform*, but his discussion is restricted to England. Albritton and Jonsson (2016) offer a detailed account of the "simple life" of John Ruskin's circle in the English Lake District, but make no connection with translocal *Lebensreform*. These historiographies marginalize Semple as a Scottish subject whose interests are strongly illustrative of *Lebensreform*, which he expressed through several visits to continental Europe, the Nordic region and the US. Additionally, unlike Ruskin and Morris in England (but not Carpenter), he enjoyed direct personal contact with an Indian source (Gandhi). To consolidate Semple's case I will briefly outline three forms of translocal contact and exchange in which he engaged.

The first form is the holding of office in a dietary reform organization. In 1938 Semple travelled to Hurdals Verk near Oslo as President of the Scottish Vegetarian Society to attend the 10th congress of the International Vegetarian Union (IVU). Semple describes this as his "first visit to a foreign shore" and it was evidently a formative experience (Semple 1957, 95). Around ninety delegates were present including Werner Zimmerman (1893-1982) who spoke on "My Way from Disease to Health" and led "early morning gymnastic exercises" described as "a popular feature of the Congress"; and Are Waerland (1876-1955) who spoke on "A Healthy Life," followed by "an interest-

---

11. A possible exception is sustained naturism, a feature of continental *Lebensreform*. For example, there is no evidence that Semple regularly took "sun baths." Nevertheless, I have been reliably informed that Semple would on occasion bathe naked in the sea beside his hut "Sunrise" on the Kintyre coast, a relatively isolated environment (Angus Martin, pers. comm.). Semple himself acknowledges that "clothes are really a compromise ... for the more we wear the farther our distance must be from the sun" and he shows his commitment to dress reform generally when he writes: "I find sandals and canvas shoes ideal in dry weather, and ... I go barefoot whilst at the seaside" (Semple 1957, 115-116).

ing discussion" to which Semple contributed (The International Vegetarian Congress 1938). Zimmermann was a leading figure in Swiss *Lebensreform* who spoke and published widely and who, like Semple, met Gandhi in London in 1931 and again in Switzerland in 1932.[12] Waerland was a prominent figure in Nordic *Lebensreform*, born in Finland but later taking Swedish citizenship, who had been introduced to readers in English through his book *In the Cauldron of Disease* (Waerland 1934). Semple himself gave the concluding address to the Congress, entitled "Vegetarianism and Peace," in which he argued that:

> Vegetarianism is not merely a matter of food reform—it is a philosophy of life, and war will only cease when we cease to live as beasts of prey ... Vegetarianism is the first great step. The killing of human beings is akin to the killing of animals and so the exploiting of animal life leads to the selfish exploitation of human beings.
> ("The International Vegetarian Congress," 1938)

Semple attended the next IVU Congress in 1947, which had been delayed by the 1939-1945 war. The venue was Wycliffe College, a private school in Gloucestershire, England. Semple gave a report on the Scottish Vegetarian Society and chaired a session on "veganism," a term coined by Donald Watson (1910-2005) in 1944 to describe a person who does not eat or use animal products. Also present were two participants at Oslo: Are Waerland, and Ralph Bircher from the Bircher-Benner centre in Zurich who gave a talk entitled "Raw Food in Health and Disease" (1947). The 1947 Congress established an international committee to which Semple was appointed as one of several Vice-Presidents. In 1955 he attended the IVU Congress in Paris with attracted "between 400-600 people" from twenty countries (Semple 1957, 101). Semple spoke on "Natural Living" and acknowledged the support shown him by Walter Sommer (1887-1985), a Vegan from Hamburg and author of *The Very First Law of Natural Food* (Semple 1952, 102).[13] He also approvingly noted the presence of a "Belgian naturalist who wore his hair long and walked sprightly with bare feet" (Semple 1957, 102). Semple also attended the 1960 Congress in Hanover where he (again) lectured on "Vegetarianism and World Peace," arguing that the "great issue to-day is to know how to promote world peace, especially when one reads about the power of the hydrogen bomb and the crushing burden of armaments" (Semple 1960). In sum, Semple's office in the IVU took him from Scotland to Norway, England, France and Germany where he rubbed shoulders with other transnational activists and exchanged views on common themes.

---

12. Pers. comm. with Stefan Rindlisbacher, 4 and 12 June 2015.
13. This is the title used by Semple: originally *Das Urgesetz der natürlichen Ernährung* (1952).

The second form is personal contact with individuals and colonies pursuing a broader vision of "life reform": that is, not limited to dietary causes nor to the IVU as an umbrella organization (although contacts could be made at IVU conferences). For example, at the IVU event in Oslo in 1938 Semple met Ralph Bircher (1899-1990), son of Maximilian Bircher-Benner (1867-1939), creator of müsli and founder of a clinic in Zurich in 1904 called "Lebendige Kraft" ("Living Power" or "Vital Force"). His son Ralph Bircher edited the Swiss *Lebensreform* journal "Der Wendepunkt" ("The Turning Point") and in 1953 he invited Semple to visit Lebendige Kraft to experience what had become known as the "Bircher-Benner diet" (Meyer-Renschhausen and Wirz 1999). Both men were by then established authorities within translocal *Lebensreform* networks, but the precise motives behind the invitation are not clear, nor whether Semple or Bircher initiated the visit. Semple stayed for a month and was evidently impressed, describing "a huge building with several large houses to meet the continual arrival of patients from all parts of the world," including "a millionaire Hindu from Bombay" who "had been in prison with Gandhi" and "a Mohammedan" who tells Semple that the Quran "means submission to the Supreme Being and reflects all Nature" (Semple 1957, 98-99). Semple gave a talk called "Fifty Years of Simple Living" which was interpreted by Bircher to "a crowded audience" including "Dr. Ebele of the Swiss Vegetarian Society, and Dr. Aristotle of Zurich" and later published in "Der Wendepunkt" (Semple 1957, 100).[14] This visit demonstrates that organizational contact, such as through the IVU, could also foster translocal exchanges between individuals.

The third medium of contact and exchange is the culture of book publishing, borrowing and reading which formed Semple's earliest entry point into life reform ideas. We have heard how borrowing books from Semple, and as a result making direct contact with an Indian publisher, enthused the young Kenneth White and probably formed a mirror image of Semple's own practice. Although only a handful of publications survive from Semple's personal library, their content is instructive. Items include *Fruit Dishes and Raw Vegetables* with the subtitle "Sunlight (Vitamin) Food" by M. Bircher Benner and Max E. Bircher (1939), which Semple may have acquired after meeting Ralph Bircher in 1938 in Oslo. There is also a booklet called *The Salad Road to Health* by the English naturopath H.V. Knaggs (1859-1954), a member of the London Vegetarian Society when Semple was secretary. Between 1887 and 1936 Knaggs wrote prolifically on reform themes from naturopathy to antivaccination informed by a vitalistic conception of health. The human body,

---

14. Thanks to Eva Locher for providing entries from the April and May 1953 issues of *Der Wendepunkt*. In the April issue (p. 179), Semple is advertised as a well-known personality who will give a talk at the clinic on 12 May, co-organized with the Swiss Vegetarian Society and the Pythagoras Youth Group. The May issue prints a German translation of Semple's talk (Semple 1953).

he writes, is like a telephone which only works when supplied by "invisible electric current":

> [I]n the same way Nature, or the universal life-energy ... feeds our bodies [and] keeps them running and if we do but let Nature do this work for us, by not meddling unnecessarily with her plans, we are always in good hands. (Knaggs 1919, 2)

The remnants of Semple's library also contain two books by Edward Bach (1886-1936) on the Bach Flower remedies which combine the naturalist and health strands of Semple's "Simple Life" bricolage (Bach 1937, 1941). Finally, there are two self-published local items: *Culinary Herbs* (Grieve c. 1920), described on the cover as "specially written to assist members of the British Guild of Herb Growers"; and "Practical Methods in Preparing Health-Building Foods," a pamphlet by the Lee Foundation for Nutritional Research in Milwaukee, US, containing recipes for potato juice and soybean milk and a 1955 address by its author to the Organic Health Foundation of America in California (Lee n.d.).[15]

In his prime Semple's personal library appears to have been fairly substantial: on leaving the "Wheelhouse" colony in 1945 he remarks on the effort involved "in removing my far too numerous books," and during his final years in Rose Cottage, Fairlie, he writes of the companionship he finds in "Shakespeare, Tolstoy, Thoreau, Emerson, Plato, Swedenborg, and the Bible" (Semple 1957, 117, 149).[16] It is quite probable that at one time his archive also contained personal correspondence, since he mentions receiving "a great many letters [on] health matters and my simple ways of living" (Semple 1957, 120) from readers in Canada, Italy, England and Australia (Semple 1957,

---

15. Semple may have acquired this pamphlet in November 1961 when he gave a talk to the "Chicago Chapter of the American Natural Hygiene Society"; Chicago is only some fifty miles from the Lee Foundation in Milwaukee, Wisconsin ("He Really Lives the Simple Life" 1961, *The Waukegan News-Sun* 29/11/61, p. 4). The same newspaper article advertises his forthcoming lecture on "Thoreau and the Simple Life" to be given at the New York Thoreau Society in May 1962 to mark the centennial of Thoreau's death. These lectures appear to have been delivered during Semple's second visit to North America, as noted in his obituaries in the Scottish press, for example in the *Kilmarnock Standard* (25 January 1964) and the *Campbeltown Courier* (30 January 1964); other obituaries appeared elsewhere in the UK and in the US, where they were syndicated in Illinois, Massachusetts, Kansas, Michigan and North Carolina, for example, providing further evidence of Semple's translocal reputation. Semple's first visit to North America appears to have taken place in 1958–1959, following publication of his memoir *Joy in Living* (1957), when he was already in his mid-seventies.

16. Mazda Munn recalls that, after Semple's death, his secretary Jessica Shepard "had quite a lot of his things in her house ... I have no idea if she took all of his books but she certainly had ... books on diet and food reform, religion and politics. Many of the books had his name on them" (pers. comm. 31/12/2017).

120-126). He was also familiar with international colonies and settlements of a broad "life reform" character, including the Llano colony in Louisiana, US, the Eden colony in Oranienburg, Germany, and the Morelly Colony in France (Semple 1933, 116-118, 147).

Although only fragments and scattered references appear to survive, Semple was evidently in regular contact with a range of transnational sources through the medium of these organizational, personal and textual exchanges. A useful comparison on the communicative power of print culture is Treitel's (2004) account of the "niche-creating function" of "occult" publishing in constructing German *Lebensreform* biographies in the early twentieth century. Publishers curated lifestyle experimentation by providing exemplary accounts of ideas and practices which readers could try out for themselves plus endpapers with advertisements for further publications and societies (Treitel 2004, 68-71). For example, the 1922 catalogue of the Nirwana-Verlag für Lebensreform in Berlin "consisted of 937 texts ... covering a wide variety of topics, including healthy living, human sexuality, nudism, occultism, spiritualism, magnetism, religion, Theosophy, occult novels, and astrology" (Treitel 2004, 75). Treitel argues that this exemplified "the new consumerist ethos" of Weimar Germany by offering "tools to help buyers achieve wisdom" (Treitel 2004, 75). Since this publisher also "ran a lending library ..., sponsored lectures and demonstrations, and carried informational brochures," it also provided a public service. Such projects "saw themselves as active agents in the vast movement for the reform of German life" (Treitel 2004, 76). In another country, under his own "Simple Life" brand, and on a smaller scale, so did Semple.

Conclusion: Semple as a Scottish "Life Reformer"

The question of whether there was a "life reform" movement in the UK to which Semple might be considered to belong has been difficult to address because of the lack of currency of such a term in English language historiography. Nevertheless, Semple's work regularly employs terms with clear translocal family resemblance such as "health," "life," "vitality," "simplicity" and "nature," and several examples of his transnational connectivity have been identified. The evidence suggests that Semple operated within a web of networks whose *modus operandi* becomes recognizable as *Lebensreform* when a comparative perspective is applied despite the fact that secondary sources have tended not to "join the dots."[17] The evidence suggests that, even if Semple amalgamated various strands

---

17. Similarly, according to Stefan Rindlisbacher, Swiss historiography "does not describe a wider movement. There are some books on Bircher-Benner, the 'Monte Verità' and other small groups, but we are the first historians who try to 'join the dots'" (pers. comm. 4 June 2015). My findings lead me to agree with Jefferies (2003, 92): "Historians have generally preferred to focus on individual organizations or specific areas of reform—diet, medicine, clothing ... [etc.]—rather than undertaking the much more

of "reform" under his own distinctive stamp, his project was neither entirely eccentric nor unique but a local instance of a recognizable wider phenomenon. Furthermore, the ideological and political content of the networks in question is considerably more variegated than the conservative or reactionary portrayal favoured by earlier historiography. Semple's individualist pacifist anarchism in Scotland follows loosely in the tradition of Tolstoy in Russia and Thoreau in New England; it also shows affinities with Swiss practitioners such as Werner Zimmermann, and to an extent with the intellectuals' colony at Monte Verità (Kuiper 2013); it approves of Gandhian non-violence and self-rule; and it finds echoes in the more individualistic expressions of German socialist *Lebensreform* (Williams, 2007). The case of Dugald Semple and the "simple life" in Scotland therefore supports Rohkrämer's view that "it is perfectly reasonable to speak of a life-reform tradition in the United Kingdom, which extends to the present, even if the concept does not exist in English" (2013, 335).[18]

Acknowledgments

I am most grateful to Roger Griffith, Mazda Munn and Kenneth White for sharing their knowledge of Dugald Semple and to Mazda Munn for preserving the Semple archive. Thanks to Joachim Gentz, Jörg Albrecht, Thomas Rohkrämer, Bernadett Bigalke and Helmut Zander for guidance on *Lebensreform* in Germany, to Stefan Rindlisbacher and Eva Locher for information on Swiss *Lebensreform*, to Inga Sanner for information on Are Waerland, and to Frans Jespers on Belgian developments. Thanks also to Rachel Hewitt and William Hetherington for information on the British military tribunal system.

References

Albritton, Vicky and Fredrik A. Jonsson. 2016. *Green Victorians: The Simple Life in John Ruskin's Lake District*. Chicago, IL: University of Chicago Press. https://doi.org/10.7208/chicago/9780226340043.001.0001

Allen, David E. 1978. *The Naturalist in Britain: A Social History*. Harmondsworth: Penguin.

Alston, Charlotte. 2014. *Tolstoy and His Disciples: The History of a Radical International Movement*. London: I.B. Tauris. https://doi.org/10.5040/9780755621187

Bach, Edward. 1937 [1931]. *Heal Thyself: An Explanation of the Real Cause and Cure of Disease*. London: C.W. Daniel.

———. 1941 [1933]. *The Twelve Healers and Other Remedies*. London: C.W. Daniel.

"Bill MacLellan, publisher." 1996. *Glasgow Herald*, 19 October 1996.

---

difficult task of overall synthesis and interpretation."

18. "... ist es durchaus sinnvoll, von einer lebensreformerischen Tradition in Großbritannien zu sprechen, die bis in die Gegenwart reicht, auch wenn es den Begriff im Englishen nicht gibt." (translation by the author with Philippe Bornet).

Bircher Benner, M. and Max E. Bircher. 1939 [1926]. *Fruit Dishes and Raw Vegetables*. London: C. W. Daniel.

Bridge of Weir Literary Society. 1910. *Lecture syllabus for the 1910-1911 session*. Acc. 3721. Papers of the Scottish Secretariat of Roland Eugene Muirhead. Box 153/2. National Library of Scotland Archives. Edinburgh.

Deacon, Desley, Russell, Penny and Angela Woollacott. 2010. "Introduction." In *Transnational Lives: Biographies of Global Modernity 1700-Present*, edited by D. Deacon, P. Russell and A. Woollacott, 1-11. Basingstoke, Hampshire: Palgrave Macmillan. https://doi.org/10.1057/9780230277472_1

"Dugald Semple Not for the Army: 'Simple Lifer' Impresses Appeal Court'." 1916. *Paisley and Renfrewshire Gazette*, 20 May 1916.

Duncan, Robert. 2015. *Objectors and Resistors: Opposition to Conscription and War in Scotland 1914-1918*. N.p.: Common Print.

Finlay, Richard J. 2004. "Muirhead, Roland Eugene." *Oxford Dictionary of National Biography*. http://www.oxforddnb.com/view/10.1093/ref:odnb/9780198614128.001.0001/odnb-9780198614128-e-40350

Fliess, Walter. 1897. *Die Magen und Darmkrankheiten und Naturgemäße Behandlung desselben*. Hamburg.

Gassert, Imogen. 2000. "C. W. Daniel: Maverick Pacifist Publisher in the First World War." *Publishing History* 48: 7-40.

Gould, Peter C. 1988. *Early Green Politics: Back to Nature, Back to the Land, and Socialism in Britain 1880-1900*. Brighton: Harvester Press.

Green, Martin. 2000. "New Centres of Life." In *Beyond New Age: Exploring Alternative Spirituality*, edited by S. Sutcliffe and M. Bowman, 51-64. Edinburgh: Edinburgh University Press.

Gregory, James. 2007. *Of Victorians and Vegetarians: The Vegetarian Movement in Nineteenth-Century Britain*. London: I. B Tauris.

Grieve, Mrs M. c. 1920. *Culinary Herbs*. Tamworth: The Author.

"He Really Lives the Simple Life." 1961. *The Waukegan News-Sun*, 29 November 1961, 4, Semple archive, c/o Mazda Munn, Great Cumbrae.

Jefferies, Matthew. 2003. "Lebensreform: A Middle-Class Antidote to Wilhelminism?" In *Wilhelminism and Its Legacies: German Modernities, Imperialism and the Meanings of Reform, 1890-1930*, edited by G. Eley and J. Retallack, 91-106. Oxford: Berghahn.

Kenefick, William. 2007. "War Resisters and Anti-Conscription." In *Red Scotland! The Rise and Fall of the Radical Left c. 1872-1932*, 132-158. Edinburgh: Edinburgh University Press. https://doi.org/10.3366/edinburgh/9780748625178.003.0006

Knaggs, H. Valentine. 1919. *The Salad Road to Health*. London: C.W. Daniel.

Kuiper, Yme B. 2013. "Tolstoyans on a Mountain: from New Practices of Asceticism to the Deconstruction of the Myths of Monte Verità." *Journal of Religion in Europe* 6: 464-481. https://doi.org/10.1163/18748929-00604007

Lee, Royal. n.d. *Practical Methods in Preparing Health-Building Foods*. Milwaukee, Wisconsin: Lee Foundation for Nutritional Research.

Leneman, Leah. 1989. *Fit for Heroes? Land Settlement in Scotland after World War I*. Aberdeen: Aberdeen University Press.

———. 1999. "No Animal Food: The Road to Veganism in Britain, 1909–1944." *Society and Animals* 7(3): 219-228. https://doi.org/10.1163/156853099X00095

Leonard, Tom, ed. 1990. *Radical Renfrew: Poetry from the French Revolution to the First World War*. Edinburgh: Polygon.

MacCarthy, Fiona. 1981. *The Simple Life: C.R. Ashbee in the Cotswolds*. London: Faber and Faber.

Marsh, Jan. 1982. *Back to the Land: The Pastoral Impulse in Victorian England from 1880 to 1914*. London: Quartet.

Matless, David. 1998. *Landscape and Englishness*. London: Reaktion Books.

Meyer-Renschhausen, Elisabeth and Albert Wirz. 1999. "Dietetics, Health Reform and Social Order: Vegetarianism as a Moral Physiology. The example of Maximilian Bircher-Benner (1867-1939)." *Medical History* 43: 323-341. https://doi.org/10.1017/S0025727300065388

Moore, P. Geoffrey 2014. "Natural History in Newspapers: Dugald Semple (1884–1964), Ayrshire Naturalist and Nature Journalist." *Archives of Natural history* 41(2): 209-222. https://doi.org/10.3366/anh.2014.0242

Munn, Mazda. 2015. "How I was introduced to Dugald Semple's Simple Life." Unpublished typescript, 3p.

Newton, R. 2014. "Semple Centre." *Fairlie Parish Church News*, March 2014, 4.

Peeters, Evert. 2011. "The Performance of Redemption: Asceticism and Liberation in Belgian *Lebensreform*." In *Beyond Pleasure: Cultures of Modern Asceticism*, edited by E. Peeters, L. van Molle and K. Wils, 21-41. New York: Berghahn Books.

Rae, John. 1970. *Conscience and Politics: The British Government and the Conscientious Objector to Military Service 1916-1919*. Oxford: Oxford University Press.

"Raw Food in Health and Disease." 1947. https://ivu.org/congress/wvc47/raw-food.html

Reid, Donald L. 2000. *Old Beith*. Catrine, Ayrshire: Stenlake.

Reid, Walter 2016. *Supreme Sacrifice: A Small Village and the Great War*. Edinburgh: Birlinn.

Rohkrämer, Thomas 2013. "Gab es eine Lebensreformbewegung in England?" In *"Lebensreform": Die soziale Dynamik der politischen Ohnmacht / La dynam-*

ique sociale de l'impuissance politique, edited by M. Cluet and C. Repussard, 319-335. Tübingen: Francke Verlag.

Rowbotham, Sheila. 2008. *Edward Carpenter: A Life of Liberty and Love*. London: Verso.

Sedgwick, Mark. 2016. *Western Sufism: From the Abassids to the New Age*. Oxford: Oxford University Press. https://doi.org/10.1093/acprof:oso/9780199977642.001.0001

Semple, Cathie. 1938. *Wheelhouse Good Health Recipes*. London: C.W. Daniel.

Semple, Dugald. 1909. *Simple Life Visitors*. Paisley: J. and J. Cook.

———. 1911. *Living in Liberty; or, The Wheelhouse Philosophy*. Paisley: Alexander Gardner.

———. c. 1912. Leaflet "Wheelhouse," Bridge of Weir. Acc. 3721. Papers of the Scottish Secretariat of Roland Eugene Muirhead. Box 153/2, National Library of Scotland Archives. Edinburgh.

———. 1915. *Joys of the Simple Life*. London: G. Bell.

———. 1919. *Life in the Open*. London: G. Bell and Sons.

———. 1925. *Diet and Good Health: A Popular Treatise on the Food Question*. London: C.W. Daniel.

———. 1933. *A Free Man's Philosophy*. London: C.W. Daniel.

———. 1935. *Scottish No-Stipend League: An Appeal for Freedom*. Beith: The Author.

———. c. 1945. *Be Your Own Doctor: Natural Cures for Common Ailments*. Glasgow: William MacLellan.

———. 1946. *Looking at Nature*. Glasgow: William MacLellan.

———. 1951. "Letter from Semple to Muirhead, 28 February 1951," Acc. 3721. Papers of the Scottish Secretariat of Roland Eugene Muirhead. Box 18/509, National Library of Scotland Archives. Edinburgh.

———. c. 1952. *The Simple Teaching of Jesus*. Largs: The Author.

———. 1953. "Wie ich das einfache Leben lebe." *Der Wendepunkt*, May 1953: 234–237.

———. 1956. *The Sunfood Way to Health*. London: Health for All.

———. 1957. *Joy in Living: An Autobiography*. Glasgow: William MacLellan.

———. 1960. "Vegetarianism and World Peace." *The British Vegetarian* 2(6). https://ivu.org/congress/wvc60/semple.html

Sharma, Avi. 2012. "Wilhelmine Nature: Natural Lifestyle and Practical Politics in the German Life-reform Movement (1890-1914)." *Social History* 37(1): 36-54. https://doi.org/10.1080/03071022.2011.651583

Shaw, Nellie. 1935. *Whiteway: A Colony on the Cotswolds*. London: C.W. Daniel.

"Simple Lifer's Appeal Refused: Dugald Semple Marked for Non-Combatant Service." 1916. *Paisley and Renfrewshire Gazette*, 1 April 1916.

Stone, Dan. 2004. "The Far Right and the Back-to-the Land Movement." In *The Culture of Fascism: Visions of the Far Right in Britain*, edited by J. V. Gottlieb and T. P. Linehan, 182–198. London: I.B. Tauris.

Sutcliffe, Steven J. 2007. "The Origins of 'New Age' Religion between the Two World Wars." In *Handbook of New Age*, edited by D. Kemp and J. Lewis, 51–75. Leiden: Brill. https://doi.org/10.1163/ej.9789004153554.i-484.21

———. 2010. "After 'the Religion of My Fathers': The Quest for Composure in the 'Post-Presbyterian' Self." In *A History of Everyday Life in Twentieth Century Scotland*, edited by L. Abrams and C. Brown, 181–205. Edinburgh: Edinburgh University Press.

———. 2018. "Absolutism and Pragmatism in the Conscientious Objection to Military Service during the 1914-18 War: The Case of Dugald Semple (1884-1964) in Scotland," *Kirchliche Zeitgeschichte* 31(1):43–57. https://doi.org/10.13109/kize.2018.31.1.43

Taylor, Antony. 2016. "The Whiteway Anarchists in the Twentieth Century: A Transnational Community in the Cotswolds." *History: The Journal of the Historical Association* 101/344: 62–83. https://doi.org/10.1111/1468-229X.12142

"The International Vegetarian Congress at Oslo and Hurdals Verk, Norway." 1938. *The Vegetarian Messenger* (Manchester, England), August 1938. http://www.ivu.org/congress/wvc38/manchester-report.html

Third Eye Centre. 1987. "William MacLellan. A Pioneer Publisher: Scottish Arts and Letters 1940 to the Present Day." Glasgow: Third Eye Centre.

Thoms, Ulrike. 2010. "Vegetarianism, Meat and Life Reform in Early Twentieth-Century Germany." In *Meat, Medicine, and Human Health in the Twentieth Century*, edited by D. Cantor, C. Bonah and M. Dörries, 145–159. London: Pickering and Chatto.

Treitel, Corinna. 2004. *A Science for the Soul: Occultism and the Genesis of the German Modern*. Baltimore, MD: Johns Hopkins University Press.

Treitel, Corinna. 2017. *Eating Nature in Modern Germany: Food, Agriculture and Environment c. 1870-2000*. Cambridge: Cambridge University Press. https://doi.org/10.1017/9781316946312

Twigg, Julia. 1981. "The Vegetarian Movement in England 1847-1981: A Study in the Structure of Its Ideology." Unpublished PhD Thesis, London School of Economics. http://www.ivu.org/history/thesis/bibliography.html

Waerland, Are. 1934. *In the Cauldron of Disease*. London: David Nutt.

Walter, Nicolas. 2011. "C.W. Daniel: The Odd Man." In *Damned Fools in Utopia and Other Writings on Anarchism and War Resistance*, edited by D. Goodway, 225-239. Oakland, CA: PM Press.

Williams, John A. 2007. *Turning to Nature in Germany: Hiking, Nudism, and Conservation, 1900-1940*. Stanford, CA: Stanford University Press.

Willis, Lonnie L. 1999. "The Thoreau Centenary in Britain." *American Studies International* 37(2): 43-68.

About the author

Steven Sutcliffe, University of Edinburgh, is Senior Lecturer in the Study of Religion. He specializes in the study of alternative religion in modernity and in the modern history of the study of religion/s. He is author of *Children of the New Age: A History of Spiritual Practices* (2003), co-editor (with Ingvild Sælid Gilhus) of *New Age Spirituality: Rethinking Religion* (2013) and co-editor (with Marion Bowman) of *Beyond New Age: Exploring Alternative Spirituality* (2000). He also edited *Religion: Empirical Studies* (2004) and is a co-editor for the Bloomsbury Advances in Religious Studies monograph series. His current research includes the archive of the Scottish conscientious objector and "simple life" practitioner, Dugald Semple (1884-1964), and the social and cultural history of the Gurdjieff-Ouspenky movement.

— 6 —

Re-discovering Buddha's Land: The Transnational Formative Years of China's Indology

MINYU ZHANG

Since its reopening up in the 1840s, China came again into contact with India, the former "Buddha's land," at different occasions in which intellectual interests were entangled with questions about China's cultural self-identity and political ideology. Modern Indology was brought into China as a part of Western studies, first indirectly via Japanese scholarship and later directly from the Europe-US Western world. The internalized Buddhist legacy and the work of diligent Buddhist intellectuals added Chinese indigenousness to this branch of Western studies. The encounter of early scholars with Western oriental studies paved the way for Ji Xianlin, who later studied Indology in Göttingen and brought back the German academic tradition to China. In addition, pragmatic concerns that appeared during the later years of World War II—with the Allies' strategic supply provided via India—encouraged the building of a special India-China relation, materialized through the creation of a Hindi programme in the new National Institute of Oriental Languages. Thus, in the formative years of China's Indology, Chinese intellectuals developed their perspectives within three major transnational networks: the revived Buddhist ancestral China-India connection, the scholarly network around Western, particularly German orientalists, and the political network based on socialist and anti-imperialist ideology. The internalization of these streams resulted in a distinct appearance of China's Indology and still influences China's perception of India.

In 1917, Xu Jishang (1891–1953), a scholarly Buddhist layman, started his class on Indian philosophy at Peking University (hereafter PKU). This is regarded as the beginning of Indology in China (Wang 1998). In the past century, a lot of prominent Chinese scholars, both Indology specialists and non-specialists, participated in the founding of Indology in China. Unlike cultural contacts between the two Asian civilizations in ancient times, modern Indology in China itself is a product of the intellectual globalization of the modern era involving grand transnational networks.

Re-engaging the Buddha's land

After retreating from the Indian Ocean in the fifteenth century, China came into contact with India again in the nineteenth century. Now a colonized territory, the former "Buddha's land" had become the frontier of European power. In order to balance trade deficits, the British East India Company turned India into a major exporter of opium. Meanwhile, around five hundred Chinese, including tea plantation labourers, craftsmen and petty merchants mostly from costal Guangdong province, had settled down in port cities like Calcutta and Bombay by the mid-nineteenth century. Conversely, in the two opium wars spanning from 1840 to 1860, thousands of Indian sepoys served in the British expeditionary force. The wars defeated not only China's outdated forces, but undermined a self-centric worldview as well. In one of his memorials to the throne demanding the construction of a modern fleet (1872), Li Hongzhang (1823–1901) said:

> I, your humble subject, have observed that since the past century or so, the European states have reached China via India and the South Sea. They intruded into our borders and heartland. Those who have never been recorded in history, who have never been in contact with us, all request to establish mutual trade ... This is an unprecedented change in the past three millenniums indeed! (Liang 2015)[1]

The unprecedented change and the humiliating defeats urged open-minded bureaucrats such as Li Hongzhang and royal princes like Yi Xin (1833–1898) to initiate importing modern military forces and re-engage the world more actively. In 1879, Huang Maocai (1843–1890) became the first official envoy to British India. Back in China, he compiled volumes of maps and reports, warning about possible British intrusion towards the southwestern frontier bordering India and Burma (Lin 1991). The bitter encounter with the British Indian forces and similar observations, thereafter, made India a frequently mentioned counter-example among the reformers, and, later, the revolutionaries. For instance, Zhang Zhidong (1837–1909), imperial governor of Huguang expressed his fear that China would become the next India if it kept on resisting new knowledge and insisted that in order to save China and "Chinese studies," learning "Western studies" should be compulsory (Zhang 1898). It was further summarized by Sun Jianai (1827–1909), the founder of Imperial University of Peking (later Peking University) in the following way: "*Chinese studies* as the core, *Western studies* as the tool" (Shi 1998; Zhongxue wei ti, xixue wei yong). After the humiliating defeat by the Japanese in 1895,

---

1. "Chen qie wei Ouzhou zhuguo, baishi nian lai, you Yindu er Nanyang, you Nanyang er Zhongguo, chuangru bianjie fudi, fan qianshi suo weizai, gengu suo weitong, wubu kuanguan er qiu hushi ... ci sanqian yu nian yi da bianju ye." Unless otherwise noted, all translations are my own.

young Emperor Guangxu (1875-1908) and reformers like Kang Youwei (1858-1927), Liang Qichao (1873-1929) and others, became impatient about the slow pace of reform and the conservative outlook of elder reformers. Their hasty Hundred Days' Reform (1898), however, failed due to conservative opposition. While in exile, Kang Youwei travelled to India and tried to draw lessons from the British colonization of India (Kang 1981).

Another humiliating defeat during the Boxer War (1899-1901) eventually convinced even the conservatives that learning *Western studies*—not only technology, but institutions and culture as well—was crucial for the endangered throne. Thereafter, philosophy was introduced into China as a discipline of study and a part of "Western studies." The early translations of foreign philosophical works laid the foundations of China's modern academic research on philosophy. The translators valued their own work, believing it an indispensable part of efforts to save first the scholarship, then the people's minds, the people, and finally the nation. At the dawn of the twentieth century, young Chinese students studying in Japan, then the role model for modernization, started to translate philosophical works with great enthusiasm. Japanese textbooks on philosophy translated by Chinese overseas students became China's first introduction to the intellectual world of the West (Xiong 2013). By then, thanks to the work of European and Japanese scholars, Indian philosophy had already been given a place within the discipline. Japanese scholarship, that of the Japanese Buddhist reformer Inoue Enryo (1858-1919) in particular, reinforced India's position. Unlike some other peers including Nishi Amane (1829-1897), a pioneer in introducing western philosophy, who would argue that there had been no philosophy in Japan, Inoue Enryo was among those who argued for the existence of philosophy within Buddhism and other oriental religions (Godart 2008). In his early work, *Epitome of Philosophy* (1886), which was among the earliest introductory books to philosophy in East and West written in Japanese, Inoue divided the world of philosophy into two parts: Oriental and Occidental. Chinese and Indian philosophies are two pillars of the oriental philosophy. Within Indian philosophy, he further placed Brahmanism and Buddhism. This book was translated into Chinese by Luo Boya in 1902. This was followed by another of Inoue's compositions, *Outline of Indian Philosophy* (1898), translated into Chinese by Wang Qin (1881-1921) in 1903.

Meanwhile, Buddhist intellectuals also started to engage India via Japan and the Western world. In 1866, at the end of the Taiping Civil War (1850-1864), a logistics officer of Zeng Guofan's (1811-1872) army and also a Buddhist layman, Yang Renshan, also known as Yang Wenhui (1837-1911), established Jinling Buddhist Publishing House together with other devout Buddhists. Initially, this was a purely Buddhist enterprise to preserve and publicize Buddhist scriptures in order to save all the living beings in the Dharma ending age

(Lv 1997). Due to historical reasons, many Buddhist scriptures were lost, damaged or contaminated. Yang and his colleagues, mostly well-educated Confucian intellectuals who favoured *Mahāyāna* philosophy, decided to discern and exclude apocryphal, suspicious, shallow and augural ritualistic works from their publishing catalogue. Resorting to the well-developed methodology of Chinese textual criticism, Kaoju Xue, they recollected, critically edited and published many important scriptures. In 1878, Yang was summoned by Zeng Guofan's son Zeng Jize (1839–1890) to join the Chinese Embassy in London as a counsellor. His exposure to the flourishing field of European Buddhology made him realize the value of foreign resources, both in terms of scriptures and scholarship. On one occasion, he met the Japanese Buddhist scholar, Nanjo Bunyu (1849–1927), then working with Max Müller (1823–1900) at Oxford. Nanjo introduced Müller's work on *Ṛg Veda* to Yang, but the Chinese Buddhist was more eager to know if Nanjo had a Sanskrit text of *Da Cheng Qi Xin Lun*, or *Mahāyāna Śraddhotpāda Śāstra* (Kaichao 2013). This was the primer that initiated Yang to Buddhism and the debate about its authenticity would involve most renowned Buddhist scholars, both Chinese and foreign, in the first half of the twentieth century. In the following years, with the help of Nanjo, Yang acquired hundreds of copies of lost Chinese Buddhist scriptures and several Sanskrit copies for his publishing house. In 1895, Yang met another foreign Buddhist, Sri Lankan monk Anagarika Dharmapala (1864–1933), who was travelling back from the 1893 Parliament of World Religions. Dharmapala's efforts and determination to revive and reform Buddhism impressed Yang. In the years to come, as Buddhist pilgrimages would be revived along both land and maritime trade routes, the Chinese Buddhists re-established a connection with the Buddhist world.[2] In 1907, Yang established Qihuan Jingshe, one of the earliest modern Buddhist institutes that would attract a growing number of Buddhist scholars and leaders.

India between China and the West

Disillusioned by the Manchurian ruling family's slow progress on constitutional reform, citizens increasingly turned towards violent revolution. In 1911, with the mutiny in Wuchang, the first dominoes fell, ending the Qing dynasty and a two-thousand-year-long monarchy. In the following years, the Republic of China (hereafter ROC) remained in a chaotic situation politically, witnessing the rise and fall of provincial warlords who had support from different external powers. Overwhelming military pressure and the need to win the support of intellectuals and the public, however, made warlords less

---

2. In 1904, the monk Qingfu traveled from southwestern Sichuan province to India via Burma. Later, another monk, Wanhui, followed in his footsteps to the Buddha's land. See *Encyclopedia of China-India Cultural Contacts, Complete Edition*, sub verbo "Zhong-Yin Fojiao Jiaoliu (Overview of China-India Buddhist Contacts)."

motivated to intervene in the scholarly world. Intellectuals were, to some extent, left free to carry out their educational experiments.

In 1916, 48-year-old Cai Yuanpei (1868-1940), former revolutionary Education Minister, returned from the University of Leipzig. He was recommended to Li Yuanhong (1864-1928), the new president of the ROC[3] who appointed him as the President of PKU, a legacy of the early Hundred Day's Reform. At that time, Cai already had a plan for PKU based on his observation of German universities. In 1910, he had already translated *The Features of German Universities*, i.e. the introductory part of *Die deutschen Universitäten und das Universitätsstudium* (1902) by the German philosopher Friedrich Paulsen (1846-1908). Cai agreed with Paulsen on how university professors' research and teaching could influence young students, thus exerting profound influence in the formation of a nation (Chen 2008). He firmly believed that his own nation would be saved through the education of the public. Now he had a platform to realize his ideal.

In his inaugural speech at PKU, Cai clearly stated that "university is where higher learning should be studied." He further asked students who wanted to pursue career development as their first priority to choose law school and business school instead of PKU. In 1917, "Indian Philosophy (Yindu Zhexue)," the first course on India in a modern Chinese university, was added to the PKU syllabus, a move which was part of Cai's initiative to strengthen research and teaching in the humanities. Having translated philosophical works and studied in Germany for years, it seemed natural that Indian philosophy would have a part to play in the PKU under Cai. He planned to invite Liang Shuming (1893-1988) to teach. However, Liang was then serving as secretary at the Ministry of Justice. Instead, Xu Jishang (1891-1953), a student of Yang Renshan, taught the course for the first year. Xu's lecture notes were largely based on then prevalent translations of Japanese and European textbooks (Liang 2013). They were handed over to Liang, who later reworked and compiled the *Introduction of Indian Philosophy* (1919). This book is divided into four parts, *Introduction, Ontology, Epistemology,* and *World View*, already in a framework much influenced by Western philosophy. Under each title, Liang introduced "The Law of Buddha" and "the Other Schools" respectively. The Buddhist-centrism of the textbook can be explained not only by Liang's personal preferences as a Buddhist layman, but also by the will to operate a reasonable choice, since Buddhist cultural legacy can be a shortcut for Chinese students. By then, Indian philosophy, Buddhist

---

3. The former Imperial Viceroy of Zhili and Minister of Beiyang Yuan Shikai (1859-1916) and his Beiyang clique took over the Republic, forcing the revolutionary government to dismiss itself. However, his later efforts to restore monarchy and to crown himself as the emperor were opposed by the revolutionaries and his subordinates alike. After his death, the Republic was restored with a fragile balance between the former Beiyang generals and revolutionaries.

philosophy in particular, had already become a platform of dialogue between the East and West, in which Liang had great interest. Using Buddhist philosophy as a yardstick and interpreting other schools by comparison, Liang was trying to bridge the gap between the Eastern and Western mind. A similar process was at work in India, where comparative philosophy (for example Spinoza and Vedānta) was often used to defend the dignity of local traditions (Halbfass 1985). For Liang and many Buddhist scholars, Buddhism was already an indispensable part of *Chinese studies*. Therefore, tracing the evolution of Buddhism was not only a way of studying India, but also of rediscovering an important part of the Chinese mentality itself. Thus, these two seemingly contradictory goals coexisted in China's study of Indian philosophy. This particular feature influenced the future development of China's Indology. Chinese students were attracted to study Indian philosophy, particularly Buddhist philosophy, whereas another main field of European Indology, Comparative Linguistics, remains relatively unpopular because of a lack of connection with the Chinese tradition.

Cai Yuanpei's reforms were supported by Hu Shi (1891–1962)[4] whose contributions to China's modern Indology cannot be underestimated despite the fact that he was not a professional Indologist. In 1918, with a recommendation from the vice-chancellor of the University of Hong Kong, Sir Charles Eliot (1862–1931), Hu invited Baron Alexander von Staël-Holstein (1877–1937) to teach Sanskrit and the history of Indian religions, joining the Department of Philosophy at PKU (Wang 2008, 12–13). Centuries after the closing of ancient Buddhist translation workshops, Sanskrit was once again formally taught in China, this time by a European Indologist who came to China incidentally.[5] His course lectures were in English and Hu would translate. Their cooperation was mutually beneficial. For Alexander von Staël-Holstein, Hu's reputation and popularity would have increased interest in his class. Meanwhile, Hu, though not a trained Indologist, started to research the intellectual history of China and begun his work on Buddhism with the help of Alexander von Staël-Holstein.[6] According to Hu, Alexander von Staël-Holstein envisaged the establishment of a "Department of Indian and Central Asian Philology" (Qian 1997), which could only, to some extent, be realized

---

4. Hu Shi got his doctor degree from Columbia University under the supervision of American philosopher John Dewey (1859–1952). His article "Some Modest Proposals for the Reform of Literature" made him famous even before his academic career started.

5. Baron Alexander von Staël-Holstein, a German-Baltic aristocrat was among the hundreds of thousands of White émigrés who moved to China in early twentieth century. However, he was not the only European teaching Sanskrit then in China. Another German scholar, Ferdinand Diedrich Lessing (1882–1961), taught Huang Shuyin Sanskrit and Pali while he was staying in Shandong.

6. For instance, it was Alexander von Staël-Holstein who told Hu Shi about Rāmāyaṇa and Hanuman, as explained in the next paragraph.

with the establishment of the "Department of Oriental Languages" after a quarter century of support of Hu and his colleagues. In 1923, Hu translated and published Alexander von Staël-Holstein's paper "The Phonetic Transcription of Sanskrit Works and Ancient Chinese Pronunciation," which, for the first time, drew Chinese scholars' attention to reconstructing the ancient pronunciations using comparative linguistics. Except for one year at Harvard, Alexander von Staël-Holstein spent the rest of his life in Beijing, where he imparted his knowledge to a number of Chinese scholars, such as Chen Yinke (1890–1969), Huang Shuyin (1898–1925) and Yu Daoquan (1901–1992).

Hu Shi's research also greatly increased scholars' interest in India. In 1923, Hu wrote his article on the critical study of Chinese fiction *Xiyouji*, a legend based on Xuan Zang (602–664)'s journey to India during the Tang dynasty. In an earlier letter to Hu Shi, Lu Xun (1881–1936), a famous progressive writer and guest lecturer at PKU, argued that a local deity, Wu Zhi Qi, was the origin of the popular Monkey King Sun Wukong. Hu, however, wrote in his article:

> I have always doubted if this omnipotent monkey is not domestic, but imported from India. Perhaps even the tales of Wu Zhi Qi themselves were produced under Indian influence. ... Following the guidance of Dr. Alexander von Staël-Holstein, I discovered one figure, Hanuman, in the oldest Indian epic *Ramayana*, which can be seen as a backdrop of the Qi Tian Da Sheng [i.e. the Monkey King] (1980).[7]

The two star intellectuals of that age triggered a long-lasting debate.[8] However, for Hu, the argument on Sun Wukong's literary prototype was but a reflection of his grand picture of an intellectual history of China and its relation to India. In the following years of teaching, Hu extended his interest beyond the pre-Qin period to China's "medieval time" that spans between 220 BCE–1020 CE. In his lecture notes (1931–1932), he summarized the features of "medieval time" as such: "1. The religionalization of thoughts; 2. The Indianization of the outlook on life; 3. The hidden struggle between the Chinese and Indian thoughts" (2013, 330). In 1937, he further elaborated this argument and published an English article "The Indianization of China: A Case Study in Cultural Borrowing." Unlike Buddhist scholars, Hu is critical towards the superstitious religious life and intellectual sophistication that

---

7. "Dan wo zong yixin zhege shentonggunagda de houzi bu shi guohuo, naishi yijian cong Yindu jinkou de. Yexu lian Wu Zhi Qi de shenhua yeshi shoule Yindu yingxiang er fangzao de ... zai Gang Hetai boshi (Baror A. von stael holstein) de zhiyin, zai Yindu zui gu de jishishi *Ramazhuan (Ramayana)* limian xunde yige Ha Numan (Hanuman), dagai keyi suanshi Qi Tian Da Sheng de beiying le."

8. Hu's argument was more popular among the intellectuals. Chen Yinke, Zheng Zhenduo, Ji Xianlin and most later Indologists supported Hu; Wu Xiaoling (1914–1995), the Chinese literature specialist and Sanskrit scholar, favoured Lu Xun's view (Ge 2002; Zhao 1986).

had hampered the development of China. He had apparently brought the concept of "medieval time," and probably its hidden implication of a "dark age," from European history and applied it to his analysis of Chinese history. He made his point clear in the article:

> Indeed, nowhere in the world, with the only possible exception of the Christianization of Europe, can one find another source of historical materials equal in extent and in length of time. I venture to say that this attempt to study the Indianization of China as a case of extensive cultural borrowing may be found at least of suggestive value to the study of the parallel, though not quite similar, story of the Christianization of Europe. (Chou 2013)

By engaging India and China in different aspects, Hu Shi successfully expanded the academic spectrum of China's Buddhist-centric Indology. His debate with Lu Xun regarding the Monkey King and other popular topics aroused general interests in non-Buddhist texts of ancient India like the *Rāmāyaṇa*. Re-evaluating Buddhism's role in China's history, he asked students to read contemporary European scholarship on Indian religions and literature, including Farquhar's [*An*] *Outline of Religious Literature in India*, Sir Charles Eliot's *Hinduism and Buddhism*, and his colleague Alexander von Staël-Holstein's lecture notes (2013, 362). "The Indianization of China," a concept he put forward, opened a new possible dialogue between the Chinese intellectuals and their Western counterparts as he envisaged it.

Another major factor that facilitated the advent of Indology in China is the "Tagore Fever," marked by the wide reception of Nobel laureate Rabindranath Tagore (1861–1941) and the poet's visit to China. Tagore was first formally introduced to the Chinese reader by Qian Zhixiu (1883–1947) just after the award of the Nobel prize (Qian 1913). Chen Duxiu (1879–1942), founder of the Communist Party, translated four poems out of *Gītañjali* (Zhang 1981). Tagore's beautiful works, particularly his poetry, became so popular among the young writers experimenting with different forms of vernacular Chinese literature— one of the main agendas of the New Culture Movement—that there would be soon various versions of different collections translated by different writers. Initiated by Zheng Zhenduo (1898–1958), Tagore's admirers even formed a Tagore Study Society under the Literature Study Society, whose periodical publication *Novel Monthly* soon became a window through which Chinese readers were introduced to the Indian poet (Wang 2011). In 1923, upon the invitation of Jiang Xue She funded by Liang Qichao, Rabindranath Tagore visited China. Being warmly welcomed, he shared with the Chinese audience his understanding of humanity, universal love and the value of the oriental culture. On the other hand, harsh criticism also emerged. For instance, Chen Duxiu and Qu Qiubai (1899–1935) criticized Rabindranath's uplift of universal love as a doomed petition in the world of imperialist oppression. Chen Duxiu, the earliest translator of Rabindranath's poetry, wrote:

> Now Tagore has come and cried out "love." Whereas my question towards you is that is it possible that such a cry for 'love' will ever move the European-US capitalists and make them practice universal human love? Will it make them nullify imperialism? Will it make them stop exploiting the working class and the weak nations? In my opinion, this is just like telling the tiger: "Do not to eat human!" (1924).[9]

For many like Chen Duxiu and Qu Qiubai, what China needed at that moment was a brave revolution against internal feudalism, capitalism and external imperialism. The combination of Marxist-Leninist ideology and strong nationalist sentiments left little patience to appreciate a "backward oriental" voice from a failed colony like India, as the southwestern neighbour was regarded by many Chinese during the nineteenth century. Nevertheless, just as Hu Shi's interventions which either triggered or participated in a series of academic debates concerning India actually helped Indology, controversies around Rabindranth Tagore, combined with his well-received poetry, helped arouse an interest in India and made it fashionable to study an India that was no longer remembered solely as the Buddha's land. Rabindranath's visit also established an important direct link between the intellectuals of the two countries. In the years to come, his Visva Bharati University played a major role in the exchange of personnel, including some future Indologists. Such exchange was also a part of Rabindranath's efforts to promote his idea of Asiatism (Stolte and Fischer-Tiné 2012).

In sum, in the early years of the twentieth century, the historical legacy of China-India contacts, the contact with European scholars and the "Tagore fever" all helped the humanities scholars in modern universities to start creating a primitive sphere of Indology in China. Though Buddhism still contributed significantly to the interest in India, some non-religious aspects of this area of study gradually emerged as well.

Indologists' journey to the "Western paradises"

Following the new roadmap of Indology drawn up by the Buddhist community, diplomats, Chinese diaspora and precedent scholars, young Chinese students set out for their own journeys to the West to study Indology. Unlike the Buddhist monks in ancient China, they have before them two "Western paradises"—the Europe-US Western world and India.

---

9. "Cishi Tai Ge'er youlai jiao 'ai', woyao wenwen ni zhe 'ai' zhi jiaosheng, nenggou gandong Oumei zichan jieji shi tamen shixing renlei xiang'ai, shi tamen ziji quxiao ziben diguozhuyi, buqu lveduo laodong jieji, buqu qinlve ruoxiao minzu ma? Wo kan dengyu xiang laohu shuo: 'Ni buyao chiren ba.'"

The new Western paradise: Europe and the US

Among the Chinese students of European Indology in the early twentieth century, a crucial figure is Chen Yinke. Though he takes more interest in Chinese history than Indology, he was among the first groups of Chinese students to study Indian philology systematically in Western institutions. He conducted a number of study trips abroad, witnessing and actively facilitating the founding of Indology in China. Chen Yinke's grandfather Chen Baozhen (1831-1900) was a former imperial governor of Hunan and a keen reformist who supported the Hundred Days' Reform in 1898. After the failed reform, Chen Baozhen and Chen Yinke's father Chen Sanli (1853-1937) were dismissed and moved back to their hometown in Jiangxi province. In 1903, two years before the official termination of the old imperial examination, Chen Sanli founded a modern primary school, Siyi Xiaoxuetang, where English, mathematics, and the sciences were taught by both Chinese and foreign faculties. The family exposure to *Western studies* explains why Chen Yinke was sent to Japan for secondary education. In 1909, his family supported him to study in Europe. He attended a wide range of courses in Berlin, Zurich and Paris. In Paris, he was introduced to Paul Pelliot (1878-1945) by Wang Guowei (1877-1927) (Yin 1998). Through his contact with Paul Pelliot and European scholarship, Chen Yinke, an enthusiast of the northwestern frontier's history and geography, realized the importance of Indian and Central Asian philology and the crucial role of textual criticism for historical study. World War I temporarily held him back but in 1918, he won a scholarship from the provincial government in Jiangxi and set out for Harvard. At Harvard, he studied Sanskrit and Pali with Charles R. Lanman (1850-1941), accompanied by a group of Chinese students supported by the Boxer Indemnity Scholarship Program, including Tang Yongtong (1893-1964). In 1921, as the situation in Europe became stabilized, he moved to Berlin to study with German orientalists like Heinrich Lüders (1869-1943) and Friedrich Wilhelm Karl Müller (1863-1930). Though Chen Yinke never got a formal degree from a university, he was offered a position in Tsinghua College (later Tsinghua University) under strong recommendation from Liang Qichao and Wu Mi (1894-1978), his classmate at Harvard. Chen taught a number of courses on Chinese history and literature in Tsinghua, one of which focused on the translation of Buddhist scriptural literature. Among the young students in this class there was Ji Xianlin (1911-2009), who majored in German.

Unlike his teacher Chen Yinke, Ji grew up in a humble peasant family in Shandong. His original reason to choose Tsinghua was simply the college's reputation for overseas connections. At the time, a foreign degree meant a well-paid job and the opportunity to improve the living standards of his family. In 1935, Ji was awarded a DAAD scholarship to study in Germany. Before his trip to Germany, he was determined to never write a thesis on China

(Ji 2008). He recalled Lu Xun's harsh criticism of the Chinese students who impressed their foreign tutors with knowledge of Kongzi and Laozi, and their fellow countrymen with Kant and Hegel. After initial bewilderment, Ji decided to study Indology at Göttingen. He wrote in his diary on 16 December 1935:

> Again, it occurred to me that I have to learn Sanskrit. Chinese culture is so heavily influenced by Indian culture. If I study the China-India cultural relation thoroughly, I may discover something. Even if I only managed to learn the certain desired languages, Sanskrit in particular, while in Germany, this is worth the long journey. Back in China, even if I should be willing to learn, there would be no one to teach. (2008)[10]

By then the idea of Indian culture casting a strong influence over China was an entirely natural one for a young student like Ji. Though Ji's understanding of the process is not necessary the same as Hu Shi's "Indianization," such widespread admission of foreign influence was itself a result of the earlier collapse of the conservative China-centric worldview.

During the following 10 years—his stay in Europe being prolonged due to World War II—Ji studied under the supervision of Ernst Waldschmidt (1897–1985) and later Emil Sieg (1866–1951). Initially, Waldschmidt suggested that he works on a thesis using Chinese texts, but Ji convinced Waldschmidt that he should study grammar and become an Indologist professionally trained in the European style. In 1941, Ji finished his dissertation, titled "Die Konjugation des finiten Verbums in den Gāthās des *Mahāvastu*." Assuring the committee of the quality of the dissertation, Emil Sieg wrote in his recommendation: "[I] firmly believe that we can proudly send this young doctor back to his homeland, where he will add the glory of German scholarship," (Chen 2009; shen xin, wo men ke yi zi hao de jiang ci nian qing de bo shi song hui qi jia xiang, ta yi ding hui zai na li wei De guo de xue shu zeng tian rong yu) an expectation that Ji certainly lived up to.

Upon the end of World War II in both Europe and East Asia in 1945, Ji set out on his return trip to China. He approached Chen Yinke, his former teacher at Tsing Hua and by now his guru-uncle.[11] Impressed with his research, Chen recommended Ji to his colleagues and friends in Beijing, including then President of PKU Hu Shi, Deputy President Fu Sinian (1896–1950) and the head of the arts faculty Tang Yongtong. In the autumn of 1946, Ji joined PKU.

---

10. "Wo you xiangdao wo zhongyu fei du Sanskrit (fan wen) buxing. Zhongguo wenhua shou Yindu wenhua de yingxiang taida le. Wo yao dui zhongyin wenhua guanxi chedi yanjiu yixia, huo neng yousuo faming. Zai Deguo neng ba xiangxue de jizhong wenzi xuehao, yejiu buxucixing le. Youqishi Sanskrit, huiguohou zai xiangxue, budan meiyou nayang de ji hui, ye meiyou nayang de ren." Apparently Ji Xianlin did not know about the Sanskrit class offered by Alexander von Staël-Holstein at PKU, whose campus was located some distance from Tsinghua.

11. Both Ernst Waldschmidt and Chen Yinke studied with Heinrich Lüders in Berlin.

The old Western paradise: India

Though individual monks started to resume the pilgrimage to India in the early twentieth century, it was not until the growth of Rabindranath Tagore's fame and his visit to China in the 1920s that young Chinese people, both Buddhist and non-Buddhist, realized that India could also be a destination for higher education. Yu Daoquan, who later became a Tibetologist, was among the group of Tagore admirers. He expressed his will to study at Visva Bharati University founded by the poet. Due to political instability, however, Yu could not make the trip and was later recommended by Tagore to work with Alexander von Staël-Holstein at PKU. At the same time, Tagore was looking for Chinese faculty teachers for Visva Bharati. In 1927, he met Tan Yunshan (1898–1983) in Singapore and invited him to teach Chinese at Visva Bharati. In the following years, Tan Yunshan shuttled between China and India. One of Tan Yunshan's major achievements was to establish Cheena-Bhavan, or the Chinese Department at Visva Bharati, in 1937, for which Tan Yunshan actively raised funding and books. Cheena-Bhavan became a transit spot for Chinese officials and scholars visiting India.

Among the first group of Chinese visitors to Cheena Bhavan was a Chinese Buddhist delegation led by Master Taixu (1890–1947). He had studied at Yang Renshan's Qihuan Jingshe and, having witnessed the decline of his nation and religion since childhood, he started to read the works of the revolutionaries along with Buddhist scripture (Shi 2011, 23). In order to rally support for China's desperate fight, Taixu headed a delegation to Southeast Asia and India.[12] Under Taixu's recommendation and guidance, Fa Fang (1904–1951) and Bai Hui (1919–2014)[13] later joined Visva Bharati to study Sanskrit, Pali, Buddhist texts and Indian philosophy.

As the Japanese occupied large parts of coastal China in the 1940s, more and more Chinese fled to Southeast Asia and India via land and naval routes. Jin Kemu (1912–2000) was one of them. He reached Calcutta via Burma in 1941. His friend and roommate, Zhou Dafu was then assisting Vidhushekara Battacharya Shastri in editing the Sanskrit text *Yogācārabhūmi Śāstra* at Visva Bharati. It was under Zhou Dafu's encouragement that Jin started to study Sanskrit and Hindi with him (Jin 1999, i–ii). In 1943, Jin moved to Sarnath, where he met Dharmananda Kosambi (1876–1947), a pro-Marxist Buddhist

---

12. Until the breakout of the Pacific War in 1941, China had to face the Japanese invasion alone. The only external support came from Germany and the Soviet Union. For the ROC government, calling international attention and rallying support from the Chinese diaspora, both financial and personal, was important. That was one of the main considerations behind the permission of Taixu's visit and Hu Shi's appointment as the Chinese ambassador to Washington.

13. Bai Hui, later known as Wu Baihui, would later join the Hindi section at PKU after the war.

who studied Sanskrit from old Sanskrit pandits in Varanasi and Pali from Sri Lankan monks. In the following years, Jin furthered his study of Sanskrit following a traditional way. He recorded a small yet international class on *Visuddhimagga* with two more classmates, a Sri Lankan monk and an English lady.

> The [Sri Lankan] monk reads out a paragraph of Pali text. The old upāsaka [i.e. Kosambi] paraphrases it into Sanskrit casually, obviously for my convenience, teaching me. Then he explains a bit in English, for the convenience of the English upāsikā. Then he adds his personal comments in an unrestrained and imaginative way. He says due to his poor sights, he cannot read under the lamp, relying fully on his memory. He does not repeat the simple sentence, whereas he may utter a whole commentary with many profound meanings and metaphors on one particular verse. This is the feature of *Visuddhimagga*. Not until did I realize that ancient Indian texts were but written records of such oral teaching. (2011)[14]

Joining Ji, Jin's arrival is thought to have brought to PKU the combination of the German Indology tradition with an Indian one (Duan 2002). However, even Kosambi was not totally disconnected from the world of Western Indology. He once worked at Harvard and helped Charles R. Lanman edit *Visuddhimagga*. Though it is not clear if he met any Chinese students studying Indology at Harvard, this is yet another example of the hybridity of Indology in modern China.

The formation of the Indology community

Alexander von Staël-Holstein was not able to see the establishment of a Department of Indian and Central Asian Philology. Till his last days, interest in Indology was still scattered around and loosely connected, sometimes overlapping intellectual groups including scholars of Chinese philosophy and history, Buddhist intellectuals, admirers of Tagore and so on. However, as India started to emerge as a nation state, and an important political partner for China, the more unified state, both wartime ROC government and its successor the People's Republic of China (hereafter PRC) stepped into the academic world. The patriotism of the intellectuals, partially predestined by the Confucian ethic of "loyalty" imbibed from childhood, also urged them to cooperate more closely with the state. State intervention and the reposito-

---

14. "Heshang xuandu yiduan baliyu yuanwen, lao jushi suikou niancheng fanwen, zhe xianran shi wei wode fangbian, ye jiushi jiao wo. Ranhou yong yingyu lvezuo jieshuo, zhe shi weile yingguo nv jushi. Jiezhe jiu shangtianxiadi de fahui tade yijian. Ta shuo yanjing laohua, meiyoudeng xia buneng kanshu, quanping jiyi beisong jingdian. Youde juzi ta renwei rongyi, jiu bu chongfu shuo shenme; youshi yiju jiyu jiu neng yinchu yipian yilun, xuduo aoyi, jiazhe piyu, cengchubuqiong. Zhe ye zhengshi *Qingjingdaolun* de tedian. Wo cai zhidao, yuanlai Yindu gushu tili jiushi zhezhong kouyu jiangshuo de fangshi de jilu."

ries of human resources accumulated in previous decades eventually gave birth to an independent Indology community, which would act as one of the core groups of China's orientalist scholarship.

When the Pacific War broke out in 1941, China had already lost all major ports and had to rely on the strategic aids supplied via the Yunnan-Burma road. Extending the supply line to India became an urgent task. In 1942, the Chairman of the National Military Council Jiang Jieshi (1887–1975) visited British India. In addition to diplomatic and military success, this visit also had an impact on China's Indology. Having realized the importance of contacts with India and Southeast Asian peoples, the ROC government established a new National Institute of Oriental Languages (hereafter NIOL) in Yunnan. Hindi was added to the curriculum. Tan Yunshan, who hosted Jiang during his visit to Cheena Bhavan, soon sent Visva Bharati student K. K. Singh to teach Hindi. During wartime, the demand for instrumental knowledge that could solve urgent problems for the nation outstripped purely intellectual endeavours such as examining the self. Young students of NIOL, instead of pursuing "higher learning," had to acquire the language as soon as possible and went on to establish the teaching system of Hindi in China.

Yin Hongyuan (1925–) is the leading figure of early NIOL students. He was born in the coastal Jiangsu province. When he set out for higher education, his homeland was already under the puppet regime headed up by the collaborator Wang Jingwei (1883–1944). Instead of studying in one of the nearby institutions, he went to the wartime capital and southwestern city, Chongqing. Due to ongoing warfare, he had to first travel northwards to Shanxi and then southwards to Sichuan, Chongqing, where the newly established NIOL had relocated. Unlike Sanskrit, which was already a cosmopolitan academic language with a highly international community of scholars, Hindi, for the Chinese students, was but a tool to save their nation. After graduation, Yin Hongyuan was hired as a Hindi teacher, dedicating much of his time to teaching, and textbook and dictionary compilation.[15]

In the autumn of 1946, only one week after joining PKU, Ji , the young doctor from Göttingen, was informed by Tang Yongtong, the head of the arts faculty, that the university administration had decided to appoint him as professor and head of the new Department of Oriental Languages. However, he soon found himself in difficulty. The scarcity of library collections relating to India threatened his career as a professional Indologist. As he would reflect in his biography:

---

15. This is based on personal interviews between Yin Hongyuan and the author. At the time of writing, Yin Hongyuan, now over 90, just completed the 2016 edition of Chinese-Hindi dictionary and is already working on a new edition of a Hindi-Chinese dictionary. His grammar books are still considered the cornerstones of Hindi teaching in China.

> My interest in the field of Indian literature is mainly on the Sanskrit language, the "hybrid Sanskrit" in particular, of the ancient and medieval Buddhist scriptures. My doctoral thesis and several other papers I wrote while in Göttingen shall prove that. However, such research work requires a large amount of specific monographs and journals. The University library of Göttingen and the collection of the Sanskrit Institute can meet such demands. ... Whereas in China, though the library collection is one of the world's largest, the situation of Indology collection is like a desert. (2008)[16]

He had no choice but to shift his research focus from "pure Indology" to the history of India-China contact and comparative literature, exactly what Ernst Waldschmidt had suggested. He studied how literature, technologies and material goods were transmitted around India, Central Asia and different parts of China and their influence on China. Some of his major contribution to this field includes *Datang Xiyuji Jiaozhu* (An annotated and critically edited version of Xuanzang's Travelogue, 1985), *Tangshi* (A History of Sugar, 1998), etc. Moreover, he started to implant the German Sanskrit teaching system into China and translate literary works like Kalidāsa's *Śakuntalā* (1956), *Vikramōrvaśīyam* (1962) and, later, *Rāmāyaṇa* (1980-1984). Had Ji chosen to remain in Europe, he could have progressed his research on hybrid Sanskrit in a more agreeable environment. However, back in China, he had to start from the very beginning.

In January 1949, the Communist army liberated Beijing. In just three months, Nanjing, the ROC capital, followed. Soon after the liberation of Nanjing, Ji received a letter from a former classmate at Tsinghua, Hu Qiaomu (1912-1992).[17] By 1946, Hu Qiaomu was already the vice president of Propaganda Department of the Communist Party of China Central Committee, the main secretary of Chairman Mao Zedong. Hu told Ji that the new government needed more specialists of oriental languages. He asked if Ji was willing to incorporate the National Institute of Oriental Languages, Department of Frontier Politics of the former National Central University and several other minor institutes into his department (Jiang 2016). Ji fully supported the decision and the NIOL was soon incorporated in July. This move may have been

---

16. "Wode xingqu zhuyao zai Yindu gudai ji zhongshi fodian fanwen shang, tebie shizai 'hunhe fanwen' shang. Duici wode boshi lunwen yiji wo zai Getinggen xiede jipian lunwen keyi weizheng. Ran'er zuo zheyang de gongzuo xuyao daliang zhuanye de zhuanzhu he zazhi. Getinggen daxue tushuguan he fanwen yanjiusuo tushushi shi jubei zhege tiaojian de ... Fanguan wo guo, suiran dianji zhi fujiatianxia, ran'er, tandao yinduxue shukan, ze jihu shi yipian shamo."

17. While in Tsinghua, Hu and Ji were close friends. In 1931, Hu had to quit Tsinghua due to his political activities. He joined the Communist Party and started his career as professional revolutionary.

influenced by the Soviet mode, but it is likely to have come down to the leadership's judgment. The leadership believed that former colonies scattered across Asia, Africa and Latin America, or "Ya Fei La"[18] would become friends of the newly liberated China and the main frontier of a future revolution against feudalism and imperialism. The department expanded rapidly and, according to Ji, the total number of faculty grew tenfold, while the number of students increased two hundred-fold (2008). During the expansion of 1949–1951, former faculty members of NIOL like Yin Hongyuan joined PKU and students from other universities and departments, such as Liu Anwu (1930–), were mobilized to study the strategic oriental languages like Hindi.

Moreover, the new state also took over the extant Hindi specialists, among them Shi Zhuyun (1917–2010), a graduate from NIOL, and her husband Yan Shaoduan (1920?–1970), a member of the Chinese diaspora in India. The couple returned to China in 1953 and joined the China Youth Publishing House. They started translating Hindi literature works, especially realistic novels. According to Shi, Yan started the translation of Premchand's *Godan* before leaving India. This translation was published in 1958. Besides, Yuan Ruo translated some of Premchand's short stories via Russian translations. The reception of Premchand further widened the scope of China-India cultural communication. The Indian village and the pathos of peasant village reminded Chinese readers of rural life in China. It invoked a non-religious progressivist affinity between the two countries. Yan Shaoduan had planned to translate other works by Premchand but this task was interrupted by the decade-long Cultural Revolution (Shi 1980). His unfinished work would be taken up by Liu Anwu and his colleagues, who would publish their translated works of Premchand, Yashpal and other progressive Hindi writers as political stability was restored.

Conclusions

Although India had been a well-remembered old neighbour for China, this shared historical experience did not greatly help China in re-engaging India in unprecedented circumstances. The emergence of Indology in China is subject to the influence of a number of factors, both internal and external. At the beginning, Indology was introduced to Chinese readers and scholars by young intellectuals, who eagerly wanted to modernize the nation, as a part of *Western studies*. Meanwhile, diligent Buddhist intellectuals, resorting to the internalized Buddhist legacy in China, added Chinese indigenousness to this branch of *Western studies*. These two currents collided and merged with each other, creating space for this scholarship of seemingly less practical value in the newly established universities following the role models of their

---

18. For the Communists, "Ya Fei La," i.e. Asia, Africa and Latin America means "the third world." It soon replaced the original rich meaning of the word "orient" given by the European.

Western counterparts. The threefold significance of early Indology was as follows: first, it helped China to re-examine and re-evaluate its own history and culture by improving the understanding of Buddhism and China's historical contact with Buddhist India; secondly, it became another minor yet important intellectual link, after Sinology, between nascent Chinese university scholarship and its Western counterparts; thirdly, it spread knowledge about India, particularly non-Buddhist India. Due to a relative lack of impetus to learn about India, still living in the shadow of the British Empire, the first two functions were more salient in early years.

However, the change in world configuration, especially the rise of India's importance to China, transformed early mutual sympathies among the revolutionaries into government policy to establish and strengthen China-India relations, which kicked off state intervention from both ROC and PRC government, and, finally, led to the evolution of China's Indology. Both the establishment of the Hindi programme in 1942 and the incorporation of it into PKU in 1946 represented state efforts to integrate the country's intellectual resources to serve the state's needs. The state ideology, whether anti-imperialism or socialism, was injected into the young Indology community. This, to some extent, enriched the then still weak first function of Indology: to learn about non-Buddhist India. Thus, in the formative years of China's Indology, Chinese Indologists developed their perspectives within three important transnational networks: the cultural network of the revived ancestral Buddhist tradition and exchange of personnel between the two countries; the scholarly network around Western, particularly German, orientalists; and the political network based on socialist and anti-imperialist ideology.

The internalization of these streams resulted in a distinct appearance of China's Indology—it was as much a product of modern globalization as it was deeply rooted in China's own historical tradition and it has a threefold religious-intellectual-political orientation. As the cold war unveiled, earlier academic connections with the Western world were halted. Then, the boundary conflicts with India in 1962 abruptly ended the direct contact that had gradually resumed since the nineteenth century. Seeking legitimacy internally via research on China-India comparative literature and socially progressive Indian literature seemed inevitable for Chinese Indologists.[19] The postponed fructification only came after 1978 when the Cultural Revolution ended. After the 1990s, as China reopened to India and the rest of the world, the three networks of Indology met different fates. China's Buddhology regained impetus as both academic and religious life resumed. Young students followed

---

19. Whereas, for instance, sociology was deemed non-Marxist "capitalist knowledge" and abolished in 1952. It was only after the Cultural Revolution that Fei Xiaotong (1910–2005), contemporary of Ji Xianlin and a student of Bronisław Kasper Malinowski (1884–1942), and his colleagues started to lecture again on sociology.

the footsteps of early Indologists and went West, with Germany and India among the most popular destinations. The biggest change took place at the foundation of the third network, the political network based on socialist and anti-imperialist ideology. For China and India, both now at greater ease with their self-identification as modern nation states, the first priorities are how to develop via economic means. The number of students learning about India, the study of Hindi in particular increased rapidly, but this time, the main impetus is the employment opportunities thanks to the booming China-India mutual trade instead of progressivist affinity. The change this development will bring to the third network, and then China's Indology, is yet to emerge.

Acknowledgments

The author would like to express his gratitude to Prof. Dr. Maya Burger and Dr. Philippe Bornet for their inspiration on this paper, to Prof. Dr. Jiang Jingkui for years of guidance, and to the Peking University-Université de Lausanne exchange programme that funded the author's visiting scholarship to Lausanne during 2013–2014.

References

Chou, Chih-P'ing. 2013. "The Indianization of China: A Case Study in Cultural Borrowing." In *English Writings of Hu Shih: Chinese Philosophy and Intellectual History*, vol. 2, edited by H. Shih and C. Chou, 147–163. Berlin, Heidelberg: Springer. https://doi.org/10.1007/978-3-642-31181-9_13

Duan, Qing. 2002. "What Does Indology Mean Specially for China." *Indology: Past, Present and Future*, edited by S. Bhate, 223–232. New Delhi: Sahitya Academy.

Encyclopedia of China-India Cultural Contacts, Complete Edition. 2015. Beijing: Encyclopedia of China Publishing House.

Chen, Duxiu. 1924 (4-25). "Ping Taige'er Zai Hangzhou Shanghai de Yanshuo" (On Tagore's speeches in Hangzhou and Shanghai). *Minguo Ribao: Juewu*, 1924.

Chen, Hongjie. 2009. "Deguo Mingshi Shouxia de Zhongguo Gaotu" (The outstanding disciples of renowned German teachers). *Dushu* (12): 49–56.

———. 2008. "Cai Yuanpei Dui Deguo Daxue Linian de Jieshou: Jiyu Yiwen *Deyizhi Daxue zhi Tese*" (On Cai Yuanpei's reception of the ideology of German universities: based on Cai's translation of *The Features of German Universities*). *Peking University Education Review* 6 (3): 2–7.

Ge, Weijun. 2002. "Xiyouji Sun Wukong Gushi de Yindu Yuanyuan" (The Indian origin of Sun Wukong's tales in Xiyouji). *Mingqing Xiaoshuo Yanjiu* 4: 36–43.

Godart, Gerard Clinton. 2008. "'Philosophy' or 'Religion'? The Confrontation with Foreign Categories in Late Nineteenth Century Japan." *Journal of the History of Ideas* 69 (1): 71–91. https://doi.org/10.1353/jhi.2008.0008

Halbfass, Wilhelm. 1985. "India and the Comparative Method." *Philosophy East and West* 35 (1): 3–15. https://doi.org/10.2307/1398678

Hu, Shi. 2013. *Zhongguo Zhonggu Sixiangshi Changbian* (An intellectual history of medieval China). Guilin: Lijiang Chubanshe.

———. 1980. *Zhongguo Zhanghui Xiaoshuo Kaozheng* (Critical study of China's chapter fiction). Shanghai: Shanghai Shudian.

Ji, Xianlin. 2008. *Ji Xianlin Zizhuan* (An autobiography of Ji Xianlin). Beijing: Dangdai Zhongguo Chubanshe.

Jiang, Huilin. 2016. "Ji Xianlin Xueshu Nianpu (Er)" (Academic chronology of Ji Xianlin, 2)." *Journal of Hunan University of Science and Engineering* 3: 16–19.

Jin, Kemu. 2011. "Tianzhu Jiushi" (Memoirs of India). In *Jin Kemu Ji* (Jin Kemu Omnibus), edited by Jin Kemu, 481–565. Beijing: Shenghuo, Dushu, Xinzhi Sanlian Shudian.

———. 1999. *Fanzhulu Ji (Jia): Fanyu Wenxueshi* (The collection of Fanzhulu [I]: history of Sanskrit literature). Nanchang: Jiangxi Jiaoyu Chubanshe.

Kaichao, Jiamuyang. 2013. "Riben Xuezhe Nantiao Wenxiong yu Zhongguo Yang Renshan Jushi de Jiaowang" (The interaction between the Japanese scholar Nanjo Bunyu and the Chinese Buddhist layman Yang Renshan). *The World Religious Cultures* 1: 73–75.

Kang, Youwei. 1981. "Yu Tongxue Zhuzi Liang Qichao Deng Lun Yindu Wangguo Youyu Gesheng Zilishu" (A letter to Liang Qichao and other comrades on how India had been conquered because of provincial independence). *Kang Youwei Zhenglun Ji* (Political Writings of Kang You Wei), edited by Tang Zhijun, 495–505. Beijing: Zhonghua Shuju.

Liang, Qichao. 2015. *Li Hongzhang Zhuan* (A biography of Li Hongzhang). Shanghai: East China Normal University Press.

Liang, Shuming. 2013. *Yindu Zhexue Gailun* (Introduction to Indian philosophy). Reprinted based on the 3rd edition, 1922. Shanghai: Shanghai Renmin Chubanshe.

Lin, Chengjie. 1991. "Huang Maocai de Yindu Youli he Tade Jizai" (Huang Maocai's journey to India and its records). *Nanya Yanjiu Jikan* 5(2): 62–67.

Lv, Jianfu. 1997. "Yang Renshan yu Jinling Kejingchu" (Yang Renshan and the Jinling Buddhist publishing house). *Fayin* 6: 23–28.

Qian, Wenzhong. 1997. "Nanjue he tade Huanxiang: Jinian Gang Hetai" (The baron and his fantasy: in memory of Alexander von Staël-Holstein). *Dushu* 1: 49–55.

Qian, Zhixiu. 1913. "Tai'e'er Shi Zhi Renshengguan" (Tagore's outlook on life). *Dongfang Zazhi* 10(4): 71–74.

Shi Quansheng. 1998. "Lun Yangwupai de 'Zhongxue Wei Ti, Xixue Wei Yong' Sixiang" (On the idea of "Chinese studies as the core, Western studies as the tool" of the self-strengthening movement). *Lishi Dang'an* 3: 86–93, 104.

Shi, Yinshun. 2011. *Taixu Dashi Nianpu* (Life chronology of Master Taixu). Beijing: Zhanghua Shuju.

Shi, Zhuyun. 1980. "Chongdu Gedan Yi Shaoduan" (Review of Godan in the memory of Shaoduan). *Dushu* 11: 113–118.

Stolte, Carolien, and Harald Fischer-Tiné. 2012. "Imagining Asia in India: Nationalism and Internationalism (ca. 1905–1940)." *Comparative Studies in Society and History* 54(1): 65–92. https://doi.org/10.1017/S0010417511000594

Wang, Bangwei. 1998. "Beijing Daxue de Yinduxue Yanjiu: Bashinian de Huigu" (Indology in Peking University: A retrospective review of the past eighty years). *Journal of Peking University (Humanities and Social Sciences)* 2: 100–106.

Wang Qilong. 2008. *Gang Hetai Xueshu Nianpu Jianbian* (A brief academic chronology of Alexander von Staël-Holstein). Beijing: Zhonghua Shuju.

Wang, Xiangyuan. 2011. "Taige'er zai Zhongguo de Yijie" (The translation and introduction of Tagore in China). In *Chinese Scholars on Rabindranath Tagore*, edited by Jiang Jingkui, 554–567. Yinchuan: Yangguang Chubanshe.

Xiong, Yuezhi. 2013. "Qingmo Zhexue Yijiere Shulun" (Review on the "philosophy translation fever" of the Late-Qing period). *Guoji Hanxue* 1: 52–71.

Yin, Zhusheng. 1998. "Chen Yinke de Liuxue Jingli yu Xiyang Dongfangxue" (Chen Yinke's overseas experience and Western Oriental studies). *Shehui Kexue Zhanxian* 3: 197–203.

Zhang, Xia. 1981. "Woguo Zuizao Fanyi de Taige'er Shige" (The earliest translation of Tagore's poetry in China). *Nanya Yanjiu* Z1: 134.

Zhang, Zhidong. 1898. *Quanxue Pian* (On learning). Guangzhou: Xihu Shuyuan.

Zhao, Guohua. 1986. "Lun Sunwukong Shenhou Xingxiang de Laili (Shang): Xiyouji yu Yindu Wenxue Bijiao Yanjiu Zhiyi" (On origins of the imagery of Sun Wukong as a holy monkey: A comparative study of Xiyouji and Indian literature). *Nanya Yanjiu* 1(4): 39–48.

About the author

Dr. Minyu Zhang is Assistant Professor of South Asian Studies at the Program of International and Regional Studies, School of Foreign Languages, Peking University. He holds a doctorate in Indian Language and Literature from Peking University and his main research area is Indian literature, Religions in India and Indian society. He is currently investigating the transmission of Kabirian works through a National Social Science Foundation Early Career Project. His main publications include *Kabir's Poems: Annotated Translation and Study* (monograph), two translated works and dozens of articles on peer-reviewed journals.

PART III

Religions on the Move

— 7 —

Charles Pfoundes and the First Buddhist Mission to the West, 1889–1892: Some Research Questions

BRIAN BOCKING

In 1889, the Irishman "Captain" Charles James William Pfoundes (b. Wexford, Ireland 1840, d. Kobe, Japan 1907) launched, under the aegis of the newly-formed *Kaigai Senkyō-Kai* (Overseas Propagation Society) in Kyoto, a Buddhist mission in London called the Buddhist Propagation Society which operated until 1892. This forgotten but highly active Japanese-sponsored Buddhist mission to London, the cosmopolitan hub of the global British empire, predates by ten years the so-called "first" Buddhist missions to the West led by Japanese immigrants to California in 1899 and by almost two decades the "first" Buddhist mission to London of Ananda Metteyya (Allan Bennett) from Burma in 1908. Recent research into Pfoundes's 1889 mission, including his confrontations with Theosophy and links to Spiritualism and progressive reform movements, offers new insights into the complex, lively and contested character of global religious connections in the late nineteenth century and particularly the early influence of Japan in the development of emerging "global" Buddhism(s). This chapter builds on existing published material to raise a number of issues surrounding Pfoundes's Buddhist activities in London, with questions which may resonate for researchers dealing with other "transnational encounters" in the field of religion.

Introduction: Charles Pfoundes and the Buddhist Propagation Society

In October 1889, Pfoundes launched the London BPS with the backing of the Kyoto-based Buddhist missionary group the *Kaigai Senkyō Kai* (Overseas Missionary Society; hereafter *KSK*/BPS), a progressive initiative of outward-looking lay Buddhists led by the English teacher Matsuyama Matsutaro (dates unknown) and associated with the Nishi Honganji Pure Land Buddhist headquarters in Kyoto and specifically the new Western-style school the *Futsū Kyōkō* sponsored by Nishi Honganji. Although the London branch of the BPS lasted for only three years before Pfoundes left London for Japan in late 1892, it remains notable as the only functioning overseas missionary project established by Matsuyama and his *KSK* colleagues during the short period of the KSK's existence. The London BPS was also, as we now know, the very first Buddhist mission to be established in the West.

In December 2014, an article co-authored by Brian Bocking, Laurence Cox and Yoshinaga Shin'ichi entitled "The First Buddhist Mission to the West: Charles Pfoundes and the London Buddhist mission of 1889–1892" (Bocking *et al.* 2014) was published in *DISKUS*, the journal of the British Association for the Study of Religions. This article, which is freely available online,[1] describes in some detail the background, launch and subsequent activities of Charles Pfoundes's pioneering and long-forgotten Buddhist mission, the Buddhist Propagation Society (hereafter BPS). The article was our attempt to restore a significant "missing chapter" in the history of modern global Buddhism. In charting the rise and decline of the BPS the *DISKUS* article provided much detailed information relevant to the present chapter which is not repeated here. The *DISKUS* article may be regarded as useful background to this chapter, especially for those new to the story of Charles Pfoundes and the Buddhist Propagation Society in London.

Given that most of the details so far known of the London BPS have been presented in the *DISKUS* article mentioned above, the main focus of this chapter will be on questions not yet answered about Pfoundes and about the London BPS; questions which are not so narrow as they might at first appear since they may be useful in interrogating other quite different examples of transnational encounters, connected histories, cross-border travels and individual appropriations of religions of the kinds addressed by fellow authors in this volume.

In what follows, I raise eight such issues, with some concluding remarks which relate the questions raised to areas for further research, including some identified by workshop participants at the "Buddhist Crossroads" conference held at University College Cork, Ireland, in September 2012. This conference addressed the late nineteenth and early twentieth-century intercontinental[2] emergence of numerous different individual and group efforts directed towards what we now call "global Buddhism." The areas for further research, identified at the end of the conference by participants with a wide range of research specialisms, informed in turn the essay "A Buddhist crossroads: pioneer European Buddhists and globalizing Asian networks 1860–1960" (Turner *et al.* 2013).[3]

---

1. See References below for links.
2. "Transnational" is anachronistic if applied to widespread Asian-Western interactions in the colonial period, although entirely appropriate for e.g. Japanese-British encounters which were between two nations and for most post-second World War developments.
3. Published subsequently in book form as Bocking *et al.* 2015.

Pfoundes's letters printed in the journal *Kaigai Bukkyō Jijō*

Although Pfoundes had good Japanese, his letters from London to his KSK sponsors in Kyoto in the period 1889-1892 were most probably written in English. They were translated and edited by Matsuyama and his colleagues for publication in the Japanese-language journal *Kaigai Bukkyō Jijō* ("The situation of Buddhism overseas"—hereafter *KBJ*)[4] which reported on global Buddhist affairs for the local readership, from 1888 until publication ceased in 1893.[5] Pfoundes's letters alone cover a very wide range of topics and will undoubtedly repay further detailed study, preferably by a team including researchers with expertise on the geography and socio-religious character of Victorian London as well as specialists in Meiji Buddhism, Japanese immigration policy and the global networks of correspondence around the KSK. The complete *KBJ* of course includes far more than just correspondence from Pfoundes. Other contributors from America, Europe, Australia and Southern Asia to *KBJ* or to its shorter-lived (1888-1889) English-French sister publication *Bijou of Asia* (both journals now reprinted with an introduction in Yoshinaga and Nakanishi 2014-2015) included Francesca Arundale, Charles Johnston, Laura Carter Holloway, Josephine W. Cables, Elliot B. Page, Edward Wolleb, Alexander Russell Webb, Dharmapala, Charles Leadbeater, Helena Blavatsky, Max Müller, T. W. Rhys Davids, Robert G. Ingersoll and Sarat Chandra Das. The most prolific contributor was Philangi Dasa (Carl Herman Vetterling) and after him Charles Pfoundes.[6] The first three issues to be considered below stem from the contents of Pfoundes's letters. He may not have expected the letters to be published in their entirety for in some respects they read as reports but at other times they sound more like personal communications, including requests for advice perhaps intended for Matsuyama alone.

Ostensible aims versus aims achieved, in Buddhist activities

When we read of someone launching, as Pfoundes did in October 1889, a religious mission in a large city, our working assumption is very probably that the instigator has embarked on the project with at least the intention that the mission will "succeed"; that people will be converted and that the institution will take root and grow. However, in a letter from London written on 4 October 1889 to his sponsors in Kyoto and published in *KBJ* in December

---

4. The 1888-1893 *Kaigai Bukkyō Jijō* is not to be confused with the much later *Kaigai Bukkyō Jijō* launched by the International Buddhist Society in 1933.
5. *KBJ* and its sister English/French language publication *Bijou of Asia* (published 1888-1889) have recently been published in three volumes (Yoshinaga and Nakanishi 2014-2015)
6. Information on this and many other aspects of Pfoundes research gratefully received from Prof. Yoshinaga Shin'ichi.

1889, Pfoundes already declares—this is before the BPS has been launched—that he would like to retire from his (humble) job as a clerk at the Admiralty and travel first to America and thence to Japan, where he would study Shingon Mikkyō (Esoteric Buddhism) and climb the sacred Mt. Koya (*KBJ* 5, 28–29). This strongly suggests that even as the BPS London mission was being launched Pfoundes did not see himself primarily as a missionary to *London*, at least not in the long term. Instead, he appears to have viewed the founding of the BPS branch in London as a way to garner a new identity for himself as a proponent of Buddhism in America and/or in Japan.

Pfoundes was not lacking in commitment to his London propagation work, for it is evident that he put all his energies into the London mission once it had started, but the insight we get into his longer-term intentions from this early letter might help to put in context the apparent "failure" of the mission after less than three years. In a second letter, written ten days after the first, Pfoundes reports that he is instructing some young men who will go to "Europe and America" as well as to "China, Siam, Burma, Ceylon, and India" to do Buddhist missionary work (*KBJ* 7, 29). Once again there is no mention of training missionaries for London itself. Examination of the UK Admiralty registries for the period reveals that Pfoundes's resignation was submitted and accepted as early as 3 March 1891, only eighteen months after the Mission started (ADM 12/1226 1891 March 3 Treasury 5.1AG, National Archives Kew). Did the London mission, short-lived as it was, perhaps last even *longer* than Pfoundes had initially planned?

We might ask similar questions of other comparable projects. A theme that has recurred in recent conference discussions around the various modernizing Buddhist projects from this period is that "failure" has for too long been simplistically defined as "forgotten by history/lineage," when even "failed" projects reflect real effort and sometimes substantial achievement in their time and may constitute a significant and potentially instructive trajectory within modernist Buddhism. Should we now revise even our revisionist understanding of failure, to allow for the fact that some projects were never intended to achieve their ostensible aims; that they were at some level designed to fail? This raises the question of how many other pioneering, cross-border ventures currently being studied by scholars across the range of religions had a larger purpose, or dual or multiple purposes, or a covert purpose,[7] which may have been fulfilled to some extent, even if the ostensible main objective was not achieved.

---

7. Shimatsu (2008) highlights Buddhist involvement over decades in covert Japanese diplomacy regarding Tibet.

Charles Pfoundes and the first Buddhist mission to the West, 1889–1892

Changing names and fluid identities

In a further letter to Matsuyama in Kyoto dispatched on 25 October 1889, a week after he launched the BPS in London, Pfoundes writes that his (Pfoundes's) name is already known to Americans, so he would like to change it to something more suitable for that country, and he asks Matsuyama for suggestions (*KBJ* 8, 29). Pfoundes was sensitive to any questioning of his name, which he had changed from his birth name of Pounds in the 1860s shortly after arriving in Japan.[8] In 1883 a US newspaper had carried the following:

> Mr Pfounder [*sic*], in a recent lecture in London, denounced the greater portion of Japanese art manufactured for the foreign market as "meretricious rubbish." And now will Mr Pfounder give us his unbiased opinion of that big P at the front of his name? ("Editorial Dots" 1883)

Much later, in 1905, writing from Kobe to the Australian police for help with enquiries about his late father, James Baker Pounds, Pfoundes hastens to explain that his own name is "officially written as such..." and then amends the typed letter by hand to read "officially *registered and* written as such..." (Pfoundes 1905).

In asking Matsuyama for his suggestions for a suitable name, did Pfoundes perhaps have in mind an "exotic" Buddhist name like that of Philangi Dasa (the American Carl Herman Vetterling), with whom he carried on a correspondence? In fact, Pfoundes already had one "exotic" name—spelled at the time "*Omoie Tetzunostzuke*" and officially conferred on him decades earlier in Japan (Bocking 2013) but perhaps he had already discovered in London that, unlike Indian-sounding names, his Japanese name, hard to read and even harder to pronounce, carried little or no advantage for him outside Japan.[9]

The above discussion of just one pioneer Victorian Buddhist's minor array of names raises the larger issue of how names and identities were deployed, and to what effect, by other modernizing religious actors of the period. Naming was an area of considerable and generally purposive fluidity among pioneer Western Buddhist monastics; U Dhammaloka (alias Captain Daylight, John Larkins, William Colvin, Laurence Carroll, Larry O'Rourke and probably other pseudonyms) being a prime example, and also among some modernist Asian Buddhists (cf. "the Anagarika Dharmapala"), in a period when personal identities, including names, were considerably less "fixed" than they are today.[10]

---

8. The surname "Pfoundes" (for a discussion of its origin see Bocking 2013) is unique. Pfounds (no e) is found elsewhere but the only other person ever called Pfoundes was Rosa Alice, Pfoundes's wife.
9. He had also published letters in the *Japan Herald* before 1875 under a remarkable variety of pen-names (see Bocking 2013).
10. While Pfoundes managed to change his name in the 1860s, an attempt in 1899 to change his nationality from British to Japanese was unsuccessful (Ruxton 2008, Bocking 2013).

Facilitating and constraining factors for modernizing Buddhist travellers

In the letter to Kyoto sent on 25 October 1889, just a week after the Buddhist Propagation Society had been formally launched in London, Pfoundes adds that he has heard that some Chinese, Koreans and Indians have been given the title of [Buddhist?] "missionary" and that if necessary he [Pfoundes] will go to America first [before Japan] (*KBJ* 8, 29). There are several possible interpretations of this statement, perhaps the most plausible being that Pfoundes thought he could be admitted to residence status in Japan more readily as a Buddhist missionary, possibly one bearing American credentials, than if he arrived in Japan from London as an ex-Admiralty clerk (which is what eventually happened in 1893). This suggests another avenue of research in emerging Buddhist (and other) modernisms. In an increasingly "global" age, but before efficient technologies and systems had been developed to trace and cross-check a traveller's identity,[11] what were the restrictions on travel to different places, to whom did they apply, and what effect, if any, did such restrictions (or the reverse) have on global Buddhist exchanges? To take an example from research on Buddhist networks in turn-of-the-century Siam, Phibul Choompolpaisal has pointed out that the completion of road and rail links from the Shan States to Bangkok in 1902 not only reduced a journey formerly of three months by river and elephant to a single day, but Buddhist monks travelling the route were not subject to strict identity checks (Choompolpaisal 2013, 102, 104). The other "Irish Buddhist" U Dhammaloka (?1856–?1913) could make himself at home in an ethnically "Tavoy" monastery whether in Bangkok, Chittagong or Rangoon. By contrast, the young American "vagabond traveller" Harry Franck, penniless by choice but undeniably white, was, despite his best efforts, actively prevented by the Chittagong chief of police from tramping overland from Chittagong to Mandalay and instead bundled onto a ship for Rangoon (Franck 1910, 373–377). Where, we may ask, could Buddhists (and Hindus, Christians, etc.) of various statuses, ethnicities and persuasions go or not go, more or less easily, in different periods of the late nineteenth and early twentieth centuries, and how did this sometimes obvious, sometimes invisible, network of favourable factors and negative constraints influence the geographical development of modernist Buddhism and other transcultural religious initiatives in different areas?

What was "Buddhism" for Pfoundes?

A reviewer of our 2014 *DISKUS* article on the BPS observed that the topic of what "Buddhism" meant to Pfoundes seemed relatively underdeveloped in our

---

11. For example, a letter from the Burma Railway police who were after Dhammaloka in April 1912 reached the Australian police only after Dhammaloka had spent three months in Australia and was safely back in Singapore ("Missing Friends" 1912).

account of the London mission. It seems reasonable to expect that Pfoundes would embody some recognizable strand of Buddhism, but in the *DISKUS* paper, *faute de mieux,* we could only articulate Pfoundes's Buddhism as he did in his published London pieces; as being above all something that Theosophy was not. Pfoundes's audiences were most likely coming to his talks with a conception—albeit very vague—of "Buddhism" derived from the contemporary "Theosophic boom," as Pfoundes described it in 1891.[12] The same public meeting halls across London could be hired by anybody wishing to present religious, political or cultural talks and performances, so an audience could listen to Pfoundes and his Theosophical adversaries giving talks at different times in the same venue, while Theosophists in the audience were known to argue with Pfoundes at the lectern (Bocking *et al.* 2014). The impact that the popular Theosophical "Esoteric Buddhist" writings and public talks of Blavatsky, Besant, Sinnett and others had on the ordinary Londoner's understanding of "Buddhism" at exactly the time the BPS was launched does appear to have been overwhelming, to the extent that a Theosophical view of Buddhism prevailed in the UK well into the twentieth century (Bocking *et al.* 2014). Hence, rather as many of our university undergraduates today come to study "Buddhism" with the hazy view that it is now, and always has been, a harmonious, egalitarian, open-minded transnational community of enlightened peacemakers, and we therefore have to devote a good deal of time explaining what Buddhism is not, so Pfoundes explained Buddhism largely as "not Theosophy."

In more positive terms, Pfoundes's impressive study habits in the British Library,[13] his informed requests to Matsuyama for Japanese books[14] (of which Pfoundes reportedly had three thousand)[15] and his declarations about the elevated character of Buddhist thought[16] suggest that Pfoundes, despite a relatively limited formal education (he must have left school aged 14 at

---

12. The extent to which Pfoundes's largely working-class and self-educated London audiences had internalized more elite literary depictions of Buddhism such as in Arnold's *The Light of Asia* (1879) also requires further research.
13. "I read books on Buddhism and religious matters at the reading room of the British Library from five to eight" (Pfoundes 1890).
14. In a letter of 25 October 1889 (published in *KBJ* 8, 1890) Pfoundes stressed the need for a publication company for (presumably English) books on doctrine, history, morality and the "middle path of the *Avatamasaka Sutra*." On 12 November 1889 (published in *KBJ* 9, 1890) he wrote asking for *Shingaku* (Heart-Learning) texts to improve his Japanese public speaking skills.
15. Kobayashi [Takakusu] Junjiro, letter from London to Matsuyama, *KBJ* 11, 30 June 1890, 24.
16. E.g. "I venture to assert that nowhere will be found more interesting material by the competent student than in Japan and its Budhistic [sic] literature" (Pfoundes 1889a, 351).

the latest), had a well-developed if largely self-taught grasp of Buddhist philosophy and history by the time he launched the BPS in London. However, despite having stayed, he says, at three temples while resident in Japan up to 1876, it appears that Pfoundes had not actually been a committed practitioner of Shingon or any other form of Buddhism in earlier years. In a letter to Matsuyama he asks whether he needs to undergo some kind of ordination in order to act as the agent of the BPS (*KBJ* 8, 29) and he underwent what was presumably a first ordination only after returning to Japan in 1893 (Bocking 2013, 34 n. 27). In his popular book on Japanese customs *Fuso-Mimi Bukuro: A Budget of Japanese Notes* published in 1875, the year before he left Japan, Pfoundes was notably disdainful of the Buddhist priesthood's encouragement of superstitious practices (Bocking et al. 2014). This suggests that Pfoundes's personal commitment to what he calls "Extreme Oriental" (i.e. Japanese) Buddhism grew largely through book-study in London, was strengthened by his increasing exasperation with the rise of Theosophy and was further reinforced by the realization that he (and probably he alone, in London at the time) had as a Westerner observed and absorbed enough of "real" Buddhism from his earlier life in Japan to see through and respond in an informed way to the idealized and imaginative Theosophist version of "esoteric Buddhism."

Further light could be shed on Pfoundes's trajectory from disappointed London man of letters to Japanese Buddhist ritualist by an examination of his subsequent fourteen-year career as a Buddhist in Japan from 1893 to 1907, including further analysis of his 1893 lectures to Japanese audiences published by his *Kaigai Senkyōkai* sponsors (Uchiyama 1893). While Pfoundes soon fell out with many of his erstwhile *KSK* colleagues after 1893, he certainly did not abandon Buddhism. We know that in 1893 he took Tendai and subsequently probably other ordinations. In 1902 he "represented" several Japanese Buddhist sects at the Oriental Congress in Hanoi, where his unusual presentation included a personal demonstration of robes and ritual items; in 1903 he participated in the great convocation of "10,000 Bonzes" at Tennoji, Osaka held to commemorate the 1300th anniversary of Shotoku Taishi;[17] in 1904 he was pictured officiating at *Shugendō* rituals for military victory over Russia and in 1907 he died a Japanese Buddhist (Bocking 2013). Pfoundes was very much his own kind of Buddhist, yet in developing his own idiosyncratic Buddhist identity he paradoxically resembled many if not most other "transnational" religious actors from the Victorian era onwards. In a transcultural context there is no "standard" Buddhist (or Christian, or Muslim, or Atheist)—and in the modern world contexts which are not in some way transcultural are becoming increasingly rare.

---

17. Printed flyer ca. 1904 advertising Pfoundes's multifarious activities and commercial services. President's office correspondence. Mss 1609, Lewis and Clark Centennial Exposition Records. Oregon Historical Society Research Library.

Colonizing the "non-denominational" space?

Writing in the Spiritualist magazine *The Two Worlds* (*TTW*) shortly before declaring himself an apostle of Buddhism in London in Autumn 1889, Pfoundes rather enigmatically describes himself as "neither a Buddhist nor a Theosophist" (*TTW* 23 Aug 1889, 494). This statement is not self-explanatory and we suggest in our *DISKUS* article (Bocking *et al.* 2014, 9, n. 25) that in making it Pfoundes wanted to position himself "above the sectarian fray"—in other words to present himself as one who is concerned with a superordinate "pure Buddhism" rather than the machinations of any institutionalized religious body. A rather similar claim is made in the bilingual (Japanese-English) London BPS leaflet (reproduced in our *DISKUS* article) which states: "[t]his Society does not desire to spread any special form of Bud(d)hism, [*sic*] but to proclaim the great truths to the whole world." Statements such as this may appear to us today grandiose, but not controversial—but this is only because in the nineteenth century a new space was generated within the "secular" sphere for "nondenominational" engagement with religion. In Britain, this secular-religious space (which presupposes some degree of private religious freedom under the state) was created in the course of successive Education Acts (principally 1870 and 1902) which legislated for a special kind of teaching about religion in Britain's schools. I have written elsewhere about this as follows (Bocking 2016, 275):

> An extensive and passionate [Westminster] parliamentary debate culminated in the Education Act of 1870 which prohibited the teaching of any particular catechism or denominational creed in government-funded schools, and allowed pupils to withdraw from religious instruction in religiously-based schools aided by taxpayers money. Pupils could be taught about Christian beliefs and could study the Bible as a text even in Board [government-run] schools, but they could not be forced to receive, in any British school, instruction in the teachings of a particular sect or church, nor could they be forced to participate in daily acts of school worship. The approach was modified in the 1902 Act but only to allow Church-controlled schools to teach their own religion while insisting on "non-denominational" teaching about religion in schools controlled by the state. ... Thus, as a result of a parliamentary compromise between different religious factions, a "non-denominational" form of schools religious education (and of schools worship) became the state's ideal.
> (Bocking 2008, 2016)

In consequence of these legislative moves—highly controversial at the time—a form of "Religious Education" or "Religious Instruction" emerged in Britain in which state-funded teachers taught (or were expected to teach) school pupils the Bible, but as history, without a particular theological slant. This practice continued for decades. Only in the late twentieth century was it superseded by teaching about multiple religions in an increasingly multicultural society; a practice itself only possible[18] because the idea that there could be a "nondeminational" kind of Religious Education seemed by then "natural" and thus went largely uncontested.[19]

In Japan, as is well known, the concept of religion as a separate category (a notion that is generally traced back to Europe)[20] took full shape in Japan only in the Meiji period.[21] To summarize a very complex set of conceptual and legislative moves, the Meiji government first adopted the Western category and term "religion," translated with the term *shūkyō*, then allocated certain institutional traditions to that new category—primarily Buddhist and Christian sects and in due course also a number of so-called "Sect Shinto" movements (i.e. officially recognized Shintoesque groups). Once the category of *"shūkyō"* was established it became possible to legislate for a further, conceptually derivative but politically and socially far more significant, sphere called *"hishūkyō"* (usually translated "non-religious")[22] to which were allocated the mainstream Shinto[23] texts and shrines as well as ritual veneration of the emperor as *kami*; matters which thus came under the control of the state, not of any "religion." This process of separating "Shinto" from "religions" became particularly visible in 1890–1891 with the promulgation of the new Meiji Constitution, which protected freedom of "religion," and the simultaneous dissemination of the *Imperial Rescript on Education*, which instituted the teaching of imperial genealogy, beginning with the age of the Gods, as his-

---

18. This is not to underplay the substantial positive efforts required to revivify RE in multicultural form in the UK from the late 1960s onwards, led by members of the "SHAP" working party connected with Lancaster University's Religious Studies department.

19. In the USA, where the line between religions and state was more sharply drawn, students could not even be taught *about* religions in the "nonreligious" sphere of the classroom unless religious teachings were reclassified as "science" (hence the endless and for many baffling debates over the scientific status of "creationism," "intelligent design" etc. in modern America).

20. Salemink (2009, 262) argues that a contest between religious authority and state authority (as in Europe) sharpened the distinction between political and religious, generated the category of the secular, and hence constructed the modern area dubbed "religion."

21. Michael Pye might disagree; see his *Emerging from Meditation* (Pye 1990) and the subsequent debate with Tim Barrett (Barrett 2016).

22. There are interesting parallels with the legal deployment of the categories "homosexual" and "heterosexual" following the invention of the terms (for quite different reasons) by Károly Mária Kertbeny in 1869. See http://www.salon.com/2012/01/22/the_invention_of_the_heterosexual

23. I use the term "Shinto" here with all possible caveats!

tory, by teachers in the nation's schools as well as the introduction of rituals of emperor veneration into the school day. While in 1891 Matsuyama was promoting non-sectarian Buddhism in Kyoto and Pfoundes doing the same on his behalf in London, the maverick Japanese Christian teacher Uchimura Kanzo was famously refusing to bow low before the portrait of Emperor Meiji newly installed in his school, on the basis that this would be a *religious* act.

What we witness here is the creation in the late nineteenth century of a new conceptual and social space in Japan called *hishūkyō* (a term which for purposes of comparison is I think far better translated "nondenominational" than its more usual "nonreligious"); a space which was actively colonized by the Meiji state in Japan to inculcate in school children, through their teachers, knowledge and understanding of the Shinto scriptures as history underpinning the divinity and authority of the Meiji emperor, over and above any regional or sectarian loyalties. The same space was at the same time being used by the British state to deliver to schoolchildren, through their teachers, knowledge of the Bible as history, while at the same time defusing sectarian tensions.

My suggestion here, which may well be seen as relevant to other figures and other contexts, is that we should see both Matsuyama's and Pfoundes's appeal to "pure Buddhism" or "no special form of Buddhism" as parallel attempts by non-state actors to colonize this new "nondenominational" conceptual and social space for Buddhism, rather than allow Buddhism to be restricted to the sphere of a particular "religion" or sect. Perhaps we can find comparable cases for a proposed transcultural "Christianity," "Hinduism" etc. in other regions in the period. Neither Matsuyama nor Pfoundes, of course, could be fully aware at the time of how the *category* of religion was being subtly transformed and we find Pfoundes struggling to make his point, using the term "religion" in three different ways in the same sentence:

> BUDHISM[24] is not a religion in the strict sense of the word, though it is religious, and in many of the sects, so numerous, there is much admixture of religion. (Pfoundes 1889b, 326)

The economics of global lay Buddhism

Promoting "Bud(d)hism" was not the only thing that Pfoundes did after the BPS was launched. For most of his thirteen years in London Pfoundes worked by day in his humble post at the Admiralty and for the first ten years or so gave his numerous lectures on Japanese art, culture and religion and participated (sometimes very actively) in learned societies and various social and political movements only in his spare time. From 1889–1892 he propagated

---

24. *Sic* in original; "Budhism" was originally a Theosophical usage distinguishing "universal knowledge" from what might be called actually-existing "Buddhism."

Buddhism on behalf of the BPS almost entirely in the evenings and on Sundays. He is insistent in his letters to Matsuyama in Japan that he does not ask for money for the work he is doing on behalf of the BPS; evidently he preferred to be self-reliant. Apart from a period around 1876–1878 when he seems to have been particularly flush following the sale of a substantial catalogue of Japanese art objects in New York, it seems that from the moment he joined the colonial navy in Melbourne as a 14-year old in 1854 until a week before his death in 1907, when he was reportedly still working as a court interpreter, Pfoundes earned his own living by hard graft.[25] The economic imperative to work undoubtedly shaped the nature and extent of his involvement in Buddhist activities—and presumably also his understanding of what a modern Buddhist life could and should be.

We might then think about how Pfoundes's particular economic situation compares with the circumstances of other modernist Buddhist figures of the period (and non-Buddhists, such as Sadhu Sundar Singh in Bornet, this volume) who subsisted on one or more of: institutionalized almsgiving, personal wealth, sponsorship, subscriptions or subventions from colleagues and followers, publications, targeted fundraising campaigns, or other less clearly identified or less openly acknowledged sources. We have yet to establish in the case of U Dhammaloka how as an observant Burmese style monk he managed to travel alone in areas where he could not necessarily rely on daily *dāna* to keep him alive (for example, his trip to Australia in 1912). In 1905 Dhammaloka told Harry Franck (who believed him) that outside Burma he, Dhammaloka, was allowed as a monk to carry just enough money for his needs and he would give any cash remaining from his trip to the first beggar he encountered back "home" in Burma (Franck 1910, 363). This begs the wider question of how far modernist monks and their lay supporters were prepared to [re-]interpret monastic rules in an age of unprecedented possibilities for routine, safe and independent travel.

The telegraph—Buddhist access to "the Victorian internet"?[26]

There is some doubt—reflected in our jointly-authored 2014 *DISKUS* article—about whether Pfoundes "jumped the gun" in launching the London BPS. Did he really have the prior permission of the *KSK* in Kyoto to do so? He announced his new role as invited representative of "Extreme Oriental" Buddhism in a letter written on 12 October 1889 which was published on 18 October in the UK Spiritualist magazine *The Two Worlds*. At this time, Pfoundes's letter of 4 October to Matsuyama which asked for permission to serve as the Kyoto BPS' London representative can hardly have begun its long sea journey to Japan;

---

25. Or sometimes just graft! (Cox 2013, 223).
26. The phrase is from Standage (1999).

it would not even reach Matsuyama until December (*KBJ* 5, 15 Dec 1889, 29). An exchange of letters between London and Japan in 1889 might take around three months, but for a matter as important as this it seems at least feasible that Pfoundes used the telegraph. This was a near-instantaneous medium of international communication which, though seldom used by the average citizen, would have been thoroughly familiar to Pfoundes who as an Admiralty employee in London and a former senior mariner in Japan would routinely expect to have access to the fastest means of communication available.[27]

We know that Pfoundes had first approached Matsuyama some weeks before, in June/July 1889, when he sent by way of introduction to the editor of *Bijou of Asia* his articles on Buddhism then being serialized in *The Two Worlds*. We also know that Matsuyama's reply to Pfoundes, though it has not survived, must have arrived in London in early October and, evidently, that it suggested in some way that Pfoundes become a London representative of the BPS; a proposal which Pfoundes was clearly eager to accept. In these circumstances a brief telegram request, sent some time before 12 October from Pfoundes in London to Matsuyama in Kyoto and saying something along the lines of "Request permission to represent BPS. Letter follows" could have received a "Yes" from Matsuyama within 24 hours. We have no evidential basis for such an exchange, which is why it is not discussed in the *DISKUS* article, but I mention it here because it seems very probable that Pfoundes would use the telegraph for something so important to him. If he did, then the narrative changes quite significantly because it means that Pfoundes launched the London BPS on 12 October with the explicit permission of Matsuyama and the *KSK*, not just in confident anticipation of approval by letter several months ahead.

This *excursus* into telegraphy in relation to the BPS may be worthwhile if it prompts us to question the assumptions we (perhaps) make about the maximum speed of global interpersonal communications in the late nineteenth century. We tend to think that in the old days everything proceeded at a more leisurely pace (which is also perhaps why we feel we have some chance of reliably reconstructing events). We know that people, goods and the mails could travel only at the speed of the fastest train or ship.[28] We may be less aware of how widespread was the telegraphic network that could spread data around the world in seconds, or of how key information conveyed this way was often available within 24 hours or less, via their breakfast newspapers, to the individuals and communities in Asia, America, Europe and elsewhere

---

27. The telegraph link between Japan and Europe had opened 17 years earlier in 1872; by 1891 Japan had a network of 435 telegraph offices (Headrick 1991). By 1903–1904 Pfoundes, back in Kobe, had a telephone number: Kobe 1383.

28. *Around the World in Eighty Days,* the title of Jules Verne's 1873 novel, suggested a near-impossible task, yet by the 1890s transactions between the London and New York stock exchanges took 2–3 minutes (Headrick 1991).

whom we study. The editors of those newspapers, along with governments, shipowners, stockbrokers, large traders, the military, and wealthy individuals made constant use of the worldwide web of telegraph lines.[29] Which (other?) "transcultural" religionists used telegrams as a means of communication, for what purposes and with what results?

Pfoundes's "family life"

A final field of potential further research concerns what might be called Pfoundes's "family life," involving a number of significant others, both male and female. Descriptions of Pfoundes right up to the last period of his life in Kobe, 1893–1907, suggest that he was a difficult person to deal with. One account from 1904–1906 has British Consulate staff in Kobe scurrying to get away whenever Pfoundes appeared (Diaries of Richard Gordon Smith cited in Rogala 2000, 999). Pfoundes seems, despite his constant public activities, to have been a loner. He had no close European friends of whom we are aware and whether he had any real friends among his many Japanese acquaintances is a topic yet to be researched. We do know that on his death a substantial tombstone was erected "by his Japanese and European friends of Kobe"[30] but not whether these "friends" were more than business associates. We also know that Pfoundes was constantly seeking to make new connections with individuals and institutions, but that few of these connections lasted long. However, positioning Pfoundes as a "loner" and thus ignoring his closest personal relationships might fit rather too conveniently with a "great man" approach to history, which of course leaves out, above all, women.

When we look more closely we see that Pfoundes had meaningful if often problematic close relationships with a number of people, both men and women. I do not have space here to deal with any in detail (for some further biographical details see Bocking 2013) but we might start with a brief mention of Pfoundes's parents, James Baker Pounds and Caroline Pounds (née Elam), and Pfoundes's only surviving sibling, his elder brother [Joseph] Elam Pounds. After the age of 14 Charles never again saw, and evidently did not want to see, his father James Baker Pounds or his brother Elam, both of whom emigrated to Australia within two years of the young Charles sailing there, quite probably in search of him since he had almost immediately run away to sea. Half a century later in 1905, long after his father had died in Australia, Pfoundes wrote to the Victoria police in Melbourne with queries about his father's burial and belongings, issuing strict instructions (ignored by the police) to keep the correspondence away from his brother Elam, still living

---

29. For the transformation wrought to merchant shipping by the introduction of the telegraph see e.g. Fayle 2013, 264–265.
30. My thanks for this information to Mr Okazaki Hideki who discovered Pfoundes's tomb.

in the locality (Correspondence with Melbourne police, 1905. Public Records Office, Victoria). We can surmise that by this time Pfoundes was not only increasingly conscious of his own mortality (even though at 65 he was many years younger than his contemporaries in Kobe believed) but perhaps also that he had imbibed a proper Japanese concern for the welfare of ancestors which led him at this rather late stage to wonder whether his father had been appropriately buried and memorialized.

Pfoundes's mother, Caroline Elam, had left the family home in Wexford in 1846 when Charles was only six years old. This was during the Famine of 1845–1852 which prompted mass emigration, but while the men of the family did emigrate to Australia in the mid 1850s, Caroline remained in Ireland until her death in 1898.[31] Charles did on several occasions make contact with his mother. He made a side visit to Ireland during a Europe-USA tour with Japanese dignitaries in 1871 and he brought Caroline out to Japan to visit him in 1874, but then allegedly took all the money she had brought with her, leaving her to find the fare home from her friends. In 1877, between leaving Japan (1876) and setting up home in London (1878–1879), Charles visited his mother twice in her home in Dublin but evidently not out of filial love. The second encounter ended up in court, with Pfoundes bound over to keep the peace after allegedly terrorizing his mother when she failed to produce certain documents he believed were in her possession. Probably these were birth or educational certificates that he needed to secure suitable employment in London.

The departure of his mother from the family home when Charles was only six is likely to have left Pfoundes with strong feelings of anger, partly directed against his mother, as well as a lifelong uncertainty about his own identity. He may have retained a feeling that his mother owed him something, but it is unlikely that in his adult years he would realistically have expected a reconciliation. An enduring feeling of deprivation might help account for his habit of accumulating objects; we know from several sources that he possessed in London a remarkable collection of Japanese artefacts, images, lantern slides, and of course books, even after the sale of hundreds of art objects in New York *en route* from Japan to London in 1876–1877. At the same time, we might reasonably infer that Pfoundes's unhappy experiences in the realm of human relationships were among the factors that drew him to embrace Buddhist teachings and a Buddhist identity in later life.[32]

---

31. Caroline Pounds is credited with being one of Australia's pioneer botanical artists on the basis of paintings attributed to her and dated 1846, discovered in the 1980s in the attic of a nineteenth-century property in Geelong, near Melbourne associated with her son Elam (https://www.daao.org.au/bio/caroline-pounds/biography), but so far the evidence, including her own court testimony, indicates that she lived all her life in Ireland (Bocking 2013).
32. I am grateful to child psychologist Shelagh Graham for a discussion on some typi-

In court in Dublin in 1877, Charles's mother Caroline sought to blacken Charles's character in support of her contention that he had threatened her with assault, by complaining among other things that he had expected her to be companion to the (presumably Japanese) woman with whom he was living in Shiba, Tokyo when she visited in 1874 ("Police Intelligence" 1877 and "Police Intelligence Yesterday" 1877). In March 1878, a few months after his court appearance in Ireland, Pfoundes married in the Liverpool Registry Office Rosa Alice Hill, daughter of a prison governor from Sandwich in the Southeast of England. Rosa was 22, Charles 38 and the newly married couple went almost immediately to live in London, where for a time Rosa accompanied her husband to some of the many lectures he attended, or delivered, around the capital in the early 1880s.

The Japanese Buddhist scholar Takakusu (then Kobayashi) Junjiro, at the time a student of Max Müller in Oxford, stayed with the couple in London when they had been married for eleven years, childless. Takakusu wrote to Matsuyama on 29 April 1890 to say that Pfoundes wanted to travel to America in a year or two and after a stay there to go to Japan, then to India and France and then again to America. Takakusu suggested to Matsuyama that it might be better to have Pfoundes stay in Japan, giving his wife a teaching job at some women's school (*KBJ* 11, 1890, 28). This suggests that Takakusu perceived Pfoundes's young wife Rosa as a woman of some education, but not necessarily sharing Pfoundes's interests. In the event, the marriage failed soon after and we find Pfoundes, without his wife, living in a radical commune called "the Fellowship of the New Life" in Doughty Street, London (Cox 2013). When Pfoundes finally left for Japan in late November 1892 he sailed to Kobe on the *Monmouthshire* alone. Although Matsuyama and his Japanese colleagues who received Pfoundes in Japan early in 1893 must have known from Takakusu's reports that Pfoundes was married, Rosa seemingly figured no more in Pfoundes's life. Thereafter, we can trace Rosa's own life in England through fleeting census and electoral register entries which indicate that she remained living, widow-like, under her married name of Rosa Pfoundes, by occupation a civil servant, until her death, destitute, at the advanced age of 80 in 1936. She is buried in a pauper's (unmarked) grave in Worthing, on the South coast of England.

Rosa was not the only woman in Pfoundes's life at the time the BPS got under way. I quote from our own *DISKUS* article:

> On March 9th [1890] at the "Progressive Association, Penton Hall, 81 Pentonville Road" at 7pm, Mrs. Frederika Macdonald (a gifted writer,

---

cal effects of maternal deprivation in early childhood; any misunderstandings are my own. On a side note, we do not know if Pfoundes took his extensive collection of books, lantern slides etc. back to Japan or if he left them in London, and whether any have survived.

intellectual and exponent of Indian philosophy who three years later publicly debated Theosophy vs Buddhism with Annie Besant and then donated her share of the evening's takings to a poor children's charity) spoke on "Buddhism." Since Sunday evening at the Penton Hall was one of Pfoundes' regular slots, MacDonald may have been that *rara avis*, a close ally of Pfoundes and a Buddhist co-propagandist. On Sunday 16th March the "Ball's Pond Branch of the N.S.S. Secular Hall 36 Newington Green Road" heard a lecture on "Buddhism or enlightenment: its gospel and doctrines." The speaker on this occasion was identified only as "the Representative of the Propaganda," so could have been either Pfoundes or MacDonald. (Bocking *et al.* 2014, 20)

Speculation again, but the appearance of the manifestly talented and *sympathique* Mrs Macdonald does appear to coincide with Pfoundes's final separation from his wife. Quite apart from any speculation on the relationship, we should note that Frederika MacDonald deserves further research as the first woman Buddhist missionary in London and certainly the only female missionary ever fielded by the Japanese *SKS*, with or without its knowledge.

In sum, we may conclude that Pfoundes, the irascible "loner," had at least one unnamed live-in female partner in Japan, was married for more than a decade to Rosa Alice Hill and somehow attracted to his otherwise one-man BPS campaign Frederika MacDonald, a remarkable woman who was capable of matching Annie Besant in public debate. In principle each of these three women closely associated with Pfoundes, as well as Pfoundes's mother Caroline, could and should be further researched. That we know so little about each is partly of course because women's lives were not so well documented as those of men in the late nineteenth century. However, the exponential growth of digital resources may in time enable us to discover far more about these "doubly forgotten" figures influencing our pioneer Buddhists, not just the pioneers themselves who are already emerging into the limelight.

More could be said about Pfoundes's inner circle, but my purpose in drawing attention to his family life is wider than Pfoundes himself, for each of the pioneer Western and Asian Buddhists encountered in the course of research inevitably has a family background and history of some kind and was influenced by personal relationships of one kind or another. In suggesting that research be directed towards Pfoundes's "family life" I am also suggesting that a study of close personal relationships in other cases might also reap rewards. In Dhammaloka's case we have no definite family history (so far), since we are not yet certain that he was Laurence Carroll (b. 1856) of Booterstown Road, Blackrock, but we are aware that he had after 1900 at least one particularly close and trusted companion. A Burmese jewel merchant, Maung Maung, accompanied Dhammaloka to Tokyo in 1902 and Bangkok in 1903, acted as his secretary and amanuensis and very probably funded and organized many of his travels. Maung Maung remains otherwise unidentified and his other deeds and motives in relation to modernizing Buddhism unknown, in part because the name Maung Maung is very common in Burma.

The senior Tokyo monk Shaka Unsho whom both Pfoundes and Dhammaloka managed to fall out with on separate occasions in 1893 and 1902 respectively[33] was the uncle of the pioneer Japanese monastic traveller to Ceylon, Shaku Kozen (Jaffe 2004) and an uncle-nephew relationship presupposes a larger family circle. We are perhaps only now becoming familiar with the idea that monks and nuns, even in Southeast Asia, may not only be married but may also continue relating closely to their family members (Clarke 2014) and in Japan of course the temple wife and hence the temple family has been, since the Meiji period, an often-present and often crucial if almost always (so far) invisible source of potential agency; a topic addressed by Richard Jaffe (Jaffe 2001) and others. Professor Yoshinaga's remarkable research on the young William McGovern (Yoshinaga 2013) dwells for good reason on the role of McGovern's mother and the "twist in the tale" of his article about "three boys on a Mahayana Vehicle" reveals unexpected Western Buddhist connections through the female line of the Everett family.

The transformation in the colonial period of some elements of Buddhism into a protestant-style missionary religion with global aspirations involved many European pioneers, not just the few earliest known Buddhist monastics such as Asoka (Gordon Douglas), Dhammaloka, Ananda Metteyya (Allan Bennett) and Nyanatiloka (Anton Gueth). This style of religiosity created leadership opportunities of many kinds not only for laymen such as Pfoundes and Olcott (as well as globally active Asian pioneers such as Dharmapala, or for Hinduism Vivekananda) but also for European laywomen, among whom the best known in this field are figures such as Helena Blavatsky and Annie Besant, Beatrice Suzuki and Sister Sanghamitta (Countess Canavarro) but there were others, even in London, who helped spread Buddhism, such as Frederika MacDonald referred to above.

On the Japanese side, because the mainstream Buddhist denominations remained relatively powerful and overwhelmingly patriarchal, opportunities for pioneering Buddhist activities by both men and women—including joint male-female leadership—have arguably most often occurred in the arena of the New Religious Movements of nineteenth- and twentieth-century Japan. If we hold up as a mirror to Japan the milieu in which Pfoundes's operated in late Victorian London—a world of spiritualists, Theosophists, esotericists, occultists, homosexuals, vegetarians, utopians, socialists, secular humanists, etc.—we might find reflected in it from Japan not "mainstream" (if somewhat marginal mainstream) Buddhists like Matsuyama, associated with the vener-

---

33. I am grateful to Okamoto Yoshiko (pers. comm.) for this and other information.

able institution of Nishi Honganji, but the founders and followers of syncretic and Buddhist new religious movements, notable Buddhist examples in the twentieth century being *Omoto, Reiyukai, Rissho Kosei-kai, Shinnyo-en, Soka Gakkai*, etc., all of which generated their own networks, sometimes global, and all of which represent intriguing "turns" in the complex history of modern Buddhism.

Conclusion

In "A Buddhist crossroads: pioneer European Buddhists and globalizing Asian networks 1860-1960" (Turner, Cox and Bocking 2013) we identified some of the broad areas and themes for further research that emerged at the 2012 Cork conference workshop in relation to modernist, globalizing Buddhism in the decades either side of 1900. These included new technologies of travel and communication, which routinized formerly difficult journeys and thus multiplied contacts and interactions; the spread of printing presses and the beginnings of global mass communication (mass production also multiplying the chance of a document surviving to be studied today); the centrality of Japan and India, albeit for different reasons, in the emergence of a pan-Asian Buddhist sense of self-confidence and identity and the corresponding lesser importance, or so it seemed, of the British imperial hub, London.

In this chapter I have drawn on the life of just one, albeit extraordinary, modernist Buddhist, Charles Pfoundes, to explore some of these areas and to suggest some further research questions which might be relevant also to other case-studies. In respect of London, I would suggest that the recent discovery of the true extent of activity of the London Buddhist Propagation Society and our better appreciation of Pfoundes's role in the BPS reminds us that London, being the hub of empire, was, with hindsight, where we should always have been looking for the very first Buddhist mission to the West. In this respect it seems strange that Notto Thelle's brief but explicit 1987 reference to Pfoundes and the London branch of the BPS in his *Buddhism and Christianity in Japan: From Conflict to Dialogue, 1854-1899* (Thelle 1987, 110) went for so long unremarked by the rest of us—why was that? At the same time, research on Pfoundes has underlined just how significant in this period was Kyoto and the "internationalizing" activity around Nishi Honganji, in which the *KSK* was a hub of a different kind, acting as a clearing-house for thoughtful communication and global networking (including via the innovative English-French Buddhist magazine *Bijou of Asia*) among modernist Buddhists and sympathisers worldwide. In calling attention to the complexities of the notion of "failure" when related to the ostensible purpose of a religious enterprise, to the fluidity of names and identities, to factors that encouraged or constrained Buddhist travellers within the new era of mass transport, to the question of "what is Buddhism?" in an era which had not yet agreed on how to spell the word, to the colonization of the new and powerful sphere of the "nondenominational," to the economics of lay Buddhist leadership, to the potential of the telegraph as the "Victorian internet" and to Pfoundes's "family life" and to gendered histories I have no doubt sacrificed depth for breadth, but consideration of each of these areas may help, I hope, to shed a little more light on a period which has shaped our present and of which, it turns out, we still know very little.

Acknowledgments

This chapter began life as a paper delivered in the workshop panel "Plural Modernities" in the conference *Asian Buddhism: plural colonialisms and plural modernities* held at Kyoto University and Ryukoku University, 12–14 December 2014. I am very grateful to Prof Yoshinaga Shin'ichi and his team for their outstanding achievement in planning and organizing the conference, conceived as a third in the "Buddhist Crossroads" series following those in University College Cork, Ireland, 2012 and Duke University, USA, 2013, and for Professor Yoshinaga's valuable comments on my paper. A revised version was presented at the XXI IAHR World Congress in Erfurt, Germany, in August 2015 in the panel "Transnational encounters and religion: following the threads of connected histories (nineteenth–twentieth century)" organized by Philippe Bornet, to whom I extend my thanks also for bringing this chapter to publication.

Abbreviations

BPS   Buddhist Propagation Society (London branch)
KBJ   *Kaigai Bukkyō jijō*
KSK   *Kaigai Senkyō Kai*
TTW   *The Three Worlds,* http://www.ehbritten.org/texts/primary/two_worlds/index.html

References

Barrett, Tim H. 2016. "Michael Pye, Translating Drunk—and Stark Naked: Problems in Presenting Eighteenth Century Japanese Thought." *Journal of the Irish Society for the Academic Study of Religions* 3: 236–249. https://jisasr.org/archive/volume-3-2016

Bocking, Brian. 2013. "Flagging up Buddhism: Charles Pfoundes (Omoie Tetzunostzuke) among the International Congresses and Expositions, 1893–1905." *Contemporary Buddhism: An Interdisciplinary Journal* 14(1): 17–37. https://doi.org/10.18792/diskus.v16i3.51

———. 2016 "Tracing the 'Non-Denominational': Japan and the UK." In *Contemporary Views on Comparative Religion*, edited by P. Antes, A. Geertz and M. Rothstein, 271–282. Sheffield: Equinox.

Bocking, B., P. Choompolpaisal, L. Cox and A. Turner, eds. 2015. *A Buddhist Crossroads: Pioneer Western Buddhists and Asian Networks 1860–1960*. London: Routledge. https://doi.org/10.4324/9781315764733

Bocking, B., L. Cox and S. Yoshinaga, eds. 2014. "The First Buddhist Mission to the West: Charles Pfoundes and the London Buddhist Mission of 1889–1892." *DISKUS* 16(3): 1–33. https://cora.ucc.ie/handle/10468/9812

Choompolpaisal, Phibul. 2013. "Tai-Burmese-Lao Buddhisms in the 'Modernizing' of Ban Thawai (Bangkok): The Dynamic Interaction between Ethnic Minority Religion and British-Siamese Centralization in the late Nineteenth/early Twentieth Centuries." *Contemporary Buddhism: An Interdisciplinary Journal* 14 (1): 94–115. https://doi.org/10.1080/14639947.2013.785241

Clarke, Shayne N. 2014. *Family Matters in Indian Buddhist Monasticisms*. Honolulu: University of Hawai'i Press. https://doi.org/10.1515/9780824840075

Cox, Laurence. 2013. *Buddhism and Ireland: From the Celts to the Counter-Culture and Beyond*. Sheffield: Equinox.

"Editorial Dots." 1883. *The Weekly Hawkeye* [Burlington, Iowa], 17 May 1883: 7. https://doi.org/10.17077/0003-4827.11948

Fayle, C. Ernest. 2013. *A Short History of the World's Shipping Industry*. Abingdon: Routledge. https://doi.org/10.4324/9781315020006

Franck, Harry. 1910. *A Vagabond Journey around the World: A Narrative of Personal Experience*. New York: The Century Co.

Headrick, Daniel R. 1991. *The Invisible Weapon: Telecommunications and International Politics 1851–1945*. Oxford: Oxford University Press.

Jaffe, Richard M. 2001 *Neither Monk nor Layman: Clerical Marriage in Modern Japanese Buddhism*. Princeton, NJ: Princeton University Press.

———. 2004. "Seeking Śākyamuni: Travel and the Reconstruction of Japanese Buddhism." *The Journal of Japanese Studies* 30(1): 65–96. https://doi.org/10.1353/jjs.2004.0019

"Missing Friends." 1912. *Victoria Police Gazette*. 20 June 1912: 317. Public Records Office, Victoria.

Pfoundes, Charles. 1889a. "Is the Bud(d)hist an Atheist?" *Lucifer* 4(22): 351.

———. 1889b. "Buddhism, What It Was, and Is." *The Two Worlds* (magazine). 17 May 1889: 326–327. http://www.ehbritten.org/texts/primary/two_worlds/1889/two_worlds_v2_n79_17_may_1889_licensed.pdf

———. 1890. "Letter from Pfoundes to Matsuyama sent 14 October 1889." *Kaigai Bukkyō jijō* 7: 28.

———. 1905. "Letter from Pfoundes in Kobe to Inspector General of Police, Melbourne." 24 February 1905. Public Record Office, Victoria.

"Police Intelligence: Extraordinary Case." 1877. *Irish Times*, 3 November 1877, 3.

"Police Intelligence Yesterday: A Strange Case." 1877. *Freeman's Journal*, 3 November 1877, 2.

Pye, Michael. 1990. *Emerging from Meditation: Being Translations of the Writings of Tominaga Nakamoto 1715-1746*. Duckworth: London

Rogala, Josef. 2000. *A Collector's Guide to Books on Japan in English: An Annotated List of Over 2500 Titles with Subject Index*. Abingdon: Routledge

Ruxton, Ian. 2008. *Sir Ernest Satow's Private Letters to W.G. Aston and F.V. Dickins: The Correspondence of a Pioneer Japanologist from 1870 to 1918*. Morrisville: Lulu.com.

Salemink, Oscar. 2009. "Afterword: Questioning Faiths? Casting Doubts." In *Casting Faiths: Imperialism and the Transformation of Religion in East and Southeast Asia*, edited by T.D. DuBois, 257–263. Basingstoke: Palgrave Macmillan. https://doi.org/10.1057/9780230235458_12

Shimatsu, Yoichi. 2008. "A Hidden History 'Free Tibet, the Lost Crusade of Buddhist Japan.'" *Japanese Religions* 33(1/2): 91–95. http://www.japanese-religions.jp/publications/

Standage, Tom. 1999 (2nd edition). *The Victorian Internet*. London: Phoenix.

Thelle, Notto R. 1987. *Buddhism and Christianity in Japan: From Conflict to Dialogue, 1854-1899*. Hawaii: Hawaii University Press.

Turner, A., L. Cox and B. Bocking. 2013. "A Buddhist Crossroads: Pioneer European Buddhists and Globalising Asian Networks 1860–1960." *Contemporary Buddhism: An Interdisciplinary Journal* 14(1): 1–16. https://doi.org/10.1080/14639947.2013.785244

Uchiyama, Torasuke, ed. 1893. *Pfoundes, Bukkyō enzetsushū* (C. Pfoundes: A collection of Buddhist lectures). Kyoto: Kobundo.

Yoshinaga, Shin'ichi. 2013. "Three Boys on a Great Vehicle: 'Mahayana Buddhism' and a Trans-national Network." *Contemporary Buddhism: An Interdisciplinary Journal* 14(1): 52–65. https://doi.org/10.1080/14639947.2013.785249

Yoshinaga S. and Nakanishi, N., eds. 2014–2015. *Kaigai Bukkyō jijō. The Bijou of Asia*. (3 vols.) Kyoto: Sanninsha.

About the author

Brian Bocking is Professor emeritus of the Study of Religions at University College Cork, Ireland and formerly Professor at SOAS, University of London. In recent years he has been researching the emergence of global Buddhism, collaborating with Alicia Turner (Toronto), Laurence Cox (Maynooth) and Yoshinaga Shin'ichi (Kyoto) on the study of two "forgotten" Irish Buddhists; U Dhammaloka (?1856–?1913) and Charles Pfoundes (1840-1907).

— 8 —

Travelling through Interstitial Spaces: The Radical Spiritual Journeys of Pandita Mary Ramabai Saraswathi

Parinitha Shetty

The exceptional circumstances of Pandita Ramabai's (1858–1922) life did not allow her to be rooted within any socio/religious space that existed in her world and denied her the certainties that come with such a sense of belonging. Her early life was nomadic as it was spent travelling across India and later to England and across America. This, in conjunction with the many difficulties she encountered in this stage of her life, forced her to inhabit radically disjunctive socio-cultural, experiential spaces, simultaneously. To be incessantly travelling is to be pushed into continually re-imagining and re-making the templates which naturalize and normalize the practices of embodied existence. It was from these liminal locations that Ramabai contoured a spiritual interiority centered on her personal emotional and spiritual needs, that would both shape and legitimize the radical material and institutional transformations she sought to bring about in her society. After the death of her husband she travelled to England where she converted to Christianity. Later she travelled across America. Existing at the cusp of histories, cultures and religions, not at ease within the institutionalized religions that she traversed, there emerged in her a radically alienated, critical seeing that shaped her attempts at creating an egalitarian and humane world for those she considered the most oppressed in her society. When she returned to India she established institutions and homes which broke denominational and caste mappings in an attempt to provide a livable community for those at the extreme margins of her society.

The Brahmin pilgrim

Pandita Ramabai (1858–1922) was born into a Brahmin family in south west India. Though born into the socio-politically powerful Citpāvan Brahmin caste,[1] Ramabai's father's simultaneous adherence as well as non-adherence

---

1. See Chakravarti 1998 for a detailed history of the dominance of the Citpāvan Brahmin Peshwai in organizing and regulating caste and gender in eigthteenth-century

to the rules of his caste community drove his family to a life of extreme physical hardship and perpetual travel. This nomadic life which often pushed Ramabai's family to the extreme edges of survival, would arguably be crucial in shaping later a kind of "religious nomadism." After the demise of her parents she travelled to Calcutta and later to Bombay and was exposed to socio-religious reform organizations like the Brahmo Samāj[2] and the Prarthana Samaj[3] which were engaged in the reform of Brahmanical Hinduism. After the death of her husband she travelled to England where she converted to Christianity. Later she travelled across America. For Ramabai, her "conversion experience" reconstructed many years after her conversion to Christianity in her autobiographical text *A Testimony of our Inexhaustible Treasure,*[4] was the apogee of what she saw as her gradual but complete acceptance of Christ. However, her Christianity was shaped on the site of her personal dissent against the orthodoxies of the caste into which she was born and the orthodoxies of the institutionalized Christianity into which she was converted. Availing for herself the interpretative freedom offered by Protestantism she validated her reform for women and her heretical critique of Anglican Christianity, through her personal reading of the Bible. Strongly believing in the possibility and efficacy of human agency in the shaping of human history, Ramabai understood her faith in Christ as a source of personal strength and a means of legitimizing the particular human and humane trajectories that she attempted to give to this history.

Through a chronologically linear narrative, *A Testimony* plotted her life from childhood to adulthood as one of continuous travel attaining closure in the establishment of the last of the institutions that she set up, namely, the Mukti Sadan. Overriding this narrative and intertwined with it is the narrative of her spiritual journey from Brahminic Hinduism to Christianity. By the time Ramabai wrote *A Testimony*, she had undergone a conversion experience which she describes in *A Testimony* as follows, "The Holy Spirit made it clear to me from the Word of God, that the salvation which God gives through Christ is present, and not something future. I believed it, I received it, and I was filled with Joy." (Kosambi 2000, 313) An overtly evangelical text, *A Testimony* conflates Ramabai's spiritual journey with her geo/bio-graphical journey, both of which are constructed as inevitably moving towards the telos of Christian enlightenment and its institutional instantiation in the Mukti Sadan. The text, in typical Christian missionary fashion, affirms the truth of the

---

Maharashtra.

2. A Hindu reform movement started in Calcutta in 1828 by Raja Ram Mohan Roy.
3. This was a socio-religious reform movement founded in Bombay in 1867 by Atmaram Pandurang.
4. Sarasvati 1907. The text will be henceforth referred to as *A Testimony*.

Christian God and the efficacy of faith leading to salvation offered through Christ. It retrospectively recasts Ramabai's life by telescoping it through the lens of Christian evangelism. However, if *A Testimony* were to be read against the background of the essays, travelogue, letters, and books that Ramabai wrote at different points earlier in her life, the self that is fashioned through this autobiographical text would reflect the opaque transparency of a palimpsest, simultaneously transparent as well as opaque to the sedimented layers of the other textualized selves. The evangelical Christian authorial self-fashioning of *A Testimony* would be disorganized, undermined, complicated and dismantled by the multiple self-fashionings that are prior to, as well as simultaneous with it. Read as a palimpsest, *A Testimony* shows the traces of the dissonantly layered social and personal history through and against which a fractured, deeply personal as well as socially radical, spirituality is shaped and comes into being. In this palimpsest, the articulations of the convert's spiritual interiority are simultaneously present in the surface spatial multiplicity of shifting, intersecting, interrogating spiritual self-fashionings, and in the diachronic depth of an evolving spiritual interiority in which only some of the multiple trajectories are acknowledged and recognized at the site of the convert's present spiritual state of being as it is discursively constructed in *A Testimony*. In what follows, I will attempt to explore the multiple strands in Ramabai's spiritual journeys, and their material/historical moorings, through a palimpsestic reading of her autobiographical text.

In *A Testimony* Ramabai writes,

> My father, though a very orthodox Hindu and strictly adhering to caste and other religious rules, was yet a reformer in his own way. He could not see why women and people of the Shudra caste should not learn to read and write the Sanskrit language and learn sacred literature other than the Vedas. (Kosambi 2000, 295)

Here, Ramabai presents her father, Anant Shastri, as a reformer through the interpretative frameworks of the nineteenth-century upper caste socio-religious reform movements (Figure 8.1). In the latter part of the nineteenth century, the education of women had become the focus of many such movements, initiated and shaped by the advent of colonial modernity and Protestant Christianity. Ramabai positions her father's reform as being at odds with his orthodox adherence to the rules of caste. However, the inspiration for Anant Shastri's educational reform did not come from the reform movements of his period but rather from a visit to the palace of the Peshwa Baji Rao II, a stronghold of Brahminic Hindu patriarchy in Maharashtra. As Meera Kosambi puts it,

> On one of his visits to the Peshwa's palace with his reputed teacher, Anant Shastri was held spellbound by the mellifluous Sanskrit recita-

Figure 8.1   Anant Shastri with his family (Dyer 1930, Frontispiece).

tion of the Peshwa's wife. He vowed to teach his own wife "the divine language" from which tradition—and allegedly scriptural injunctions as well—had mandated the exclusion of women and Shudras.

(Kosambi 2000, 4)

In her autobiography, Ramabai Ranade, a contemporary of Pandita Ramabai, writes about Anasuya Bai and tells us that she, "was well-versed in Sanskrit and gave discourses on the *Purāṇas*." (Ranade 1963, 105) Anasuya Bai's knowledge of Sanskrit and her ability to discourse on the Puranas is not seen as extraordinary or exceptional by Ramabai Ranade. This indicates that a regulated access to the Sanskrit language and Sanskrit texts, though rare, was available to high caste Hindu women and that, as in the case of the newly introduced European models of education for women, this traditional education could have an instrumental purpose for women. When Anant Shastri was questioned by the caste preceptor for teaching Sanskrit to his second wife, Ramabai's mother, he successfully defended his action by taking recourse to traditional *śāstras*.[5]

---

5.   In a Kannada biography of Ramabai, the author M. Lakshmana Harihara Joshi writes

The discursive formations within which the categories of reformed modernity and orthodox tradition were being constituted in the nineteenth century, relegate Anant Shastri to the latter category and describe him as being confined by the tyrannical authority of an unchanging set of caste and religious rules. Ramabai's retrospective attempt at legibilizing her father's reform through this discourse displays its inadequacy in capturing the fluidity of intra caste distinctions that were structured on temporally and geographically variant practices of Brahminism. What is indicated by what Ramabai presented as her father's educational reform, is that seemingly transgressive extensions of, or inclusions into a specific repertoire of Brahmanical practices were, in actuality, part of the process of internal borrowings and exchanges that were taking place between geographically distinct groups of the same caste. Such transgressions from caste rules could be legitimized by proving that they were sanctioned by the sacred texts of the Hindus. Since, the Hindu *śāstras* comprised a collection of texts which could be selectively chosen and interpreted, a Sanskrit scholar like Anant Shastri would be able to strategically use these texts to authorize his deviations from the customary practices of his caste.[6]

---

that Anant Shastri was summoned by the pontiff of the Madhva Peeta in Udupi and was upbraided for going against his religion by teaching Sanskrit to his wife. Anant Shastri replied that he could defend his action since it was sanctioned by the *śāstras*. According to Joshi's biography, Anant Shastri was asked to defend himself before an assembly of 400 Sanskrit scholars and did so by quoting passages from *śruti* and *smṛti* literature, the *Rāmāyaṇa* and the *Mahābhārata*. (Joshi 1964, 9-10) Joshi also states that Ananta Shastri quoted the foundational *śloka* of the *Vyoma Saṃhitā* to defend himself. The *śloka* goes as follows: "Since, women, *śūdras* and Brahmins who have failed to fulfill their duties as Brahmins, have the authority to read and interpret the *Dharmaśāstras*, except for the Vedas, they can be initiated into the study of these texts." (Joshi 1964, 13, translation mine).

6. It is interesting to note that the British colonial administration in the nineteenth century also legitimized its legislations against upper caste Hindu practices like *satī*, child marriage, the interdiction against widow remarriage, through the production of scriptural justifications, as suggested in the work of feminist historians like Lata Mani (Mani 1986, 37) and Uma Chakravarti. According to Chakravarti, Henry Colebrooke's first pieces of research titled "On the Duties of the Faithful Hindu Widow" (1799), which focused on the practice of *satī*, compiled evidence bearing on women from the ancient texts. She writes: "The essay reflects all the characteristic features of the historiography of the women's question: the reference to a variety of ancient texts, the special authority given to texts over custom, the search for the 'authentic' position as contained in the older and more authoritative texts and the confusion in reconciling contradictory evidence. However, it is significant that there is nothing in Colebrooke's essay to suggest that the Vedas were recognized as either the oldest or the most authentic texts; the past was as yet unstratified and was perceived as one homogenous whole." (Chakravarti 1989, 30-31).

In a similar manner, the converted Ramabai was to smudge the boundaries between religions and between Christian sects, precisely through such borrowings and mixings across religions and across Christian sects, in the process of contouring her personal practices of Christianity and instituting her reforms for Hindu women.

The regulated access to Sanskrit texts[7] which her reformer father, as Ramabai described him, had allowed to his wife and daughters was for Ramabai the beginning of a radical opening up of access to other prohibited texts. On the suggestion of the leader of the Brahmo Samāj, Keshub Chandra Sen, Ramabai was to read the *Veda*s which had been forbidden to her by her father,[8] and her English lessons led her to reading the Bible.[9] These new readings and her participation in the Brahmo Samāj's and Prārthanā Samāj's reformist projects for women were to provide her with a critical perspective which led to her feminist reading of the *Dharmaśāstra*s.[10] With her conversion to Christianity and her introduction to American feminists, this reading developed into a trenchant criticism of upper caste Hindu patriarchal practices as seen in her book *The High-Caste Hindu Woman* (Sarasvati 1981 [1887]) written in America.

We come to know of Ramabai's early travels, before her conversion, through her autobiographical writings namely *Famine Experiences* (1897) and *A Testimony* (1907). In *A Testimony* Ramabai legibilizes the Hindu past of her

---

7. In her essay titled "Indian Religion," which was published in the Cheltenham Lady's College Magazine, Ramabai writes: "I remember, when a child, being forbidden to repeat the sacred texts, which I had picked up by hearing my brother and other pupils of my father repeat them. The Aranyaks are so sacred that not a single text from them is pronounced in the presence of women, even of the Brahman caste, much less in that of a Sudra" (Ramabai 1886, 115).

8. Recounting her visit to the house of Keshub Chandra Sen, Ramabai writes in *A Testimony*: "He and his family showed great kindness to me, and when parting, he gave me a copy of one of the Vedas. He asked if I had studied the Vedas. I answered in the negative and said that women were not fit to read the Vedas and they were not allowed to do so. It would be breaking the rules of religion, if I were to study the Vedas. He could not but smile at my declaration of this Hindu doctrine. He said nothing in answer, but advised me to study the Vedas and the Upanishads." (Kosambi 2000, 304)

9. In his biography of Ramabai, Basil Miller tells how Ramabai learnt English along with Ramabai Ranade, the wife of chief justice Ranade, from Miss Hurford, principal of the government female training school at Poona. He writes: "Miss Hurford had agreed to teach English to the wife of the Chief Justice on the condition that she be permitted to teach her the Bible also. Although Miss Hurford was not a missionary, she was a devout Christian. Pandita Ramabai was invited to join the Chief Justice's wife in these English classes. She found the English grammar extremely simple, for the Sanskrit grammar was much more intricate, and years earlier she had mastered it. The Bible lessons interested her intensely" (Miller 1949, 33).

10. A genre of Sanskrit texts enumerating the right behavior within ritual, moral and social spheres.

childhood as a futile pilgrimage spent in the rigorous practice of meaningless rituals. She writes:

> We had fulfilled all the conditions laid down in the sacred books, and kept all the rules as far as our knowledge went, but the gods were not pleased with us, and did not appear to us. After years of fruitless service, we began to lose our faith in them and in the books which prescribed this course, and held out the hope of a great reward to the worshippers of the gods. We still continued to keep caste rules, worshipped gods and studied sacred literature, as usual. (Kosambi 2000, 300)[11]

In both these autobiographical texts Ramabai's self-fashioning is mediated through the missionary Christian othering of non-Christian faith traditions as heathen and their gods as false. Describing her present spiritual state as one of complete and joyful communion with her personal savior Jesus Christ (Kosambi 2000, 314), she hollows out her erstwhile faith practices of all spiritual or religious significance. In *Famine Experiences* Ramabai establishes the truth of the Christian God as the one and only true God through denying the very existence of her father's Hindu God of "stone and metal images" (Kosambi 2000, 248) except as the product of false belief. Recounting her father's last words to her she writes:

> "Remember, my child," he said, "you are my youngest, my most beloved child. I have given you into the hands of our God, you are His and to Him alone you must belong and serve all your life." He could speak no more. My father's prayers for me were, no doubt, heard by the Almighty, the all-merciful Heavenly Father whom the old Hindu did not know. The God of all flesh did not find it impossible to bring me, a great sinner and an unworthy child of His, out of heathen darkness into the saving light of His love and salvation. (Kosambi 2000, 250)

As Ramabai recasts and critiques her relinquished Hindu past, and retrospectively gives a meaning to that past from the site of her Christian present, she re-cognizes the god whom her father addressed, yet failed to recognize, as the Christian God. Seemingly Ramabai's conversion is complete. She also writes in *A Testimony*:

> The low-caste people are never allowed to enter the temples where high-caste men worship gods. So the poor degraded people find shapeless stones, broken pots, and smear them with red paint, set them up under trees and on roadsides, or in small temples which they build themselves, where Brahmans do not go for fear of losing their caste, and worship, in order to satisfy the cravings of their spiritual nature.
> (Kosambi 2000, 303–304)

---

11. See also Joshi 1964, 17–18, about the family progressively becoming disillusioned by traditional religious practices.

Here Ramabai's upper caste Brahmin denigration and denial of the reality of the gods worshipped by the lower castes, and her unfamiliarity with the belief systems that orient their practices of worship, merge with and replicate the Christian missionary denial and denigration of her father's gods. Structurally, the missionary Christian relegation of other religions to heathenism is analogous with the upper caste relegation of lower caste practices of religion to primitivism.

However, the intense physical sufferings of her early travels and the absence of any sense of rootedness within a community or a geographical location, contributed to Ramabai's lifelong discomfort with the hierarchies and dogmas of caste as well as those of institutionalized religions. Ramabai's early travels were pilgrimages to holy Hindu shrines across India, where the family performed elaborate religious rituals. Though marked by constant movement through unfamiliar geographical and socio-cultural spaces, the mapping of this journey as a pilgrimage, the family's strict adherence to its caste practices, and the sacralization of this travel through its intended purpose of gaining religious merit through the performance of rituals and practices of ascetic self-discipline, sequestered them within the familiarity of a mode of being structured through the religious regulations of caste. However, the physical sufferings that the family endured as a result of the rigours of their ascetic self-disciplining and the extreme poverty leading to starvation and the death of her parents, destabilized the familiarity of that caste-structured mode of being and the legibility that was inscribed into it. Again, however rigidly mapped, travel, especially the kind of unplanned meandering pilgrimage undertaken by Ramabai's family, makes it impossible to sequester oneself within the confines of sanctioned spaces. It was equally impossible to avoid unfamiliar sights and to prevent contact with strangers through unsanctioned and unfamiliar modes of acquaintance. These epistemological disruptions contributed to Ramabai's proneness to new religious influences in an attempt to make sense of what it was to be human and humane. At the age of sixteen Ramabai saw her parents die of hunger. A year later her elder sister Krishnabai died of cholera. Ramabai herself suffered a partial hearing loss because of the intense cold faced by her and her brother while travelling on the banks of the river Jhelum which required them to bury themselves neck-deep in sand to keep warm. The demands of caste did not allow them the flexibility required to adapt to the novel and changing requirements of the journey and deal effectively with their increasingly impoverished condition. From Ramabai's experience of extreme corporeal suffering at the edge of starvation and death, there emerged a recognition of the radical equality of human beings based on their common vulnerability to corporeal suffering. Describing her rescue work during the famine of 1896, in *Famine Experiences*, Ramabai writes:

> None of my friends can ever understand what my feelings are for the famine people unless they know that I have had once to go through the same experience as that of the starving thousands of Central India. Yet I must say that suffering alone is not able to produce sympathy for other sufferers.—Unless God changes our hearts through the wonderful regenerating action of His Holy Spirit, we never have true love and sympathy for our fellow men. (Kosambi 2000, 253)

Here, Ramabai attributes her self-transforming recognition that she belongs to the human community and is linked to her fellow men through bonds of love and sympathy, to the regenerating action of "His Holy Spirit." Through this conceptualization of God and his creation, and the socially recognizable structures through which the relationship between God and his creation could be known and lived, Christianity provided Ramabai with a critical perspective on suffering. Christianity's conceptualization of the equality of all human beings and their common origin as the children of God shaped Ramabai's criticism of social inequalities that existed in her own times.[12] In her other writings, Ramabai locates human suffering in the debilitating hierarchies of caste, gender, race and religion, that fractured her society and those she visited. For Ramabai, the radical egalitarianism propounded by Jesus became the founding principle on the basis of which a humane human community, based on mutual and reciprocal concern and care, could be both envisioned as well as put into practice. In the institutions that she established, the effort towards the spiritual regeneration of the women who were sheltered there was consequent to the fulfillment of their physical needs and restoration of their bodily health (Shetty 2012, 36–37, Figure 8.2).

In her text *The Word-Seed* (1908), Ramabai narrates how she first heard and received the name of Christ, "about 40 years ago,"[13] while she was a child on a pilgrimage to Benares with her parents. She writes of her parents:

> As orthodox Brahmans, they most religiously avoided coming in contact with Christians and Mlechchhas, i.e. the foreigners. But one day in the providence of God, a Christian man came to see my father while we were at Benares. I do not remember whether he was an Indian or an European

---

12. According to Judith Becker, this conception of human equality based on its common origin, was shared by most Protestant Mission societies of the nineteenth century. She gives the example of Gustav Warneck, "the doyen of (German) mission studies," as articulating the broad theological framework within which this idea of humanity was structured. Elaborating on this framework she writes, "Warneck taught the unity of all humankind as created in God's image and that all humankind was of the same blood. This means that it shared descent from Adam and Eve and was meant to be saved by the love and blood of Jesus Christ" (Becker 2016, 109).
13. Sarasvati 1908, 325. Hence it must have taken place in 1868, since this text was written in 1908.

Figure 8.2 Photograph of an inmate of Mukti Sadan "before and after" her arrival (Dyer 1930, 72).

Christian, nor what he spoke to my father. But I remember two words which I heard him say while he was conversing with my father. The words were: "Yeshu Khrista," i.e. Jesus Christ. He shook hands with my father when taking his leave, and said something which I do not remember. But I found myself repeating the two words "Yeshu Khrista," which I heard from him, after he went away. I must have repeated them many times, because my sister was much alarmed and drew my mother's attention to what I was whispering to myself. Mother asked me what it was that I had been repeating; but I was afraid to answer her question and kept silence. She warned me against repeating the name of the God of the Mlechchhas, and told me not to bring His name to my lips again. But I never forgot that Name. (Kosambi 2000, 325–326)

In these autobiographical texts, Ramabai narrativizes her Brahmin past as always already moving towards the telos of Christian conversion. Events and incidents from that Brahmin past are retrospectively imbued with meanings and significances that are generated from her evangelical Christian location in the present. From this location, she assumes epistemological control over her past and consequently achieves legibility over her present. Describing her first encounter with the rituals of Christian worship during her visit with her brother to a Christian gathering in Calcutta, Ramabai writes in *A Testimony*:

> We looked upon the proceedings of the assembly with curiosity, but did not understand what they were about. After a little while one of them opened a book and read something out of it and then they knelt down before their chairs and some said something with closed eyes. We were told that was the way they prayed to God. We did not see any image to which they paid their homage but it seemed as though they were paying homage to the chairs before which they knelt. Such was the crude idea of Christian worship that impressed itself on my mind. (Kosambi 2000, 301)

Here Ramabai implicitly acknowledges that the practices and rituals of worship of a particular faith tradition become meaningful only for the insider who exists within and through the explanatory schema and belief system of that faith tradition. However, as an evangelical Christian, Ramabai asserted that the Christian religion was the only true religion. But in her practice of Christianity she was unable to gloss over the polarities and tensions inherent to her religious heritage. Through a notion of "spirituality," she creatively traversed all these contradictory sites in order to put into practice a humane society. Ramabai's critique of Brahmanical patriarchy and its debilitating grip on the upper caste woman's life also emerged from the site of these contradictions (Shetty 2012, 30–31).

A difficult transition

In April 1883, Ramabai set off to England to study medicine. On 29 September of the same year, Ramabai and her daughter Manorama were baptized by Canon Butler. Shortly before Ramabai's conversion, Anandibai Bhagat who had accompanied her on her trip to England committed suicide by swallowing poison (Kosambi 2000, 9). Kosambi writes that "the suddenness of Ramabai's conversion remains a mystery" (Kosambi 2000, 14), adding that she was baptized when in a state of disappointment, depression and even despair. Pressure had been exerted on her and Anandibai by the Wantage Sisters to convert, in the genuine belief that she was an "inquirer." According to Kosambi, when Ramabai visited Max Müller about the time of her conversion, "he found Ramabai in a state of 'nervous prostration' because Anandibai Bhagat had been so frightened by the possibility of forced conversion that she had tried to save Ramabai by attempting to strangle her one night and finally killed herself" (Kosambi 2000, 14). During this phase of her life, the contradictions, conflicts and contestations between her Brahmin past and Christian present were held in a state of creative and critical tension.[14] Occupying an indistinct religious space, comfortable neither with her Brahmanical past nor with her Christian present, she developed a trenchant criticism of institutionalized religions. This was the period when she was shaping a tenuous, yet-to-be-formed spiritual interiority, which was at odds with the institutionalized structures and hierarchies within which she was being compelled to place and recognize herself as an Anglican Christian. In *A Testimony* she writes:

> No one can have any idea of what my feelings were at finding such a Babel of religions in Christian countries, and at finding how very different the teaching of each sect was from that of the others. I recognized the Nastikas of India in the Theosophists, the Polygamous Hindus in the Mormons, the worshippers of ghosts and demons in the Spiritualists, and the Old-Vedantists in the Christian Scientists. Their teachings were not new to me. I had known them in their old eastern nature as they are in India; and when I met them in America I thought they had only changed their Indian dress and put on Western garbs, which were more suitable to the climate and conditions of the country. (Kosambi 2000, 308)

As a new convert, Ramabai attempted to intellectually legibilize her adopted religion through the conceptual categories of her relinquished religion. However, Christianity provided a set of moral and social values that opened for her alternative possibilities on moral and social levels. The radical egalitarianism offered by Jesus through the equal offer of salvation, and equal personal access to God, and the universal access to the Bible, was something that Ramabai found to be deeply enabling. The interpretive freedom offered by Protestant Christianity allowed Ramabai to contour a creatively accommodative spiritual interiority while straddling religions and sects. The Protestant belief in the "priesthood of believers," and the conception of the individual conscience as the location of individual choice, judgment and personal and direct access to God, empowered Ramabai to shape a spiritual interiority in consonance with her spiritual longings. Ramabai conceptualized this interiority as the location where Christ directly intervened into her life and where she was brought into his guiding presence. By making this spiritual interiority the location of her vision for humane practices and egalitarian human relationships, Ramabai legitimized her reforms for the most marginalized in her society and affirmed their right to humane concern and care, thus re-defining the category of the human in egalitarian ways. To her Christian mentors, the catholicity of Ramabai's Christianity and its openness, to what they considered as dissenting sects of Christianity as well as reform-

---

14. According to Maya Burger, the conflicts and oppositions that characterized the early years of Ramabai's life as a Christian convert are "marks of transcultural conversion as characterized by misunderstanding and irreconcilable positions" (Burger 2013, 1171).

ist Hindu movements like the Brahmo Samāj, posed the constant threat of losing a prized Brahmin convert/missionary. In a letter to Rev. C. Gore, dated July 1885, Sister Geraldine, a member of the religious order of the "Community of Saint Mary the Virgin" and Ramabai's spiritual mentor at Wantage writes, "I fear the love of popularity is a very great snare to her, and that she has been of late in correspondence with some of her old Brahmo friends[15] and has some idea of working with them in the future. A diluted Christianity without Christ is what I feel she is in danger of drifting into" (Shah 1977, 82).

Ramabai's translation of Christianity as a Hindu Brahmin convert was considered as heretical by the Anglican church authorities. For Ramabai it was this very possibility of heretical dissent that was liberating about Protestant Christianity. In a letter to Dorothea Beale she writes,

> Ajeebai (Sister Geraldine) ran almost mad with anger when I said that she had no right to call the Dissenters heretics, because she herself belonged to a Church which is but a Dissenting sect of the Roman Catholic. I should like to know what kind of an answer she would give to Dr. Bruno if she heard him saying the English Church is a heresy. I am sure I shall hear the answer will be given in the same way by her to a Roman Catholic as by a Baptist or Wesleyan, if they were called a heretic by her or by Dean Butler. Missionaries who want to convert the Hindoos to their own religion would do well to take care not to call themselves the only inheritors of truth, and all others "the so-called false philosophers," for the Hindoos as a rule will not be content to look or hear only one side, and it is quite natural that they should not. (Shah 1977, 170)

On the one hand, Ramabai's spiritual self-fashioning which sanctioned her reform for women was made possible by the alienating Brahmin perspective she brought to her new religion and to which it was amenable. On the other hand, Christianity offered a new template of intelligibility which allowed her to include those at the extreme margins of her society within the category of the Human. Thus, her visit to a Rescue Home run by the CSMV sisters at Fulham was to give her a new perspective on those who were termed as "fallen

---

15. A similar critical point of view was expressed in Helen S. Dyer's biography of Ramabai, writing as follows regarding the reception of Ramabai after she returned from America: "But the foremost welcome to India came to Ramabai from the Reform Hindus, known as the Brahmo Samāj. The leaders in this fraternity were largely the product of missionary education. They had been trained in missionary colleges. Their intellects had been convinced of the benefits of Christianity and of its social superiority to Hinduism; but they had rejected the Lord Jesus Christ. They no longer believed in the preposterous fables of their Hindu Shastras. They adopted many Christian and Unitarian doctrines; laid down rules permitting the remarriage of widows, and raising the age which girls might remain unmarried. In short, they established a sort of halfway-house to Christianity which turned many a promising youth aside and deadened his conscience as effectually as if he had remained in the toils of idolatry" (Dyer 1930, 10).

women." Their status of "fallen women" was a recognition which Christianity shared with Ramabai's Brahminism. But the recognition of these women by Christianity as deserving of care and kindness, and their institutional rehabilitation was something that deeply touched Ramabai. For her, that the egalitarianism of Christ could accommodate even these women within the category of the human, was a startling revelation of a deeply humane conceptualization of the Human. In *A Testimony* she writes,

> I asked the Sisters who instructed me to tell me what it was that made Christians care for, and reclaim the "fallen" women. She read the story of Christ meeting the Samaritan woman, and His wonderful discourse on the nature of true worship, and explained it to me. She spoke of the Infinite Love of Christ for sinners. He did not despise them but came to save them. I had never read or heard anything like this in the religious books of the Hindus; I realized, after reading the 4th Chapter of St. John's Gospel, that Christ was truly the Divine Saviour He claimed to be, and no one but He could transform and uplift the downtrodden womanhood of India and of every land. (Kosambi 2000, 307–308)

It was this revelation of a new legibility to the Human that was to mark and inscribe the institutional spaces that Ramabai shaped for the most oppressed and marginalized women and men in her society.

In 1907 Sister Geraldine decided to publish the letters that Ramabai had written while in England as well as the letters those others had written in connection to Ramabai. It is through this dense network of letters that Ramabai's stay in England is available to us. These letters constitute a dialogue, very often acrimonious, in which the new convert is attempting to shape herself into a Christian mould, even as she is contesting institutional and clerical attempts to regulate her practice and understanding of Christianity. This collection also gives us access to letters to which Ramabai herself did not have direct access but whose intentions were conveyed to Ramabai through Sister Geraldine. These letters reveal that the context within which the new convert was being shaped was deeply racist and traversed by colonial power. In her brief biographical sketch of Ramabai, which prefaces the collection of letters, Sister Geraldine describes the unconverted Ramabai who had just made her acquaintance with missionaries of the Community of St. Mary stationed in Pune, thus, "Impulsive and energetic, and at that time quite undisciplined, she was swayed by every passing thought" (Shah 1977, 7). For her mentors in the Church of England, Ramabai was a "Christian Hindoo"[16] and a

---

16. Expanding on the concept of "contact zone" first developed by Mary Louise Pratt in her book *Imperial Eyes*, Judith Becker writes that this concept could be broadened to include the aspect of "a personalized contact zone" in which a single person becomes a kind of contact zone in himself or herself by integrating aspects of different cultures. Becker terms them as "cultural brokers" who facilitate contact between

colonial subject. In December 1883, Ramabai was enrolled in the Cheltenham Ladies College and she decided to give Sanskrit lessons in order to support her education. This did not go well with her Anglican mentors. Responding to this decision, the Rt Rev. Thomas Valpy French, Bishop of Lahore, then in England wrote to Dorothea Beale,

> *As a rule* I have protested against young Christian Hindoos being sent over to England, as they have almost uniformly scorned work among their own countrymen, and become wholly denationalised.
>
> The remaining quietly for a while in the Sisterhood (if I understand the Bishop [of Bombay] rightly) is not what he objects to, so much as the undertaking a Professorship among English young ladies, which might lead to a little undue self-exaltation. (Shah 1977, 42–43)

Ramabai's conception of Christian liberty, as she had interpreted it through her reading of the Bible, went contrary to her experience of being a Christian subjected to the authority of the Anglican Church and the racism of a colonial power. In her letter to Sister Geraldine she writes, "The things which come from the Most High and which are ordered by Him for my good come directly to me and then I am prepared for them. But they do not come through persons whom I do not or little know" (Shah 1977, 51). If the interpretative freedom offered by Protestantism enabled a private shaping of her spirituality, her agency to do so was considered as heretical by her Christian mentors. The problem was further exacerbated by the fact that Sister Geraldine who belonged to a Christian order expected from Ramabai the obedience required of members of such an order. As the Rt. Rev. Dr. Mylne, Bishop of Bombay, writes to Sister Geraldine:

> Wrong and obstinate she may be; I think, she is. But the question is how to minimise an evil which we cannot wholly prevent. And that I think can be secured by not pressing upon a woman in the world, the kind of obedience which is proper to a Community. (Shah 1977, 57)

As a member of a Christian religious order Sister Geraldine's understanding of God and her relationship to him was structured and authorized through the disciplinary regimes of her order. For the Brahmin Ramabai such an institutionally located disciplinary authorization of a knowledge and relationship to God was alien. When Sister Geraldine attempted to shape Ramabai's Christianity through such institutional regimentation Ramabai saw it as a curbing of her freedom of conscience.

In a sense, Ramabai converted Christianity through her conversion. She extended the meanings of Christian symbols by wresting them out of their

---

different cultures but pay the price of not being accepted by either of the cultural groups that they partially represent and bring together (Becker 2015, 10).

European setting and recasting them through the cultural world into which she had been born and through which Christianity was understood by her. In a letter to Sister Geraldine she conveys her reluctance to wear the cross[17] because as she writes, "So I am not inclined to do any such thing, which will lead my fellow (Indian) Christians into wrong ideas" (Shah 1977, 28). Even if she were to agree to wear the cross, she writes, she would like it to be inscribed in Sanskrit rather than Latin. For as she writes, "I stick fast to Sanskrit, not because I think it to be sacred or the language of gods, but because it is the most beautiful, and the oldest language of my dear native land" (Shah 1977, 28).

There is a deeply personal and untranslatable dimension to spiritual experience. It morphs into longings as yet unnamed and its meaning, even to the person whose experience it is, is always tenuous and unclear. Yet, spirituality emerges and fulfills itself through the material contexts within which human subjectivity is shaped and its longings and possibilities of being are generated. The historically specific legibility of spirituality is always social and institutional. As a longing for a reformed community, within which an ideal self-formation is possible, spirituality very often articulates what is historically marked yet is also deeply personal, through socially radical yet socially recognizable transformations of the material life. It is an attempt at scripting the self by re-scripting the social/material sites, institutionalized religion with its rituals and sacral texts being one of them, through which this self comes into being and is represented.

Ramabai's spiritual journeys are given through a generic spread of texts. The generic diversity of these texts attests to the diversity of her spiritual journeys and their inaccessibility to any single one of these textualizations. It is only by taking into account this generic range of texts that we can begin to recover the complexity of Ramabai's spiritual journeys. Thus, *A Testimony* which is structured as a spiritual autobiography attempts to give a stable, recognizable shape to her spiritual interiority and in the mode of the missionary tract makes it an exemplar message for the "heathen world." While the letters that Ramabai exchanged with her Christian mentors in the early conflictual stage as a new convert are in the form of interrogations and debates, which bring an alienating and critical perspective to Anglican Christianity in its institutionalized form. As a new convert who occupied a liminal location between religions and cultures, Ramabai was acutely sensitive to the proselytizing fervor and authoritarian structures of the Anglican Church of her times. In a letter to Canon Butler she writes: "If a Hindoo theologian—

---

17. Meera Kosambi explains this refusal as follows: "As a mark of her personal blend of the Indian culture and an alien religion, Ramabai focused attention on indigenization of the Christian ritual and practices. This was consistent with her view that the universal elements in Christianity could and should be presented to different countries of the world through the indigenous cultural idiom." (Kosambi 1992, 67)

however learned and holy and good he may be—comes and tells you that your religion was a false one, and that you were to accept humbly everything that he taught, could you do it?" (Shah 1977, 75). Canon Butler's response to Ramabai's claims to liberty of conscience within her new religion is seen in his letter to Miss Beale: "But to a neophyte in the Faith that self-reliance is intensely dangerous" (Shah 1977, 76). For her Christian mentors Ramabai's questions verged tempestuously on heresy[18] and very often slipped her back into heathenism as seen from Sister Geraldine's letter to Ramabai: "The germ of the new life given to you in holy Baptism which at first sprang up and gave such fair promise, has been over-grown by rank and poisonous weeds of heresy" (Shah 1977, 92).

Discovering America and an egalitarian Christianity

In 1885, Ramabai travelled to America on the invitation of Dr. Rachel Littler Bodley, the dean of Women's Medical College in Philadelphia, to attend the graduation ceremony of Anandibai Joshi, her kinswoman. Ramabai stayed in America for more than two years during which she extensively travelled across the country. Shortly after her return, in 1889, she published a travelogue in Marathi on her travels in America (Frykenberg 2003).[19] Colonial modernity had introduced and normalized the cognitive world within which the meaning and purpose of Ramabai's travels to England and America were structured and its narrativization through the genre of the travelogue was made possible. Beginning in the 16th century, the interlinking of colonial, missionary and trade interests led to the travels of Europeans to the "New World" and introduced that world to new legibilities and templates of travel. On the part of Europeans, such journeys very often resulted in ethnographic texts in which the indigenous cultures were described through a European racist stereotyping and missionary heathenizing perspective (Rubies 2002). According to Talal Asad the problem for European travellers, missionaries and ethnographers was how to establish the kinship between the "savages" found in the new world and Christian Europeans. Quoting Margaret Hodgen, Asad writes,

> The eventual solution adopted in the late seventeenth and early eighteenth centuries, according to Margaret Hodgen, was a synthesis of two old ideas: the chain of being and the genetic principle. In this way,

---

18. In her chapter on Pandita Ramabai, titled "Silencing Heresy'" Gauri Viswanathan elaborates on this aspect of Ramabai's conflictual relationship with the Anglican Church to which she converted (Viswanathan 1989, 12).

19. According to Meera Kosambi, Ramabai started writing the book in the USA in 1887 and completed it after returning to India in early 1889. (Kosambi 2002, 209). Kosambi also tells us that illustrations of the textbooks that Ramabai started preparing in America for her proposed school were paid for from the sale proceeds of this travelogue (Kosambi 1988, 42).

"a spatial arrangement of forms [was converted] into an historical, developmental, or evolutionary series" (Hodgen 1964, 389–390). A common human nature was thus accorded to all human beings, but one that was assumed to exist in various stages of maturity and enlightenment.
(Asad 1993, 20)

Much of the European travel writing that emerged from such mobility was also implicated in the European colonial enterprise. As Helen Carr puts it "The period from 1880 to 1940 was the heyday of British Empire, and much travel writing shows the complicity with imperialism—if not its outright support—that Mary Louise Pratt identifies in her study *Imperial Eyes*" (Carr 2002, 71). Indians travelling to Europe or America saw themselves as accessing the choices made available to them by the coming of colonial modernity, and marking out their modern subjectivities as the site of choice and mobility. The purpose of such travels was predominantly seen to be educational, through exposure to both western educational institutions and western culture. Very often, these travels were made possible through the special interest taken, and support given, by missionary organizations and the colonial government, in "promising natives." When Indians travelled to the colonizers' world under the patronage of colonial or missionary institutions, as was the case with Ramabai, they were controlled by the intentions of such patronage.

At the outset of her journey Ramabai legibilized her travel to England as the exercise of agency in the service of her country.[20] She allayed the fears of her fellow Hindus that this journey might lead to her conversion to Christianity, by explaining to them that the journey was initiated by her desire to study medicine and serve her fellow country women, even though it was being organized and supported by the members of a Christian order. The mobility of Ramabai is seemingly an indication of the exercise of agency by the modern subject while her conversion to Christianity is seemingly an abrogation of this agency to the institutional regimentation of religious belief. However, for Ramabai, conversion enabled a reclamation of agency through the site of the individual conscience. Ramabai defines conscience as "the conscious faculty (*buddhi*) in the human heart that distinguishes good from evil" (Frykenberg 2003, 74). It was from this location that she contested the authority that institutionalized Christianity attempted to wield over what she considered as her Christian liberty of individual conscience. She recuperated the prerogative of individual agency from within Christianity and legitimated the material practices initiated by that agency as being sanctioned by God. In England,

---

20. In the section titled "A Word to the Reader" which precedes the main section of the book, Ramabai writes: "If the reading of this book instills even a little more love of hard work and goodwill toward the service our Mother Bharath in the hearts of the dear brothers and sisters of my homeland than what they have at present, I shall know that this small effort of mine has been worthwhile" (Frykenberg 2003, 56).

dissenting factions within Protestant Christianity had appropriated a similar agency to question the nexus of political and religious power within the Anglican church. In America, Ramabai found a Church free of state control and a horizontal spread of Protestant sects existing in a relationship of democratic equality. Ramabai's description of the evolution of American democracy is structured through and assumes the post-enlightenment belief in human rationality and historical progress. In America she found the political instantiation of the radical equality preached by Christ.[21] In the functioning of the American social and political system she saw a modern instantiation of a liberating Protestant conception of individual freedom. The evolutionary history of the young American democracy is described by her as the product of human agency shaped by Christian influences. For Ramabai this evolutionary history was moving towards a Christian Utopia. According to Asad,

> It was in Europe's eighteenth century that the older, Christian attitudes toward historical time (salvational expectation) were combined with the newer, secular practices (rational prediction) to give us our modern idea of progress (Koselleck 1988, 17). A new philosophy of agency was also developed, allowing individual actions to be related to collective tendencies.
> (Asad 1993, 19)

However, Ramabai's self-conscious admission, at the beginning of her travelogue, of the relativity of the ethnographic perspective in general and of hers in particular, inflected and structured as it is by the historical and cultural location of the ethnographer,[22] denies the ethnographic narrative the authority of epistemological control.[23] Though Ramabai believed in the possibility of a Christian Utopia she undermined the possibility and authority of a single

---

21. In her travelogue Ramabai writes: "The public spiritedness in the system of government of the United States is the chief reason for the concern for the common good in almost all other things" (Frykenberg 2003, 114). Regarding the education of American children Ramabai writes, "They are not educated to think that one person, by virtue of his social group (*jāti*), is superior within their society while someone else is inherently inferior. They are educated to understand that they are all *human beings* and should treat one another with humanity" (Frykenberg 2003, 115).

22. According to Mary Baine Campbell, the study of travelogues written by women "as writing, as records, as narratives, has provided considerable material for discussion of the gendered nature of subjectivity and the positionality or 'situatedness' of all knowledge" (Campbell 2002, 264).

23. In her travelogue Ramabai writes, "When you have read the description of our customs, traditions, and living conditions by the English and American people who have traveled in Hindustan, it is easy to understand how any foreigner visiting another country must see its people in a very different light. So instead of asserting a rigid theory that the living conditions of the American people are of exactly such and such a kind and of only so many types, my aim in this chapter and in the entire volume is to tell you how I myself thought them to be" (Frykenberg 2003, 113).

Christian Truth by giving historical instances of how Christians and Christian nations had legitimized unchristian acts by claiming for them a Christian provenance and purpose. Ramabai appropriates a genre that was central to the western colonizing project of exploiting and ruling the new world and gives it an estranging perspective.[24] As a colonial subject and an erstwhile Brahmin, she defamiliarizes the historiography that legitimated and normalized the colonial enterprise as a necessary part of an evolutionary history of human beings, and historicizes the practices of European and American Christianity. Highlighting the dual history of America as both a colonized as well as a colonizing nation she dismantled the authority of "Christian Truths" by tracing their material historical origins and purposes. Thus in her travelogue she writes, "To call oneself a follower of a certain religion and actually to practice that religion are two altogether different things" (Frykenberg 2003, 217). Describing the slaughter of Red Indians by the early settlers she writes,

But it pains me grievously to tell you that those who called themselves religious and who said they came to give knowledge to the ignorant and to show the way to heaven to the hell-bound, adopted an evil ethic of deceit, persecution, cruelty, and dishonesty from start to finish so as to destroy these poor and blameless Indians (Frykenberg 2003, 80).

The travelogue gives its readers an insight into the newly converted Ramabai's excited discovery of a political system in which she saw the possibilities for the realization of the principles of equality and freedom propounded by Christ. Ramabai's perspective in this text is always comparative. Coming from a caste based feudal society under the yoke of colonialism, and having recently struggled against the authority of the Anglican church, for Ramabai, the young American democracy demonstrated a political system which privileged and was structured through the innate merits of individual citizens, just as the denominational democracy of American Christianity represented for her a spirituality based on and structured through the Protestant individual's relationship with her God. She saw in America the creative shaping of a young nation through the two principles of the equality of all human beings and the freedom of conscience—principles she saw as the foundations of a Christianity that was faithful to the message of Christ. She saw the functioning of these two principles in the smallest social unit of the American nation namely the American family. Not only did the functioning of the American political and family system provide her with the Archimedean location for critiquing what she saw as the tradition bound, in-egalitarian political and socio-religious institutions in India, it also provided her with a model on which to base her own reformed communities and institutions for women when she returned to India.

---

24. Thus, Ramabai saw a similarity between the treatment of lower castes in India and slaves in America (Frykenberg 2003, 200).

In her review of Ramabai's travelogue Kashibai Kanitkar, a contemporary, writes:

> It would be hardly surprising if all our countrywomen who read this book mutter dejectedly that such a golden day will never dawn for us! However, we must swallow these words quick before they reach anyone's ears for fear of committing "treason against men," just as our men are afraid of committing treason when they discuss the [British] government.
> (Kanitkar 2011, 72, tr. by Kosambi, originally published in 1889)

That Ramabai's America was seen as a feminist Utopia by a contemporary Maharashtrian Brahmin woman and that Kanitkar should fear that her longing for such an Utopia would be considered as dangerously incendiary by the patriarchal society in which she lived, is telling. It indicates to us that the America of Ramabai's travelogue was amenable to radical feminist and political projects and interrogations of even a non-Christian modernizing world. Though Ramabai sees in America a democracy based on Christian principles, she structured the history of America as a history of the evolutionary progress of human beings, wrought through human agency. The telos of such a history was a utopian society in which men and women enjoyed equal privileges and rights because of their human struggles. Ramabai describes this evolutionary process as the gradual elimination of men's *raṇati* ["uncivilized"] nature.

Finding Christ

In *A Testimony* Ramabai writes: "I came to know after eight years from the time of my baptism that I had found the Christian *religion*, which was good enough for me; *but I had not found Christ, Who is the Life of the religion,* and 'the Light of every man that cometh into the world'" (Kosambi 2000, 309). In 1895 Ramabai claimed that she felt the personal presence of the holy spirit. Referring to this event that happened at a Lonavala camp meeting, Ramabai writes in *A Testimony*, "I found it a great blessing to realize the personal presence of the Holy Spirit in me, and to be guided and taught by Him." (Kosambi 2000, 316) Ramabai's biographer Padmini Sengupta terms Ramabai's experience of finding Christ a mystical experience. Such "mystical" turning points in Ramabai's life were marked by events like her second baptism in the river Bhima.[25] On 6 November 1897 Ramabai travelled to the River Bhima with 17 cartloads of converts where they immersed themselves in the river and were baptized. Sengupta writes that Ramabai might have travelled to this river because of

---

25. Regarding this event Frykenberg writes: "By then, Ramabai had come a long way in her religious journey. She had migrated from High Church affiliations in England and distinguished and theologically liberal supporters in America to dissenter and populist links with strong Anabaptist and Pentecostal overtones. Yet, while all these groups tried to 'own' her and use her, she stoutly remained free of all" (Frykenberg 2003, 47, fn 107).

Figure 8.3   Ramabai at work on her translation of the Bible into popular Marathi (Butler 1922, Frontispiece).

the significance it had within Maratha Vaishnavite devotional poetry and also because of associations with her childhood. (Sengupta 1970, 248). With these "mystical" experiences, Ramabai's practice of Christianity acquired an increasing denominational eclecticism.[26] According to Frykenberg, later in her life Ramabai showed a leaning towards sects which were not accepted by mainstream Christianity, like the Pentecostal movement. The final part of this journey was her translation of the Bible into Marathi for which she did not use the Sanskrit of her earlier years (Figure 8.3).[27]

In the 1909 November issue of *The Mukthi Prayer Bell,* Ramabai writes:

> The present mixture of the Marathi Bible—half old and half new, which must of necessity be bought and read by Marathi Christians who would read the Bible at all—is arbitrarily forced upon us by the agents of the Bible Society. The Marathi revision of the New Testament, though very excellent in certain passages, is grievously unintelligible to the unlearned in most places. The women and children and simple village

---

26. According to Philippe Bornet, the notion of "mysticism" is a construct that gets a wider currency in the beginning of the twentieth century, precisely as a way to delineate a space of freedom, not constrained by either institutional religion or colonial politics. This, according to him, is "also illustrated by the re-readings of Tamil devotional Shaiva literature in the same period, as 'mystical'." (personal correspondence)

27. In his biographical introduction to Ramabai's travelogue Frykenberg writes, "All language, Ramabai believed, and hence all languages, had the capacity, as gifts from God, to be divine. It followed from such reasoning that each human being should have immediate access to the Word of God in her or his own mother tongue. That was the ultimate message of Pentecost and of 'speaking in tongues.' This then meant that Marathi was potentially as divine and sacred as Sanskrit" (Frykenberg 2003, 54).

people do not understand this language half as well as they understood the old translation. (Basil Miller 1949, 102)

Ramabai was attempting to translate her God into her mother tongue. This was the final phase of her lifelong attempt to translate her belief in a transcendental power and the promptings of this belief, into a culturally specific, politically enabling, socially humane, historically located, human legibility. Ramabai's autobiographical text marks a temporal point in her long and difficult spiritual journey. She attempted to structure the telos of her spiritual journey through this text. However, it is but one among the many texts through which she attempted to legibilize her spiritual longings through scripting her tenuous, fluid, changing relationship to her God. In none of these texts did she achieve spiritual closure or completion, and each of them carried the cumulative traces of the texts that had preceded them. These traces complicate her autobiography and indicate the many trajectories of her spiritual journeys. In the last of her texts she was attempting to translate the Bible from Greek and Hebrew into a Marathi version that could be understood by those she considered as the humblest believers. It was a continuation of her life-long effort to disrupt and break through religious institutions and human languages in an attempt to articulate the essence of what she believed.

References

Asad, Talal. 1993. *Genealogies of Religion: Discipline and Reasons of Power in Christianity and Islam.* Baltimore, MD: The Johns Hopkins University Press.

Becker, Judith. 2016. "Conceptions of Humanity in Nineteenth-Century German Protestant Missions." In *Humanity: A History of European Concepts in Practice from the Sixteenth Century to the Present*, edited by F. Klose and M. Thulin, 107–129. Gottingen: Vandenhoeck and Ruprecht. https://doi.org/10.13109/9783666101458.107

———. 2015. "Introduction." *European Missions in Contact Zones: Transformation through Interaction in a (Post-) Colonial World*, edited by J. Becker, 7–24. Gottingen: Vandenhoeck and Ruprecht. https://doi.org/10.13109/9783666101410.7

Burger, Maya. 2013. "Transcultural Conversion: The Life of Pandita Ramabai." *Asiatische Studien Etudes Asiatiques* 67(4): 1155–1177.

Butler, Clementina. 1922. *Pandita Ramabai Sarasvati: Pioneer in the Movement for the Education of the Child Widow in India.* London: Fleming H. Revell Company.

Campbell, Mary Baine. 2002. "Travel Writing and Its Theory." In *The Cambridge Companion to Travel Writing*, edited by P. Hulme and T. Young, 261–278. Cambridge: Cambridge University Press. https://doi.org/10.1017/CCOL052178140X.016

Carr, Helen. 2002. "Modernism and Travel (1880–1940)." In *The Cambridge Companion to Travel Writing*, edited by P. Hulme and T. Young, 70–86. Cambridge: Cambridge University Press. https://doi.org/10.1017/CCOL052178140X.005

Chakravarti, Uma. 1989. "Whatever Happened to the Vedic Dasi." In *Recasting Women: Essays in Colonial History*, edited by K. Sangari and Sudesh Vaid, 27–87. Delhi: Kali for Women.

———. 1998. *Rewriting History: The Life and Times of Pandita Ramabai*. New Delhi: Kali for Women.

Dyer, Helen. S. 1930. *Pandita Ramabai: A Great Life in Indian Missions*. Glasgow: Pickering & Inglis.

Frykenberg, R. E., ed. 2003. *Pandita Ramabai's America: Conditions of Life in the United States*, translated by K. Gomes. Michigan: William B. Eerdmans Publishing Company.

Joshi, M Lakshmana Harihara. 1964. *Bharathada Agresara Mahile Pandita Ramabai* (in Kannada). Mala: Sharadha Press.

Kanitkar, Kashibai. 2011. "Review of Pandita Ramabai's *The Peoples of the United States* (December 1889)." In *Feminist Vision or "Treason Against Men?": Kashibai Kanitkar and the Engendering of Marathi Literature*, edited by M. Kosambi, 67–82. New Delhi: Permanent Black.

Karlekar, Malavika. 1986. "Kadambini and the *Bhadralok*: Early Debates over Women's Education in Bengal." *Economic and Political Weekly Review of Women's Studies* 21(17): 25–31.

Kosambi, Meera. 1988. "Women, Emancipation and Equality: Pandita Ramabai's Contribution to Women's Cause." *Economic and Political Weekly* 23(44): 38–49.

———. 1992. "Indian Response to Christianity, Church and Colonialism: Case of Pandita Ramabai." *Economic and Political Weekly* 27(43/44): 61–71.

———. 2000. *Pandita Ramabai through Her Own Words: Selected Works*, compiled, translated and edited by M. Kosambi. New Delhi: Oxford University Press.

———. 2002. "Returning the American Gaze: Pandita Ramabai's *The Peoples of the United States, 1889*." *Meridians* 2(2): 188–212. https://doi.org/10.1215/15366936-2.2.188

Mani, Lata. 1986. "Production of an Official Discourse on *Sati* in Early Nineteenth Century Bengal." *Economic and Political Weekly* 21(17): 32–40.

Miller, Basil. 1949. *Pandita Ramabai: India's Christian Pilgrim*. Michigan: Zondervan Publishing House.

Ramabai Sarasvati, Pandita. 1886. "Preface: Indian Religion." *Cheltenham Ladies College Magazine* 4.

———. 1981 [1887]. *The High-Caste Hindu Woman.* Bombay: Maharashtra State Board for Literature and Culture.

———. 2000 [1897]. "Famine Experiences." In *Pandita Ramabai Through Her Own Words*, edited by M. Kosambi, 247–260. New Delhi: Oxford University Press.

———. 1907. *A Testimony of Our Inexhaustible Treasure.* Prahran, Vic.: Fraser & Morphet.

———. 1908. *The Word-Seed.* Kedgaon: Ramabai Mukti Mission.

Ranade Ramabai. 1963. *Ranade: His Wife's Reminiscences*, translated by Kusumavati Deshpande. Delhi: Ministry of Information and Broadcasting Government of India.

Rubies, Joan Pau. 2002. "Travel Writing and Ethnography." In *The Cambridge Companion to Travel Writing*, edited by P. Hulme and T. Young, 242–260. Cambridge: Cambridge University Press. https://doi.org/10.1017/CCOL052178140X.015

Sengupta, Padmini. 1970. *Pandita Ramabai Saraswati: Her Life and Work.* Bombay: Asia Publishing House.

Shah, A. B., ed. 1977. *The Letters and Correspondence of Pandita Ramabai*, Bombay: Maharashtra State Board for Literature and Culture.

Shetty, Parinitha. 2012. "Christianity, Reform and the Reconstitution of Gender: The Case of Pandita Mary Ramabai." *Journal of Feminist Studies in Religion* 28(1): 25–42. https://doi.org/10.2979/jfemistudreli.28.1.25

Viswanathan, Gauri. 2001. "Silencing Heresy." In *Outside the Fold: Conversion Modernity and Belief*, 118–152. Oxford: Oxford University Press.

About the author

Parinitha Shetty is professor at the Department of English, Mangalore University. Her areas of research include gender studies and missionary studies. She has published a number of articles, among which are included "Missionary Pedagogy and the Christianisation of the Heathens: The Educational Institutions established by the Basel Mission in Mangalore," *The Indian Economic and Social History Review* 45(4): 509–551(2008) and "Medical Mission and the Interpretation of Pain" in *Cultural Ontology of the Self in Pain*, edited by Siby K. George and P. G.Jung, 269–283 (New Delhi: Springer, 2016).

— 9 —

A "Christian Hindu Apostle"? The Multiple Lives of Sadhu Sundar Singh (1889–1929?)

PHILIPPE BORNET

The chapter deals with Sadhu Sundar Singh and the way his life and experiences have been shaped by multiple influences, co-constructed by himself and his admirers, and made possible by a concept of *sādhu* that functioned as a key to unlock an "interstitial space" that was not controlled by any authority. In order to delineate the contours of that space, it is necessary to go back to Sundar Singh's early years in India, to re-contextualize his biographical trajectory in the framework of early twentieth century revivalist (politico-) religious movements and to consider him in relation with initiatives to delink Christianity from its colonial background. Focusing then on his tour in Switzerland, 1922, it is argued that the tour's organizers were both projecting intentions on Sundar Singh, and overwhelmed with the actual performance and its effects. Furthermore, members of several religious movements were equally attending the meetings, producing various kinds of encounters: some leading to creative reconfigurations and some to open conflict. In sum, Sundar Singh is an excellent case study for a "connected religion" framework: since he made himself available for interpretations reflecting the different intentions of his interlocutors, the sources telling us about him are often written from very divergent standpoints—making a "connected religion" approach that brings the pieces of the puzzle together particularly appropriate.

Introduction

The present chapter is part of a larger research on a Swiss missionary organization called the Kanarese Evangelical Mission (KEM). This Protestant mission took over from the Basel mission when it had to leave India in 1918, because being considered as a German, and hence hostile, society on British soil. Even if the KEM was certainly not a major success from a missionary point of view, it had lasting effects in both India and Switzerland during its

10 years of activity and beyond. I will not deal with the mission and its activities in Karnataka, but will focus on one event in Switzerland that it organized and that appeared prominently in the propaganda literature: Sadhu Sundar Singh's (1889–1929?) 1922 tour.

In the only book providing an (apologetic) history of this mission, written by one of its Swiss German proponents and published in 1930, one can read the following statement:

> It is possible to see in the Indies, still today, the grossest forms of paganism. Thus are the Sannyasis, mendicant monks who spend their life wandering around the country. Deeply mystic, they practice meditation. Indifferent to their appearance, dressed with a saffron robe, they entirely neglect their body. Their messy hair, their nails which, not being cut, look like claws, the sufferings they inflict to themselves: this all gives them the appearance of sanctity and grants them the general admiration.
> (Zimmermann 1930, 76)

This image of a wild India, epitomized by its homeless and wandering mendicant monks, was rehearsed on several occasions in the mission's widely-diffused propaganda. This was connected to a notion of Christian mission as a "civilizing project," as can be clearly seen in the visual discourse of the following "Sammelkarte" (a card used for collecting funds from donators): white angels pouring water received by dark skinned people showing their thankfulness to their generous patrons—a dark picture that was typical of the propaganda literature that circulated among the Swiss donators of the mission (Figure 9.1). In addition, the diffusion of this image in a network of protestant churches (some of which state-sponsored) gave it an institutional and "mainstream" validation.

By the necessities of the situation, however, the missionaries working in the field acquired a quite different perspective, in which they not only had to recognize that what they wanted to "give" was not always welcome, but also that the local groups they were trying to appeal to were often less preoccupied by their own spiritual salvation than by concrete economical, social and political issues. Sundar Singh's period of activity coincides with a time of crisis for Christian missionary societies and with contemporary attempts to delink Christianity from its colonial background. I will argue that it is against this backdrop that Sundar Singh should be first contextualized, resulting in an image that differs from that offered by most biographies which tend to present him under the light of an individual spiritual quest exclusively. In this context, his tours in Europe reveal a deep ambiguity: despite having been introduced by Western missionaries and using their networks of communication, Sundar Singh revalorized the notion of a spiritual and authentic Oriental Christianity and propagated on a global scale a message critical of

Figure 9.1 "I was thirsty and you gave me to drink" in *Mitteilungen des Schweizerischen Hilfskomitees für die Mission in Indien* 4(2), March 1922, 12 (35'000 copies).

the West. This hybrid message was certainly open to divergent interpretations: while enjoying some popularity in evangelical circles until present day, Sundar Singh also triggered major controversies in other circles.

To reconstruct a balanced account of the phenomenon, it is then necessary to recontextualize the case in both its Indian and European settings and to bring together sources written from various situations. I will first focus on Sundar Singh's North Indian background, in order to identify different aspects—also social and political—that were combined in the construction of his largely idiosyncratic religious profile. I will then look at the image projected during his tour in Switzerland, suggesting that the tour was carefully manufactured to produce the image of an "authentic Oriental" spiritual figure, carrier of an "authentic form of Christianity," but that it ended up escaping the organizers' intentions. In so doing, it will be stressed that Sundar Singh's performances are not only the result of a complex history of politics and religion between India and Europe, but also that they entered into resonance with a striving (at the time) web of alternative religious currents in Switzerland, producing various creative combinations and controversies, much as in a kaleidoscope.

The case is a perfect example, then, for a tentative approach in "connected religion" that pays attention to documents stemming from various cultural, geographical, linguistic backgrounds, even if it will not be possible to deal with everything in the limited framework of the present contribution.

Sadhu Sundar Singh (1889-1929?): The North Indian background

Biographical sketch

We need first to give a few biographical indications about Sundar Singh who, except for two studies by Eric Sharpe (2003) and Timothy Dobe (2015), and despite his importance in Europe during the interwar period and in India until now, has not been in the center of many studies. For this biographical part, we should remember that we rely extensively on documents that reflect reconstructed biographies to be received by specific audiences—a point that is of course always to be kept in mind, but is particularly crucial in Sundar Singh's case (Bourdieu 1986 and Trakulhun 2013).

Sundar Singh's early years are particularly difficult to reconstruct, because the events entirely rely on Sundar Singh's own retellings. According to the standard narrative, Sundar Singh was born in 1889 to a Jāṭ Sikh family in a small Punjabi village called Rampur, in the princely state of Patiala. His mother insisted to give him a traditional upbringing and provided him with both a Sanskrit pandit and another man whom he calls an "old Sikh sādhu."[1] Unfortunately, we do not know much about who these teachers were and what exactly was taught to him at this point. In 1903, after the death of his mother and brother, he was sent to the American Presbyterian mission in Rampur and revolted against the Christian framework of the institution, burning the Bible. At this point, the autobiography continues, he would have felt remorse and, on a desperate search for a spiritual way, Jesus would have appeared to him (Singh 1929, 117-118) and convinced him to become a Christian. After having been rejected by his father, he went to the American Mission of Ludhiana before fleeing away from the school and going to Subathu in the hills. In Subathu, Sundar Singh came into contact with an American millionaire, a missionary named Samuel Evans Stokes *alias* Satyananda Stokes (1882-1946) who had just resolved to live a life of full renunciation, longing after the ideal of St. Francis of Assisi.[2]

Sundar Singh was baptized soon after in 1905 in Shimla and stayed then in Kotgarh. With Stokes and another Scottish missionary, a certain C.F. Andrews (1871-1940), Sundar Singh was the third member of a society they had founded together: the "Brotherhood of the Imitation of Jesus" (Emilsen 1998, 97). Even if the society insisted to be strictly apolitical, the profile of its members tends

---

1. "The pundit taught me simple lessons out of the Hindu *Shastras*, and, when he died, another pundit, Kashi Nath, taught me the Sanskrit scriptures. The venerable Sadhu taught me the Granth, or Sikh scriptures." (Singh 1929, 107) This is Sundar Singh's last text and probably the version of his auto-biography which he wanted to be the definitive one.

2. Stokes' rather tumultuous life is recounted by Sharma (2008) and Emilsen (1998), for his progressive "conversion" to Ārya Samāj.

to show the exact contrary.³ Andrews would later get involved with the independence movement and—among other things—teach in Tagore's University in Shantiniketan.⁴ Stokes gave up his life of renunciation in 1911, married an Indian woman, fought for the independence on Lala Lajpat Rai's (1865–1928) side and later (1932) converted to the Ārya Samāj (Sharma 2008, 64 and 241). Even if Sundar Singh himself did not frontally engage in politics, he arguably shared with both Andrews and Stokes the same sense of revolt and a general disgust for institutions imported from the West.

In 1908, Sundar Singh left the Brotherhood and went preaching by himself. One year later, he was invited to attend the St. John theological school of Lahore. Again, he failed at school and abandoned his studies, but was exposed there to some books, among which *The Imitation of Christ* by the medieval mystic Thomas à Kempis (1380–1471), probably in a nineteenth-century Urdu translation.⁵

From then on until 1916, we do not know much: Sundar Singh was on his own, without having to account for his activities to any institutional authority. Regular letters reached the editorial committee of a Ludhiana-based Urdu journal called *Nūr-i Afshan* (published from 1877 to 1944) from 1913 on.⁶ The letters were reporting about repeated encounters with the Maharishi of Kailasa, a Christian seer of more than 300 years old, and about secret groups of Christian *saṃnyāsin*s living in the Himalaya.⁷ In 1916, Sundar Singh met a

---

3. Sharma (2008, 31–58) gives a vivid description of these years.
4. Andrews is the author of "recollections" on Sundar Singh: (Andrews 1934).
5. Since Sundar Singh was not proficient in English yet, one must assume that he read books in Urdu. A partial Urdu translation of the *Imitatio Christi* had been produced earlier by the Roman catholic bishop of Esbonen, the Capuchin Antonino Pezzoni, around 1850 and could very well have been in the collections of the Lahore school library (Rusconi 2006, 231). As a sign that Kempis' book was enjoying a certain popularity by the end of the nineteenth century in India, within and without Christian circles, Vivekananda published a partial Bengali translation of Kempis in a magazine (*Sāhitya Kalpadrūma* 1889), writing the following in the preface: "We happen to be the subjects of a Christian government now. Through its favour it has been our lot to meet Christians of so many sects, native as well as foreign. How startling the divergence between their profession and practice! ... There he [the Christian missionary] says that he follows him who 'hath not where to lay his head', glibly talking of the glorious sacrifice and burning renunciation of the Master, but in practice going about like a gay bridegroom fully enjoying all the comforts the world can bestow! Look where we may, a true Christian nowhere do we see. The ugly impression left on our mind by the ultra-luxurious, insolent, despotic, barouche-and-brougham-driving Christians of the Protestant sects will be completely removed if we but once read this great book with the attention it deserves." (Vivekananda 1989 [1889], 160).
6. The journal was recently fully digitized and is accessible at the following address: https://eap.bl.uk/project/EAP660/search
7. The figure of the Maharishi of Kailash, albeit a source of debates on the soundness

person called Alfred Zahir who would publish a well-diffused book reporting about these events in Urdu and then in English, with a quotation of Thomas à Kempis in epigraph[8] (Zahir 1917) and the following sentence on the front page: "My body will I sacrifice, my life will I lay down, in the service of my Master and my Motherland," with an unmistakable political subtext about self-sacrifice for the good of the nation. In his book, Zahir introduced Sunder Singh as "a Christian *Sadhu* or itinerating friar"—translating *fakir*, in the Urdu version, with *sādhu*, being the first to call him that way in a publication. As we will examine below, all three expressions of *fakir*, *sādhu* and "itinerating friar" convey the notion of a role located in the fringes of institution. This is also the sign of future tensions between Sundar Singh's highly idiosyncratic form of Christianity and any institutional form of religion.

In 1918, and with the support of an Anglican mission, Sundar Singh came to South India and Sri Lanka (Madras, Vellore, Trichinopoly, Calicut, Jaffna, Colombo, Trivandrum etc.) and continued to Japan and China (Appasamy 1958, 104).[9] This tour seems to have been a major turning point in the sense that he began to present himself as an "apostle" to large Christian communities, apparently constructing an image and a preaching after the model of biblical apostles—in particular St. Paul. In addition, he is often reported to have performed miracles, as for example in Colombo where he was thought to have healed a twelve-year-old boy (Appasamy 1958, 107 and Dobe 2015, 153–154). In 1920, he went on a first European tour that took him to Great Britain, France and Ireland, before sailing to America and Australia (on the tour in Great Britain, see Mukherjee 2017). He toured again Europe in 1922, sailing first to Palestine and visiting holy Christian sites. He continued to Switzerland and one month after his arrival, left for Germany, Sweden and Holland. This was his last trip to Europe and from 1923 to 1929, he stayed in Subathu where he was running a school. During this time, he remained in epistolary contact with different European scholars, such as Friedrich Heiler and Nathan Söderblom.[10] On April 4, 1929 he left for Tibet and was never to be seen again.[11]

---

of Sundar Singh's religious views, still aroused interest much later, as witnessed for example in Goetz (1954)'s curious book.

8. The quotation is the following: "There is no health of the soul nor hope of eternal life, but in the Cross. He died for thee On the Cross, that thou mayest also bear thy Cross and love to die on the Cross." It seems to be directly translated from an Urdu (or at least non-English) version.

9. Appasamy is a South Indian Christian thinker. For his theological views, see Schouten (2008, 116–117).

10. See an example in the appendix.

11. All known elements about the circumstances of his disappearance have been collected by Andrews (1934, 158–182).

A "Christian Hindu Apostle"?

What is meant by sādhu?

At the outset, there is one difficult point to be clarified: what is meant by *sādhu* (or *fakīr*) in this context? Avril Powell noted that Sundar Singh drew his authority "not from Sanskritic and Brahmanical sources and models but from ... paths of devotionalism." (Powell 2003, 226–227, cited in Dobe 2015, 98) This is probably an accurate description but it is certainly possible to speculate about different and more precise sources of influence. We know that there was an important Nirmala Sikh monastery in Patiala (created in 1861), an institution that can be labelled as "conservative," as opposed to contemporary reformist Sikh organizations such as the Lahore Singh Sabha.[12] This tradition is known in particular for its "missionary" activities conducted by touring Nirmala *sādhu*s who observe strict rules (Oberoi 1994, 125). This might have been in the background, as a possible model, even if Heiler's reading of Sundar Singh against the Sikh tradition is evidently too narrow (Heiler 1925 on which see Sharpe 2003, 123).

Secondly, one could also think about the political subtext of ascetic movements, as popularized by Bankim Chandra Chattopadhyay in his *Ānandamaṭh* (1882): the ascetic idiom as a way to manifest political discontent, connecting with a long tradition that conceives itself as insubordinate to any political power.[13] Not reducible to any easy and stable meaning, the notion of *sādhu* can function as a key for unlocking and valorizing a space of freedom that would otherwise have remained out of reach. In that sense, it is very much reminiscent of Homi Bhabha's political reading of "hybrid spaces," the only place—according to him—out of which truly subversive discourses can be produced.[14] A Christian iteration of this idiom was precisely Samuel Stokes' "neo-Franciscan" *saṃnyāsin* which eventually turned into an active involvement with the Ārya Samāj. Here, the challenge was to disentangle Christianity from the colonial context in order to transform it into an ideology compatible with the national struggle.[15] Against the image of Christian missions as the spiritual arm of colonial powers, Sundar Singh's role as a *sādhu*, backed with strong personal religious experiences that remained his own, constructed a militant message strengthened by the appropriate authority to preach it. It was the main function of a narrative such as that of the

---

12. Oberoi (1994, 125–126) gives a precise description of Sikh monastic orders in Patiala at the turn of the nineteenth century.
13. This is evident in Pinch's study about "warrior ascetics" (2006).
14. As Bhabha noted (1994, 28): "Here the transformational value of change lies in the rearticulation, or translation, of elements that are *neither the One nor the Other but something else besides*, which contests the terms and territories of both" (emphasis in the text).
15. See also Novetzke 2007 on the writing of biographies about saints.

Maharishi of Kailash to substantiate the anti-colonial idea of a perfectly "indigenous Christianity" to be traced back to Saint Thomas, and, in a sense, more authentic than Western Christianity. Following in the footsteps of Keshub Chandra Sen (1838–1884) and Protap Chandra Mozoomdar (1840–1905) in their attempts to present Christianity as an Asiatic religion, the notion of a hidden Christian community in the Himalayas was a powerful device in the construction of a religious authority that was not relying on (Western) missionary Christianity or on a tradition started by a Western theologian. This also explains Sundar Singh's later statement that the Gospel of John was actually the source of the *Bhagavad Gītā*—something he declared to the Bishop (and scholar of religion) Nathan Söderblom who vigorously but vainly protested against such a claim.[16]

Finally, there is the model of Indian religious activists traveling across the world in the beginning of the twentieth century. One can think of Vivekananda, who had been in Lahore in 1897 and left a strong impression on another future Punjabi charismatic figure, Rama Tirtha (1873–1906).[17] One can also think of contemporary movements developing in Punjab and sending representatives all around the world, in particular Hindu and Muslim activists. Inspired by Christian evangelical practices, these movements—for example the Ārya Samāj or the Muslim Aḥmadiyya movement—began to have "missionaries" of their own. As writes Nile Green:

> Just as...the Arya Samaj exchanged trains for steamships to seek followers among the Indian diaspora in South Africa and Burma, so in turn were members of the Ahmadiyya Movement dispatched on preaching tours of their own, from South Africa to south London.[24] Within around a decade of the death of its founder in 1908, the Ahmadiyya Movement had dispatched missionaries to Britain, Germany, Singapore, China and West Africa.
> (Green 2015, 213)

Echoing this pattern of Indian globe-trotters, Sundar Singh is sometimes portrayed as an anti-Vivekananda (especially for America), and in several of his speeches to Westerners, he takes a critical stance against Europeans becoming Hindus.[18] Nevertheless, his profile as a travelling guru and the socio-political implications of his message for India do not radically diverge from those of Vivekananda, much on the contrary—and as Beckerlegge

---

16. On Söderblom's protestation, see Sharpe 2003, 109.
17. Dobe (2015) compares the figures of Ram Tirtha and Sadhu Sundar Singh and shows many similarities between both, despite the different religious affiliations.
18. He said: "Instead of seeking something in Indian religion and books, people should study the lives of the Indian people. If their doctrine has done nothing good for them, what good can Europeans get out of it? The knowledge of Christ can satisfy but a Gospel-hardened people wants something new." (Goodwin 1989, 39)

underlines in this volume, it would be mistaken to imagine Vivekananda's audience in the West as systematically committing to one or the other form of "Hinduism."[19]

The 1922 Swiss tour

Before the tour

To my knowledge, the first encounter between Sundar Singh and Swiss missionaries goes back to 1918.[20] In March of that year, a conference of missionaries took place in Calicut, a conference during which it was decided to re-center the activities on the regions of Mangalore and Dharwad and to leave Kerala to other organizations, in the wake of the Basel Mission's demise after the War. Attending the meeting, one of the main protagonists of the KEM, the doctor Pierre de Benoît (1884-1963) met and hosted Sundar Singh.[21] In a text published before Sundar Singh actually came to Switzerland, he insisted on the similarity with Jesus, who "was equally fearing popularity and was constantly withdrawing when the crowds were pressed around him." (De Benoit, introduction to Parker 1923, 8)[22] Certainly Sundar Singh was not fearing popularity, much on the contrary, but De Benoît already read him according to his own, Calvinist, interpretation of the biblical narrative. This actually coincided with Sundar Singh's own shift in representing himself, as can be seen in the change of the narrative about his conversion: from the story of a progressive interest for the Bible (in Zahir's text), it became a sudden revelation, so as to better fit the Paulinian scheme of an unexpected conversion (in the South Indian speeches).[23]

Another antecedent is the circulation of publications. The relatively modest written production of Sundar Singh himself (7 booklets, all in Urdu)[24] is to be

---

19. Beckerlegge in this volume, p. 68.
20. Calicut had been an important center for the Basel mission until the war and in 1918, still had a College that had been founded in 1908 by the Basel mission, the Basel German Mission College which was about to be merged with the Malabar Christian College run by the Scottish Church.
21. On this encounter, see De Benoit 1973, 142-143.
22. Similarly, giving his own reading of the figure, De Benoit insisted that Sundar Singh did "not represent a kind of new ascetic teaching, but preaches Jesus Christ, the crucified and resurrected" (in the *Mitteilungen der Kanaresischen Mission* 1 (1920), 6), therefore showing that he was aware of other possible readings.
23. Dobe (2015, 153-154) describes precisely the Paulinian elements in Sundar Singh's conversion narrative.
24. These are: 1. *Maktab-i Masīh* [*The School of Christ*], tr. *At the Master's Feet*, 1922; 2. *Ḥaqīqat aur Mazhab* [*Reality and Religion*], 1924, 3. *Talāś-e Ḥaqq* [*The Search After Reality*], 1925, 4. *Rūḥānī Duniyā* [*The Spiritual World*], tr. *Visions of the Spiritual World*, 1926; 5. *Ḥaqīqī Zindagī* [*The Real Life*], n.d.; 6. *Dur-i Ḥaqīqī* [*The Real Pearl*], n.d. and 7. *Baghair Masīh aur*

contrasted with the abundance of works *about* him, already before his European tours. This can already hint at a process of an "external" construction of his identity by people interested to present him under a specific angle—first among them, missionaries eager to show that evangelization was producing positive results on Indian soil. An early book about Sundar Singh, using excerpts of speeches noted down in India, was published by an employee of the London Missionary Society, Rebecca Parker (1865-1946).[25] The book was originally written in Malayalam (1917), intended for Christian women in the region of Trivandrum, and was subsequently translated to English (but also in Tamil, Telugu, Marathi, Urdu) under the title *Sadhu Sundar Singh, called of God* (1918). It was brought back to Switzerland by De Benoît and a French translation was published soon after, under the curious title *Un apôtre hindou: Le Sâdhou Sundar Singh* (1920), erasing the "divine call," introducing the notion of apostle and the usual confusion between Indian and Hindu.[26] It is remarkable that the notion of "apostle" was used to give a Christian frame to the "sadhu" in the subtitle—even if that involved taking some freedom with the notion of "apostle" itself, using it for characterizing a person beyond the canonic circle of biblical apostles.

It is also noteworthy that one of Sundar Singh's booklets was not translated by the KEM but appeared only 10 years later, in 1936: his *Visions of the Spiritual World* (1926). In that text, Sundar Singh described the visions he had been having since his time in Kotgarh. He wrote:

> At Kotgarh, fourteen years ago, while I was praying, my eyes were opened to the Heavenly Vision. So vividly did I see it all that I thought I must have died, and that my soul had passed into the glory of heaven; but throughout the intervening years these visions have continued to enrich my life. I cannot call them up at will, but, usually when I am praying or meditating, sometimes as often as eight or ten times in a month, my spiritual eyes are opened to see within the heavens, and, for an hour or two, I walk in the glory of the heavenly sphere with Christ Jesus, and hold converse with angels and spirits. Their answers to my questions have provided much of the material that has already been published in my books, and the unutterable ecstasy of that spiritual communion makes me long for the time when I shall enter in permanently to the bliss and fellowship of the redeemed. (Sundar Singh 1926, xi-xii)

---

us ke sāth [*Without Christ and With Him*], 1929. A German translation of his complete works has been published by the Basel mission: Melzer 1946.

25. On the quasi "maternal" relation between Sundar Singh and Parker and their correspondence, see Mukherjee 2017, 27-28.

26. Parker 1920, French version: Parker 1923. The sixth edition contains additional material from the Swiss tour: an "extract of a discourse" held in Geneva, exchanges with students in Neuchâtel, as well as an account of the tour itself by G. Secrétan.

A "Christian Hindu Apostle"?

This part of Sundar Singh's "message" was particularly sensitive and there are clear indications that both himself and the tour organizers downplayed everything about visions and miracles.

The tour's logistics

The idea to invite Sundar Singh for a Swiss tour was a suggestion of William Paton (1886–1943), former secretary for the YMCA in India (1916–1919) and then Secretary of the Student Christian Movement in London. It is however the KEM and its general secretary, the pastor Gustave Secrétan (1867–1945) who concretized the plan.[27] To make sure that the tour would be met with success, Secrétan launched a wide advertisement campaign. Letters sent to various newspapers explained that: "The Sadhu's deep experiences, as narrated in the biography published by our Secretariat [Parker 1922] bring us back to apostolic times and will awaken the faith of many, in our century of doubt and tepidity" ("Visite en Suisse" 1922, 5).

The goal was to raise the general awareness about the necessity of mission—and with the awareness, of course, to raise actual funds.[28] The KEM collected more than CHF 12'000.- in the mere French speaking area and adding donations from the German speaking area, it probably collected about 10% of its yearly budget (a total of CHF 322'489 that year).[29] The question of who paid for Sundar Singh's travels is not entirely clear, except that we know he was hosted for free by sympathizers and that he certainly did not have to pay anything for himself.[30]

---

27. The practical aspects of the tour were organized by the pastor G. Naymark, associated to the KEM committee (Zimmermann 1930, 92).
28. Dobe (2015, 151)'s observation is valid, at least from the point of view of those who were organizing the tour: "Sundar Singh reaffirmed key tenets of the Christian missionary project increasingly under the attack of global-trotting Indian sadhus and subject to Christian self-doubt and debate: the need for and success of Christian missions; salvation in a unique Christ over against non-Christian religions, and the shortcomings of modernist biblical criticism in favor of a biblical world of the supernatural."
29. Basel Mission Archives, box CC-3. Donations were however not only for the KEM, but also for Sundar Singh's own activities in India. For example, in Geneva, he managed to raise a significant sum of money (CHF 2150) for a school run by a friend of his in the area of Lhassa. His remark about the money transfer is somewhat odd: "He was much troubled as to how he should send the money to Tibet, and at last decided to have it given to a faithful Tibetan trader, one of the 50 odd Tibetans who had once seen him surrounded by angels when they had made up their mind to kill him. It was one of the many miracles the Sadhu had experienced" (Goodwin 1989, 25).
30. See the comments of Secrétan in Parker (1923, 145): "He arrived in Lausanne with a little bag that was containing two yellow robes and one or two books. He had no money, no watch." On the financial aspect, see Bocking's remark in this volume, p. 181–182.

Sundar Singh arrived in Lausanne from Marseilles on 27 February 1922. As soon as he disembarked from the train, he was welcomed by the tour's organizers and everything had been planned.[31] From February to March 1922, he gave lectures in 15 different locations, and about the double of speeches, to large audiences.[32] He spoke in English but was introduced and translated in French and German by different pastors such as a former missionary in Hubli, Emil Schwab.[33] As to the venues, Sundar Singh used three kinds of spaces: (1) he spoke in churches and Cathedrals; (2) in rooms that are part of the Protestant Church infrastructure; (3) and in open air venues in the public space. If a number of venues were chosen for practical reasons or "because the Sadhu prefers speaking in the open air,"[34] in some places, he was clearly not offered to speak in a church when he could have. For example, in Geneva, he did not give any speech in the Cathedral—but in adjacent rooms including the large "Salle de la Réformation" which was also being used for meetings of the League of Nations.

As to the physical appearance and dress, it would be easy to argue that Sundar Singh wanted to give an orientalized image of himself, or maybe more to the point, the image of an "authentic" Indian Jesus. Alys Goodwin, the secretary hired to typewrite Sundar Singh's speeches during the tour noted,

---

31. See Parker (1923, 120–121): "At 5.30 pm, we meet again with a marching plan throughout Switzerland for March. The map is on the table. After a while, the sadhu understood; he did not take any note, but the dates and the places are in his mind. He accepted our plan, which had been submitted to him in the broad lines before his departure from the Indies, but he asked to cancel certain meetings: 'Do not have me speak more than once a day, except Sunday; this is not the same as teaching a class at school; this would become something like mailing a letter at the post office, and there would be no benediction. But we want it to be fruitful'"

32. The dates are the following: Bienne (28 February, Protestant Temple), Tavannes (March 1), Saanen (2 March, Protestant Church), Lausanne and Morges (3 March, English Church; 5 March, Chailly Church and kids of the Sunday school; 5 March (afternoon), Public meeting for young people, Montbenon; 6 March (afternoon), Morges Church; 6 March (evening), Lausanne "Salle de réunion"; 7 March, Lausanne Cathedral), Geneva (9 March, Salle de la Réformation; 10 March, Consistoire and Salle centrale; 12 March, Salle de la Réformation), Neuchâtel (13 March, Public square), La Chaux-de-Fonds (14 March, open air) and Le Locle (15 March, open air), Basel (16 March, 2 meetings, one in the "Vereinshaus"), Zurich (17 March; 19 March, Grossmünster), Schaffhausen (21 March), St Gall, Aarau and Berne (26 March, Münster).

33. Later, Schwab led an enquiry about Sundar Singh (see the response addressed to him by Samuel Evans Stokes, in the appendix) and was in contact with Sundar Singh's biographer, A.J. Appasamy.

34. Goodwin (1989, 26), who continues: "He does not care for buildings, and particularly dislikes Anglican Churches, because there are 'too many pillars, they come between me and my hearers'. '–Would you object to speaking in a Catholic Church?' '–Not at all, but there are so many pictures, there would be no room for me'."

A "Christian Hindu Apostle"?

Figure 9.2 Eugène Burnand (1850–1921), "Go forth into all the world and preach the gospel to all creatures" 1915, painted for the centenary of the Basel Mission [Basel Mission archives QS-30.026.0171].

looking at Sundar Singh in Saanen: "While he was speaking the Sadhu leant back against the grey stone pillar, with hands folded, and one could not help thinking of the portraits of Christ; there was such a striking resemblance." (Goodwin 1989, 12) There is indeed some similarity between a painting of Jesus by Eugène Burnand (1915) and Sundar Singh's appearance (Figures 9.2 and 9.3).[35]

A detail confirming this worry to appear authentic is that, when given a watch in Geneva, he politely thanked for the gift but remarked that it would be appropriate for "this country" (Switzerland) but not for India.

The Sadhu's messages

With this performance framed, indeed, to bring the audience back to "apostolic times," came naturally a harsh criticism of Western modernity and Western Christendom. Sundar Singh declared, in a speech given next to La Chaux-de-Fonds:

> I was believing that all inhabitants of Christian countries were reading the Bible and were similar to angels. In going around these countries, however, I realized my mistake. Most of them have a white face and a

---

35. Dobe (2015, 149–151) similarly emphasized the similarity between Sundar Singh and contemporary representations of Jesus.

Figure 9.3   Sundar Singh in Lausanne, *L'Illustré*, April 1922.

black heart. In heathen countries, I see people going to their temples. They fear God. Here, I mostly see people looking for their own pleasure.
(Sundar Singh, "Le Locle, 15 mars 1922" in Singh 1922c)

After the Great War which, for many, had undermined the idea of a European civilizational superiority, this type of discourse could definitely find a sympathetic audience.[36] Another *leitmotiv* of his speeches was the emphasis on prayer and the personal relation to the divinity. Sundar Singh concluded almost every speech by insisting that no guide, adviser, priest or guru can act on the behalf of someone else. He shocked a pastor in Saanen who had asked him "to pray for one of his sick parishioners" by replying: "We must not pray for others, they must go themselves straight to God." (Goodwin 1989, 10). Also characteristic is a karmic conception of "action" and "sin." For example, when asked (in Lausanne) what his opinion was on the "forgiveness of sin,"

---

36. On this point, see Duara (2007, 214) and Sharpe (2003, 78) who observes: "In 1920, a fair proportion of Christians in the West, disillusioned by their culture's failures, were longing for 'light from the East.' If it came through a Tagore or a Gandhi, all well and good. If it came speaking the language of Christendom, so much the better."

he answered: "There is no difficulty: Be free from all kinds of sin and then there will be no need of forgiveness. Salvation is not only forgiveness of sin, but freedom from sin" (Goodwin 1989, 18, 28, 33 and 34). No inherently sinful mankind in need to be redeemed then, but good and bad actions, achieved by individual persons: a notion very much reminiscent of the Indian karmic retribution system.

These different elements already suggest that Sundar Singh used the opportunity of these speeches to distill a slightly subversive message, or at least one that did not entirely overlap with what was expected from him. While some of the organizers were close to evangelical circles—and ready to criticize the lack of spirit in the "state church"—others were certainly not. Sundar Singh's trenchant critique is evident when looking closer at specific speeches: his interventions were framed to produce a specific effect on local audiences—reminding one of Beckerlegge's notion of "imported localism," in which the ideal of a "universal religion" contrasts with the shape the doctrine or practice of the same "universal religion" takes in specific locations (in the West), through a specific rejection of local forms of religion and concomitant attribution of the imported religious doctrine or practice to a remote location (e.g. "Oriental," "Hindu") (Beckerlegge 2004, 314).

Geneva: Witnesses and not scribes

In the city of Calvin, Sundar Singh underlined that "many know Him [Jesus] through theology or history and do not have any time to spend with Him and do not know Him" (Singh 1922a, 7). The next day, a smaller meeting was organized specifically for the "Corps pastoral," and as people were entering, the official secretary heard two elderly men saying, with condescendence: "We should not hit too harsh." Not minding to accentuate the gap between his own views and those of his learned audience, Sundar Singh repeated that for him, "truth is not in dogma or doctrine, but in the living Christ" (speech of 10 March 1922, morning, in the "Consistoire," Goodwin 1989, 20). In the evening, at another public event, he emphasized once again that Christians should be "witnesses," not "scribes" (speech of March 10, evening, in the "Salle centrale," Singh 1922a, 12). In the time of questions, some asked about the Maharishi of Kailash, to what he abruptly replied that "it was very interesting but not useful" (Appasamy 1958, 174). Secrétan wrote that the public was slightly disturbed by these negative statements about theological studies—probably an understatement.[37] A more radical criticism is found among liberal Protestant theologians writing in the Zurich journal *Neue Wege*, such as one of its co-founders, Leonhard Ragaz (1868–1945):

---

37. "They might have been disappointed by certain stances of the Sadhu concerning studies and surprised by his emphasis on certain points, such as miracle and the divinity of Christ" (Parker 1923, 125).

> When one is introduced and protected by theologians, is it possible to destroy theology? ... If what I heard and read is right, he came to us as a kind of "higher religious inspector" [religiöser Oberinspektor]. Then I need to ask: where is he taking the competence for this from?
>
> (Ragaz 1922, 237)

Invited to speak in front of a small group of wealthy Genevois, Sundar Singh again adapted his speech and warned his audience that "people try to satisfy the comfort of this physical body which is going to be eaten up by worms in the grave; they ignore the desires of the soul which is going to live forever." (Goodwin 1989, 23)

Basel: Hold fast what you have!

In Basel, he spoke in front of an audience comprising Swiss missionaries who had been working in India. His first speech was about a text of Revelation 3, 11, "I am coming quickly; hold fast what you have, so that no one will take your crown." The text is indeed fitting for the situation of the Basel mission itself, considering its extremely critical situation at the moment, having lost almost all its mission fields (Cameroon, Ghana, India). Sundar Singh's development emphasized that God's word needs to be carefully listened to, possibly suggesting that the present situation might be the result of people not listening well enough.

As we learn in the official the magazine of the Basel mission, the *Evangelische Heidenbote*, the speech was disturbed by what is described as an odd and regretful "missionary demonstration." It was an event organized by the Salvation army, in the framework of a tour at roughly the same time in Switzerland. Contemporary newspapers indicate that 20 "Hindu young girls" were paraded around, and instructed to sing and play scenes of the "Indian life." An advertisement printed in the *Neue Zürcher Zeitung*, entitled "Indien in der Schweiz," deemed it of ethnographic interest (see *Der Evangelische Heidenbote* 95/5, 1922, 73, and *Neue Zürcher Zeitung* 20 March 1922). This is yet another sign that Sundar Singh's appearance contrasted with the paternalist image of an India in need of external intervention—an image that was of course, as we saw, very much shared by the missionary institution which had invited him.

Saanen and the mountains

There is one part of the trip that Sundar Singh particularly enjoyed: the travel in and through the Swiss alps. He did not only appreciate the landscapes—inspiring and reminiscent of the Himalayas—but also emphasized the simple life in the mountains and in nature in general, in opposition to the urban lifestyle (Figure 9.4).

As C. F. Andrews writes in recollections about his friend:

A "Christian Hindu Apostle"?

Figure 9.4   Sadhu Sundar Singh in Saanen, March 1922, *En pays hindou: Ténèbres et lumière* 2, 1923, 28.

Of all the countries he visited abroad, Switzerland came nearest to his heart. It reminded him daily of his own Himalayas, which rise up from the valleys, on a still vaster scale of grandeur than the Alps. He loved best of all the Swiss village people, who flocked in to see him from the remote recesses of the mountains; for he seemed to be far more at home with them than with the crowds in the great cities in Northern Europe. (Andrews 1934, 133)

In this, Sundar Singh again represents an "anti-modernist" view, idealizing the simplicity of countryside people opposed to the evils of urban life (Appasamy 1958, 48). This was reflected in parts of his speeches, when expressing the wish to go back to a better, pre-industrial age, as an image illustrating a publication of his speeches in Switzerland powerfully suggests (Figure 9.5).

A mixed reception

Let us now examine the reception of the performance. The mediatic exposure was unparalleled elsewhere, so that the Swiss tour can be considered

Figure 9.5 "As you look for me wholeheartedly, I will let myself be found by you [Jeremiah 29: 13],″ *Mitteilungen der Kanaresischen Mission* 4.4, July 1922, 13. Note the chimneys on the bottom left and the South Indian temple on the bottom right.

as a turning point in Sundar Singh's career (Appasamy 1958, 168–169). With the label of "Hindu Christian sadhu" opening a wide semantic field, and under the spotlight during one full month, Sundar Singh attracted lots of attention, exposing himself to well-disposed hearers, of course, but also to serious misunderstandings and, in at least one case, open hostility. Not surprisingly and even if Sundar Singh's public appearance had been carefully framed by his hosts, many saw more (or less) than what they were supposed to see.

A "Christian Hindu Apostle"?

Evangelical missionaries

A first group of interested people was of course evangelical missionaries. The KEM published French and German translations of transcriptions of speeches in Switzerland,[38] postcards, illustrated sayings with a poem *about* Sundar Singh, a biography written by a Swiss German pastor (Schaerer 1922, 15'000 copies!) and an important number of articles in its propaganda.[39] In all these publications, the tendency was to downplay the "surnatural" elements and to emphasize the moral message—using it against what they perceived as intellectualist theology. Sundar Singh was coming from India to restore Christianity to a purer form of itself, a form of Christianity that was strongly echoing the image evangelicals wanted to give of themselves. Up to today, Sundar Singh remains an important figure in Swiss evangelical circles, as witnesses the continuous republication of yet another biography (Van Berchem 1982).

In India, Swiss missionaries saw Sundar Singh as a sign of hope in a dire situation. The KEM missionary Paul Burckhardt wrote a theatre play about the upbringing of Sundar Singh in his family and his conversion—a play written in German but probably meant to be translated in Kannada and performed in the missionary context.[40] The ambiguity of the figure of a "Christian *sādhu*" was however already perceivable in that context: in March 1923, a young employee of the KEM, Nelly Gruffel, wrote from Bettigeri that there had been a Christian *sādhu* in their church, but in no way comparable to Sundar Singh, the only "real Christian *sādhu*"—a sign that Christian *sādhus* "need not fall into outright heresy to challenge mission and church discipline."[41]

---

38. Initially in five independent booklets, Singh 1922a, Singh 1922b, Singh 1922d and then gathered in one book: Singh 1922c.
39. For example: "The Sadhu is a Christian who brings to us, Westerners, the purity, the freshness, the deepness and the beauty of the original faith and life, with no mediation, while our Christianity has gone through an ecclesiastical and religious evolution of 2000 years and has undergone many transformations" (Rippmann 1922, 10).
40. Burckhardt, Paul, "Indische Szenen," kept in Basel Mission archives CC-1, 4.
41. Cox 2003, 227 (about "Christian fakirs"). The full description of the mission employee reads: "Last Sunday, we had a *sādhu* in the morning at church. He spoke Tamil and was translated in Kannada by our biblical colporteur. He was no Sundar Singh, though! He was full of himself and was looking more like an actor than a real *sādhu*. We did not like him: he was doing such a theatre with his hands and arms while speaking, that we were almost sick having to watch him during 1.30 hour. He disappointed us very much. He said to Ms. Stokes [she is not related to S.E. Stokes] that in the whole India, there were only three real *sādhu* and he was counting himself among them. To his eyes, Sundar Singh was not one. In his predication, he compared himself to John the Baptist. This made me think that for this life of Christian *sādhu*, it was like for everything which stands slightly over the ordinary: we need really special people, who have directly received a superior vocation from God. Otherwise, it becomes pure charlatanism" (Letter of N. Gruffel to her parents, March 1923, Basel Mission archives, CC-1,4.).

Broader public

Even if organized by a Christian Protestant organization, people who were not directly involved in religious activities got interested. Some were clearly puzzled by an exotic figure such as Sundar Singh—as had been the crowds who had attended Tagore's meetings one year earlier. Tagore had drawn huge crowds fascinated by his charisma, in the context of a disillusioned post-War Europe and quite logically, Sundar Singh appealed to the same general public.[42] In Lausanne, several thousands of people participated, "of all social classes" if we are to believe a newspaper report about the event. In a good neo-romantic fashion, some probably also came with expectations of a more religious nature, looking for the spiritual teachings of an Oriental Sage. While some might have entertained the hope to be introduced to a more universalistic and revised form of Christianity, others touched Sundar Singh's dress or looked for his gaze (Goodwin 1989, 7 and 17). Secrétan noted with regret:

> We were witnesses of regrettable scenes which reveal the background of gross superstition that is still lurking in our old protestant populations: people came to ask the Sadhu to pray, so that they find back a lost ring, or other similar requests. I had to pass a letter addressed to "the Sadhu: the Saint of India"! Ah, if the Sadhu had wanted to start a cult or heal the sick, what for a movement he would have provoked! (in Parker 1923, 133–134)

This is actually very similar to what happened in Sundar Singh's Indian meetings, with crowds coming for *darśan*, especially in South India, and this is a first indication of the event escaping the control of its organizers. It went however much beyond.

Swedenborgians

The society of Swiss Swedenborgians which had an important branch in Lausanne took notice of the tour and the journal *Le Messager de la nouvelle Eglise* (The Messenger of the New Church) reported extensively about Sundar Singh's visit. The report was subsequently translated in English and published in the British Swedenborgian Journal, *New Church Life* (Mayer 1984, 133–134 and Sharpe 2003, 147, who, curiously, seems to assume that Sundar Singh travelled to Switzerland *after* his Swedish stay). A pastor of the New Church in Lausanne, Norman Mayer, wrote:

> Lausanne has just received the never-to-be-forgotten visit of Sadhu Sundar Singh, and we have witnessed the stirring spectacle of crowds thronging to church eager to hear the message brought to them from the East by the new apostle of the Lord ... He has come from the far-off

---

42. On the fascination for Tagore in this context specifically, see Kämpchen 2014, 396–400. This aspect of the reception of Sundar Singh is in the center of Mukherjee's study of his British tour (2017).

Orient to proclaim aloud in simple and beautiful language the fundamental verity of the New Church: "Jesus Christ is the living God, the one and only God. There is no other. Jesus Christ is the Father manifested to men. There is no other Lord." ... The respectful attention with which the crowds listened to him, and the insistence with which they followed him, seem to us of good augury. And the several members of the New Church who were present rejoiced from the bottom of their hearts to think that the light which they have so long tried to disseminate was perhaps on the point of dawning. ... Here is a man who, like Swedenborg, has had his spiritual eyes opened. As in Swedenborg's case, the Lord was pleased to manifest Himself before him. He has been in the spiritual world, and there learned by experience that the angels of all the heavens acknowledge no other Father than the Lord Jesus Christ ... . This is what mankind today has been needing to rouse it from the torpor into which it has fallen—a second prophet (may we not venture to give him this title?) addressing himself directly to the masses, and speaking a tongue within reach of all."
(Mayer 1922, 49-53, translated and reprinted in *New Church Life* 1922)

It is striking that Sundar Singh is here "used" to give an authority to Swedenborgians: the fact that crowds listened to him was read as a sign that more and more people would develop an interest for their own Spiritualist views. However, not all Swedenborgians were as enthusiastic: William H. Alden, an American Swedenborgian, thought that if Sundar Singh had been experiencing a "strong emotional experience," he was only superficially repeating statements of Evangelical Christianity.[43] Even if Sundar Singh had not known this group so far, it would later play a significant role in his career (Mayer 1984, 134). Initially "used" by them, he would in turn use Swedenborgian networks to promote his views and sell books, and would claim to have conversations with Emmanuel Swedenborg (1688-1772) himself.[44]

Along with the Swedenborgians, Sundar Singh was noticed in circles interested in psychological studies, and further in psychical societies. In Geneva, one person asked: "what is the possibility of fellowship with those in the other world? Are they near to help us?" Sundar Singh answered in a sibylline way: "It will not help you much if I answer that. You will think I am a spiritualist. Unseen things are not so useful." (Goodwin 1989, 25).[45] The magazine of

---

43. Alden comments: "One can discern, throughout this strange experience, the background of the Hindoo character, with an injection of Christian theology, and, mixed with these, some true conceptions respecting the Lord and the spiritual world; but all interwoven with a straining after martyrdom which is hardly sane, and with some notions that are utterly false" (Alden 1922, 637, on which see Sharpe 2003, 148).

44. Sharpe (2003, 18) notes that Sundar Singh expressed this in a letter sent to Nathan Söderblom.

45. Sundar Singh was visibly worried to distinguish a good (Christian) form of conversation with spirits from contemporary "spiritualist" experiences. This is evident in the

the "Spiritualist Association of London," *Light: A Journal of Spiritual, Psychical & Mystical Research*, published a very sympathetic review of an article about Sundar Singh published in the Hibbert Journal of the same year ("The Miracles of Sundar Singh" 1921, 125, on Emmett 1920–1921). Similarly, the *Occult Review* positively reviewed Streeter and Appasamy's book on Sundar Singh (Streeter & Appasamy 1921), taking Sundar Singh's "visions" at face value and describing him as "a Christian mystic living a life of absolute poverty, seeing visions, entering into the state of ecstasy, essaying a complete fast of forty days, and experiencing deliverances from the hands of his enemies which are truly miraculous in the sense that no obvious explanation is forthcoming." (Hubbard 1921, 374). A later issue of the same *Occult Review* focused on oriental conceptions of Jesus and on Sundar Singh's emphasis on prayer:

> Perhaps the most striking feature of Sundar's gospel is his emphatic insistence on the vital importance of prayer in the Christian life. [...] In the light of occultism, prayer is seen to be the very Path itself. From the humble petition for spiritual enlightenment, to the heights of mystical contemplation, prayer is the very life of the soul. In prayer the deepest, purest essence of the man is freed, and floating upward draws nearer to its Source. (Strutton 1927, 224)

There is evidence that members of the Anthroposophical society (founded in 1913) were also aware of Sundar Singh. In an article published in the German-speaking journal of the Anthroposophical society, *Die Drei*, the author complained about Heiler presenting Sundar Singh as an inspiration for a Christian revival in Europe, whereas at the same time, Rudolf Steiner's conception of Christ—which could be used to the same effect—had been ignored by European theologians (Kühne 1925).

Pfister

The main detractor of Sundar Singh was a Swiss theologian, President of the Swiss General Mission Society in Zürich but also a friend of C.G. Jung and bet-

---

introduction to his booklet *Visions of the spiritual world* (1926), in which he feels it necessary to formulate the following caveat: "Some may consider that these visions are merely a form of spiritualism, but I would emphasize that there is one very essential difference. Spiritualism does presume to produce messages and signs from spirits out of the dark, but they are usually so fragmentary and unintelligible, if not actually deceptive, that they lead their followers away from, rather than to, the truth. In these visions, on the other hand, I see vividly and clearly every detail of the glory of the spiritual world, and I have the uplifting experience of very real fellowship with the saints, amid the inconceivably bright and beautiful world made visible. It is from these angels and saints that I have received, not vague, broken and elusive messages from the unseen, but clear and rational elucidations of many of the problems that have troubled me" (Sundar Singh 1926, xi–xii).

ter known for his correspondence with Sigmund Freud: Oskar Pfister (1873-1956). He published a first article in 1922 and other soon followed. These attacks in turn triggered reactions from Sundar Singh's defenders, such as Friedrich Heiler and his book, *Sadhu Sundar Singh: Ein Apostel des Ostens und des Westens*, published the same year (1922). Things quickly escalated, to the point that one could soon speak of a *Sadhustreit* (Heiler 1925 on which see Sharpe 2003, 123). Pfister wrote a critical review of Friedrich Heiler's book (Pfister 1922) which was followed in 1926 with a full book entitled *Die Legende Sundar Singhs*, in which he tried to "debunk" the Sadhu's phenomenon with the help of psychoanalysis.[46] In an article of synthesis, supposed to bring a definitive end to the whole affair, he wrote:

> Anybody [who will study the case of the Sadhu] will perceive with astonishment what enormous amount of Asiatic astuteness and European pseudo-science was provided to paint the image of a moderately saint apostle of the East and the West. ... Today, the apostle does not hallucinate anymore as often as before, the level is alarmingly lower and the danger of a real craziness [wirkliche Verrücktheit] in the psychopathological sense has increased. The last booklet of Sundar, entitled: "Visions of the spiritual World" (1926) is a regrettable sign of this intellectual and religious decline. In the place of biblical figures appear now good and bad spirits, with whom the Sadhu has visual and auditory intercourse, and in whose mouth he sets his childish wishful fantasies, tirades without any spirit, as one can often hear from psychopaths, for example within the walls of an asylum filled with failed cult founders. (Pfister 1928, 177 and 179, my translation)

It is remarkable that despite this total rejection of Sundar Singh, Pfister still felt necessary to write an answer. Judging by his 1926 book, he spent major time and efforts on this. In any case, this crude assessment reflects divergent views and a real fear that Sundar Singh's iconoclast views might cast a shadow on the local ecclesiastical institution and theological studies.

Swiss freethinkers

A last note before closing: Pfister's article was read by Swiss freethinkers, who took it as the proof of Sundar Singh being "a fake," notwithstanding the fact that they were citing the work of a Protestant pastor—but they urged Pfister to apply the same critical approach to Jesus (*Der Freidenker* 12/14, 1929, 106–108). Oddly enough, a later issue of the same journal printed a quotation of Sundar Singh's speech in Tavannes, this time as communicating a message they could fully endorse, about Christians having a "white face and a black heart" (*Der Freidenker* 14/10, 1931, 1).

---

46. Pfister 1926; for a thorough summary of the controversy, see Bonnard 1926.

These critical voices arouse doubt even among the tour's former organizers, and in 1927, Emil Schwab wrote a letter to Samuel Stokes asking about Sundar Singh. The answer to that letter managed to keep out of the dull debate of whether Sundar Singh was a "fraud" or not, giving elements of context and insisting on the mediatic phenomenon that was built around him, from which he could hardly extricate himself (see Appendix 1).

Concluding thoughts

I would like to conclude now on three issues: (1) on Sundar Singh's "message" and his use of institutions, (2) on the Indian specificity of the figure and (3) on the Swiss context of the tour.

(1) There is of course a deep ambiguity in using the network of an institutional religion for spreading a message that, in the end, is radically opposed to any form of institution. One must conclude that from Sundar Singh's point of view, Protestant networks were doubly interesting: on the one hand, they were providing an infrastructure to spread his own views on a global (and local) basis; on the other hand, and once recognized as the recipient of a revealed message, he could benefit from a certain doctrinal freedom—given the Protestant emphasis on the absence of mediation between humans and the divinity (for a similar pattern in the case of Pandita Ramabai, see above p. 204). In that sense, even if the syntagm "Christian sādhu" has no easy univocal meaning, it can be considered as a strategic key to unlock the benefits of both an institutional network and the freedom to articulate a personal message.

It is this fundamental "hybridity" in the message that explains the multiple creative combinations that could be made out of it, depending on the circles that received the message and their intentions, and the situations (also in terms of locality) in which specific discourses were produced. This also explains why any attempt to control the phenomenon, that is, to give it a univocal meaning, was bound to fail. From the point of view of semiotics, it exemplifies U. Eco's search for a middle way between two opposite models of interpretation: on the one hand, that of a signifier (the public image of Sundar Singh) corresponding to one single meaning (e.g. an Indian evangelical Christian), and on the other hand, that of a signifier open to *any* meaning that its readers could give to it (Eco 1994, 23-24). The metaphor of a kaleidoscope, in which the resulting images are products of a creative reconfiguration of finite elements under the action of the viewer, is probably an apt visualization of this process.

(2) Secondly, one must emphasize that the formative years of Sundar Singh in India have been crucial in the shaping of his authority. Two aspects specific to the Indian context should be underlined here: on the one side, he learned how to perform as a guru / sādhu, with a particular attention to the

A "Christian Hindu Apostle"?

visual and material presentation of himself. As Dobe underlines (Dobe 2015, 180–181), the notion of "sanctity" is here not so much related to charisma as it is to the acquisition of a vocabulary for "performing a tradition" and constructing the authenticity of his message. Building on that expertise, Sundar Singh proved himself as a virtuoso in appearing as an Oriental Jesus to wide and diverse audiences. On the other side, one should mention the narrative of Christianity as an indigenous Indian religion and of Jesus as an oriental yogi. Pushed to their ultimate logical consequence, Sundar Singh's views not only make theology and institutions useless, but also imply that the West cannot contribute much to the East, at least religiously—and probably politically as well. Despite saying being apolitical, it has, then, definitely an anti-imperialist coloration that is actually not that far from the views expressed by Vivekananda. As Cox noted,

> His [of Sundar Singh] celebrity served, like mission institutions, to give the urban Indian Christian community some status, particularly as the rise of the national movement in the twentieth century left them more vulnerable to charges that they were "denationalized" by their Christianity. (Cox 2012, 232)

As a counterexample to the negative propaganda of the missionaries about a wild India in need of civilizing forces (ironically typified by wandering ascetics), Sundar Singh was successful in delivering an opposite message to an international audience. It is interesting to note that around the same time, such a voice of contestation did not manage to get heard in the context of the Swiss missions in South Africa—even if local converts equally toured Switzerland and were invited to give speeches, as did Calvin Mapopé in 1927.[47]

(3) Thirdly, and even if a more precise comparative study would be needed, the diversity of audiences met in Switzerland should be emphasized: a diversity that contributed to fuel the controversy, but which is also emblematic of post-first World War Switzerland as a major hub for a number of transnational intellectual and religious circles. Theosophy, Anthroposophy, Lebensreform movements (see Sutcliffe in the present volume), Spiritualist Churches such as the Swedenborgians were all developing quickly, so that Jean-François

---

47. On Mapopé's visit, see Harries 2007, 247. For a comparison with Sundar Singh, see the announcement in the *Feuille d'avis de Lausanne*, 27 March 1925, by the pastor Louis-Samuel Pidoux (1878–1953): "It is worth retracing in broad strokes the career of a man, who, born in the African jungle and the pagan savagery, will in a few days speak from Pierre Viret's pulpit, in the Cathedral of Lausanne—a living witness of a work of spiritual colonization of which our country can be proud. ... We will however not expect from this son of the remote Africa, stemming from a people without culture which just opened itself to civilization, the same as what we can receive from a religious personality such as Sadhu Sundar Singh, son of an India that has a long past of life and light." (Pidoux 1925).

Mayer can speak about a striving Swiss *cultic milieu* in the beginning of the twentieth century (Mayer 1993, 82–91 and Stark and Bainbridge 1985, 499, about Geneva). All this—added to a neo-romantic attraction for oriental spirituality and to Sundar Singh's own expertise in performing as an "authentic" oriental Jesus—composed a powerful resounding box for an event such as his tour. It explains why the tour's organizers were quickly overwhelmed with what happened. If the case can be compared to Tagore's tour one year earlier, it certainly had a more lasting impact because of its encounters with the Swiss religious scene and the multiple transcriptions of the speeches held there which were then translated and widely diffused.

As the unsettling character of a title such as "Hindu Christian Sadhu Apostle" well shows, any attempt to categorize Sundar Singh within the boundaries of a specific register is bound to fail. To see him as an Oriental Jesus, a fraud, or as a mystic having regular intercourse with spirits obliterates other dimensions and almost inevitably ends up with a normative judgment. Similarly, and despite attempts to make it fit a Christian (Protestant) framework, the case clearly exceeds clearcut religious boundaries, whether one examines Sundar Singh's formative years, his actual teachings, his performances as a guru or the reception of his work. This is exactly why a "connected religion" approach is appropriate here: by bringing together sources that are told from different points of view and geographical spaces, it becomes possible to build a "thicker" scholarly narrative and to construct a common space of intellegibility for making sense of Sundar Singh's decidedly multi-faceted, versatile and (at least in part) translocal life.

References

Alden, W. H. 1922. "Sadhu Sundar Singh," *New Church Life* 1922: 634–642.

Andrews, Charles Freer. 1934. *Sadhu Sundar Singh: A Personal Memoir*. New York: Harper & Brothers.

Appasamy, Aiyadurai Jesudasen. 1958. *Sadhu Sundar Singh: A Biography*. Lutterworth Press. London.

Beckerlegge, Gwilym. 2004. "The Early Spread of Vedanta Societies: An Example of 'Imported Localism'." *Numen* 51(3): 296–320. https://doi.org/10.1163/1568527041945526

Benoit (de, née Van Berchem), Renée. 1973. *Souvenirs et Lettres*. Saint-Légier: Emmaüs.

Bhabha, Homi. 1994. *The Location of Culture*. Routledge. London.

Bonnard, Maurice. 1926. "Questions actuelles: Une polémique sur le Sadhou Sundar Singh." *Revue de Théologie et de Philosophie* 14: 148–155.

Bourdieu, Pierre. 1986. "L'illusion biographique." *Archives de la recherche en sciences sociales* 62–63: 69–72. https://doi.org/10.3406/arss.1986.2317

Cox, Jeffrey. 2002. *Imperial Fault Lines: Christianity and the Colonial Power, 1818–1940.* Stanford, CA: Stanford University Press.

Dobe, Timothy S. 2015. *Hindu Christian Faqir: Modern Monks, Global Christianity, and Indian Sainthood.* Oxford: Oxford University Press. https://doi.org/10.1093/acprof:oso/9780199987696.001.0001

Duara, Prasenjit. 2007. "The Imperialism of 'Free Nations': Japan, Manchukuo, and the History of the Present." In *Imperial Formations*, edited by A. L. Stoler, C. McGranahan and P.C. Perdue, 211–240. Santa Fe, NM: School for Advanced Research Press.

Eco, Umberto. 1994 [1990]. *The Limits of Interpretation.* Bloomington: Indiana University Press.

Emilsen, William. 1998. "'The Great Gulf Fixed': Samuel Stokes and the Brotherhood of the Imitation of Jesus." In *Religious Traditions in South Asia: Interaction and Change*, edited by G. A. Oddie, 91–106. Surrey: Curzon Press.

Emmet, C. W. 1920–1921. "The Miracles of Sadhu Sundar Singh." *The Hibbert Journal* 19: 308–318.

Goetz, Albert. 1954. *Der 300 Jährige Maharishi vom Kailas als Prophet Biblischer Wahrheiten.* Hamburg: Mehr Licht Verlag.

Goodwin, Miss Alys. 1989. *Sadhu Sundar Singh in Switzerland*, edited by A.F. Thyagaraju. Madras: The Christian Literature Society.

Green, Nile. 2015. *Terrains of Exchange: Religious Economies of Global Islam.* Oxford: Oxford University Press. https://doi.org/10.1093/acprof:oso/9780190222536.001.0001

Harries, Patrick. 2007. *Butterflies & Barbarians: Swiss Missionaries & Systems of Knowledge in South-East Africa.* Athens: Ohio University Press.

Heiler, Friedrich. 1925. *Apostel oder Betrüger? Dokumente zum Sadhustreit.* Basel: Friedrich Reinhardt.

Hubbard, Harry Lovett. 1921. "Review of *The Sadhu: A Study in Mysticism and Practical Religion.*" *The Occult Review* 33(6): 374.

Kämpchen, Martin. 2014. "Germany, Austria and Switzerland." In *Rabindranath Tagore: One Hundred Years of Global Reception*, edited by M. Kämpchen and I. Bangha, 389–410. Delhi: Orient BlackSwan.

Kempis, Thomas A. 1881. *The Imitation of Christ.* London: Kegan Paul Limited.

Kühne, Walter. 1925. "Friedrich Heilers Schrift über Sadhu Sundar Singh und ihre Untertöne: Ein Symptom der geistigen Welt." *Die Drei: Zeitschrift für Anthroposophie in Wissenschaft, Kunst und sozialem Leben* 5(3): 230–236.

Mayer, Jean-Francois. 1984. *La nouvelle Eglise de Lausanne et le mouvement Swedenborgien en Suisse romande des origines à 1948.* Swedenborg Verlag. Zürich.

———. 1993. *Les nouvelles voies spirituelles: Enquête sur la religiosité parallèle en Suisse.* Lausanne: L'Age d'Homme.

Mayer, Norman E. 1922. "Le Sadhou Sundar Singh." *Messager de la nouvelle Eglise* 6(4): 49–53.

Melzer, Friso. 1946. *Sadhu Sundar Singh: Gesammelte Schriften.* München: Neubau.

Mukherjee, Sumita. 2017. "The Reception Given to Sadhu Sundar Singh, the Itinerant Indian Christian 'Mystic', in Interwar Britain." *Interwar Britain, Immigrants & Minorities* 35(1): 21– 39. https://doi.org/10.1080/02619288.2016.1246966

Novetzke, Christian Lee. 2007. "The Theographic and the Historiographic in an Indian Sacred Life Story." *Sikh Formations* 3(2): 169–184. https://doi.org/10.1080/17448720701726413

Oberoi, Harjot. 1994. *The Construction of Religious Boundaries.* Chicago, IL: University of Chicago Press.

Parker, Mrs Arthur. 1920. *Sadhu Sundar Singh: Called of God.* London: Fleming H. Revell Company.

———. 1923. *Un Apôtre Hindou: Le Sâdhou Sundar Singh.* Translated by Ch. Rochedieu. 6th edition. Lausanne: Secrétariat de la mission suisse aux Indes. http://livres-mystiques.com/partieTEXTES/SundarSing/Parker/table.html

Pfister, Oskar. 1922. "Sundar Singh und Albert Schweizer: Zwei Missionare und Zwei Missionsprogramme." *Zeitschrift für Missionswissenschaft und Religionswissenschaft* 37: 10–25.

———. 1926. *Die Legende Sundar Singhs: Eine auf Enthüllungen Protestantischer Augenzeugen in Indien Gegründete Religionspsychologische Untersuchung.* Bern / Leipzig: Paul Haupt.

———. 1928. "Der Bankerott eines 'Apostels': Eine vorläufige Schlussabrechnung mit dem Ex-Sadhu Sundar Singh und Prof. Dr. Friedrich Heiler." *Zeitschrift Für Missionswissenschaft und Religionswissenschaft* 43: 1–15, 33–48, 129–145, 166–189.

Pidoux, Louis-Samuel. 1925. "Calvin Matsivi Mapopé: Berger de chèvres, pasteur de noirs." *Feuille d'avis de Lausanne*, 27 March 1925.

Pinch, William. 2006. *Warrior Ascetics and Indian Empires.* Cambridge: Cambridge University Press.

Powell, Avril. 2003. "'Pillar of a New Faith': Christianity in Late-Nineteenth-Century Punjab from the Perspective of a Convert from Islam." In *Christians and Missionaries in India: Cross-Cultural Communication since 1500*, edited by R. E. Frykenberg, 223–255. Grand Rapids, MI: Eerdmans.

Ragaz Leonhard. 1922. "Wie Gott zu uns kommt und wir zu ihm." *Neue Wege* 16: 233–241.

Rippmann, Ernst. 1922. "Sundar Singh's Heimkehr." In *Mitteilungen der Kanaresischen Mission KM* 4(6): 9–11.

Rusconi, Giuseppe. 2006. *Ecclesiastici ticinesi a Roma nel Settecento*. Locarno: A. Dadò.

Schaerer, Max. 1922. *Sadhu Sundar Singh: Ein Apostel Jesu Christi in Indien*. Gütersloh: C. Bertelsmann.

Schouten, Jan Peter. 2008. *Jesus as Guru: The Image of Christ among Hindus and Christians in India*. Amsterdam: Rodopi. https://doi.org/10.1163/9789401206198

Sharma, Asha. 2008. *An American in Gandhi's India*. Bloomington: Indiana University Press.

Sharpe, Eric J. 2003. *The Riddle of Sadhu Sundar Singh*. New Delhi: Intercultural Publications.

Singh, Sundar. 1922a. *Connaître le Christ dans la souffrance: Témoins de Jésus Christ. L'expérience Chrétienne*. Lausanne: Secrétariat de la Mission Suisse aux Indes.

———. 1922b. *Le Christ vivant*. Lausanne: Secrétariat de la Mission Suisse aux Indes.

———. 1922c. *Par Christ et pour Christ: Discours de Sadhu Sundar Singh*. Lausanne: Secrétariat de la Mission Suisse aux Indes. http://livres-mystiques.com/partieTEXTES/SundarSing/table.html

———. 1922d. *Repentez-vous. Perdus... puis sauvés*. Lausanne: Secrétariat de la Mission Suisse aux Indes.

———. 1926. *Visions of the Spiritual World: A Brief Description of the Spiritual Life, Its Different States of Existence, and the Destiny of Good and Evil Men as Seen in Visions*. London: Macmillan. https://ia800605.us.archive.org/4/items/VisionsOfTheSpiritualWorldBySadhuSundarSingh-1926-UploadedBy/VisionsOfTheSpiritualWorldBySadhuSundarSingh-1926.pdf

———. 1929. *With and Without Christ*. London: Harper & Brothers. http://archive.org/details/WithAndWithoutChristBySadhuSundarSingh-1929-UploadedByPeter-john

Stark, Rodney and William Sims Bainbridge. 1985. *The Future of Religion*. Berkeley: University of California Press.

Streeter, Burnett Hillman and Aiyadurai Jesudasen Appasamy. 1921. *The Sadhu: A Study in Mysticism and Practical Religion*. London: MacMillan.

Strutton, Harry J. 1927. "Notes of the Month: Christ Through Eastern Eyes." *The Occult Review* 46(4): 217–226.

"The Miracles of Sundar Singh." 1921. *Light: A Journal of Spiritual, Psychical and Mystical Research* 41(2093): 125.

Trakulhun, Sven. 2013. "Negotiating Biography in Asia and Europe." *Asiatische Studien/Etudies Asiatiques* 4: 1075–1088.

Van Berchem, Alice. 1982. *Le Sadhou Sundar Singh*. St-Légier: Emmaüs.

"Visite en Suisse du Sadhou Sundar Singh." 1922. *Mission aux Indes, Bulletin du Comité Suisse de Secours* 1(1922): 5.

Vivekananda. 1989. *The Complete Works of Swami Vivekananda*, vol. 8. Calcutta: Advaita Ashrama.

Zahir, Alfred. 1917. *A Lover of the Cross: An Account of the Wonderful Life and Work of Sunder Singh, a Wandering Christian Friar of the Punjab*. Agra.

Zimmermann, Arnold. 1930. *La mission canaraise évangélique*. Lausanne / Chêne-Paquier: Comité suisse de Secours pour la Mission aux Indes.

Acknowledgements

The research for this chapter has been conducted in the framework of a project funded by the Swiss National Fund (SNF 147342). Entitled "Travels, missions, translations: Mechanisms of encounter between India and Switzerland (1870–1970)." The project was directed by Professor M. Burger (Lausanne) and Professor A. Malinar (Zurich). I thank them and the collaborators of the project for fruitful comments and suggestions on the material presented here.

About the author

Philippe Bornet is Senior lecturer in South Asian studies at the Department of South Asian Languages and Civilizations, University of Lausanne, Switzerland. After stays in Tübingen and at the University of Chicago, he completed a PhD in the comparative history of religions on rituals of hospitality in Jewish and Indian texts. His current research deals with interactions between India and Europe and more specifically, Swiss missionaries in South India in the beginning of the twentieth century. Recent publications include *Rites et pratiques de l'hospitalité*, 2010, *Religions in Play*, 2012 (edited with M. Burger) and *L'orientalisme des marges*, 2014 (edited with S. Gorshenina).

Appendix: Letter from S. Stokes to E. Schwab

(UTC Bangalore, VPC 19, Box SSS 1)
33 Church Road, Delhi
10 Feb. 1927
To Rev. E. Schwab

Dear Mr. Schwab,

I received your letter this morning, and shall reply to the best of my ability, though I must request you to consider what I write as personal and confidential. I have definitely determined that it is not my duty to be drawn into this controversy and that were I to take part in it I should have to tell *everything* that I know. Should I do this it would result in Sundar's influence and reputation being further weakened.

My point is that S. S. would not deserve the impression that would be given to ordinary people by what I should be compelled to say. In general men fail to view such a character understandingly; either he must be a faultless superman, or he must be a liar and a hypocrite. To my mind, Sundar is neither, and it is just because people have rushed to raise him to an unnatural pedestal that they will now be ready to deny all that is wonderful and admirable in his life when they discover that he is unable to occupy it.

What has impressed me most, as I review the reaction of people both here and in the West to S.S., is their eagerness for signs and wonders—the avidity they still display for miracles. It wonderfully illustrates how little human nature changes.

To me the wonder of S.'s life lies in the thought of where it started and what it has come to include. He was only a small Sikh boy—the son of farmers in a Punjab village, with no education beyond what he could receive in an ordinary village school. Practically whatever he has now of mental and spiritual growth is, humanly speaking, an independent achievement. That which in the first place made him leave house and family, has carried him all over the world, and made him a force in the lives of many men of many lands.

To me it would have been a real miracle had he come out of the influence which surrounded his boyhood—the communal religious atmosphere of a Sikh village where the spiritual and the miraculous are inextricably blended—without looking for and expecting to find the miraculous closely associated with his awakened spiritual life. He probably looked for them and doubtless was convinced that he found them. That surely was natural to medieval experiences, and we must remember that he was not the product of mission-education but of medievalism reacting to the urge which he found in the life of Christ. We must also remember that for several years after becoming a Christian—during the earlier years of his sadhu-life, before people began to pay attention to him—he still lived and thought medievally, and grew upon his own thoughts and dreamings rather than by contact with the life and thought typical of this century.

Personally, to this period and to the long periods of solitary thinking that belonged to it I would be inclined to attribute what often appear to me the failure to distinguish the subjective from the objective—whether what he had experienced was 'in the spirit or out of the spirit' as Paul puts it. But Paul was a far maturer man and saw that the two had to be clearly distinguished.

Then there seems to me to have followed a period when S—still hardly more than a boy—suffered as a result of the universal enthusiasm and almost hysterical hero-worship of a group of people in this country, both European and Indian. It was a heavy and unfair tax upon the spiritual strength of the boy—one that might well have worked the destruction of a saint much more mature, that he has not been entirely undone commands my admiration.

During this period—of course I may be in error—it appears to me that he gave rather free rain to his imagination, and in attempting to satisfy his admirers' voracious hunger for signs and wonders, probably was consciously guilty of untruths from which he subsequently found it almost impossible to extricate himself. This might never have happened were he not the victim of others' unwisdom. It would have resulted in the complete spiritual destruction of most men; what makes me respect Sundar is that it does not seem to have so resulted in his case.

He has not, I conceive, the spiritual strength of Francis or Gandhi, who doubtless would have felt impelled to "throw ashes upon their heads" and confess their weakness to all the world, but he has continued to climb. Probably, that period is a chapter of hidden grief in his life. Possibly, knowing what the effect of such a confession would be upon many whom he has helped, he may feel that his right course is to suffer alone rather than seek their stumbling and doubtless, it is true that the many would not understand the greatness of the spiritual victory won by such a confession. My reason for thinking that he has advanced beyond this period is that I have noticed that during the last few years he has come to talk less and less of Sundar, and more and more of Sundar's Master. This is a good sign, surely.

As to your questions:

1. I personally do not remember the vision of Christ you refer to, but this does not imply that he may not have mentioned it.
2. The first time S attempted to go to Tibet. He went from Kotgarh, and returned shortly after reaching the border, telling us that he had tried to go in but that he had not got more than two or three miles when the people took him by the arms and led him back into British territory. I know that since then he has been over the border but do not know how far. A friend of mine with whom he has made the trip

up, and to whom he refers in one of the books, does not believe that he has been far over the border, or that he has had the adventures in Tibet that he speaks of—or most of them. This man has the reputation of absolute honesty, and is much at home in Tibet—all parts of it—as he is this side of the border.

3. I first met S when, shortly after he left his people, he was sent up to me by Mr. Fife of the A.P. Mission, Ludhiana, because of the disturbance that his people were making there. He stayed with me for some months, if I remember correctly, at Sabathu, at his request. I then arranged for his baptism by the Rev. Redman at Simla. Shortly after that he said that he wished to serve Christ as a sadhu. We had the "choga" made for him and he left me. I forget how many months later he came up to Kotgarh where I was spending the summer.

4. I do not remember hearing of his taking any vow not to have a house or property. Doubtless he did not contemplate having one at the time, but we must remember that he started a medieval and that his progress in subsequent years involved a growing contact with modern life and ideas. Personally I don't see why people should worry about his house, if all else be well.

S. should be permitted to evolve in his own way. The trouble has been that his admirers expect him to live as they think he should.

Sincerely yours, S.E. Stokes

— 10 —

The Chen Jianmin (1906–1987) Legacy: An "Always on the Move" Buddhist Practice

FABIENNE JAGOU

> According to his website, Chen Jianmin followed thirty-seven masters before establishing his own school, called *Adi Buddha Mandala*. Chen Jianmin's Buddhist life impressed a large range of people, from his co-disciples in the 1930s and 1940s to his today's Taiwanese and American disciples. He first lived among Tibetans in Kham province before spending 25 years in Darjeeling meditating and producing hundreds of Buddhist booklets. He created new Buddhist symbols mixing Tibetan and Chinese traditions, and finally died in the United States. His remains are kept in Taiwan. The aim of this paper is to follow the life of Chen Jianmin and to analyze the way his created Buddhist legacy is practiced and understood among his followers, Taiwanese people mainly, who founded yet another Buddhist identity revealing a mechanism of religion that is "always on the move."

Chen Jianmin's (1906-1987) spiritual achievements are myriad. Amongst other things, he studied with thirty-seven masters before establishing his own school called *Adi Buddha Mandala*; he travelled from China to Taiwan via Tibet, India, and the United States meditating, teaching and producing hundreds of Buddhist booklets; he finally created new Buddhist symbols by combining elements from Japanese, Tibetan and Chinese traditions. Nonetheless, before charting these aspects of his life any further, he needs to be understood within both historical and religious contexts. Indeed, Chen Jianmin's destiny was not an individual one. Many other Han persons took the same spiritual path turning towards Tibetan Buddhism in the 1930s and 40s to travel and teach then in Asia and in the United States, mainly from the beginning of the 1960s. Each of these individuals had a spiritual aspiration that historical circumstances helped them to accomplish. Chen Jianmin specifically learnt from Gangkar Rinpoché Karma Chökyi Senggé (Chin. Gongga qutuγtu, 1893-1957) in the 1930s-1940s, because of history and travel. Then, and that will be the second point of analysis, he contributed to the transmission of the Tibetan teaching received from Gangkar Rinpoché to Chinese disciples from 1960 onwards, mainly outside of Mainland China, but also in the United States thanks to Westerners he met in Kalimpong. However, his ways of teachings were different from the methods of Gangkar Rinpoché: creating new techniques of meditation, he also adjusted the received Tibetan teachings to the needs of his public, in accordance with his own spiritual achievement. As a matter of fact, and that will be our conclusion, the school created by Chen Jianmin represents an original synthesis whose main branch is established in Taiwan today. There, his adaptations of Tibetan esoteric Buddhism were the reason for Tibetan Buddhism to be categorized as one of the "new religious movements" (*xin xing zong jiao tuan*) in the Taiwanese religious classification system.

From the local...

Buddhist masters between Tibet and China

Surely, it would only have been a matter of time before the two Buddhist communities of the Chinese laity and the Tibetan clergy would encounter each other. This actually occurred at the suggestion of some lay Buddhists, among whom members of successive Chinese governments. They were largely warlords eager to gain power and strength from Tibetan esoteric teachings and practices, and initiated the contact during the 1920s. They looked first for Tibetan masters already on the move in China, such as the 9th Panchen Lama (1883-1937), Bai Puren (1870-1927), Dorjé Chöpa (Chin. Duojie Jueba, 1874-? and Norlha qutuγtu (Chin. Nuona Hutuketu, 1865-1936). These Tibetans were members of the first generation of Tibetan masters to offer their teachings to the Chinese civil society and they met with success in China. They all had important political men as their disciples and were actively supported by them.[1] From the Chinese side, although the Buddhist approach to Tibetan Buddhism (among others religions) was mostly a practical one, some were interested in searching for Tibetan tantric texts and attempted to collect as many of those as possible in order to revive esoteric Buddhism in China. Subsequently, this interest in Tibetan Buddhism extended to the Chinese clerical world, with some Chinese monks going to Tibet to learn directly from Tibetan masters, the most famous among them being Dayong (1893-1929), Fazun (1902-1980), and Nenghai (1886-1967). These monks not only received

---

1. For example, the 9th Panchen Lama was the master of Dai Jitao (1891-1949) a prominent figure within the KMT government, Duan Qirui (1865-1936), president of the Republic of China between 1924 and 1926. Gangkar Rinpoché was the master of Li Zongren (1891-1969) who will be the last president of the Kuomintang in China.

teachings from Tibetan masters but also learnt the Tibetan language. After they returned to China, they translated many Tibetan texts that are still in use today (Bianchi 2004, 2014; Tuttle 2005; Sullivan 2008 and 2014).

These first interactions were not connected with political history. They merely signal that Chinese Buddhists, both lay people and clerical, were interested in Tibetan Buddhism and took the opportunity to visit some prominent Tibetan masters in China to get closer to them. Subsequently, monks began to consider travelling to Tibet to learn with Tibetan masters.

Chen Jianmin's background and formative years

The history of Modern China is an "always on the move history," that is to say a time of migration for at least a part of the Chinese people and Chen Jianmin's life is a perfect example of this. At the time of Chen Jianmin's birth (1906) and during his early years, China was a theatre of turmoil and revolution. His apocryphal biography reveals that the year of his birth the plum trees bloomed twice, so that his father gave him the name of "Born from the plum tree" (Meisheng). Emphasizing again the sacred signs surrounding his birth, the same biography mentions that he was born lucky. He is the fourth boy of a family in which three previous children had died (Chen Haowang 1998, 24-27).[2] He witnessed the beginning of the new Republic in 1912 and Yuan Shi-kai's (1859-1916) monarchic regime (1915-1916). He seems to have been too young to have truly understood the significance of these events. In consequence, his early life is portrayed as happy, and he is said to have received an education from a private teacher. Once an adult, he changed his name to Chen Jianmin and became engaged with Chen Xiangyou (dates unknown) while also being involved with political life. He entered the military academy (Huangpu) opened in the Guangzhou province by Sun Yat-sen with Chiang Kai-shek (1887-1975) as its head from 1923, and became a propaganda section head during the Northern Expedition (*beifa*, 1927-1928) (Chen Haowang 1998, 55, 65). After the end of the first united front between the nationalists and the communists, his section was dissolved as too many of its members were suspected to be communists. Chen Jianmin himself was arrested but was soon released thanks to the efforts of his father, even if doubts about his political affilia-

---

2. I have chosen to work on this biography of Chen Jianmin written by Chen Haowang, Chen Jianmin nephew, because it is the first one related to Chen Jianmin in Chinese language. This author does not reference his work to the autobiography of Chen Jianmin's that may have been the introduction of the book *Buddhist Meditation, Systematic and Practical* written by B. Kantipalo and published on the website dedicated to him. I have not been able to trace the original version of this Autobiography (http://www.yogichen.org/gurulin/gc/sa0012e.html). However, the content looks the same. For an analysis of the form of this autobiography of Chen Jianmin compared to the autobiographies of Billy Graham and the 14th Dalaï Lama, see Payne 2016, 33-82.

tions remain up to today. Then, at the foundation of the Nanking government (1928), he returned to civil life. His life began to take a new turn. He became one of the secretaries of the Education Commission of the Hunan province, based in Changsha. Changsha was endowed with a huge library where Chen Jianmin spent much time reading books on Taoism and the works of Taixu (1890-1947), the Buddhist monk reformer. There he began to practice meditation. Taixu became Chen Jianmin's first master, with whom he took refuge and from whom he received the dharma name of Fajian (Chen Haowang 1998, 89). During that period, at the beginning of the 1930s, he met Tibetan masters in China, such as Norlha qutuγtu, from the Nyingma School, who transmitted to him esoteric teachings ("The Great Seal," Chin. *da shou yin*, Skt. Mahāmudrā) and the "Great Perfection" (Tib. *dzokchen*, Chin. *da yuan man*). He also participated to the building of his *stūpa* in Mount Lu in 1936 where he met Gangkar Rinpoché, Norlha qutuγtu's successor, for the first time.

Gangkar Rinpoché was well-known in China under the name of Karma Shedrup Chöki Senggé (Meinert 2009, 216). He was the fifth of the lineage of reincarnation attached to the Bo Gangkar monastery in the Tibetan province of Kham (today located in Ganzi Tibetan Autonomous Prefecture in Sichuan province) and a disciple of the 15th Karmapa Khakhyap Dorje (1871-1922), the religious leader of the Karma kagyü School before being named junior tutor of the 16th Karmapa Rangjung Rikpe Dorje (1924-1981) in 1930. He had not been to China yet. Fulfilling Norlha qutuγtu's wish to see him come to China, Gangkar went to take care of Norlha's relics and built his reliquary (Mi nyag Mgon po 2007, 60-61). At Mount Lu, he met Chen Jianmin and Chen Xunlin (dates unknown), Chen Jianmin's father-in-law, a fervent lay Buddhist who supervised the building of the reliquary (Wang Desheng 2006, 72). He finally taught Tibetan Buddhism to a Chinese audience and contributed to Chinese efforts to pacify Chinese territory by providing teaching in aid of the country (Meinert 2009, 224-225).[3] Norlha qutuγtu thus illustrated his trust in Gangkar Rinpoché, and significantly, the latter was then recognized as Norlha's heir in China. On the one hand, Norlha's Chinese disciples could continue their spiritual path, and on the other, Gangkar was allotted a Chinese audience as soon as he arrived in China. Beyond his newly acquired reputation among Chinese disciples, Gangkar also went to the Sino-Tibetan Buddhist studies Institute (*Han Zang jiaoli yuan*) opened by Taixu to transmit esoteric teachings to the Chinese laity there (Wang Desheng 2006, 81). After studies with Taixu, Chen Jianmin was first a disciple of Norlha qutuγtu. In 1937, he chose to quit his position as a Chinese professor at the Sino-Tibetan Buddhist Studies Institute

---

3. Gangkar Rinpoché was granted different titles by the KMT government: the one of "Master of the Chinese nation" (Tib. *rgyal khab kyi bla ma*) and the one of "Omniscient Master, benefactor for the propagation of Buddhism" (Tib. *bstan pa spel ba'i bshes gnyen kun mkhyen bsam gtan gyi slob dpon*).

in order to follow Gangkar Rinpoché to Kham. However, Gangkar Rinpoché forbade him to do so, emphasizing the duty to take care of one's family. Chen Jianmin found a protector who helped him go to Bo Gangkar and who would take care of his family in his absence. On his return to his monastery after his stay in China (1939), Gangkar Rinpoché founded the Minyak Mahāyāna and Vajrayāna Buddhist Studies Institute (*Muya xian mi foxueyuan*), offering an educational structure identical to the one which had been created in China and to which Chinese people were now accustomed to thanks to the efforts of Taixu who organized classes in monasteries (Wang Desheng 2006, 105). This institute welcomed more than forty Chinese and Tibetan students every year. Mahāyāna and Tantrayāna teachings were given, mostly by Tibetan teachers among which the abbot of the Dege monastery, Thubten Dendrang (Mi nyag Mgon po 2007, 46). From then on, Gangkar's reputation was made and because of this educational structure that suited Han Chinese, many Chinese lay Buddhists went there to study, with Chen Jianmin being one of them.

Then, after living with his family (he had three children) and working as a teacher in Changsha during the subsequent ten years, Chen Jianmin followed Gangkar Rinpoché to Tibet to meditate in the Bo Gangkar hermitage (Mi nyag Mgon po 2007, 60-61). He would stay six years there, receiving the highest esoteric teachings from Gangkar Rinpoché and meditating (Wang Desheng 2006, 72-115). While he was in the Tibetan mountains, the political situation in China became increasingly perilous. Soon, the Nationalists were challenged by the Communists. The Japanese invasion (from 1937 to 1945) with a non-interventionist policy adopted by the nationalist government (Kuomintang, KMT), at the head of the Republic of China from 1928 to 1949, prevented any further unification either within China or with the outer territories. Thus, the KMT government was forced to move from Nanking to Wuhan first, and later to Chongqing. Exiled in the southwest of China while the North and the South of China were occupied by the Japanese or the Communists (from 1937 to 1945), the KMT government did not succeed in regaining Mainland Chinese territories at the end of the Japanese occupation when the Republic engaged in a civil war with the Communists and were subsequently defeated. This retreat of the KMT government in the province of Sichuan from 1938 to 1949 put them in a position of a never-before-experienced proximity with the Tibetan territories. This provided the KMT government with new perspectives regarding these territories and new possibilities for lay people who followed the KMT in this retreat and who may have aspired to a spiritual life.

While he was at Bo Gangkar, Chen Jianmin met Zhang Chengji (1920-1988), another lay Chinese disciple of Gangkar Rinpoché. As Chen Jianmin, Zhang Chengji had met Gangkar Rinpoché at Mount Lu where he entered into a one-hundred days retreat at the age of 16. When he was 18, his father Zhang Dulun (1892-1958) (who would become the Chongqing mayor a few years later) helped him financially to join his master in Khams where he studied the Tibetan language and Tibetan Buddhism. He married a Tibetan woman and had two sons. At Bo Gangkar, Chen Jianmin and Zhang Chengji received teachings from Gangkar Rinpoché and when Chen Jianmin entered into retreat in the Bo Gangkar hermitage, Zhang Chengji stayed with him for one week. For Gangkar Rinpoché's disciples today, both had a real "dharma brother" link. When the People's Republic of China was founded (1949), both went on a pilgrimage to India (Chen Haowang 1998, 139). Subsequently Zhang Chengji went into exile, first in Hong Kong and then to the United States.

Despite the fact that Chen Jianmin and Zhang Chengji were at Bo Gangkar at the same time, Zhang Chengji does not quote Chen Jianmin in his writings and Wang Desheng, a Chinese biographer of Gangkar Rinpoché, does not link them at all. Instead, Wang Desheng linked Chen Jianmin to Shen Shuwen (1903–1997), later known as Elder Gongga (Gongga laoren), a lay Buddhist woman and another Gangkar Rinpoché disciple, adding that the presence of Chen Jianmin was a determining factor in her coming to Bo Gangkar (Jagou 2018 and forthcoming). According again to Wang Desheng (Wang Desheng 2006, 124), Shen Shuwen went to Bo Gangkar after learning that Chen Jianmin was conducting a spiritual retreat there but no such information is quoted in Shen Shuwen's autobiography (Jagou 2018 and forthcoming). This probably means that Chen Jianmin was already well-known for his religious achievements. After a few years of practice in Bo Gangkar, Chen Jianmin came back to his village where he found his family in total despair after the Japanese had destroyed the place. He stayed there for two years meditating in a cave outside his town (from 1944 to 1946) (Chen Haowang 1998, 129).

As a matter of fact, Chen Jianmin's Buddhist experiments were already very impressive at this early stage. His activities reveal how much they were the fruit of a Buddhist experience that began mainly at the beginning of the twentieth century, when policies to reform Buddhism were implemented, and as monasteries were taken by the government to be used as public spaces. Indeed, Taixu, for example, played an important role in the effort to preserve Buddhist monasteries for a traditional Buddhist purpose. He also reorganized the form of these monasteries as schools or institutes to avoid them being destroyed or occupied by the military. The Sino-Tibetan Buddhist Studies Institute in Chongqing was thus a pivotal place for all Chinese Buddhists eager to learn more about Tibetan Buddhism and to get first-hand knowledge of the Tibetan language. As a logical next step, Chen Jianmin went to Tibet. The master-disciple relation he established with Gangkar Rinpoché among other Tibetan masters, for want of a Chinese Buddhist connection, gave him the credentials needed to formally practice Tibetan Buddhism. In turn, this experience helped him to become acquainted with other disciples of Gangkar Rinpoché. This specific relationship between Chen Jianmin and a Tibetan master probably could not have happened apart from the political history of China, and this decision to go on a pilgrimage to India was decisive for his future. He was incentivized to act on a more global scale and to contribute to the spreading of Tibetan Buddhism everywhere in the world in multiple ways.

... to the global

The pilgrimage to Indian Buddhist sacred sites that occurred two years before the KMT government immigrated to Taiwan became a twenty-five years sojourn.[4] After touring the sacred sites, Chen Jianmin decided to stay in Kalimpong, a choice that he does not explain. Kalimpong, an Indian hill town south of Sikkim, lays close to the southern tip of the Tibetan Chumbi valley and was a strategic place for all sorts of exchanges. As Andrew Duff noted in his study about the kingdom of Sikkim's modern history: "Located on a trading crossroads between Tibet, Bengal, Sikkim, Bhutan and even Nepal (trade was conducted through the Jelep pass into the Chumbi Valley), Kalimpong had housed a vibrant trading community over many centuries, with thousands of semi-resident Tibetan muleteers" (Duff 2015, 61). These crowded surroundings did not prevent Chen Jianmin living "as a hermit in a small bungalow at the bottom end of the lower bazaar, to never go outside his front door, and rarely receive visitors" (Sangharakshita 2011, 289).

The only reason that looks acceptable for Chen Jianmin to settle in this populous town while he was accustomed to practice retreats in caves or in hermitages was the presence of a large number of Tibetans, including reincarnated masters among them. Indeed, the Tibetans used to send their children to study at the English School of Kalimpong as early as the beginning of the 1940s. Moreover, Tibetans converged to Kalimpong as it was at the confluence of trade roads. At some point, the 14th Dalaï Lama (born in 1935) also went there and stayed for a month in 1956. Tibetan masters and monk refugees came in even greater numbers after the exile of the 14th Dalai Lama to India in 1959. Eventually, Chen Jianmin would meet accomplished Tibetan masters such as Dudjom Rinpoche Jikdrel Yéshé Dorjé (1904–1987) and Dilgo Khyentsé Rinpoche Gyurmé Tekchok Tenpé Gyeltsen (1910–1991) from the Nyingma School, or Kalu Rinpoche aka Kyabjé Dorjé chang (1905–1989) from the Kagyü School, and received teachings from both of them. This sojourn in Kalimpong and the contact with Tibetan masters from various schools of Tibetan Buddhism would allow him to say that "he received teachings from thirty-seven masters from the seven schools of Tibetan Buddhism," thus affirming an ecumenism on the basis of which he created his own school, the *Adi Buddha Mandala*.

---

4. As Zhang Chengji went back to China, Chen Jianmin decided to stay there helped by generous donators, such as Mr Khoo Poh Kong of Malaysia, and supported by the Overseas Chinese Indian Office (*Zhu Yin huaqiao*).

Duff adds that "by the mid-1950s, Kalimpong had ... started to attract an extraordinary assortment of characters." (Duff 2015, 62) Individuals we may term as "hippies" arrived with Chen Jianmin: for example, he wrote poems dedicated to them and met Allen Ginsberg.[5] More importantly for his fame abroad, Western monks converted to Buddhism also came to study there. In particular, two monks decided to transcribe Chen Jianmin's spiritual biography and teachings in English: the British Bikkhu Khantipalo (born in 1932) and Sangharakshita (born in 1925) (Khantipalo 2002; Sangharakshita 2011).[6] While Sangharakshita himself stayed fourteen years in Kalimpong, Khantipalo only remained a few months in 1962. It was during this time that they used to meet and interview Chen Jianmin in his hermitage called the "Five Leguminous Tree Hermitage." Khantipalo (2002, 141) describes the place as composed of two small rooms:

> the larger room — whose walls were covered with thangkas and contained many shrines overflowing with offerings—was where he practiced, while the smaller, rather dingy one, can be glimpsed through its window bars.

At that time, Chen Jianmin looked like:

> a short, plump, round-faced man in his middle or late fifties, the yogi had an ebullient manner not usually associated with a hermit, least of all one who spent the greater part of each day engaged in various forms of meditation. Nor was he without his eccentricities. Sometimes he wore the traditional dress of a Chinese scholar, complete with black skullcap, sometimes an anorak and baseball cap. (Sangharakshita 2011, 289)[7]

He was:

> of a short and stocky build and when I met him was perhaps in his forties [1962]. Even if he was older he gave the impression of vigour and good health. His face was generally cheerful, often adorned with a wide smile, but it could also manifest grief at others' sufferings. (Khantipalo 2002, 141)

Sangharakshita (2001, 289) added that

> despite his eccentricities, he possessed a thorough knowledge of the Buddhist scriptures (he had twice read through the entire Chinese Tripitaka), a comprehensive grasp of Buddhist doctrine, and a rich and varied inner life which included in its gamut not only insights and ecstasies of

---

5. Chen Jianmin translated poems written by Hanshan (hermit and poet whose existence is doubtful) as he thought they were suitable for hippies, see http://www.yogichen.org/cw/cw30/bk049.html
6. Both would later come back to the West and open new Buddhist schools.
7. It is from that time in Kalimpong that Chen Jianmin became to be known as Yogi Chen, probably because of the long time he spent there meditating.

a more spiritual nature but also strange psychic experiences. Over the years I must have asked him hundreds of questions about the Vajrayana, about Chan, and about Chinese Buddhism in general; and many were the times he had clarified a philosophical doctrine, or explained a meditation practice, in a way no one else had been able to do. For this reason I had come to regard Yogi Chen as one of my teachers.

Khantipalo (2002, 141) shared this opinion on Yogi Chen:

> When he spoke Dharma it was with a tranquil but occasionally forceful seriousness. His sincerity, born of deep practice, did not preclude a certain impishness which could only be called eccentricity if one did not know him well. He was kind and generous to others but very content with his simple lifestyle as a hermit. He was immensely learned, as well as being a Dharma practitioner, and was accessible because his "hermitage" was situated in the middle of Kalimpong and also because he spoke English in an understandable if peculiar manner. He was known locally, in fact, as an amiable eccentric, but also respected for his obvious devotion to practice.

This respect led Sangharakshita to interview and transcribe Chen Jianmin's teachings with the active participation of Khantipalo. The book would finally be entitled *Buddhist Meditation, Systematic and Practical* and first published in Malaysia in 1966. In the introduction of the book in English, Khantipalo (2002, Introduction, 142) describes the following process of which the book is the result:

> In this book, the words of our Buddhist yogi, C.M. Chen, have first been noted down and particular care taken to preserve something of his original expressions and peculiar style. So that nothing is missed, two persons have met him every week, one listened, that is Ven. Sangharaksita, and another recorded, Rev. B. Kantipalo. The next day, the subject still being fresh in the mind, these notes were converted into a rough draft which then was given to the Ven. Sthavira, and another recorded, that is the writer. After revising as he suggested they were typed and then taken along to the next meeting with Mr Chen. He read the text carefully adding or deleting material where necessary, resulting a final manuscript which is certainly well-checked and we hope, an accurate presentation of the Buddha teachings and Mr Chen practical experience of these.

This text compiled the teachings of Chen Jianmin on the fundaments of Buddhism. It is divided into sixteen chapters:

I. Reasons for Western interest in the practice of meditation
II. What is the real and ultimate purpose of practicing Buddhist meditation?
III. The exact definition of some Buddhist terms concerning meditation
IV. Should meditation be practiced directly without preparations?

V. What is the relation of different Buddhist principles and how do they center upon meditation?
VI. Why emphasize the whole systems of meditation in the three-yanas-in-one?[8]
VII. Samatha[9] must be practiced to obtain the result of Samapati[10]
VIII. The Five fundamental meditations to cure the five poisons[11]
IX. The Four foundations of mindfulness: a good bridge to Mahayana meditation[12]
X. Part one: All the Mahayana meditation are sublimated by sunyata[13]
XI. Part two: Supplementary details of the sunyata meditations
XII. Meditations of the Chinese Mahayana schools
XIII. Meditation in the lower three tantras of the Eastern Vajrayana tradition
XIV. Part one: Meditation in Anuttarayoga tantra found only in the Western Vajrayana tradition[14]
XV. Part two: Meditations of the third and fourth initiations of Anuttarayoga
XVI. The highest meditation in the tantra-mahamudra and the great perfection
XVII. Is Chan a meditation?
XVIII. How to recognize and treat all sorts of meditation troubles and how to know false realizations

Appendices: Questions and answers (Khantipalo 2002, 143-148).[15]

Aimed at beginners, the book contains much for experienced practitioners in Buddhism as well. It gives advice on meditation while paying a special attention to various methods and schools. In addition, some parts are clearly designed for a Western audience. The book met with success and inscribed Chen Jianmin's legacy in the West. He was soon invited to the University of Berkeley, California where he gave lectures and taught to a Western audience. According to his biographer (Chen Haowang 2001, 157), outside of this public life, he preferred to stay alone and to meditate. He would stay twenty-five years in the United States giving Buddhist teachings there, or occasion-

---

8. Here the *three-yanas-in-one* refer to the three Buddhist vehicles (Hinayāna, Mahāyāna and Tantrayāna) and to the wish of Chen Jianmin to convert these three Buddhist vehicles into a single one.
9. Meditation on a single point practiced by every Buddhist school.
10. The correct acquisition of truth.
11. The five poisons are: ignorance, desire, anger, pride, and jealousy.
12. The four foundations of mindfulness are: mindfulness of body, of feelings, of consciousness, and *dhammās*.
13. *Śūnyatā* could be translated as *emptiness*.
14. According to the new Tibetan schools (Kadam, Kagyü, Sakya and Géluk), the *Anuttarayoga tantra* belongs to the superior class of tantra.
15. See the following page: http://www.yogichen.org/cw/cw35/bmlist.html

ally returning to Asia for brief spells. Soon, the first edition of his work was out of print and a reprint edition was produced in the United States ten years later and distributed for free. Two appendices were added: "How to transform the human body into the Buddha body" and "how to transmute the human consciousness into the Buddha's wisdom." This latter edition definitely attracted the attention of religious studies scholars working under the umbrella of the Institute for Advanced Studies of World Religions in New York, who decided to standardize the Sanskrit transliterations and to clarify some passages with Chen Jianmin directly.[16] The revised edition was published in 1980 and reprinted in 1989. At the same time, disciples of Chen Jianmin, notably Lin Yutang (dates unknown), his main disciple in the United States and successor, worked on a Chinese version of the book that would be published under the title *Fundamentals of Chan Buddhism* (*Fojiao chan ding*) in Taiwan in 1980.[17] Chen Jianmin himself remained active. He decided to write short books on Buddhism which people could carry in the pocket with a first publication of that kind entitled *A Talk on Preaching* (*Tan fo fa zhi hong hua*) (Figure 10.1). It is difficult to obtain an accurate idea about the number of volumes published. According to a biography written by Lin Yutang, Chen Jianmin's works (without letting the reader know what kind of works he is talking about) include 48 volumes, 154 booklets in English and 17 in Chinese. Later in the biography, he mentions that over 50 books have been published in English or in Chinese without specifying the nature of these books (http://www.yogichen.org/gurulin/efiles/mb/mbk02.html).

Figure 10.1 Chen Jianmin, from Chen 1998.

---

16. The team headed by Dr. Christopher S. George was composed of Vicki Brown who went to Berkeley, California, where she worked with Chen Jianmin for over eight months revising the text. The 1980 edition is the result of the joint effort made by the members of the team which included Teresa Szu, Alice Romanelli Hower, Larry Hower, Vasiliki Sarantakos and Janet Gyatso.

17. The full Chinese version of the text is readable on http://www.yogichen.org/cw/cw46/CW46.pdf

Apparently, considering the texts available on the website dedicated to Chen Jianmin, his work has been compiled in Chinese under the title *Collected Works of Chen Jianmin* (*Qu gong ji quanji*) but in this compilation, only 100 booklets in English are to be found (and not 154). The confusion is complete when later published works refer to a specific volume of the *Qu gong ji quanji* under a classificatory scheme that does not exist in the works of Chen Jianmin.[18] As a matter of fact, Chen Jianmin was a prolific writer whose works range from Buddhist teachings to Buddhist history through poetry and daily life teachings. He had an equally eclectic practice: he used to perform public rituals such as the fire offerings (Tib. *homa*) almost every day; he frequently meditated in cemeteries and practiced the "transference of conscience" (Chin. *kaiding*, Tib. *'pho ba*) in order to purify wandering souls. He moreover regularly freed animals (*fang sheng*) and is well-known too for his practice of *karmamudrā*, a vajrayāna Buddhist technique of sexual practice with a physical or visualized consort.[19]

His writing and his decision to move to the United States contributed greatly to his fame. He subsequently taught in the United States, Canada, Malaysia, Philippines, Hong Kong and Taiwan. His achievements are there for all to see with the foundation of communities of disciples, the building of monasteries and various books, all of which testify of his spiritual achievement. However, the ways he taught Buddhism or the way he conducted his spiritual life gave birth to new forms of teachings that his disciples-heirs still practice today. Under the influence of Chen Jianmin's adaptation of Tibetan Buddhism, some Taiwanese Tibetan Buddhism centres were classified as "new religious movements" (*xin xing zong jiao tuan*) in official terminology, meaning that the ways these centres taught Tibetan Buddhism in Taiwan look like alternative teachings rather than Tibetan Buddhism. This phenomenon is even more obvious today.

... to the local again

Much more delicate is the fate of the second generation of disciples following Chen Jianmin's death. It appears that if the masters who were disciples of Gangkar Rinpoché were eager to prove their legitimacy as his heirs travelling and going abroad to teach Buddhist philosophy, or Buddhist teachings, their own disciples were much more local. Keeping Chen Jianmin's life in mind, we should recall the fact that he was a lay person and lived in a hut in Kalimpong, but this did not prevent him to have his own disciples. Today, his

---

18. For example, a 1992 publication entitled "Shiye shouyin jiaoshou juewei" referred to this text as it had been already published in the *Qu gong ji quanji* as the 11th volume (*ce*) while this teaching on *karmamudrā* is in the 10th volume.

19. This said 11th volume had a specific edition in Taiwan entitled *Shiye shou yin jiao shou juewei* (Yuan ming chu ban: Hong tai tu shu zong jing xiao, 1992), see also http://www.yogichen.org/cw/cw11/cw11_102015.pdf. About Chen Jianmin practice and teaching of this tantra, see Khantipalo (2002, 145).

The Chen Jianmin (1906–1987) Legacy

legacy is claimed in the United States and in Taiwan by Lin Yutang, his main disciple, as proclaimed on the website dedicated to Chen Jianmin he created. Lin Yutang met him in the United States and introduced himself as his successor in Taiwan. He got a PhD in Logic and the Methodology of Science from the University of California, Berkeley (1983).[20] He contributed to the foundation of a Buddhist centre called *Adi Buddha Mandala* (*fo jiao yujia shi*) in California which became the headquarters of Chen Jianmin's new order. In Taiwan, people do not mention him or only whisper his name as some scandals seem to have occurred a few years ago. Some of the more controversial elements of his personal practices, notably the *karmamudrā*, seem to have been at the origin of the public scandal.

Another of Chen Jianmin's disciples, Hsu Chin-ting (Chin. pinyin Xu Qinting), a dynamic old man over 80, is also very active in Taiwan. He holds a doctorate in Chinese philosophy and is recognized as being well-versed in the Yijing philosophy and practice. He taught at the university and is a recognized professor.

When Chen Jianmin died and his corpse was cremated in the United States, his skull remained intact and many pearl relics emanated from the ashes. The relics were divided between Lin Yutang (who kept the skull) and Hsu Chin-ting who left some of them in a *stūpa* built in a cemetery in the North of Taipei, as a reminder of Chen Jianmin's practice of meditating in a cemetery during his lifetime. Close to this *stūpa* is another one: this is a creation of Chen Jianmin and is shaped as an object of meditation.

This *stūpa*, whose building was finished in 1983, is the "trademark" of Chen Jianmin in the Chinese cultural area (Figure 10.2): as soon as one sees it, one knows that the place is connected with him although a *stūpa* with such a specific form is known as a commemorative monument in Japan, notably by the esoteric schools such as Shingon. Chen Jianmin's disciples call it *The Five Elements Stūpa to Protect the Country under a Benevolent King* (*Ren wang huguo wu lun ta*) alluding to the apocryphal Buddhist scripture entitled *The Humane King Sutra* (*Ren wang huguo Boreluomi duo jing*) and was built to protect the country. This sutra, first translated into Chinese during the Tang dynasty (618–907), is dedicated to the protection of human beings, but also of the lands and countries, and was written as a guide for the authorities. The *stūpa* combines the Chinese five elements (water, air, fire, wood, and earth) and the Tibetan four great elements (the five Chinese elements without the wood), the symbol of the universe, the moon and the sun, and an esoteric teaching (the *Sarvatathāgata-adhiṣṭhānahṛdayaguhyadhātukaraṇḍamudrādhāraṇī*).[21] Characters derived from

---

20. About Lin Yutang, see http://www.yogichen.org/gurulin/elist/glin_e.html
21. Taisho 1022A, 19: 712a–b. I thank my colleague, Kuo Li-ying for giving me this information.

Figure 10.2 Chien Jianmin's *Five Elements Stūpa*, Taipei, photograph of F. Jagou.

Siddham script engraved on the *stūpa* specify these elements. For Chen Jianmin's disciples (even if they do not give much explanation), the monument is dedicated to the three following religions: Confucianism, Taoism and Buddhism and symbolizes the three corpses of the Buddha (Hsu Chin-ting 1988, 10) too. The *stūpa* and its bronze bell—both objects that seem to have been ordered by Chen Jianmin and considered as precious donations for the monastery—are supposed to act for the protection of the country, mostly against natural disasters. And indeed, it demonstrated its efficiency when several typhoons that were initially headed towards Taiwan ended up taking another course (Hsu Chin-ting 1988, 21). As we noted, the *stūpa* is not his reliquary but it holds relics from the Karmapa inside. Most interesting is that this *stūpa* is duplicated in multiple supports, such as paper, painting, sculpture as if Chen Jianmin really reinvented it from the Japanese model and his disciples today really made it his trademark.

The Chen Jianmin (1906–1987) Legacy

A small temple has been built in the vicinity of this *stūpa*, still within the cemetery, with a beautiful view from the mountain over Taipei city.[22] This place resembles to a small hall where people meet to receive teachings from Hsu Chin-ting and explanations from his main disciple, Lin Ziyang. Hsu Chin-ting also taught the "Great Perfection" doctrine, the one he is said to have received from Chen Jianmin and in whose lineage he inscribed himself when beginning his transmission. Every listener has the same book in his or her hands, which has been compiled by Hsu Chin-ting himself who taught from it. His disciples continue to read from the book without much master assistance. His younger disciples contributed to locate this teaching within contemporary ways of life, often adding humour: this helps to apply *dzokchen*, but also Buddhism, to everyday life, with disciples and students alike often escaping to the local Taiwanese language when the narratives become too funny.

Today four generations of the lineage remain extant:

- Gangkar Rinpoché (the master),
- Chen Jianmin (the disciple of Gangkar Rinpoché),
- Hsu Chin-ting (the disciple of Chen Jianmin),
- Lin Ziyang, the main disciple of Hsu Chin-ting, who is part of today's practitioners with nobody designated as the future heir yet. None of them took monastic vows: they are all lay people.

Despite this lineage extended over four generations, it seems obvious that a new Buddhist school with its own symbols in use has been created not from the legacy of Gangkar Rinpoché but from that of Chen Jianmin, who is officially recognized as the master and the founder of the new school.

In fact, from various spiritual experiences shared with a Tibetan master (Gangkar Rinpoché) of the Karma Kagyü School in Tibet, new schools emerged all over the world that do not deny their first Tibetan link but on the contrary gain their legitimacy from it. Then, why did Chen Jianmin become himself leader of a new school that identifies itself with Tibetan Buddhism, but not only? The Taiwanese religious context and the way Chinese people practice their religion are very important factors. In Taiwan, despite the establishment of martial law between 1949 and 1987, religion continued to exist and was practiced. Secret societies flourished and still exist today. Taiwanese people succeeded in circumventing state control over religion by founding associations or community groups. For example, the Chinese Buddhist lay Society was created and recognized by the KMT government. As such it could conduct religious activities addressed to lay people. For instance, a room organized as a Tibetan Temple main hall was established and dedicated to the transmission of Tibetan teachings by Tibetan masters in the Chinese Buddhist lay Society office.

---

22. Two names are given for this small monastery: *Puxian wang rulai tancheng* and *Renwang huguo youming si*.

Another example is the creation of an association dedicated to the Tibetan Karma Kagyü School in Tainan that allowed Tibetan masters from this specific School to be invited to Taiwan at the beginning of the 1980s, well before the end of martial law. Moreover, the *Five Elements Stūpa* was built in 1983, again before the lifting of martial law and the establishment of freedom of religion. It was then possible to organize religious activities under a collective name registered and recognized by the government and not under a merely personal endorsement.

After the lifting of martial law (1987), religions and religious movements flourished in Taiwan. Tibetan Buddhism was one among them. Older generations of Taiwanese had been familiarized with Japanese esoteric Buddhism, present on the island from 1905 to 1945 when Taiwan became a Japanese colony. The departure of Japanese Buddhist masters with their compatriots at the end of World War II left a gap that had not been filled yet despite of the arrival of Chinese Buddhist monks from Mainland China and Tibetan esoteric Buddhism offered an opportunity to do so. Moreover, Taiwanese people received favourably esoteric practices and, according to Zheng Zhiming (2011, 198), saw the Tibetan deities as intermediaries that could provide a swift help with practical vows. According to Jiang Canteng (2012, 165-166), Taiwanese people are also fond of retreats and thus very appreciative of people who conduct them. Having spent more than twenty-five years of his life meditating, Chen Jianmin could have been seen as an example. Although it seems obvious that if the parents of a Taiwanese family practice a specific religion, their children will follow the same tradition, Taiwanese people practice a "spiritual nomadism" (*you zong*). They can be affiliated with many religions without having any need to question such a multiple affiliation. They are simply attempting to improve their life in practical and pragmatic ways. People can then very well attend a Tibetan tantric initiation in high numbers without being systematically members of the community. Moreover, I observe that many of these Tibetan Buddhist centres lost their Tibetan characteristics in a way: some had Tibetan masters coming to perform rituals or esoteric initiations, but the Chinese practitioners do not understand the meaning of these rituals or of these initiations. Very few of them practice the teachings they have received, with the language of communication being a real obstacle: how could they practice an initiation if they cannot communicate with the master who would guide them during their retreat?

Most disciples from Gangkar Rinpoché's first generation were fluent in Tibetan or at least were said to understand it. This skill has been lost. As such, the transmission is limited. The third and fourth generations of disciples do not speak Tibetan and teach exclusively in Chinese and Taiwanese. Actually, as in Western countries, the transmission of Tibetan teachings tends to be oversimplified and located within the context of everyday life instead of a spiritual realm. Indeed, although Chinese devotees are impatient to receive Tibetan tantric initiations, the masters devote most of their time to teaching general Mahāyāna ideas and explaining the benefits of adopting good behaviour in everyday life for the present and future lives of everyone. Still, the "Tibetan" label remains very important, especially when the ideas of death and rebirth are at stake. As such, initiations involving the transference of consciousness ('pho ba) are followed by numbers of Han people.

From the first generation of a Tibetan master's Chinese disciples to the present generation of Han disciples, many changes have occurred. The legacy of the Tibetan master tends to be set aside to favour a more general understanding amongst lay groups. These changes have given birth to a hybrid Sino-Tibetan Buddhism, at the origins of new schools which emerged from Tibetan Buddhism but practice according to their own ways and adapt to their audience. These schools are however recognized as teaching and practicing Tibetan Buddhism by the Taiwanese and are considered as being part of the "New religious movements." Then, we are left with somewhat of a paradox in that these schools are identified as belonging to an institutional and traditional religion but regarded as new religious groups.

Acknowledgments

For the Tibetan transcriptions, the phoneticization system developed for the Tibetan and Himalayan Library by David Germano and Nicolas Tournadre has been used. For Chinese transcriptions, the Pinyin system has been chosen.

References

Bianchi, Ester. 2004. "The Tantric Rebirth Movement in Modern China: Esoteric Buddhism Re-vivified by the Japanese and Tibetan Traditions." *Acta Orientalia Academiae Scientiarum Hung* 57(1): 31–54. https://doi.org/10.1556/AOrient.57.2004.1.3

Bianchi, Ester. 2014. "A Religion-Oriented 'Tibet Fever'. Tibetan Buddhist Practices among the Han Chinese in Contemporary PRC." In *From Mediterranean to Himalaya. A Festschrift to Commemorate the 120th Birthday of the Italian Tibetologist Giuseppe Tucci*, edited by Dramdul and F. Sferra, 347–374. Beijing: China Tibetology Publishing House.

Chen, Haowang. 1998. *Chen Jianmin - hanjian de xiandai ku xing seng* (Chen Jianmin: A contemporary extraordinary ascetic). Xindian: Shuixing wenhua.

Duff, Andrew. 2015. *Sikkim: Requiem for a Himalayan Kingdom*. Edinburgh: Birlin.

Hsu, Chin-ting. 1988. *Forever in Our Hearts: A Memorial to Guru C.M. Chen*. Chung-li: International Buddhist Association.

Jagou, Fabienne. 2018. "Tibetan Relics in Taiwan: A Link between Past, Present, and Future." In *The Hybridity of Buddhism: Contemporary Encounters between*

Tibetan and Chinese Traditions in Taiwan and the Mainland, edited by F. Jagou, 67–90. Paris: École française d'Extrême-Orient.

———. forthcoming. *Gongga Laoren (1903-1997): Her Role in the Spread of Tibetan Buddhism in Taiwan*. Leiden: Brill.

Jiang, Canteng. 2012. *Renshi Taiwan bentu fojiao. Jieyan yilai de zhuanxing yu duo yuan xin mao* (About the local Taiwanese Buddhism. Changes and new forms since the lifting of martial law). Taiwan shangwu: Taipei.

Khantipalo, Laurence. 2002. *Noble Friendship: Travels of a Buddhist Monk*. Cambridge: Windhorse Publications.

Meinert, Carmen. 2009. "Gangkar Rinpoché between Tibet and China: A Tibetan Lama among Ethnic Chinese in the 1930s to 1950s." In *Buddhism between Tibet and China*, edited by M. Kapstein, 215–240. Boston, MA: Wisdom Publications.

Mi nyag Mgon po. 1997. *'Bo Gangkar sprul sku'i rnam thar dad pa'i pad dkar bzhugs so* (Biography of 'Bo Gangs dkar Tulku: The white lotus of faith). Beijing: Mi rigs dpe skrun khang.

Payne, Richard K. 2016. "Self-Representation and Cultural Expectations: Yogi Chen and Religious Practices of Life-Writing." *Entangled Religions* 3: 33–82. https://doi.org/10.46586/er.v3.2016.33-82

Sangharakshita, Urgyen. 2011 (2nd edition). *Moving Against the Stream: The Birth of a New Buddhist Movement*. https://www.sangharakshita.org/_books/against-stream.pdf

Sullivan, Brenton. 2008. "Venerable Fazun at the Sino-Tibetan Buddhist Studies Institute (1932–1950) and Tibetan Geluk Buddhism in China." *Indian International Journal of Buddhist Studies* 9: 199–241.

Sullivan, Brenton. 2014. "Blood and Teardrops: The Life and Travels of Venerable Fazun (1901-1980)." In *Buddhists: Understanding Buddhism Through the Lives of Practitioners*, edited by T. Lewis, 296–304, Malden, MA: Wiley-Blackwell.

Tuttle, Gray. 2005. *Tibetan Buddhists in the Making of Modern China*. New York: Columbia University Press.

Wang Desheng. 2006. *The Reincarnated Master Gangkar (Gongga huofo)*. Kunming: Yunnan minzu chubanshe.

Zheng, Zhiming. 2011. *Taiwan zongjiao de fazhan yu bianqian* (Development and changes of the Taiwanese religions). Wenjin: Taibei.

About the author

Fabienne Jagou (Habilitation Paris, École Pratique des Hautes Études, PhD Paris, École des Hautes Etudes en Sciences Sociales) is senior associate professor at the École française d'Extrême-Orient. She teaches at the École Normale Supérieure in Lyon and at the Lyon Institute of Political Studies. She is the author of *Le 9e Panchen Lama (1883-1937): Enjeu des relations sino-tibétaines* (EFEO, 2004), published in English under the title *The Ninth Panchen Lama (1883-1937): A Life at the Crossroads of Sino-Tibetan Relations* (Silkworm/EFEO, 2011). She is also the editor of *The Hybridity of Buddhism: Contemporary Encounters between Tibetan and Chinese Traditions in Taiwan and the Mainland* (EFEO "Études thématiques n°29," 2018). Her forthcoming book is entitled *Gongga Laoren (1883-1937): Her Role in the Spread of Tibetan Buddhism in Taiwan* (Brill, Series Studies on East Asian Religions).

PART IV

In Summary

Afterword

Maya Burger

The truest cosmopolitanism goes with the intensest local colour, for otherwise you contribute nothing to the human treasury and make mankind a featureless monotony.

(Rabindranath Tagore)

An afterword is a suitable moment to reflect on the achievements of the book it is supposed to end, at least physically. It is an occasion to relate to the ideas, strands and perspectives the book contains and to see how they may nurture curiosity and stimulate the imagination to enrich further debates. It is also an invitation to travel in the stories of connections studied in it and go beyond them by asking new questions to stir new thoughts. The present volume reveals intriguing destinies, of travellers, thinkers, religionists who, in one way or another, are part of a history of religions in the late nineteenth and twentieth century in Asia and Europe. We are invited to take part in their various itineraries and follow their intricate pathways as they interact, as individual actors, with various aspects of religions. The stories in the book stage actors who utilize religious frameworks or reconfigure them as religious entrepreneurs. The documentation of the variety of religious, entrepreneurial activities and debates is, in many ways, the strength of the book. However, the breathtaking multiplicity of the fields investigated invites scholars to ask how we are to understand their selection together in an edited volume: what do these stories have in common? To put it in other words, what are we to learn for the *study of religions* from these multiple case studies of entangled histories between Asia and Europe? And how are we to envisage the passage from micro-stories to global debates or large-scale phenomena? What happens to religions in the processes of exchange and translation, and how are we to reflect on it?

Looking back: Impressions from the book

If the history of religions is full of stories of cultural transfers that have unfolded over centuries, this volume gives a privileged attention to this topic by carefully observing what chosen actors do in designing for themselves alternative ways of "being religious" or in dealing with religions as strategic artefacts. We become witnesses to a great diversity of unexpected and fresh connections, which trigger new knowledge on what all "religion" can be.

If contemporary theories and critical approaches have pointed out, in the modern period, phenomena like fluidity, exchange, circulation, transnational flow, hybridity, or the global, the study of individuals who are circulating somewhere in this net of connections, writing their own personal narrative, has received comparatively little attention. These singularized, particular figures are central vectors, however, to grasp the mechanics, strategies and forms of the processes of encounters in constant circulation between Asia and Europe. To follow their tracks and precise stories adds details to the descriptions of global movements and theorizing, rendering the general picture more complicated, more complex also.

The book also represents a step towards acknowledging the importance of minor figures and their impact on global processes, even if such an impact cannot be measured rigorously but only suggested through their stories, their lives, through emerging questions and problems, or more so through their strategies to deal with their life. Thus, a crucial aspect of the history of religions working with individual stories consists in reflecting on ways and strategies that turn out to be more than individual, but frequent enough to constitute trends and patterns that incite us to embark on theorizing attempts. Paying close attention to individual agencies avoids the stiffness and rigidity (or supposed unity) of a term such as Hinduism (for instance) and may bring us closer to the immense diversity that characterizes South Asia, especially in the realm of "religions."

Further, the South Asian context illustrates the need to tread new paths. In the field of Indian studies, many critical contributions have taught us the amount of misunderstandings that still exist, revealing the volume of unreflective and insufficiently researched studies that have been produced in, about and towards South Asia. Many and very deeply misleading ideas, if not blunt errors, about the Indian social and religious background exist and even if one can understand the reasons behind their genesis, they leave us with many problems.

Especially in the field of the study of religions, the paradigm of world religions has worked as a master narrative, leading to doubtful apprehensions of the South Asian context and of the relations between Europe and South Asia. Despite critical voices that have pointed the problems of this paradigm since over a few decades now, it continues to be used, as if precautions and criticisms had never been voiced. We may employ quotation marks to indicate that something is contestable, but how many studies continue to offer comparative surveys of transversal subjects, such as space, women, authority, etc. in the

Afterword

so-called world religions? With the approach privileged in this book under the label of "connected religion" we become even more aware of the limits lurking in categories such as those of world religions. This is not to say that encompassing categories such as Hinduism, Buddhism, etc. do not have their role and reason, especially for theology, but a bottom-top approach through the dynamics of exchange is helpful for redirecting our focus and shuffle frozen perspectives. When we look at religions from the angle of connected histories and pay attention to individuals, the knowledge gained turns out to be somehow more provocative and critical. This is especially important when working in domains such as Asia, where large areas escape our knowledge.

What, then, is this promising "connected history" approach?

First of all, we have to distinguish between connected history and the history of connections. A starting point is to establish a connection between events. Once this has occurred, it is possible to develop a "connected history" framework, by bringing sources that document these events together. Kant was translated into Bengali in the nineteenth century, and when we study how Bengali authors read and pondered about his philosophy, we are in the realm of connected history which in turn entails the potential of critical examination. We may, for instance, compare how Swami Vivekananda interprets Kant with how William James does it.

Sanjay Subrahmanyam explored the connected history approach in the pre-modern period. He thought it would be also applicable to modern times in terms of transnational histories. Studying religions not in their dogmatic confinement only, but under the angle of their dynamic processes of encounter, means we can also go back and forth between centuries to compare in a most fruitful and interesting way how these processes unfold, change or adapt in given cultural, social and political contexts. An important heuristic level is reached when connections are re-established where they have been disconnected for various reasons (this point is developed below).

From the point of view of the study of the sources, a more balanced history, what R. Bertrand called a symmetric history, is required by studying various and complementary sources. On the one hand, local sources related to encounters are studied along those of, for instance, invaders and colonizers. On the other side, local historical interpretations (with their own perspectives) are studied together with "western" approaches.

A different and crucial contribution of the book consists in its wide scope of archival investigation. The connected history approach engages the reader to delve into various specific (and not general) domains and to confront various contexts at the same time. This is a promising effort, contributing to opening horizons and viewing stories from different angles. If for some this may sound self-evident, there are too many examples revealing a lack of decentred investigation. Comparing cross-cultural encounters viewed from different angles is an invitation to develop a more nuanced understanding about the so-called "others," and this in a pragmatic and exemplary way. It invites us to taste and enjoy different cultures and, to quote J. Ganeri reflecting on the immersive cosmopolitanism of K. Bhattacharyya, intercultural encounters act as a sort of "cognitive nutrition, the route to a balanced intellectual diet and health of mind, a precondition of any truth-directed inquiry" (Ganeri 2017, 7). It is an enlargement that may be viewed as the condition for developing fresh ideas. If translations are the reason for the survival of good texts (Walter Benjamin), the encounter of *differences* works as an antidote to intellectual stagnation. However, this book does not deal with encounter in general, but with newly studied connections, which induce the reader to rethink evidence.

The various examples presented in this book read not only as good stories but also as forgotten histories. These life stories present a very human face of what is at stake for those who have recourse to religion to arrange their existence. It is certainly a counter-approach to the more theological and dogmatic approach of religion by focusing on those who do "something" with what we are used to calling religion. Even if these cases are unique, they are not isolated and constitute the living context of problems, attitudes and actions that can recur in different places and times. Their in-depth study can lead towards a better understanding of global issues. It is a prerequisite for a connected history approach that one needs to be well informed about local customs and cultures to play skilfully with the possibilities. In this respect, we may want to include, whenever possible, anthropological investigations. Contrasting strategies and understanding the reasons for success or failure show how within a few miles and a few years possibilities can evolve. It is a kind of reclaiming agency for those who make history.

A few key points

The rich examples of "connected religion" share a concern to present detailed archival and historical investigations to bring out connections hitherto neglected or unknown. The book certainly gains its "raison d'être" with the introduction provided by Bornet where the micro-stories are thought of with the ambition to rethink global moves as well as exploring the meaning of a connected history approach for the study of religions.

In the introduction (this volume, p. 3), it is suggested to reconsider the classical issue of comparison in the study of religions from under a new light. The evaluation of the comparative endeavors is sound and we may requote here Gruzinski's critical point which is particularly appealing in the effort to give priority to historical analysis.[1]

---

1. I do not find it redundant to give some quotes here again, since they are important and deserve attention.

Afterword

> Comparative history appeared for a long time as a workable solution and it was at the origins of fruitful exchanges. The perspectives it brings to light, however, are sometimes only illusions: the choice of objects to compare, the selected frames, criteria and determinisms ..., the interpretative frameworks of underlying problems ... still rely on philosophies or theories of history that already provide the answers to the raised questions. In the worst case, comparative history is only an insidious resurgence of Euro-centrism.
> (Gruzinski 2001, 86, quoted by Bornet, this volume, p. 5)

Reconnecting histories and following specific cases studied in their own context can be seen as an antidote to some of the dangers often pointed out about the comparative approach (I will come back to this in the concluding remarks). Bornet lists three aspects that are crucial for the heuristic potential of the approach: 1. A focus on micro-histories which are re-contextualized into larger and global frameworks; 2. Attention to change as observed in various situations of interaction; 3. A multiple contextualization to shed light on the divergent local or regional dimensions of an object (or a person) in movement (this volume, p. 6). Further, the investigation of transnational itineraries of individuals active in the field of religion allows us, on the one hand, to reestablish contacts that have been overlooked or artificially separated and, on the other, invites us to reflect on concepts, practices, or taxonomies in use in the study of religions. This approach, Bornet pleads, opens new ways into the historiography of the study of religions which can be considered as the result of interactions with different circles of religious (and non-Christian) actors, texts or practices on a global scale. It may seem irritating that at this stage, we still have to plead for the acceptance of the contribution of extra-European material in the construction of the discipline of the study of religions, or for that matter of the religions themselves, but standard textbooks tend to show that this is not so evident. Once this is recognized, however, as Bornet argues, "it becomes possible to go beyond a mere criticism of the 'orientalism' that characterized much of the early production in the study of religions and towards a less Eurocentric conception of the discipline's own genealogy." (this volume, p. 23)

Bornet's well-thought introduction frames the various stories of the book and serves as a guideline to appreciate more critically the material presented. Some articles are more descriptive than others, yet they all bring fresh material to the accumulated knowledge of connected religions. As each chapter is provided with an abstract, I will not sum up their contents, but rather hint at nine key points that clearly show the impact of this approach on the study of religions, and link the stories to the promised benefits stated in the introduction for the history of religions.

1. A first point reveals the importance of connecting historiographies, as shown in "Re-discovering Buddha's Land" (this volume, p. 149). Chinese Indology came into existence with various intermediaries such as, for example, Western Studies, to finally find a contemporary Chinese way to perceive India, elucidating which networks are necessary to understand Chinese Indology, via Western Indian studies and Buddhism.

2. The approach reveals strategies to handle religions in a strategic and beneficial way. The "Curious Case of the Drs. D'Abreu" (this volume, p. 89), demonstrates how we should pay attention to the agency and skill of migrants to find their ways to develop strategies to integrate in to a new place. The story of the D'Abreu brothers may have been forgotten but, once discovered, becomes instructive in teaching us about the strategies of a Catholic family to make their way into England, the heart of the Empire, from their Indo-Portuguese origins. It shows how Catholic networks, among other strategies, could be used as a tool of integration in a migration situation. The Mangalore Catholics, protagonists of their exile stories, were already familiar with a hybrid culture and hence had no difficulties in playing with situations requiring adaptation and working with the means of religion such as the networking of Catholicism.

3. An important step is achieved when and where the approach outgrows the world religions model by showing the impact of individual appropriations and their influence on a larger scale, blurring the boundaries of defined religions. In "The Chen Jianmin legacy" (this volume, p. 253), we follow the life of a Buddhist master and discover how his legacy became a testimony to a sort of religion that is "always on the move." Buddhism is appropriated in various ways by individual followers from diverse regions of the world, changing constantly in the process, showing, for instance, the birth of a Sino-Tibetan Buddhism oscillating between the global and the local. The pattern that ensues is that of a moving religion.

4. The approach allows for a vivid handling of religions as part of life stories that allow the historian of religions to construct his or her own story to interpret the case studies. Semple's case (this volume, p. 123) shows this in the realm of the *Lebensreform* movement and emphasizes the function of biographies. It is by studying and constructing connections, and bringing together stories that knowledge is produced in such a precise way. Semple's story operates inside a wider story, connecting Scotland to other reform movements and pointing at several means, such as congresses, publications and discussions, through which connections were

Afterword

established. In order to draw a wider picture of *Lebensreform* events, collaborative work is needed to compose a fuller picture encompassing all those individual actors who forged their ways towards a new way of life.

5. The approach moves around continents, giving equal importance to the history of Asia and Europe: Sadhu Sundar Singh's odyssey (this volume, p. 221) shows the benefit of bringing together different stories which are not obviously connected, but once brought together, allow us to understand the Swiss tour of the Sadhu. It equally shows the necessity to re-contextualize trajectories, with *close reading*, to understand what is at stake, by looking at unexpected vectors of contacts, in India as well as in Europe. The benefit is to build a vast hermeneutic framework that is not bound by classical (and often imperialist) delimitations.

6. Life stories are a central focus for connected history and they are vectors to better understand the complexities of entangled events. Beckerlegge (this volume, p. 57) shows that Margaret Noble was not a mere adept formed by Vivekananda, the Indian master, but was deeply impregnated in her British life to adopt a critical view on the British Empire and to be a figure of inspiration to the Bengali society of her time. Her religious life was hybrid, unorthodox and critically reflected before she decided to be a Hindu disciple - Nivedita. Hence, by joining the two parts of her life, British and Indian, the latter part can be better appreciated by the researcher, and her life is restored to the full potentiality of a woman enrolled in many projects, social, political and educational. Paying attention to her "translocal space" across borders, shows her various modes of coming to terms with her religious quests and her socio-political engagements, be it here or there and allows the scholar to be informed about the meaningfulness of her connected religion.

7. Yet another benefit is in the approach's acceptance of the highly complex reality of interactions, refraining from inadequate simplistic models. Antony Firingi (this volume, p. 33) turns out to be the creator of European *Kālī-bhakti*, e.g. of appropriation of local structures (religious) by a transcultural subaltern. By living in two or more worlds, inhabiting the liminal and often precarious interstices of globalizing spaces, Firingi appropriates new intellectual and religious spaces in the early colonized Calcutta, testifying to one of the multiple agencies of the individuals who lived and reacted towards these new spaces.

8. Through the connected history angle we discover mechanics of encounters and strategies to survive in new global settings, hence revealing new networks, in history and in the present. The chapter

on Charles Pfoundes and the first Buddhist Mission to the West centres on the intrepid life of an Irishman and leads us to the founder of the Buddhist Mission in London called the Buddhist Propagation Society. It depicts global religious connections in the late nineteenth century and the influence of Japan in the development of the emerging global Buddhism. By suggesting eight levels of reflection to ponder over the introduction of Buddhism to the world, the author bridges in a remarkable way the micro with a macro dimensions (this volume, p.173). With the ambition to systematize trends and strategies operating in connected histories, the author proposes several tracks to reflect on cross-border religious strategies, to quote as examples: how are names and identities developed along cross-borders; what is the identity of a traveller before the present age? How were people allowed to travel and how not? etc. This serves not only as a useful reminder that things change from decade to decade with the transformation of technology, but also that specific technologies and media have an effect on the ideas, practices and people that use them as conduits. Through such questioning the author builds bridges to the other articles in the volume, allowing for a larger picture of strategies to emerge.

9. Establishing new connections gives a voice to people who have not been heard of. The nomadic life of the often forgotten Pandita Ramabai (this volume, p. 195) enables us to travel around India, Europe and America, constructing connections with Christianity viewed from the point of view of a female Indian convert. Once those connections are established, a fruitful comparison may start, for instance with Annie Besant (Malinar, 2013) who can be seen as a counterpart to the Ramabai story, or with Margaret Noble / Sister Nivedita. Another approach would be to compare Ramabai's views on Europe with those on America. As in the case of Sadhu Sundar Singh, Ramabai's is a story entangled between India and Europe and deserves an investigation delving into the historical archives of the two poles of encounter and reaction. Once more, an individual is at the centre of a wider story of religious clashes between Europe and India.

Looking forward: Perspectives

From here, I would like to pick up two central issues related to connected histories or connected religions, which come up, in one way or the other, in all chapters and deserve a special attention: comparison and translation.

Afterword

Comparison

Comparison has long been a companion to the study of religions. It had its glories and its misfortunes. Indeed, what would the study of religions be if it did not include a comparative dimension? Detractors often forget that it is not comparison that is at fault, but more often the way it is done. The present book provides a way to do and (re)think comparison, even though the various authors, while telling their stories, do not use the term comparison explicitly (with the exception of the editor, of course). What can we learn from this?

At first glance, we might consider the "connected approach" as an instantiation of the genealogical type of comparison described by J. Z. Smith, which, in opposition to analogical comparison, is a comparison based on two entities having been in contact. However, what is being dealt with here is rather another type deriving from a specific category of contacts. Religions in a genealogical relation show a great interdependency, such as Hindu and Buddhist traditions in the early centuries of South Asian History. In this book, the contacts are established by the serendipity of encounters. I would argue that these kinds of encounters encompass an important potential of creativity. Comparison through connected histories, turns out to be a tool of great heuristic potential. Once we have established a connection between, for example, the meetings of Vivekananda and William James, which occurred two times in America in 1894 and 1896 (Norris Frederick 2012, 38), we may start to compare and differentiate the practical Vedānta of Vivekananda and James's pragmatism. We may also want to investigate how James reads Vivekananda's Vedānta, as compared to his followers in Bengal. Or how an Indian such as Anirvan (1896–1978), who is a Bengali philosopher and yogi with a strong Vedic background, reads Kant, compared to a French philosopher who reads Anirvan and Kant. The path to follow in this comparative ambition would go from small detailed stories to large scale perspectives. The latter may trigger important issues for contrasting philosophical or religious interpretations and produce fruitful research questions.

If we look at just one more example, this time outside these pages and involving Anirvan—the above-mentioned Bengali philosopher well-versed in Western philosophy—we may learn about important knowledge transfers between India and Europe (Burger 2018). The Swiss writer, Lizelle Reymond (1899–1994), met Anirvan in a small village in India, where she became his disciple for many years before returning to Switzerland. Through Anirvan, who read Ouspensky, she came into contact with the Gurdjeff circle in Paris, and provided the latter with Anirvan's interpretation of Sāṃkhya philosophy. At the same time, Reymond wrote about Anirvan and provided the Bengali society with a new version of his life and his Sāṃkhya interpretation translated into Bengali. Each of the protagonists in these encounters gives his or her own interpretation of Sāṃkhya philosophy, which in turn receives an entirely new audience, worldwide. Starting with an encounter in the Himalayas on the micro-level of a Swiss traveller, the story turns out to become a chapter in the global history of philosophy and esotericism. Once the connections are established, we will have to ask what relation Anirvan saw between his Sāṃkhya and the thinking of Gurdjeff; or how much Sāṃkhya and what kind of Sāṃkhya has gone into the thinking of the disciples of Gurdjeff once they encountered the teachings of Anirvan through Lizelle Reymond. These would be questions on a conceptual level, but we could include the treatment of the body in the esoteric dance of Gurdjeff and Anirvan's yoga and learn something about very concrete body practices in diverse circles.

In the contributions of this book, comparison starts out "naturally" with the very fact that people move into contacts; it becomes a methodological tool however, when the connections are constructed and reflected, and rendered meaningful and challenging for the study of religions.

Translation

Even before we can think of comparing, we may have to confront the question of translation, which is a core problem in the study of religions. Since the translational turn and the increased awareness of how central this perspective is, we may view translation as inseparable from comparison and certainly *the* fuel of connected histories. How to imagine encounter without translation and how to imagine comparison without the effort of those who measure the gaps and the bridges between cultures through their efforts to build commensurability and make them understandable? This book contains samples of translation, located in various geographical and historical situations, and deals with those tackling the conceptual difficulties of untrans-latability.

Recent investigations in translational studies have taught us not to search for the original text which is itself already and always a translated item—such as for example the Rāmāyaṇa of Vālmīki, which comes from a large oral tradition—but rather to accentuate the processes of translation. It is possible to connect translation questions/problematics with the realm of connected histories. Translation may operate on a pragmatic and linguistic level, or on a more abstract level of ideas, be it in the context of the source of translation or the target that are connected. A good amount of creativity may let us engage in new ways to apprehend old questions or be inspired by different ones. If today many types of translations are being considered acceptable (from literal to various transpositions), we cannot avoid first of all acknowledging that there is translation from one item to another in the data itself (established connections). From there, we will decide what type of translation we shall pursue (connected histories) by comparing and evaluating the various layers of subtlety involved in the dynamic process to think in several languages and adapt words and ideas to semantic and philosophical constraints. Just as encounters yield a potential for innovation, so does translation fruitfully stimulate our imagination and force us to measure the distance between what is translated and recreated.

The connected histories approach invites us to depart from claims of cultural ownership, which of course may have their importance in given political situations, and to accentuate rather the comparison of various modes of appropriation through time and space. In the present situation of intensified circulation of ideas and cultural transfers, it is almost impossible to trace back anything to its origin; what seems to stem from India, might well be the fruit of many-layered processes of exchange and encounters, and vice versa. A good example could be the terms "religion" and "yoga." "Religion" (though related to Latin in its etymology) does not belong any longer to western culture but has travelled around the world and been appropriated in many ways—as such or in translation—as much as it has changed over the centuries by thought provoking contacts. The same holds true for yoga (though originally a Sanskrit word): it has gone into the world to be associated with so many things; in its Indian history, it has incorporated layers of stimulating contacts, its recent world expansion being part of that. This development is testimony to the changes that have characterized a globalized world, but no doubt it was no different in previous epochs. We might compare how yoga and religion changed through encounters and processes of translation, and hence reveal many significant steps in their conceptual histories.

Further, translation work points at those figures who work between societies, languages and culture and we are back to our actors who connect religions over time and space, who tell us stories we may turn into a grander narrative.

Concluding thoughts

Where does this book, its examples and perspectives lead us?

Much work has been done lately examining the relations between Europe and Asia, widening the knowledge of the interaction between Europe and Asia. However, I am still pondering whether relations between the scholarly work done in India, and the one done in Europe are functioning as parallels rather than as related operations. Clearly more collaborative work is needed and would be useful. In this respect, the present book strikes a healthy balance by giving voice to Asian scholars as well as to European.

Rather than speaking of mixture or hybridity (with ambiguous overtones), I would emphasize the creative character of cultural transfers and adaptations. People do not mimic others and are not only products of European imperialism, they have their own ways to deal with cosmopolitan situations. Why should a Bengali reformer stick to Western philosophy only when his own tradition and his own imagination has as much to offer? Those working on the relations and connections between several fields (translators), are often those who come closest to a cosmopolitan attitude which avoids reducing one to the other, and are open-minded enough to view the intellectual challenges and benefits that may arise from pondering over differences. These figures of the in-between are the most interesting protagonists to show us new ways to understand what is happening in the realm of exchanges, for example between India and Europe since Antiquity, using ever new tools to approach concrete encounters. The most creative writers may turn out to be those who are circulating between countries and languages.

The Indologist and philosopher W. Halbfass, in his seminal work on India and Europe, took up the notion of neo-Hinduism from Hacker to qualify those Indians who in the nineteenth century would rethink India having reflected on Western philosophies and *Weltanschauungen*. The situation is indeed quite different now and we may want to accentuate a model of circulation to describe the continuous processes of exchange back and forth from India to Europe, and there could be many more examples worldwide. The notion of cosmopolitan thinkers, understood as thinkers who have been deeply exposed to several ways of viewing the world, would be more adequate today. S. Rushdie speaks of the translated person, to qualify those being constantly at home in multiple cultural backgrounds. His notion includes the dimension of translation, meaning the effort to include the capacity to think and speak in another medium. A cosmopolitan thinker does not necessarily need to travel, but the dimension of translation should be there, as shown by Bornet's example of Max Müller (this volume, p. 13).

Further, the cases recounted in the book include stories with an interpretative dimension and illustrate the provisional and dynamic nature of the understanding of the processes at stake. Against a paradigm emphasizing the incommensurability of the cultural spheres in relation, they show a willingness to learn from each other which seems the best starting point for the awareness of the connectedness between the worlds we are dealing with.

When Yehudi Menuhin (1916–1999) and Ravi Shankar (1920–2012) tried to play classical Western and Classical Indian music together in the 1960s (in their Album *West Meets East* in 1967), their start was timid and characterized by a juxtaposition of two very different musical forms.[2] If we listen today to contemporary ways of combining these two musical traditions, we may be quite startled by the proficiency artists have acquired to express themselves fluently in both the mediums and by their adaptations and operations that clearly show that a new music emerged, no longer a mere combination

---

2. This is of course not to say that music styles have not met and mingled over centuries. The more classical styles have been particularly careful to keep a defined style and hence their exponents face greater difficulty to accept trans-creative processes.

Afterword

or juxtaposition. The analysis of the cultural circulation on the level of religion may bring up new religious configurations which may or may not leave todays paradigms far behind. To understand this *historically* we need the approach developed in the present volume.

These individual destinies have relevance for the theorizing on religion and they have an impact on the *study of religions*. These stories are all chapters of the history of religions. Perhaps, one can note that their relevance appears at a certain point because they are put together in one volume. The way scholars create new and their own stories about them is equally important, and turns out to be history of religions. This volume is an example of how knowledge is produced by putting together individual stories as testimonies to create a shared pattern. To examine the effects of encounter on individual actors and what they do with it, is certainly no new preoccupation in the field. But studying contextualized stories brings material to the understanding of the mechanics at work, and those in turn can be compared to other situations at different moments in time and space. Thus, they can contribute to the discipline on an abstract and more theoretical level, replying to questions of a more philosophical nature. The study of various stories on a micro level helps to create a macro story of the encounters and processes of exchange. What pattern do these connected histories render? Even if there may be no pattern at all, but a zigzagging of roads, this may be informative to illustrate what religions are in a cosmopolitan frame. It is *not* global history we are dealing with in this book, but a restitution of historically contextualized stories which are rich enough to have us reflect on the role individuals play in and with religion. It is the *connections* that turn that into a larger picture leading to new perspectives.

There is actually less a common theme in the book, but above all an ambition: the ambition to reconnect stories and present examples of micro-stories concentrating on religion not as systems or closed categories or dogmatic enterprises, but on religion as a story to deal with life, turning religions into mostly unexpected "new things." With the improvement of our knowledge and expanding areas of investigations, certain approaches will have difficulties in serving the purposes of research and we will have to revisit evidence. Religions have borders only when analyzed and postulated in an emic perspective. The intertwined character of religions makes them the most interesting objects to study, as they differ from other cultural goods and their fruitful trans-fecundation, through the claim of a specific kind of "truth." On the one hand, there is a claim to a religious identity, on the other, in the perspective of a connected history, there is nothing more than composite agglomerations which may or may not draw a picture of "something."

The vast scope of the book encourages the reader to step out of his or her field of specialization and to delve into other stories and other trajectories. It is still quite hard for an Indologist or a Sinologist to attend a conference in *the study of religions*, as he or she can rarely present material that goes beyond generalities. Stereotypes that have come with the world religion model might be a handicap for those who work in the field and are confronted with views learnt from common knowledge about the topic, often quite far from the research done in the field. The reverse is also true that specialists do not bother to see how theoretical points or comparative material would improve their own ways of going about their research. This book is an antidote to the religionist approach to religions and we must thank the editor for letting us look at the valuable new material brought together through this lens. It is also a landmark in its efforts to avoid nationalistic or "area-based" approaches to religions. The perspective of the connected histories is a step towards accepting that ideas do not bloom in one place, but are blown over the continents, producing entangled stories. It teaches us to cultivate a cosmopolitanism—in its basic sense of openness towards other cultures—a capacity to think and reflect about the foreign and the traditional as diversities on the same line. Connected stories lead towards this capacity to think not solely of one or the other, but to cultivate an informed perspective made by the other, with the other, against the other with a particular attention to quality, detail and curiosity.

Acknowledgements

I have chosen to write this afterword as an essay, in a rather free style and format. However, this does not mean that I am not indebted to many authors who have profoundly inspired me. Their thoughts have mingled with mine and I fully acknowledge their inspiration. I quote those who have most inspired me in the present subject: H. Bhabha, K. Bhattacharya, Ph. Bornet, J. Ganeri, C. Ginzburg, S. Gruizinski W. Halbfass, M. Hennard Dutheil, A. Malinar, S. Rushdie, J. Rüpke, J. Z. Smith, S. Subrahmanyam. And, of course, those who have written papers in this volume and given me food for thought, particularly Philippe Bornet whose introduction provides an analytical and conceptual frame to the entire enterprise. May they all be thanked for their ideas and scholarly work which allowed me to brew my own mixture.

References

Burger, Maya. 2018. "Sāṃkhya in Transcultural Interpretation: Shri Anirvan (Śrī Anirvāṇa) and Lizelle Reymond." In *Yoga in Transformation: Historical and Contemporary Perspectives*, edited by K. Baier, P. Maas, K. Preisendanz, 463–483. Göttingen: V&R Unipress.

Ganeri, Jonardon. 2017. "Freedom of Thinking: The Immersive Cosmopolitism of Krishnachandra Bhattacharya." In *The Oxford Handbook of Indian Philosophy*, edited by J. Ganeri, 718–736. Oxford: Oxford University Press.

Malinar, Angelika. 2013. "'Western-Born but in Spirit Eastern ...'—Annie Besant between Colonial and Spiritual Realms." *Asiatische Studien, Études Asiatiques* 67(4): 1115–1155.

Norris, Frederick. 2012. "William James and Swami Vivekananda: Religious Experience and Vedanta/Yoga in America." In *William James Studies* 9: 37–55.

About the author

Maya Burger, University of Lausanne, studied Anthropology, Indology and History of religions in Switzerland, India and United States. She is presently professor for Indian Studies at the Department of languages and civilizations of South Asia. Her field of specialization is pre-modern Hindi literature, history of yoga, history of the relations between Europe and India, as well as Indian religions. Recent publications include *Early Modern India. Literatures and Images, Texts and Languages* edited by Maya Burger and Nadia Cattoni (Heidelberg: CrossAsia-eBooks, 2019); *Religions in Play: Games, Rituals, and Virtual Worlds*, edited by Philippe Bornet and Maya Burger (Zürich: Pano Verlag, 2012); *India in Translation through Hindi Literature: A Plurality of Voices*, edited by Maya Burger and Nicola Pozza. Worlds of South and Inner Asia. (Bern: Peter Lang, 2010).

Index

Numbers in *italic* denote pages with figures.

A

actors
  types of 12–13
Aḥmadiyya movement 226
Alavi, Seema 106
Albritton, Vicky 138
Alden, W. H. 239
Alston, Charlotte 132
analogical comparison of religion 9–10
Andrews, Charles Freer 222, 223, 235
Anglicanism 65–66, 70, 90–92, 204, 207, 208
Anglo-Indians 109–110, 111
Anirvan 283–284
Anson, Peter 102 n. 7
anthroposophy 240
anti-colonial movement 42, 49
Antony Firingi 36–45, 49–52, 281
  Antony Firingee (film, 1967) 40–41, *41*
  biographical details 36, 38–39
  colonial modernity and 39–40, 42–44
  cultural mobility of 37
  Hinduism of 46
  songs of 36, 39, 46–47, 51, 52
  transcultural subalternity of 37–38, 44–45, 49–52
apostle, notion of and *sādhu* 228
archives 6, 126, 141
art, Indian 83
Arunachalam, Ponnambalam 128

Ārya Samāj 17 n. 32, 225, 226, 258
Asad, Talal 9 n. 11, 209–210, 211
ascetic movements 225
Atmaprana, Pravrajika
  Sister Nivedita (1977) 58, 59, 60, 67, 71, 76
Australia 110–114

B

Bach, Edward 141
Bai, Anasuya 196
Bai, Hui 160
Barran, Veronica (née d'Abreu) 98
Basel Mission 21, 219, 227, 227 n.20, 234
Basu, Sankari Prasad 59, 60
Bayly, Christopher A. 4 n. 2
Bayly, Susan 107
Beatty, Octavius 82, 82 n. 20
Becker, Judith 201 n. 12, 206–207 n. 16
Beckerlegge, Gwilym 16, 61–62 n. 6, 233
Beijing, China 155
  see also Peking University
Beith, Scotland *125*, 135
Bengal
  Antony Firingi and 35, 36–45, 49–52, 281
  Charles "Hindoo" Stuart and 45–46
  Derozio, poetry of 48–49
  folk-idiom and urbanization of 44, 47–48
  Friedrich Max Müller and 15 n. 25, 17, 17 n. 30
  reform movements 48–49

291

Bengal Renaissance 38, 38 n. 6, 42
Benoît, Pierre de 227
Bertrand, Romain 6, 277
Besant, Annie 72, 187, 282
Bhabha, Homi 225, 225 n. 14
Bhagavad Gītā 226
bhakti 37, 37 n. 4, 225
  see also Antony Firingi
Bhārat Mātā (Mother India) 71
Bible translations 214–215
Biggar, John M. 135
Bijou of Asia 173, 183
biographies
  role of 276, 277–278, 281
  of Antony Firingi 36–45, 49–52
  of Charles Pfoundes 171–190
  of Chen Jianmin 253–269
  of d'Abreu family 92–105, 112
  of Dugald Semple 123–143
  of Pandita Ramabai 193–215
  of Sister Nivedita 58–61
  of Sundar Singh 219–244
Bircher, Ralph 139, 140
Birmingham, England 92, 103
Blackburn, Stuart 38
Bloch, Marc 4–5
Boehmer, Elleke 71
Boer War 82
books, as medium of exchange 140–142
Booth, Eric Herman 112
Booth, Kathleen (née d'Abreu) 112
Booth, Norman Parr 112
Booth, Phillip 112
Booth, Winifred (née Denny) 112
Bowes-Lyon, Ann 98, *98*
Bowes-Lyon family 98
Brahminism 193–194, 197, 205–206
Brahmo Samāj 14, 15, 19, 47–48, 198, 205, 205 n. 15
Bridge of Weir, Scotland 133
British Empire 69, 80, 210, 281
British India and Kanara Catholics 109
Broad Church Anglicans 65–66
Brontë, Charlotte
  Jane Eyre (1847) 62–63
Buddhism
  Chinese 151–152, 153–154, 164–165
  Dugald Semple and 129
  globalization of 172, 173–174, 181–182, 188–189
  Indian 160–161
  Tibetan 254–255, 256–259
  Tibetan in India 259–261
  Tibetan in Taiwan 264–270
Buddhist mission of Charles Pfoundes 171–190
  aims, ostensible vs. achieved 173–174
  Buddhism, meaning of 176–178
  communication networks 182–184
  economics of global lay Buddhism 181–182
  family life and other relationships 184–189
  introduction 171–172
  letters of 173
  names and identities 175
  non-denominational engagement with religion 179–181
  travel, restrictions and opportunities of 176
Buddhist practice of Chen Jianmin 253–269, 280
  appearance of 260, *263*
  background and formative years of 255–259
  books by 261, 263–264
  influence in Taiwan 264
  introduction 253–254
  in Kalimpong, India 259–260
  legacy of in Taiwan 265–269, *266*
  Tibetan and Chinese masters 254–255
  travels of 259–264
  in the USA 262–263, 265
  as Yogi 261
Buddhist Propagation Society (BPS) 171–172, 179, 182–183, 189
Buddhist Studies Institutes 256, 257, 258
Burckhardt, Paul 237
Burger, Maya 203 n. 14
Burke, Marie Louise 61, 66
Burnand, Eugène 231, *231*

C

Cadbury 112
Cai, Yuanpei 153
Calcutta, India 35–52, 281

Index

Antony Firingi and 36–45, 49–52, 281
  Charles "Hindoo" Stuart and 45–46
  Derozio, poetry of 48–49
  folk-idiom and urbanization of 44, 47–48
  name of 44 n. 10, 44–45
  reform movements 48–49
Calicut, Kerala, India 227
Campbell, Mary Baine 211 n. 22
Canara, India *see* Kanara, India
Carpenter, Edward 128
  From Adam's Peak to Elephanta (1892) 128
Carr, Helen 210
Casanova, Pascale 40
caste systems 108, 195, 197, 197 n. 6, 199–200, 201
Catholics
  in Britain 92–94, 97, 100–104, 280
  in India 106–110
  migrants from India 105–106
Chakravarti, Uma 197 n. 6
Chatterjee, Partha 43
Chattopadhyay, Bankim Chandra 225
Chaudhuri, Rosinka 36 n. 2, 39, 40–41, 42, 43–44
Chen, Baozhen 158
Chen, Duxiu 156–157
Chen, Haowang 255 n. 2
Chen, Jianmin 253–269, 280
  appearance of 260, *263*
  background and formative years of 255–259
  books by 261, 263–264
  influence in Taiwan 264
  introduction 253–254
  in Kalimpong, India 259–260
  legacy of in Taiwan 265–269, *266*
  Tibetan and Chinese masters 254–255
  travels of 259–264
  in the USA 262–263, 265
  as Yogi 261
Chen, Sanli 158
Chen, Yinke 158, 159
Chidester, David 20 n. 39
China
  Buddhism in 254, 256–257, 258
  Chen Jianmin early years in 255–256
  occupation by Japan 160 n. 12, 257
  philosophy, study of 151, 153–154
  Western studies 151, 158, 164–165

China, Indology in 149–166, 280
  community, formation of 161–164, 165
  conclusion 164–166
  cultural borrowing from India 155–156
  Europe and the USA, students in 158–159
  India, contacts with 150–152
  India, students in 160–161
  Indian philosophy, study of 153–154
  Sanskrit, study of 154–155
  Tagore, reception of 156–157
Chinese Nationalist Party 257
chocolate 112
Choompolpaisal, Phibul 176
Christ *see* Oriental Jesus
Christian *sādhus* 237 n. 42, 237–238
Christianity
  Anglicanism 65–66, 70, 90–92, 204, 207, 208
  Catholicism 92–94, 97, 100–110
  indigenous Christianity 226
  Jesuits 99, 100, 101, 102 n. 7, 103–104
  nonconformism 65, 137
  Oriental Christianity 220–221
  Presbyterianism 136–137
  Protestantism 73, 194, 205, 207, 210–211, 212, 233–234, 242
  Swedenborgians 239–240
Church of Scotland 136
Collet, Sophia 16
Collins, Angela Louisa 62, 65
colonial modernity of India 39–40, 42–44, 48, 209–210
communication networks 182–184
communities, translocal 12
comparative history 4–5, 278
comparisons of religion 9–13, 283–284
Conlon, Frank 107 n. 11
connected histories 3–23, 277–278
  from comparative to connected histories 4–8
  definition of 5–6
  from early to late modernity 7–8
  of empire 6 n. 5
  of Friedrich Max Müller 13–20
  of Jakob Urner 21–22
  of "religion" and religion 8–13
  translation and 284–285, 286
connected religion approach 11–13, 23, 283–284

conscientious objection 131–132, 134
contact zone 206–207 n. 16
conversions
   of Pandita Ramabai 194, 199–200, 202–204, 207–208, 210
   of Sundar Singh 227
cosmopolitanism 285, 286, 288
Cox, Jeffrey 237 n. 42, 243
creativity 37, 46, 52, 283, 284, 285
cross-border religious strategies 282
   see also Pfoundes, Charles
cross-contextualization 6, 6 n. 7
Crossley Heath School, Halifax 61–62, 61–62 n. 6, 63
cultural mobility 37
cultural transfers 5, 285

D

d'Abreu, Abundius 103, 105
d'Abreu, Alphonsus "Pon" 94–96, 97, 105
d'Abreu, Ann (née Bowes-Lyon) 98, *98*
d'Abreu, Clare 97–98
d'Abreu, Elizabeth (née Throckmorton) 97, *97*
d'Abreu, Felicity 98
d'Abreu, Francis "Frank" 94–95, 96, 98–99, *98*, 104
d'Abreu, John Francis 92–93, *94–95*, 99–101, 102–103, 104–105
d'Abreu, Kathleen 112
d'Abreu, Teresa (née Noonan) 92–93, 94, *95*
d'Abreu, Veronica 98
Dahl, Felicity (née d'Abreu) 98
Dalmia, Vasudha 38
Daniel, C. W. 124–125, 134
Deacon, Desley 6, 63, 64, 124
Deb, Radhakanta 17, 17 n. 31
Denny, Winifred 112
Derozio, Henry Louis Vivian 42, 42 n. 8, 48–49
Dhammaloka, U 176, 182, 187
Dharmapala, Anagarika 152
discriminatory legislation 110–111
Dobe, Timothy S. 229 n. 28, 231 n. 35, 243
doctors 92, 104
   see also d'Abreu, Alphonsus "Pon"; d'Abreu, Francis "Frank"; d'Abreu, John Francis

Dodson, Michael S. 17 n. 32
Doyle, Sir Arthur Conan 91, 92
Duff, Alexander 44
Duff, Andrew 259, 260
Durgā, Goddess 36
Dyer, Helen S. 205 n. 15

E

Eco, Umberto 242
Edalji, George 90, 91
Edalji, Shapurji 90, 91–92
Edalji family 90–92, 99
Edinburgh, Scotland 100–102
education 195, 196–197 n. 5, 211 n. 21
   see also schools
Education Act (1870) 62–63, 179
Education Act (1902) 179
Elam, Caroline 185, 185 n. 31, 186, 187
empire, connected histories of 6 n. 5
Espagne, Michel 5
ethnography of travellers 209, 211
Eurocentric history 11, 23, 279

F

Fa, Fang 160
famines 200–201
Fernandes, Peter 111–112
firingi 36 n. 2
First World War 132, 134
Fischer-Tiné, Harald 50
Five Elements *Stūpa* of Chen Jianmin 265–266, *266*, 268
Fliess, Walter 127–128
folk-idiom of Calcutta 44, 47–48
Foxe, Barbara
   Long Journey Home: A Biography of Margaret Noble (Nivedita) (1975) 58, 59, 60, 63, 64–65, 72, 75–76, 77–78
Francis, Edward Carey (alias Angelo Francis J. Saldanha) 113–114, *114–115*
Franck, Harry 176, 182
freethinkers 241–242
French, Thomas Valpy, Bishop of Lahore 207
Frykenberg, R. E. 213 n.25, 214 n. 27

G

Gama, Vasco da 7, 13 n. 22, 106

Index

Gambhirananda, Swami 60–61
Gandhi, Mohandas 20, 125, 129–130, *130*
Ganeri, Jonardon 278
Gangkar Rinpoché 256, 257, 258, 259, 267
Geertz, C. 9
genealogical comparison of religion 9, 9–10 n. 12, 10–11, 283
Geraldine, Sister 205, 206, 207, 209
Germany 153, 158–159
Ghose, Aurobindo 70
Ghosh, Sunil Behari 60
global history 6
Goa, India 107, 107 n. 10, 108, 111–112
Golwalkar, Madhav Sadashiv 71 n. 15
Goodwin, Alys 230 n. 34, 230–231
governess novels 62
Great Wyrley, Staffordshire 90–91
Green, Nile 226
Greenblatt, Stephen 37
Griffith, Roger 125–126, 126 n. 2
Gruffel, Nelly 237, 237 n. 42
Gruzinski, Serge 5, 278–279
Guangxu, emperor of China 150–151

H

Halakatti, Phakirappa Gurubasappa 21
Halbfass, Wilhelm 12, 286
Handsworth, Birmingham 92, 103
Harvard University 158, 161
Heehs, Peter 71
Heiler, Friedrich 225, 240, 241
heretics 207
Hill, Rosa Alice 186, 187
Himalayas 223, 226
Hindi 162, 164
Hinduism
  Antony Firingi and 46, 51–52
  caste systems 195, 197, 197 n. 6, 199–200, 201
  Charles Stuart and 46–47
  Friedrich Max Müller, work of 13–20
  Pandita Ramabai and 193–194, 195, 198–200
  Sister Nivedita and 57, 60, 64, 66–67, 68, 69–70, 82
hippies in India 260
history
  comparative history 4–5, 278

connected history 5–6, 277–278, 284–285, 286
connected history, examples of 13, 22
connected history of "religion" and religion 8–13
global history 6
symmetric history 6, 277
Hodgen, Margaret 209–210
Hsu, Chin-ting 265, 267
Hu, Qiaomu 163
Hu, Shi 154–156
Huang, Maocai 150
hutting 135–136
hybrid spaces 225

I

identities, fluid 175
identity-formation 39
  see also self-identification
imported localism 233
India
  Bengal Renaissance 38, 38 n. 6, 42
  Chen Jianmin in Kalimpong 259–260
  China, contacts with 150–152
  colonial modernity of 39–40, 42–44, 48, 209–210
  education in 195
  hippies in 260
  independence of and Sister Nivedita 71, 80–81, 82–83
  influence on Semple 128–129
  paternalist image of 234
  religion in South Asia 276
  see also Calcutta
Indian Christians 89–117
  Catholics in India 106–110
  conclusion 115–117
  d'Abreu family in Britain 92–105
  Edalji family in England 90–92, 99
  migrants, Catholicism of 105–106, 107
  migration to Australia 110–114
  migration to the USA 114–115
indigenous Christianity 226
individual stories 276, 277–278
  see also biographies
Indology in China *see* China, Indology in
Inoue, Enryo 151
intermarriages 93

295

International Vegetarian Union (IVU) 138–140
Ireland
  Irish Home Rule 74, 77, 78, 79, 80
  Irish Literary Revival 82
  Irishness of Sister Nivedita 72–74, 79
Islam 106, 226

J

Jackson, Carl T. 60
Jaffe, Richard 188
James, William 283
Japan
  Buddhism in 188–189, 268
  and Buddhist missions to the West 171–172, 173, 178
  Charles Pfoundes, Japanese name of 175
  communication networks 182–183
  concept of religion 180–181
  Friedrich Max Müller, contacts of 20
  and India 151
  occupation of China 160 n. 12, 257
Jayawardena, Kumari 81
Jefferies, Matthew 142 n. 17
Jesuits 99, 100, 101, 102 n. 7, 103–104
Jesus *see* Oriental Jesus
Ji, Xianlin 158–159, 162–164
Jiang, Canteng 268
Jiang, Jieshi 162
Jin, Kemu 160–161
Jinling Buddhist Publishing House 151–152
John, gospel of 226
Johnson, Ethel Ashton 70
Jonsson, Fredrik A. 138
Joshi, M Lakshmana Harihara 196–197 n. 5

K

Kaigai Bukkyo Jijō (Situation of Buddhism Overseas, KBJ) 173
Kaigai Senkyō Kai (Overseas Missionary Society, KSK) 171, 189
Kailasa, Maharishi of 223
Kālī, Goddess 36, 44–45, 52, 69
Kalimpong, India 259–260
Kanara, India
  Catholics in 107–110
  John Francis d'Abreu, early years 99
  migration to Australia 111–112, 113–114
  migration to the USA 114–115
  networks of migrants 105–106
  Portuguese in 106–107
  students in Britain 101–102, 103–105
Kanarese Evangelical Mission (KEM) 219–220, 227, 229, 237
Kang, Youwei 151
Kanitkar, Kashibai 213
karmic retribution 232–233
Karnataka, India 21, 22
Keyes, Charles 59
Khantipalo (Laurence Mills) 260, 261
Kippenberg, Hans 16 n. 28
Knaggs, H. V. 140
  The Salad Road to Health (1919) 140–141
Kolkata *see* Calcutta
Kopf, David 15 n. 25, 38 n. 6, 48
Kosambi, Dharmananda 160–161
Kosambi, Meera 195–196, 203, 208 n. 17, 209 n. 19
Kropotkin, Peter 81, 81 n. 19
Kuomintang (KMT) 257
Küpper, Joachim 42

L

language barriers 268–269
Lanman, Charles R. 158, 161
Lebendige Kraft, Zurich 140
Lebensreform (life reform) 132, 138–142, 280–281
legislation, discriminatory 110–111
legislation on education 62–63, 179
Lessing, Ferdinand Diedrich 154 n. 5
Li, Hongzhang 150
Liang, Qichao 151, 156, 158
Liang, Shuming 153–154
  Introduction of Indian Philosophy (1919) 153
life stories *see* biographies
Lin, Yutang 263, 264–265
Lin, Ziyang 267
Lincoln, Bruce 8, 10 n. 13
London
  Buddhism in 177, 178
  Buddhist Propagation Society (BPS) 171–172, 174, 182, 189
  Charles Pfoundes in 181–182, 186
  communication networks 182–183
  Dugald Semple in 134–135

Index

Sister Nivedita in 65–66, 80, 81
London Vegetarian Society 133–134
Lu, Xun 155

M

MacDonald, Frederika 186–187
MacLellan, William 127
Maharashtra, India 195
Malabari, Behramji 19
Mangalore, India 99, 103–104, 106–107
Marathi translation of the Bible 214
master-disciple relationships 258, 267
Masuzawa, Tomoko 13
Matless, David 126
Matsuyama, Matsutaro 171–172
Maung, Maung 187–188
Maurice, F. D. 66
Mayer, Jean-François 243–244
Mayer, Norman 239–240
McGovern, William 188
McLaren-Throckmorton, Clare (née d'Abreu) 97–98
mediators
  types of 12–13
Menuhin, Yehudi 286
micro-histories 6, 279
migrants 105–106, 107, 110–115, 280
  see also d'Abreu, John Francis
Miller, Basil 198 n. 9
missionaries
  in India 45–46, 106–107, 219–220
  from India 226, 237
  Jakob Urner 21–22
  roles of 12
  from Switzerland 227, 234
  see also Pfoundes, Charles
monasteries, Buddhist 258
Monkey King 155
Monteiro, Ignatius 115
Moore, P. Geoffrey 126, 132
Muirhead, Roland 126–127, 130, 132, 134, 136
Müller, Friedrich Max 13–20, 203
  contacts and networks of 13–14, 15–16, 20
  and reform in India 18, 19
  theories of religion 14–15
  works, impact in India 17–19
  WORKS OF

Auld Lang Syne: My Indian Friends (1899) 14
India, What Can It Teach Us? (1883) 19
Lectures on the Origin and Growth of Religion (1878) 14–15, 18–19
Ṛg Veda (first ed. 1849–1875) 17–18, 152
Müller, Henrietta 69–70
multiple contextualization 6, 279
Munn, Mazda 126, 141 n. 16
music 286
  see also songs
Muslims 106, 226
Mylne, Dr., Bishop of Bombay 207
mysticism 214

N

names, changes of 175
Nanjo, Bunyu 20, 152
National Institute of Oriental Languages (NIOL), Yunnan 162, 163–164
nationalism, Irish 74, 77, 78, 79, 80
natural history 132
networks
  communication networks 182–184
  for *Lebensreform* 138–142, 280–281
  of Friedrich Max Müller 13–14, 15–16, 20
  Jesuits 103–104
  migrants 105–106
  of Sister Nivedita 81–82
  of Sundar Singh 242–243
Neue Wege 233–234
New Church 239–240
new religious movements 188–189, 264
Nishi Honganji 171, 189
Nivedita, Sister (Margaret Noble) 57–84, 281
  biographies of 58–61
  and Boer War 82
  and Christianity 65–66, 70
  conclusion 83–84
  correspondence about 75–76
  England, identification with 72
  Hinduism and 57, 60, 64, 66–67, 68, 69–70, 82
  independence of 64–65
  and Indian art 83
  and Indian independence movement 71, 80–81, 82–83
  introduction 57–58

297

and Irish Home Rule 74, 77, 78, 79, 80
Irishness of 72–74, 79
life as a translocal space 63–64, 72
life of service to India 69
networks of 81–82
school life in Britain 61–63, 79
seeking of 67
social attitudes of 81
Noble, Isabel 75, 76, 77
Noble, William 75, 76–77, 77–78, 79
nonconformism 65, 137
Noonan, Teresa 92–93, 94, *95*
Noonan family 93, 94
Norlha qutuytu 256
Noronha, Isidore 103
Nūr-i Afshan 223

O

Occult Review 240
O'Doherty, Malachi 61–62 n. 6, 67 n. 10
Oriental Christianity 220–221
Oriental Jesus 230–231, *231–232*, 243
orientalism 9, 13, 20, 279

P

pacifism 131–132, 134
Parker, Rebecca 228, 230 n. 31
Paton, William 229
Paulsen, Friedrich
  Die deutschen Universitäten (1902) 153
Peeters, Evert 138
Peking University (PKU) 149, 153, 154, 159, 161, 162–163, 164
Pelliot, Paul 158
Pereira, Joseph Michael 101, 102, 105
Pernau, Margrit 45
Peterson, Indira Viswanathan 39
Pfister, Oskar 240–241
Pfoundes, Charles 171–190, 281–282
  aims of 173–174
  Buddhism, meaning of 176–178
  communication networks 182–184
  economics of global lay Buddhism 181–182
  family life and other relationships 184–189
  introduction 171–172
  letters of 173
  names and identities of 175
  non-denominational engagement with religion 179–181
  travel restrictions and opportunities 176
Pfoundes, Rosa Alice (née Hill) 186, 187
philosophy, study of in China 151, 153–154
pilgrimages 200
Portuguese doctors 92, 104
Portuguese in India 106–107, 108–109
postcolonial studies 7–8
Potter, Simon J. 6 n. 5, 63
Pounds, Caroline (née Elam) 185, 185 n. 31, 186, 187
Pounds, Elam 184–185
Pounds, James Baker 184–185
Powell, Avril 225
prayer, Sundar Singh and 232, 240
Premchand 164
Presbyterianism 136–137
print, as medium of exchange 140–142
Protestantism 73, 194, 205, 207, 210–211, 212, 233–234, 242
pseudonyms 175
psychical societies 240
Pye, Michael 11

Q

Qian, Zhixiu 156
Qihuan Jingshe 152, 160
Qu, Qiubai 156–157

R

Rabault-Feuerhahn, Pascale 20
racial hierarchies in Britain 104–105
Ragaz, Leonhard 233–234
Rama Tirtha 226
Ramabai, Pandita 193–215, 282
  on America 211–213
  autobiographical writings 194–195
  Bible, translation of 214–215
  Brahmin background 193–194
  caste systems and 197, 197 n. 6, 199–200, 201
  Christ, finding of 213
  Christianity, conversion to 194, 199–200, 202–204, 207–208, 210
  cross, wearing of 207–208
  on father and education of women 195,

Index

196–197 n. 5
Hinduism, denial of 198–199
and human suffering 200–201
humanity, understanding of 205–206
pilgrimages and travel of 200–201
reading of Sanskrit texts and the Bible 198
travelogues 210, 211 n. 23
treatment of, by Christians 206–207, 208–209
Ramakrishna Math and Mission 57–58, 70
Ramakrishna movement 16, 60, 69
Ramusack, Barbara 69, 70
Ranade, Ramabai 196
Reid, Donald 126
Reid, Walter 132
relics 265
religion
 boundaries in study of 8–9
 comparative and connected religion 9–13
 education in schools 179–180
 in Japan, concept of 180–181
 and translation 285
Reymond, Lizelle 283–284
 The Dedicated—A Biography of Nivedita (1953) 58–59, 59 n. 3, 60, 61, 62–63, 71, 74, 75–76, 77, 78, 79
Rindlisbacher, Stefan 142 n. 17
Ripon, Henrietta Robinson, Lady 66
rituals 200, 203
Robinson, Rowena 108
Rohkrämer, Thomas 132, 138, 143
Roy, Ram Mohan 15–16
Rushdie, S. 286
Russell, Edmund 129

S

sādhu, meaning of 225–227, 228
Saha, Jonathan 6 n. 5, 63
Said, Edward
 Orientalism (1978) 7
Saldanha, Angelo Francis J. (alias Edward Carey Francis) 113–114, *114–115*
Saldanha, Camille 101, 102, 103, 105, 116
Saldanha, Christina 114–115
Saldanha, Martin Sebastian 114
Saldanha, Wilfred 115
sandals 128, *129*
Sangharakshita, Urgyen 260–261

Sanskrit 154, 155, 159, 160–161, 163, 196, 198
schools
 in England 61–62, 6361–62 n. 6, 63, 94, 104, 179–180
 of Tibetan Buddhism in Taiwan 267–268
 see also education
Schwab, Emil 242
Scottish National Congress 130
Scottish No-Stipend League 136
Scottish Vegetarian Society 138, 139
Secrétan, Gustave 229, 233, 238
seeking, process of 67
Seiwert, Hubert 37
self-identification 104–105, 109–110
Semple, Dugald 123–143, 280
 conclusion 142–143
 introduction 123–124
 in North America 141 n. 15
 Simple Life as *Lebensreform* 138–142
 Simple Life, how to live 133–138
 sources for 124–132
 WORKS OF
 A Free Man's Philosophy (1933) 124–125, 133, 134, 137
 Joy in Living (1957) 133, 136, 138
 Joys of the Simple Life (1915) 137
 Living in Liberty (1911) 136, 137
 Scottish No-Stipend League (1935) 136
 The Simple Teaching of Jesus (1952) 128–129
Sen, Keshub Chandra 15, 15 n. 25
Sengupta, Padmini 213
Seuldane, Wilfred 115
Shaka Unsho 188
Shankar, Ravi 286
Sharpe, Eric J. 66, 232 n. 36
Shastri, Anant 195, 196–197, 196–197 n. 5, *196*, 199
Shen, Shuwen (Elder Gongga) 258
Shepard, Jessica 126, 141 n. 16
Shi, Zhuyun 164
Shinto 180–181
Sieg, Emil 159
Sikh background of Sadhu Sundar Singh 222, 225
Simple Life *see* Semple, Dugald
Simple Life Fellowship 135
sin 232–233
Singh, Maina 59, 65

Singh, Sundar 219–244, 281
  appearance of 230–231, *231–232*
  context of the Swiss tour 243–244
  conversion of 227
  Indian background 222–225
  Indian specificity of 242–243
  introduction 219–222
  messages of 231–236
  networks and messages 242–243
  reception of 237–242
  sādhu, meaning of 225–227
  Switzerland, tour of 220, 227–231
situations of interaction 6, 279
Sivasundaram, Sujit 6, 6 n. 7
Slade, Madeleine 130, *131*
Smith, J. Z. 9–10, 9–10 n. 12, 10 n. 16, 283
Söderblom, Nathan 226
Sommer, Walter 139
songs 36, 39, 46–47, 51, 52
South Asia, religion in 276
South Kanara, India *see* Kanara, India
spiritual nomadism in Taiwan 268
Spiritualism 239–240, 239–240 n. 45
spirituality 208
Staël-Holstein, Alexander von 154–155, 161
Stokes, Samuel Evans (alias Satyananda Stokes) 222, 223, 225
Stone, Dan 132
Stonyhurst College, Lancashire 94, 104
Stuart, Charles "Hindoo" 45–46
  Vindication of the Hindoos (1808) 45–46
study of religions 9, 23, 276, 278, 279, 282, 284, 286–287
stūpa of Chen Jianmin 265–266, *266*, 268
subalternity of Antony Firingi 49–52
Subrahmanyam, Sanjay 5, 7, 13 n. 22, 277
Sun, Jianai 150
Sun Wukong 155
Sutcliffe, Steven. 67
Swedenborgians 239–240
Switzerland, *Lebensreform* (life reform) in 140
Switzerland, tour by Sundar Singh
  introduction 220
  logistics of the tour 229–231
  messages of Singh 231–236
  reception of Singh 237–242
  before the tour 227–229
symmetric history 6, 277

T

Tagore, Dwarkanath 14
Tagore, Rabindranath 48, 156–157, 160, 238
Taiwan 254, 264, 265–269, *266*
Taixu 160, 256, 258
Takakusu, Junjiro 186
Tan, Yunshan 160
Tantrism 262, 264, 269
Tasmania, Australia 112
Tavakoli-Targhi, Mohamad 13
teaching of religion in schools 179–180
telegraphy 183–184
Thelle, Notto R. 189
Theosophy 177, 178
Thomas à Kempis
  The Imitation of Christ 223, 223 n. 5, 224
Thoms, Ulrike 132
Thoreau, Henry 133, 141 n. 15
Throckmorton, Elizabeth 97, *97*
Throckmorton family 97
Tibet
  Chen Jianmin in 257, 257–258
  Chinese monks in 254–255
  Sundar Singh in 225, 252–253
Tibetan Buddhism 254–255, 256–259
tin prospecting in Australia 112–113
tithes 136
Tolstoyan movement 132, 134, 135, 137
translation and connected histories 284–285, 286
translocal communities 12
translocal spaces 63–64, 72, 281
transnational itineraries 279
transnational turn 4
travel writing 209–210, 211, 211 n. 22, 211 n. 23, 212
Treitel, Corinna 142
Trine, Ralph Waldo
  In Tune with the Infinite (1897) 127
Tsinghua University 158
Tuckwell, Cathie 135
Twigg, Julia 131
Two Worlds, The 179, 182, 183

U

United States of America
  Chen Jianmin in 262–263, 265

Chinese students in 158
Dugald Semple in 141 n. 15
migration to 114–115
Pandita Ramabai in 209–213
universal religion 66, 68, 233
universities in China 153
see also Peking University
Urner, Jakob 21–22
Uttangi, Channappa 21, 22

V

Valéry, Paul 40
Van der Veer, Peter 18 n. 34
Vedas
  reading of by women 195, 196–197 ns. 5–6, 198, 198 ns. 7–8
  Ṛg Veda (Müller, first ed. 1849–1875) 17–18, 152
veganism 139
vegetarianism 131, 133–134, 138–139
Vīraśaivas 21
visions 228–229, 240
Visuddhimagga 161
Visva Bharati University 157, 160
Vivekananda, Swami
  and Sister Nivedita 57, 60, 64, 66–67, 68, 69–70, 82
  Sundar Singh compared to 226–227
  translation of *The Imitation of Christ* (Kempis) 223 n. 5
  and William James 283

W

Waerland, Are 138, 139
Waldschmidt, Ernst 159
Wang, Desheng 258
Western studies in China 151, 158, 164–165
White, Gilbert
  The Natural History of Selborne (1789) 128
White, Kenneth 127
Whiteway, Gloucestershire 135
Whyte, E. D. W. 102
Wilson, Ruth Olave (Grancy) 75–76, 77
witnesses not scribes 233–234
women, education of 195, 196–197 n. 5
world history 6
world religions paradigm 9, 276–277
World War I 132, 134

X

Xu, Jishang 149, 153
Xuan, Zang 155

Y

Yan, Shaoduan 164
Yang, Renshan 151–152
Yin, Hongyuan 162
yoga 285
Yoshinaga, Shin'ichi 188
Yu, Daoquan 160

Z

Zahir, Alfred 223–224
Zhang, Chengji 257–258
Zhang, Zhidong 150
Zheng, Zhenduo 156
Zheng, Zhiming 268
Zhou, Dafu 160
Zimmerman, Werner 138, 139

www.ingramcontent.com/pod-product-compliance
Lightning Source LLC
Chambersburg PA
CBHW071957220426
43662CB00009B/1164